Deity and Domination

By the same author

*Deity and Domination: Divine Analogy and Political Rhetoric in the
Seventeenth and Eighteenth Centuries*
(Routledge, forthcoming)

Haiti in Caribbean Context
(Macmillan, 1985)

From Dessalines to Duvalier
(Cambridge University Press, 1979; 2nd edn Macmillan, 1988)

The Pluralist State
(Macmillan, 1975)

Three Varieties of Pluralism
(Macmillan, 1974)

Church and State in Britain since 1820
(Routledge & Kegan Paul, 1967)

Deity and Domination

Images of God and the State in the Nineteenth and Twentieth Centuries

DAVID NICHOLLS

ROUTLEDGE
LONDON AND NEW YORK

First published 1989
by Routledge
11 New Fetter Lane, London EC4P 4EE
29 West 35th Street, New York, NY 10001

Disc conversion by Columns Typesetters of Reading
Printed in Great Britain by T.J. Press
Padstow, Cornwall

British Library Cataloguing in Publication Data
Nicholls, David
Deity and domination
Images of God and the state in the 19th
and 20th centuries.
1. Religion. Related to Politics
I. Title II. Series III. Series 200

ISBN 0 415 01171 X

Library of Congress Cataloging in Publication Data
Nicholls, David.
Images of God and the state in the 19th and 20th
centuries.
(Deity and domination ; v. 1)
"Hulsean lectures, 1985–6, first series."
Bibliography: p. 293
Includes index.
1. Christianity and politics – History – 19th century.
2. Christianity and politics – History – 20th century.
3. Church and state – History – 19th century. 4. Church
and state – History – 20th century. I. Title.
II. Series: Nicholls, David. Deity and domination ; v. 1.
BR115.P7N38 vol. 1   322'.1s   88–23944

ISBN 0 415 01171 X   [322'.1'09034]

In memory of Cheslyn Jones (1918–1987)

Contents

Preface

This volume represents a much expanded version of the first series of Hulsean Lectures which I gave at Cambridge University in 1985. My interest in the topic, however, goes back many years and formed the subject of a 'Civic Sermon' at Milton Keynes in 1978, subsequently published in the *Oxford Diocesan Magazine* and as a separate pamphlet under the title *Principalities and Powers*. The second series of Hulseans dealt with the relationship between images of divine and civil authority in the seventeenth and eighteenth centuries and will form the basis for my forthcoming volume *Deity and Domination: Divine Analogy and Political Rhetoric in the Seventeenth and Eighteenth Centuries*. I am grateful for the kind hospitality of John Sweet, Nicholas Lash and Stephen Sykes.

Embracing four centuries, two continents and several disciplines, this study is something of an adventure. I have been encouraged to continue by recalling a poster which I saw on the wall of an office in Littlemore. It pictured a tortoise, with the caption: 'Behold the tortoise! who only moves forward by sticking out his neck.' As the work is addressed to those interested in political science as well as to theologians I have thought it necessary to explain certain terms and the background to certain events which may be quite familiar to many readers. All I can do is to ask their indulgence.

The section in chapter 2 on William Temple is based on my article in *Crucible*, October–December 1984; chapter 5 is a revised version of an article published in *Modern Theology*, July 1988; and the final section of the Introduction contains passages which will be printed in my essay on 'Christianity and Politics' in a forthcoming book edited by Robert Morgan, celebrating the centenary of the volume of essays *Lux Mundi.*

Friends have given suggestions and advice on different chapters, and I am particularly indebted to Bernard Crick and David Price, also to Robert Morgan, Colin Matthew, Valerie Pitt, Robin Cohen and Randall Morris. I am grateful to the British Academy, for financing visits to the USA for work on chapter 5, and also to the staff of the following libraries: Cambridge University, Harvard Divinity School, Episcopal Divinity School, British Library, British Library of Political and Economic Science, and in Oxford: Nuffield College, Manchester College, Exeter College, the Bodleian, the Taylorian, Pusey House and other faculty libraries. I have been helped and encouraged by Nancy Marten of Routledge. Writing this book has been made possible only by the love and support of my wife, Gillian, and of my parishioners.

David Nicholls
St David's Day 1988

Littlemore Vicarage, Oxford

1

Introduction

The ceiling of the Sheldonian Theatre in Oxford is decorated with an impressive painting. The central theme is the portrayal of 'Truth' with the various disciplines, including 'Theology', imploring her assistance. The existence and status of truth was seen as straight-forward; all intellectual activity was ultimately a search for truth.

Three centuries later, truth is more problematic – its nature unclear. As we have become increasingly aware of the relative status of our knowledge, as pragmatic and instrumental theories of truth have been advanced, as a materialist conception of history and a sociology of knowledge have been proposed, as our understanding of the various non-literal modes of communication has become more sophisticated, the notion of truth has been called into question. Even in the natural sciences, which for centuries were seen by positivists as providing the pattern which other disciplines should follow, the fundamental role played by metaphor, paradigm and model has been recognised, and the issue of truth has become correspondingly complex.[1] Yet it is an issue which refuses to go away.

This volume will focus on the history and sociology of an idea, and yet it will not avoid questions of truth, validity and appropriateness. As we consider each particular topic, these issues will never be far below the surface and I confront them more explicitly in the Conclusion. The primary concern of this volume is, however, to discover 'what is going on' – to borrow a phrase from Richard Niebuhr[2] – rather than to determine what we ought to do or think about God and the state. It is not that these latter questions are unimportant, but that when light has been shed on 'what is going on'

1

we may wish to reformulate the 'ought' questions, or even find that the answers to them become obvious. Some of the most hotly contested debates which agitate the contemporary world – in the areas of individual and social ethics – would evaporate if only the relevant facts could be established.

'Religion and politics are necessarily related', declared Mr Ronald Reagan, while addressing an ecumenical prayer breakfast of 17,000 people in Dallas. But how are they connected? Conventional ways of conceptualising the relationship suggest that ethics provides the link. Right political action depends upon correct ethical norms and these are derived, at least in part, from religion. I am far from wishing to deny that the political actions people take are influenced by their moral judgments, nor that these judgments are linked to their religious beliefs or more generally to their world-view. But this is by no means the only way that politics and religion are related. Subtle connections are made and conclusions drawn as a result of the analogy – sometimes explicit, frequently implicit – between God and the state. A people's image of God affects political behaviour and conceptions of civil authority influence religious behaviour. Ideas and assumptions about the nature of authority in one sphere necessarily affect beliefs and actions in the other. Karl Marx insisted that, in his day, the analysis of religion was the premise of all analysis and that, in an enlightened approach to history, 'the criticism of heaven turns into the criticism of the earth, the *criticism of religion* into the *criticism of law* and the *criticism of theology* into the *criticism of politics*'.[3] Today the need for a more dialectical approach to the relationship is perhaps apparent.

THE SOCIAL CONTEXT

'Pictures of God', wrote Friedrich Meinecke, 'often contain an element of definite historical thinking.'[4] Indeed, much of our language about God is political in its primary reference. A moment's consideration of common images used of God – king, lord, judge, ruler – and common concepts applied to him – might, majesty, dominion, power, sovereignty and so on – should convince us that this is so. In this work I wish to examine, in some detail, how this language has been used in different periods of history, to consider the ways in which successive concepts and images of God have been related to political rhetoric and how they have to some degree echoed, or at times heralded, changes in the social structure and dynamics – in the economic, political and cultural life – of given communities.

We shall note how the links between divine and political images are by no means one-way causal relationships but assume a dialectical character. Language used about God has habitually been adopted in political discourse and has in turn influenced the course of events at the institutional level. Not only did seventeenth-century clergy address God as 'high and mighty, King of kings, Lord of lords, the only Ruler of princes, who dost from thy throne behold all the dwellers upon earth', but they witnessed King James I telling his son that he was 'a little god' and noted Thomas Hobbes's reference to the sovereign as a 'mortal god'. In addition to all this it will, as I have suggested, be necessary to ask how far particular images or conceptions of God are true, whether they are consistent with Christian faith and what criteria might be used to determine this question.

A vast undertaking! and one which will call upon such disciplines as theology, sociology, history, political science, anthropology and literary criticism. It is an enterprise that will expose us – perhaps I should more frankly say expose me! – to criticism from experts in all these fields. 'De higher monkey climb de more 'im exposed' is an old Jamaican proverb.

One reason for proceeding on this risky enterprise is that, although it is frequently asserted by modern theologians that 'Christian doctrine is socially conditioned', few attempts have been made (in the English-speaking world at least) to show exactly how this is so, in respect of particular Christian doctrines. Even those who write on 'the social context of theology' fail to look in detail at specific Christian doctrines and tell us little about how the social context in which these doctrines developed has influenced their formulation, or how once formulated they have affected social structures and processes.[5] 'Theologians', writes Gregory Baum, 'often tend to regard the variations of doctrine and theology simply as a development of ideas, without paying sufficient attention to the socio-political reality, of which this development is a reflection.'[6] Writings about God, in English, are concerned almost entirely with abstract philosophical concepts, and generally fail to look critically at the concrete images used of God and at the social context from which these images are drawn.[7]

In so far as theologians and church historians have considered the importance of non-theological factors in the development of doctrine, they have concentrated their attention either on ecclesiastical politics – on imperial might and episcopal spite – or on the influence of purely philosophical movements. The classical accounts of the development of doctrine see it as occurring in a vacuum of philosophical and religious ideas. A modern writer points out that the creeds of Christendom are 'products of their time' but sees them as conditioned by 'the world of thought' in which their authors lived.[8] So little is Christian theology related to the economic, political, legal and cultural experience of the time that it might almost have taken place on the moon or on a rugby field. Much of what passes for 'patristic scholarship' in Britain suffers from this inadequacy. 'By putting forward a separate "History of the Kingdom of God" ', as Friedrich Engels put it, these writers 'deny that real history has any inner substantiality, and claim that this substantiality belongs exclusively to their other-worldly, abstract and, what is more, fictitious, history.'[9] Among continental writers, however, some attention has been paid to these matters. Gonzalo Puente Ojea, Louis Boisset and Georges Casalis have examined the theological significance of Marxist critiques of ideology, while José Vives, Alfredo Fierro, François Houtart, Adolphe Gesché, Pierre Watté and J. van Haeperen have considered in more detail how social formations and social thinking have related to concepts of God.[10]

I have chosen the doctrine of God because of its evident centrality to Christian life and to theological discourse. As a contemporary theologian has written, 'it is not only itself the basic Christian doctrine; it enters into and affects every other doctrine'.[11] Clearly, for example, our understanding of sin and atonement are tied to our doctrine of God. Is sin seen essentially as breaking the law of a celestial legislator or as disobedience to the command of a divine sovereign, or is it to be thought of rather in terms of a civil offence against a fellow citizen requiring some kind of compensation or perhaps as the breaking of delicate personal relationships? Does God then function in the role of judge or of ruler and lawgiver, as the injured party in a lawsuit or as father and friend? The answers to these questions will manifestly affect doctrines of the atonement. Can God simply remit the punishment at his whim, as many Socinians – with their autocratic image of God – maintained, or must he in some way see that the law is followed and that punishment is meted out? Hence theories of vicarious punishment. Incidentally the atonement is one aspect of Christian doctrine which has been studied by some theologians in its social context. I think particularly of the work of

Shailer Mathews, David Smith and earlier the massive study of
Albrecht Ritschl.

Much language used about God is, then, political in its primary
reference, and Christian conceptions of God have clearly been
influenced by political experience. Discussing ideas of God held by
primitive people, Hegel wrote: 'They formed their conception of him
on the model of the master that they knew, the fathers and chiefs of
families ... and', he continued wryly, 'the ideas of the majority of
men in our times of renowned enlightenment are no differently
constituted.' The relationship between political and religious rhetoric
is, however, two-way and it should not be forgotten that the
vocabulary of politics may be viewed, in large part, as a secularised
version of religious images and conceptions.[12]

Anthropologists, as we shall see, are manifestly more aware of this
relationship than are theologians. Having examined the divine
analogy in Elizabethan England, Java and Morocco, Clifford Geertz
– with a glance at the contemporary USA – writes: 'Thrones may be
out of fashion, and pageantry too; but political authority still requires
a cultural frame in which to define itself and advance its claims, and
so does opposition to it. A world wholly demystified is a world
wholly depoliticized.'[13] With respect to the latter point I examine the
relationship between atheism and anarchism in chapter 7.

Images, analogies and other tropes

When, in this work, I speak of 'images' I mean concrete terms like
king, lord and judge; when speaking of 'concepts' I refer to abstract
nouns like sovereignty, power and domination. The political images
used of God are essentially relational rather than descriptive,[14] and
analogies have frequently been drawn between God's government of
the universe and the earthly ruler's government of his realm. At times
the analogy has assumed the former as known, maintaining that
God's government is a model which should be followed on earth; at
times it is the earthly system which is given and the heavenly
kingdom is portrayed as an idealised analogue. Sometimes the
analogy is openly drawn, at other times it is implicit, and often – as
we shall see – it is explicitly rejected. In the course of this book I
shall sometimes speak about the analogical 'argument', yet the
argument can never be conclusive. Analogy speaks to the imagination
and to the practical judgment rather than presenting a definitive
logical case. Analogy persuades rather than coerces.[15] It is the kind

of argument used by lawyers when appealing to common law: surely this new factory, which causes vibration to neighbouring houses, is more like a factory producing smoke (which all agree may be held liable) than like an ugly factory (which may not).

The meaning of the various non-literal forms of expression, such as type, simile, metaphor, analogy and so on, should be clear from the context in which they are used. The images of which I speak are sometimes *similes* (kings are 'like gods'), or more usually *metaphors* (God is referred to as 'judge'). They function relationally, as *analogies* ('God relates to the universe as the earthly king relates to his kingdom'), and often depend upon a *model*, which is a more comprehensive representation, allowing for *allegorical* inferences. We could say, then, that the picture of heaven – as a feudal court, characterised by hierarchy, order and law, in which God sits on the throne, surrounded by ranks of angelic beings and saints, some of whom may represent the interests of their devotees – is a model. From this model are drawn analogies (the saint is to his devotee as the earthly patron is to his client) and metaphors (the saint is patron). I do not wish at this stage to get bogged down further in defining varieties of tropes, nor in an attempt to distinguish between literal and non-literal language, bearing in mind how the persistent application of terms like 'law' and 'power' both to the civil and to the physical world lead us to wonder which indeed should be called the literal use.

In recent centuries, when the prestige of the physical sciences has been high, it is sometimes assumed that the normal procedure is for other disciplines to borrow images and concepts from the vocabulary of the natural sciences. Historians refer to the mid-nineteenth-century movement in social theory associated with the name of Herbert Spencer as 'social Darwinism'. Yet Darwin himself stated that it was his reading of Malthus's *Essay on Population* which suggested to him the concept of natural selection.[16] Much of the language used in the natural sciences has, indeed, been borrowed from elsewhere.

Parameters

Before embarking on this enquiry it would be well for me to outline some of the parameters within which I shall move and the limits which it will be necessary to observe. Although, as I have said, the enterprise will be inter-disciplinary, it will generally be limited to *Christian* doctrines of God; I have neither time nor competence to look in any detail at the way these issues apply to other religions. Further, I shall restrict myself to the modern – post-Reformation – period in a European and North American context.[17]

I have said that much of our language about God is political, but this is not the case with some of the most common images, like rock, sun, shield, rampart or mighty fortress, which are drawn from the natural or architectural world. 'Blessed be the Lord my rock', sings the author of Psalm 144, 'my strength and my stronghold, my fortress and my deliverer: my shield to whom I come for refuge.' Other images – father, shepherd and spouse – are indeed social, but not political in their primary reference. Yet these latter have from time to time also been appropriated by earthly rulers. The emperor Charles V claimed the title of shepherd and used the text 'there shall be one shepherd and one flock' to legitimate his imperial ambition. Ancient and medieval examples could be given of the ruler's relationship to his realm being portrayed in terms of marriage. The coronation ring in French sixteenth-century ceremonial was, as Kantorowicz informs us, a symbol of the king's marriage to his realm.[18] King James I told Parliament in 1603, 'I am the husband, and all the whole island is my lawful wife; I am the head, and it is my body; I am the shepherd and it is my flock.'[19] With respect to the title 'father', Erasmus wrote:

> The good prince ought to have the same attitude towards his subjects as a good *paterfamilias* towards his household – for what else is a kingdom but a great family? What is the king, if not the father to a great multitude? We have been taught by Christ our teacher that God is the unquestioned prince of all the world, and we call him 'father'.[20]

Even a ruthless political dictator, like Haiti's François Duvalier, claimed a paternal relationship with his people and was pleased to be called 'Papa Doc'.[21] These social images – shepherd, father, spouse – should not therefore be excluded from our discussion, for they customarily function as double analogies, applied to both God and the king.

The image of God as 'father' raises the much-debated question of the 'sexist' language of Christian liturgy and theology. This is not an issue which I shall confront directly, again for reasons of space. Nevertheless much of what is said in this work has a relation to the male images which are normally used of God, for they are often patriarchal images having very definite political connotations of rule and domination.[22] The Aramaic, Hebrew and Arabic word for 'spirit' is, of course, feminine and in the early church the Holy Spirit was generally referred to among Syriac and other Middle Eastern Christians as 'she'. It is interesting to note how, on the basis of this linguistic feature, feminine images of the Holy Spirit were developed. When the church became a political power, however, these became unfashionable and were generally replaced by images of domination and patriarchy.[23]

Concepts of divine and civil authority have been related closely to ideas of church government. This is an area with which I shall be concerned only incidentally, as an exhaustive treatment of ecclesiastical structures from this standpoint would take too much space. On the one hand, monarchical images of God have certainly been used to justify papal claims to absolute power, while a heavenly hierarchy has served as the model for episcopal government of the church. Yet we must be careful here. On the one hand Christian Duquoc has recently observed that 'nothing is less certain than that monotheism sustains the Catholic Church's ideology of uniformity'. Agreeing that monotheism has sometimes been used in this way, he concludes that its true meaning – 'that the God of Jesus Christ is the Father of all men, that he bestows his Spirit on whom he wills' – constitutes a clear bulwark against a monolithic ecclesiastical particularism.[24]

On the other hand, while there is some evidence to suggest that the 'democratic' idea of a God within each believer and the doctrine of the inner light have been related to decentralised systems of church government, anyone who has had experience of organisations in which there is a strong Quaker influence will know that real power is commonly held by a self-perpetuating oligarchy. The Puritan idea of a God who limits himself by covenant was indeed related to the growth of democratic and constitutional ideas in both church and state – notably in the American colonies – yet many Congregationalists and Presbyterians held identical beliefs about God, while their model of church government was quite different. It appears, then, that the relationship between the images and concepts of God entertained by a particular ecclesiastical group and its form of church government is complex and may be unsusceptible to generalisations.

My enquiry will concern itself with the language of popular religious expression found in hymns, prayers and sermons as well as with the more sophisticated language of theologians, just as I shall include reference to the popular rhetoric of political practice as well as to the writings of political theorists. The connection between theology and popular religion is itself a matter for serious investigation, as is indeed the relationship between popular politics and political theory. Although undoubtedly practice generally precedes theory, the ideas and interpretations of theorists have influenced developments at the practical and popular level. While Barthian theology, for example, must be seen as a product of its time, it also became an active and significant force in practical religion. Pastors carried the message out from seminaries into the parishes where it was propagated among the laity. The present study will, however, concentrate on the way language has been used by leading religious and political thinkers, who may be said to reflect and make explicit many of the assumptions widely held in their day.

This book will in large part be devoted to a discussion of the *political* language used of God; surely a necessary preliminary to this is an exhaustive consideration of whether and, if so, how we can speak about God at all. I do not, however, think that I can add anything useful to this extended debate. The fact we may begin with is that people do speak in political language about God. Let us try to make sense of this language by considering the practice in more detail. 'Alas', wrote Karl Barth, 'for the theologians, who in order to speak of God truly and as Christians, must first strive "to speak of God at all"!'[25]

Allegorical elaborations

On occasions, as I have already noted, analogy becomes allegory and detailed similarities between divine and civil rule are elaborated, or implied. Saints, for example, fulfil the role of patrons, who represent the interests of their dependants in the heavenly court. Peter Brown has indicated the parallels in the world of late antiquity, pointing to the fact that in the second and early third centuries the practice of peasants directly petitioning the imperial court died out. All attempts to influence affairs had to pass through a local 'patron' who exercised influence at court. 'The medieval idea of the "patron saint", intervening on behalf of his servants at a remote and awe-inspiring Heavenly Court, is a projection upwards of this basic fact of late Roman life.' Writing of a subsequent period, J.M. Sallmann observes, 'The link joining the saint to the faithful reproduces, transposed into the supernatural domain, the link of clientship which joins the powerful to their dependants.'[26]

Parallels can be cited in modern Europe and Latin America. 'There are', writes Jeremy Boissevain,

striking similarities between the uses of intermediaries in the

religious field and the brokerage and patron–client relations which
are particularly strong in Catholic countries. The importance of
intermediaries, especially in the political field, is summed up neatly
in the proverb often quoted by Sicilians and Maltese: 'You can't
get to heaven without the help of saints', for political patrons in
both cultures are referred to as saints. In Catholic countries the
use of such intermediaries to reach valued ends is regarded as
quite normal, and there is no moral stigma attached to doing so.[27]

Similar conclusions are reached by Kenny and Bax in their studies of
patronage in Spain and Ireland respectively.[28] In countries where
Protestant culture predominates, and where 'a person does not need
the help of others to obtain salvation', such forms of patronage
would be called 'corruption' and viewed with considerable disgust.

John Donne saw angels performing the task of ministers and royal
ambassadors, while, with respect to devils, that remarkable theologian Shailer Mathews observed:

> As rulers of the Middle Ages had their torture chambers and their
> force of torturers, so God had hell and the Devil. Punishment was
> not inflicted on the dead by God. He was judge and sovereign, but
> his role, like that of the feudal lord, ended at the passing of the
> sentence.[29]

Shelley and Godwin pictured devils – like the figure of Satan in the
book of Job – as God's informers, who even act as *agents
provocateurs*, as did the spies of Lords Eldon and Sidmouth.

Anthropologists and historians

Theologians, then, have generally paid scant attention to the
significance of the political language used about God, but this would
not be true of ancient historians and anthropologists. A number of
theories have been enunciated on the relationship between conceptions of God and social or political structures in the ancient world
and in so-called primitive communities.

In his chapter on 'Civil Religion', in the *Social Contract*, Rousseau
had asserted that primitive polytheism was a consequence of political
fragmentation, for each people had its own god. Ludwig Feuerbach
and Mikhail Bakunin agreed, claiming that the national gods of
paganism reflected a fragmented political structure and that – with
the growth of empire – these were gradually replaced by a universal
God. The destruction of national autonomy was, they argued, a

necessary condition for the development of monotheism.[30] This position was elaborated by Karl Kautsky in his 1908 essay on Christian origins. There he stated that 'the image of the sole God as it grew up in Christianity was not less a product of imperial despotism than of philosophy' – the celestial hierarchy was a reflection of the imperial court.[31] Max Weber was, however, characteristically more cautious in stating the relationship between imperialism and monotheism. 'The growth of empire', he observed, '. . . has by no means been the sole or indispensable lever for the accomplishment of this development.'[32]

Later, James Breasted examined the relationship between political organisation and conceptions of divinity in ancient Egypt. Although he recognised the importance of a historical, dynamic, approach to understanding this relationship, he generally assumed that the influence was all one way, from political to religious. He put the position rather crudely as follows:

> The forms of the state began to pass over into the world of the gods and an important god would be called a 'king'. . . . It was universalism expressed in terms of imperial power which first caught the imagination of thinking men of the Empire and disclosed to them the universal sweep of the sun-god's dominion as a physical fact. Monotheism was but imperialism in religion.[33]

This latter point was echoed by Erik Peterson in his essay 'Monotheismus als politisches Problem', when he referred to the concept of divine monarchy as 'merely the reflection of the earthly monarchy' in the Roman empire.[34] Peterson was, of course, a theologian and is better known for his claim that Christian monotheism has functioned as an ideology for politically authoritarian regimes from the days of Eusebius on. I shall return to this issue in the Conclusion.

Counter-examples to the theory that monotheism is merely a reflection of imperialism can, of course, be cited both from the ancient world and from so-called primitive communities today. In some present-day African communities, the Kikuyu for example, God is recognised as 'the ruler and governor of the universe', even though there is no centralised monarchical tradition, and political power is held by groups of elders. Guy Swanson observes that in ancient Israel the development of monotheism predates the monarchy.[35] Whether he is right here depends partly on what one means by monotheism. Certainly the *worship* of one God (monolatry) predates the monarchy, but many scholars would insist that a fully developed monotheism (that denies the *existence* of other gods) does not go back further than the reforms under King Josiah. Bernhard Lang has recently echoed the claim of Bakunin, Kautsky and Feuerbach that 'The history of the rise of monotheism is part of a broader history: that of the destruction of the small State.'[36] He thus relates the rise of monotheism in Israel less to monarchy among the Jews than to their perception of imperial power in Assyria and Babylon.

Be this as it may (and I am in no position to adjudicate), Swanson goes on to suggest that the co-relation is not between monotheism and monarchy, but rather between monotheism – or belief in a 'high god' – and communities with a complex and hierarchically organised political structure. His work is, however, marred by the lack of historical perspective. He attempts his analysis in a static mode, looking only for synchronic co-relations, effectively ignoring the dynamic historical relationship between divine and political images. His Durkheimian assumption that 'An idea or attitude or belief must correspond to current experiences with the environment if it is to continue across the generations' is an unwarranted piece of functionalist dogma and his consequent assurance that 'forces which produce and support current beliefs are present along with those beliefs', if not tautological, is misplaced.[37]

More recently social scientists have elaborated the supposed connection between complex social organisation and belief in a high god. Ralph Underhill has maintained that economic – even more clearly than political – complexity is positively related to mono-theism.[38] François Houtart and Adolphe Gesché have pursued similar lines of research, but have tended to adopt a functionalist approach, generally failing to recognise the importance of a historical perspective in understanding the relationship between political and religious concepts and images.[39]

In this connection it is worth introducing a distinction, made by Raymond Williams, which will prove useful in subsequent discussions. That is between dominant, residual and emergent ideas.[40] *Residual* ideas, almost by definition, are survivals from a previous age and may bear little relation to the prevailing social structure, notwithstanding their powerful influence upon current behaviour and interpretations of reality. It might indeed prove to be the case that many of the *dominant* images and concepts of God in a given situation are related to the social conditions prevailing at the time. It should also be emphasised, however, that even some fairly dominant images may be more closely related to past social conditions than to present ones. Residents of long-standing republics still speak and think of God as 'king' and socialist Christians talk endlessly about the 'kingdom' of God. *Emergent* ideas again should be seen less as reflections of the predominant social arrangements of the day than as the imaginative response of individuals or small groups to these arrangements. Needless to say, most residual ideas are the dominant ideas of an earlier epoch and all dominant ideas are the emergent ideas of yesterday.

Divine images as independent variables

It would assuredly be a mistake to see the influence always flowing one way – from the political to the religious employment of such images and concepts. As Carl Schmitt asserted, somewhat overstating the case, 'All the pregnant concepts of the modern theory of the state are secularised theological concepts.' The link is not merely historical; the systematic structure of these political concepts, he insisted, is affected by their origin. A knowledge of their origin is therefore necessary in order to understand how they function in the political world. In the eyes of Schmitt's hero, Donoso Cortés, this was not merely a description of how concepts are borrowed by one discipline from another, but was part of a normative theory; he ascribed all evils of the modern world – particularly the French Revolution – to the theological errors of the Protestant Reformation.[41]

Furthermore religious conceptions may influence developments at the level of political institutions. In the USA, for example, liberal theology, with its God of caring and concern, predated any widespread acceptance of the idea of a welfare state in that country. This theology (and the effects which it had on popular religion) helped mould the context within which Franklin Roosevelt could successfully introduce the welfare legislation of the thirties.

In the development and refinement of religious concepts it is important to emphasise the dialectic at the level of theological ideas as well as the relationship of these developments to the political structures of the day. While he perceptively referred to the federal theology of seventeenth-century Puritans – which stressed the covenant (Latin: *foedus*) relationship between God and his people – as 'the lengthened shadow of a political platform', Perry Miller was careful to recognise the active role which the concept of covenant played in the theological controversies of the day, particularly in the debate between antinomianism and Arminianism. It was no mere importation of a political term into theology; the idea of covenant had a theological dynamic which in turn had influenced thinking on civil affairs.[42]

Erich Fromm's *The Dogma of Christ* attempts to explain the development of Christological dogmas in terms of social psychology, asserting that ideas of divine sonship result from an 'unconscious hostility to the Divine Father' and from the 'fantasy of a suffering, oppressed class'. He makes the somewhat surprising assertion that religion has the effect of encouraging psychic dependence on the part of the masses, of intimidating them intellectually and of inducing in them a 'socially necessary infantile docility towards the rulers'.[43] While it would be churlish to deny that this is frequently the case, it is far from the whole truth. As we read in our newspapers of the activities of the Revd Ian Paisley and of militant Catholics in Northern Ireland, of the Tamils in Sri Lanka and of the various Christian, Muslim and Druze militia in Lebanon, to mention but three contemporary situations, we may well doubt whether 'docility' is among the principal characteristics of these religious groups and conclude that the book might more appropriately have been entitled 'The Dogma of Erich Fromm'. Furthermore, recent work on the social composition of the early church leads us to doubt the assumption – shared by Kautsky and Fromm and derived from Engels – that 'Christianity . . . first appeared as a religion of slaves and freedmen, of the poor, of the outcasts'.[44]

The working hypothesis adopted in this study is, then, that images and concepts of God are commonly borrowed from political discourse and carry with them political connotations; but, having come into being, they assume a life of their own and will indeed affect the way later generations think, not only about God, but also about their social and civic life. Theological rhetoric, child of political experience, may also be mother of political change.

Writing history 'backwards'

In this two-volume work I plan to begin by discussing the divine analogy in the contemporary world and move – in what may be called, for want of a better expression, an anticlockwise direction – to a consideration of earlier periods. When contemplating the problem of where to begin this study I encountered a biblical scholar, who said, in distinctly weary tones, 'I suppose you will be starting with a chapter on the Old Testament.' In fact any attempt on my part to start at the beginning, say in the ancient Near East, would never get off the ground. Or who, deciding to commence a study of this kind in the complex world of Byzantium, would ever emerge to consider medieval and post-Reformation developments, let alone those in the modern world?

Perhaps a further word of explanation is in order. While many contemporary historians will readily agree that the writing of history cannot properly be conceived as a reconstruction of past events 'as they happened', and that the significance of such events is at least in part determined by their outcome, there does seem to be a general assumption that history must be written 'forwards' rather than 'backwards'. Why is this so? Why not begin with the present, if that is indeed where we are, and proceed by tracing antecedents, rather than begin at some arbitrary date in the past, working towards the present and looking for consequences. If we proceed anticlockwise are we not in grave danger of committing one of the most grievous of historical sins and adopting a 'Whig interpretation of history'? I see no reason for thinking so. The Whig historians themselves followed a strictly clockwise method of writing about the past. Another peril to which an anticlockwise approach might be thought to succumb is that of selectivity. But all history writing must involve a constructive selection of what is thought to be significant about the past.

How, it might be asked, is it possible to write about the nineteenth century before dealing with the eighteenth? Surely we must understand the earlier before attempting to explain the later. A moment's reflection, however, should convince us that this prescription for an infinite regress can be no guide to the writing of history. In any case a good argument can be made for asserting that it is only in the light of our knowledge of the nineteenth century that we can understand the meaning of events in the eighteenth. How many of those angry Frenchmen who broke into a Paris gaol on 14 July 1789 could comprehend the significance of what they were doing? 'Hindsight', writes a present-day scholar, 'is often the curse of the historian.'[45] But where would the historian be without it? By following an anticlockwise method, then, historians may at least be delivered from a spurious pretence of telling the story just as it happened without interpretation or selection and from a simulated ignorance of the consequences or an affected surprise at the outcome of the movements they are attempting to explain.

CONTEMPORARY IMAGES OF GOD AND THE STATE

Undoubtedly one of the most common characteristics applied in our modern West European and North American world, both to God

and to the state, is that of welfare. Liberal theology and political
theory agree in picturing God and the state in terms of bureaucratic
benevolence. Both are assumed to be centres of 'power and might',
but pursuing policies which maximise welfare – which 'seek the
common good', as the Church of England's *Alternative Service Book*
puts it. To be sure, the concept of the welfare God and of the
paternal state are by no means exclusively modern. Jon Elster has, for
example, argued that the particular analogy is anticipated in the
writings of Leibniz.[46] Yet they do seem to have acquired a
prominence in our own century which is significant; they have
generally become the dominant images of divine and political action.
So deeply is the idea embedded in North Atlantic thinking that any
concept of God and the state which neglects welfare is incredible.

Here are just two illustrations. The first concerns welfare views of
the state. I have suggested elsewhere [47] that the failure on the part of
most western observers to understand how François Duvalier, of
Haiti, could have continued in power so long is due – at least in part
– to this inability to comprehend a view of the state which is not
centred on welfare. What, they demand, had Duvalierism done for
the people? The answer, of course, is nothing. But no other Haitian
government has done anything for the mass of the people; thus
popular expectations of the state's role are different from those in the
countries of the OECD. The state exists to tax, to confiscate, to
control, to imprison. The less people see of it the better. A friend of
mine in Haiti once returned from a visit to the countryside and could
not find his gardener. Eventually the frightened man emerged from
behind some bushes at the end of the garden. In explanation he said
(in Haitian Kréyol), 'The state arrived and I hid.' Further questioning
revealed that one single army officer had come to the door. When
Haitians use the proverb 'Apré bondie sé léta' (after God comes the
state), they do not refer to the benevolence of God but to his power,
unpredictability and remoteness.

My second example concerns the welfare image of *God*, and I cite
words of that prophet of benevolent bureaucracy Max Weber.
Discussing the Calvinist conception of God (as he understood it) as a
celestial despot, he wrote, in contrast, of 'The Father in heaven of the
New Testament, so human and understanding, who rejoices over the
repentance of a sinner as a woman over a lost piece of silver'.[48] This
clearly selective picture of the New Testament God – who is also
represented in the Gospels as a king who dispatches those on his left
hand to everlasting fire and a master who casts his worthless servant
into outer darkness – is assumed by Weber not so much as the only

acceptable image of the Christian God but as the only *conceivable* one.

In the second and third chapters I shall consider how welfare images of God and the state have come to assume such prominence in the modern capitalist world and suggest that this phenomenon has to be seen, on the one hand, as a consequence of certain economic and social developments at the institutional level and, on the other, as related to received concepts and images of divine and political authority.

By the mid-nineteenth century, industrial capitalism had developed in such a way, in the advanced countries of western Europe, that revolution was a distinct possibility. Something was required, in addition to repressive measures, to maintain the economic and social system. Urgent action was taken by the state to mitigate some of the more flagrant consequences of unrestricted capitalism. Gradually the state took over more and more of the features of a friendly society. Parallel developments took place in Christian thinking about God. The benevolent God of liberal theology reflected and also was used to legitimate the welfare role of the state. These tendencies can be seen to have reached their apotheosis in the thinking of William Temple, but continue to predominate. Only recently, in connection with the controversy over statements by the Bishop of Durham, David Jenkins, one fellow diocesan bishop was reported in the *Church Times* as follows:

> The bishop thinks people would do well to remember Archbishop Temple's words: that to admit acrimony in theological discussion is more fundamentally heretical than any erroneous opinions upheld in the course of discussion.[49]

In other words, truth and straight talking must take second place to 'caring and concern'. Consider, in contrast, the words Jesus used about his adversaries: 'blind guides', 'blind fools', 'hypocrites', 'whited sepulchres', 'liars', 'serpents', 'brood of vipers'; he referred to the king as 'that fox'. There is more than a sniff of acrimony here! The image of a welfare God who stands for peace at any price is manifestly lodged in the bishop's subconscious.

The development of a welfare image of God must be seen also as the reaction to movements going back much further. The positivist doctrines of God and the state, dating from the late Middle Ages and becoming dominant during the sixteenth and seventeenth centuries, had retained their influence. Divine and political authority were both thought of in terms of unlimited power, exercised in an arbitrary way according to the will of the sovereign. Welfare images assume the omnipotence of both God and the state but insist that it must be exercised benevolently.

All the concepts and images considered in this work can – in part – be seen as either reactions to, or restatements of, this positivism, or 'decisionism', as I have called it. I shall suggest in chapter 7 that the political atheism, or rather anti-theism, of certain nineteenth-century writers is to be explained in this context. The rejection of God by such libertarian writers as Shelley, Proudhon and Bakunin was clearly political in its inspiration. They were denouncing a particular notion of authority and saw, in the God of their day, a celestial tyrant who governed his realm in the same way as did those earthly rulers against whose injustice they rebelled. The rule of this God was being used by the governing classes as a model and as a legitimation of political oppression.

Scepticism and authority

Authoritarianism both in politics and in religion has frequently been backed by philosophical scepticism. As both Hobbes and Hume had recognised, if reason can be shown to be impotent in establishing truth and stability in these two basic areas of human life, then the resort to some form of external authority – if only that of custom and habit – becomes necessary. In religion, W.G. Ward, H.L. Mansel and Arthur Balfour could be cited as examples of this pattern of thinking. God's way is known by conscience, papal pronouncements, scriptural revelation validated by supernatural signs or, in the case of Balfour, by custom and tradition. Scepticism clears the ground for positivism.

Balfour extended this sceptical approach into the political sphere and, drawing on the insights of such men as James Fitzjames Stephen and Henry Maine, asserted the inevitability of a governing elite and the need for traditional structures of political authority. Even when customs and habits which provide stability for human life appear to be consonant with reason, they have not been established as a result of rational processes, nor is their fate bound up with 'the extremely indifferent arguments by which, from time to time, philosophers, politicians and I will add divines, have thought fit to support them'. Such theories as the divine right of kings and social contract – 'both of extraordinary absurdity' – must be seen as attempts 'to bolster up by argument the creed which authority had been found temporarily insufficient to sustain'.[50]

The analogy questioned

A number of contemporary theories, mostly stemming from churches of Africa, Asia or Latin America, reverse the analogy between God and the state, picturing God in an analogous position to the *victims* of political authority rather than to the ruler. He is the suffering God, the crucified God, the servant God: 'El Dios humano y sencillo; el Dios que suda en la calle' (the human, simple God; the God who sweats in the streets).[51] These ideas of God are often current among oppressed minorities. They may be found in parts of the Old Testament. Again, in the early church the image of Christ the good shepherd was popular with Roman Christians in the age of persecution; the catacombs contain many pictures of the good shepherd. This image of Christ was also prevalent among Syriac Christians, who have rarely found themselves in a dominant political position. On the other hand, the only icons – produced in an age when the church had become politically powerful – which use the text 'I am the good shepherd' have a *picture* of Christ the high priest in glory, and the parable of the lost sheep is illustrated by a vacant throne in heaven.[52]

It is well to remember, however, that the God of the oppressed is not always the suffering, the powerless, the crucified God. For the Hebrews under pressure he was a God of war, and for Gerrard Winstanley and the seventeenth-century diggers he was the military captain. The diggers indeed looked to the model of the Exodus for inspiration and they spoke of a time when people would 'own no other God, or ruling power, but one, which is the King of Righteousness'. 'Let Israel go free' was their cry.[53] The slaves of the French colony of Saint-Domingue pictured many of their Voodoo spirits as military officers and even today they are frequently painted in the costume of eighteenth-century French officers.

Other contemporary rejections of the analogical relationship between God and the state would be found among totalitarian theorists, who collapse the analogy, effectively identifying God with the state or the race or the movement, which they turn into an object of ultimate concern. As anticipated by some earlier absolutist systems, the worship of any God other than the state is viewed as equivalent to treachery. The state demands the total allegiance of the citizen. In the face of such claims many Christians, as we shall see in chapter 4, saw the total state as a demonic force and rejected any analogical relationship between God and the state.

Autarky and absolutism

One of the most persistent concepts applied by Christians to God has been that of self-sufficiency. It goes back, of course, to Greek philosophers like Plato and Aristotle and was paralleled in their writings by the notion of the *polis* as autarkic. Perfection, in the divine as well as in the political sphere, was characterised by self-sufficiency. The idea, implying that God is not subject to change in any way – that he is impassible (without passions) – was difficult to reconcile with the frankly anthropomorphic language of the Old Testament and with the evident suffering of Jesus Christ the Son of God. How could the wrath of God, the love of God and the suffering of the incarnate Son be compatible with divine impassibility? The idea has consequently been influential in the formulation of Christological and Trinitarian doctrines.

The concept of God as self-sufficient has rarely been absent from Christian understandings of God, but emerged particularly strongly among German idealists of the early nineteenth century. Fichte, Schleiermacher and other thinkers of the time were preoccupied with the question of German unity and the relationship of the small German states to the nation. Many thought that the ideal political unit should follow the borders of the nation and should be economically – as well as legally and culturally – self-sufficient. The concept of autarky – not to be confused with 'autarchy', meaning absolute sovereignty[54] – has become a feature of much modern nationalism and formed part of the rhetorical apparatus of both Italian Fascism and German Nazism.

It is surely no accident that the principal challenge to autarkic images of God has come from the United States, a country which has for centuries experienced the interdependence characteristic of a federal constitution. In the writings of William James, Walter Rauschenbusch, and above all in the work of Charles Hartshorne and other Whiteheadians, this notion of perfection as involving self-sufficiency has been persistently questioned. Chapters 5 and 6 will be devoted to this theme.

We may think of the autarkic image as reinforcing the absolutism of the Reformation period. Not only was power within the state centralised at one point and characterised by sovereign will, but the state itself was a self-contained and independent unity. The fact that England was seen as an island played an important symbolic role in the patriotism of Shakespeare and his contemporaries (who appear to have shared Enoch Powell's confusion between England and Great

Britain); John Donne spoke of England as 'a little world of our own'.[55] Anxiety about the dangers of dependence follows naturally from a disturbance in the political order such as occurred in continental Europe in the sixteenth century or in the years following the French Revolution. This latter period also witnessed a striking revival in divine and political decisionism in the writings of Catholic reactionaries like Joseph de Maistre, Louis de Bonald and the remarkable Spanish writer Juan Donoso Cortés.

Stability and structure

Eighteenth-century England, in contrast, had enjoyed a considerable degree of political stability. 'Englishmen were becoming used to the idea of reading about their domestic politics, rather than fighting about them.'[56] The turmoils of the seventeenth century were passing. The need for peace and order at all costs was less obvious. God and the state were thought of as operating in the context of a system of law. 'The spacious firmament on high' manifested an order which was replicated in civil relationships; both were 'the works of an almighty hand', but a hand which was not continually meddling with what it had made. The government should interpose only in exceptional circumstance, playing the role of the night watchman – just as the divine architect allowed the universe to proceed according to its eternal laws, with only an occasional intervention. This dominant idea of divine and political government is present in Locke and the Newtonians, but is perhaps best seen in the political theology of William Paley and in the assumptions of political economists like Adam Smith and Robert Malthus. I plan to discuss these writers in the second volume of this work.

While these eighteenth-century thinkers can be seen as developing their political and religious thought in response to the changing social and political context in which they were living, their ideas must also be seen in relation to the ideology of a previous century, against which their theories were quite explictly directed. Their emphasis upon law and harmony was in reaction to the decisionism which had marked the political and religious systems of the mid-seventeenth century, among both royalists and parliamentarians. The way the analogy between divine and political sovereignty operated among theorists like Hobbes, publicists like James I and theological poets like Donne and Milton will be examined in the sequel. The notion of a divine sovereign was employed by many royalists to legitimate a system of political absolutism, and parliamentarians, in consequence frequently rejected any idea of an analogy between divine and political authority. Some of the more radical Puritans, especially in the American colonies, employed the notion of the covenant – by which the sovereign God limits himself to act in predictable ways – to explain how a sovereign people can limit itself to live under a civil constitution.

The rise of the decisionist model

These images of God and the state are related on the one hand to human perceptions of the economic and political conditions prevailing at the time and on the other to ideas inherited from the past. The dominant sixteenth- and seventeenth-century notion of authority as command, will and sovereignty has played an important role in later conceptualisations. In some cases it is a question of rejecting these images, in others of reinforcing them, in others again of modifying them.

But what of the 'decisionist' images of the post-Reformation world themselves? They must surely be seen in the context of the search for some modicum of peace and order in a world threatened by widespread disruption and disorder. With the breakdown of feudal relationships and even more with the disturbances which the Reformation brought in its wake, there was an apparent need for strong centralised government which could impose some kind of order. In such a situation the claim that anyone may challenge the validity of laws on the ground that they were contrary to reason was an invitation to further confusion.

Among nominalist writers of the late Middle Ages moral laws too were increasingly seen as dictates of an inscrutable deity rather than as norms rationally deducible from a knowledge of his nature and purposes. So with Jean Bodin and later – and more radically – with Thomas Hobbes the positivist theory of a divine and human law, constituted by the command of the sovereign, was enunciated. Both these writers quite explicitly related their image of a monolithic God to that of the earthly ruler.

The medieval picture of God, presiding over a heavenly court, had generally reflected the hierarchical structure of the earthly realm.

> What are the monarch, his court and his throne,
> What are the peace and the joy that they own.[57]

Like the earthly ruler, God operates within a quasi-legal structure that recognises the fundamental principles of justice and order.

God's laws are no arbitrary commands but reflect his eternal nature. The natural law which binds earthly rulers is that part of the eternal law relating to human affairs, which can be discovered by reason. Any civil decree which contradicts this natural law was not considered as law, nor as binding on subjects. In a relatively stable feudal state such a system could work. Those in positions of power had enough of a shared outlook and a mutual interest in the status quo for them to be able to debate the issues in the lawcourts. As in the Britain which Arthur Balfour described in his preface to Bagehot's *British Constitution* the elites had enough in common that they could safely bicker about details.

CHRISTIANS AND THE AUTHORITY OF THE STATE

'The State is sacred', wrote W.J.H. Campion in a celebrated volume of essays. He went on to assert that it possesses, like the church, a 'divine sanction'.[58] This understanding of the relation between Christianity and politics is one that has gained wide acceptance and is indeed assumed almost without question by many today. The church's job is to strengthen the authority of civil government and generally encourage obedience to the law by those it can influence. Its leaders, moving within the corridors of power, use their influence to uphold and strengthen 'Christian values in public life'. The church is viewed as part of the social cement which binds the country together and as a principal supporter of its 'value system'.[59] Some would restrict its proper sphere of concern to issues of piety and personal morality. Others, while allowing it the right to comment on public policy, insist that it should speak only of general principles.

There are three strands to this position: first a belief that the state is God's creation, possessing authority derived ultimately from him; second that it is the state's purpose to effect the common good; third that the lineaments of this common good and the limits of the state's legitimate authority are determined by moral principles and ideals, deduced from Christian faith and prior to any political order. The principal link between theology and politics – between God and the state – is believed to be ethics.

The political realm, and in particular that collection of institutions known as the state, is thought to receive legitimacy from its role in a divine plan. Both church and state are ordained by God as part of his creative or redemptive purpose. Whether the state is a result of the Fall – a remedy for sin – as Augustine believed, or a part of the created order, as Aquinas taught, it is seen in both traditions as divinely ordained. The leading Protestant reformers of the sixteenth century did nothing to challenge this position and it has continued to dominate mainstream Christian thinking on the subject since that time.

The fundamental task of the state is, according to this view, to secure the conditions of an ordered and civilised life. Its successful performance will, however, involve a recognition that many citizens are susceptible only to the lowest motive, a fear of punishment. Coercive force is therefore one of the state's chief instruments; but this inhibits its appeal to higher motives and at this point 'the Church steps in to supplement the moral action of the State'.[60] The other principal role of the church in its relations with the state is, in the words of Charles Gore, 'to throw herself into the sanctification of each new social order'. However, attempts to Christianise or sanctify the secular order, breaking down any distinction between sacred and secular, have totalitarian implications, particularly in situations of cultural and social pluralism.[61]

Although the state is viewed as ordained by God, exercising an authority derived ultimately from him, any idea of the divine right of kings is firmly excluded. Rather Christianity is in a somewhat vague and unspecified manner thought to provide religious backing for ideas of social contract and 'representative' government, where the object of state policy is the common good – a substantive condition under which the good of all citizens is subsumed. A government which has as its aim anything other than this common good is not a true government at all. Welfare is thus built into the very conception of the state.

In the view I am here criticising, a legitimate state 'rests upon and gives expression to a group of moral principles and ideals'[62] which are postulated as prior to political institutions and derived from theology. Later thinkers in this tradition have argued that these general principles or rules are applied to practical political issues with the aid of 'middle axioms'. It is the church's role to enunciate moral rules and encourage those of its members who are appropriately qualified to examine how these can properly be 'applied' to concrete issues. The experts state the 'facts', the theologians bring their principles, and together – with the aid of middle axioms – they relate the two.

Biblical perspectives

In contrast to this belief in the divine origin of political authority and the presumption that the Christian's duty towards the state is 'first and foremost, the duty of obedience', a duty 'invested with the same sanctions as the most sacred claims',[63] biblical writers are much more ambivalent about political matters. The early life of the people of Israel manifested a notion of authority as dispersed among the different tribes. There was no conception of a sovereign state; ultimate authority was found in Yahweh. The idea of a strong centralised system of political domination, which characterised some of the neighbouring states, was indeed seen as endangering the traditions and liberties of the people. James Barr has contrasted their situation with that of certain Mesopotamian peoples: 'kingship was not lowered from heaven in the beginning, on the contrary there had been a long time in Israel before kingship began. . . . The idea of having a human king was a revolt against God.'[64] Under Saul and his successors an ideology of kingship developed, in terms of 'the Lord's anointed', but the king's powers were severely restricted and were later effectively superseded by the authority of prophet and priest.

The New Testament writings too are equivocal about systems of political domination. In the Johannine tradition, the 'kingship' of Jesus plays a crucial role and calls into question all earthly claims to sovereignty. The cry of the chief priests, 'We have no king but Caesar' (John 19: 15), is seen as the ultimate betrayal of their divine calling. In the book of Revelation, Babylon – which symbolises the kingdoms of this world (Rome) – is doomed to destruction and has no claim on Christian loyalty. Many critics see, in the Pauline writings, a close connection between earthly, political authorities and the 'principalities and powers', rulers of darkness in the heavenly spheres. They point out that every time the term *exousiai* (authorities) is used in these writings it refers, with one exception, to spiritual (demonic) powers. That exception is when Paul uses the term with explicit reference to civil authorities in Romans 13: 1–7. It is thus unlikely that the spiritual, demonic connotation of the term is absent from this passage.[65]

Much debate has taken place on the interpretation of Romans 13, particularly in Germany, where it had been used by some Christians to justify obedience to Hitler. Most modern commentators argue that the statements made there, urging Christians to be 'subject' to the powers that be, must be read as advocating a response to specific historical circumstances, rather than as setting out general rules or providing a theology of the state. 'Paul is not advancing any theoretical considerations,' writes Ernst Käsemann. 'He is certainly not making exhaustive statements about the relation to authorities. Thus he is silent about possible conflicts and the limits of earthly authority.'[66] Paul's advice to Christians in Rome has illegitimately been erected into the foundation of an ideology of political domination, alien to the spirit of the New Testament, with its suspicion of 'the rulers of this age' who – ignorant of God's hidden wisdom – had 'crucified the Lord of glory' (1 Cor. 2: 8). The apostle may not rightfully be seen as here supplying Christians with a political theory, nor may it be claimed that there is a single 'biblical' doctrine of the state.

I am not then arguing that the Bible provides justification for an alternative system of government to that of kingship, such as populism, democracy or republicanism. Far from it. As Barr notes, it was *the people*, in the days of Samuel, who clamoured for a king. There is nothing in Scripture or in the history of the early church to suggest that consent of the governed bestows authority on a person or body of persons. Consent is seen as neither a necessary nor a sufficient condition of moral obligation, and political theories which base authority on contract can make no claim to a specifically Christian foundation. Apart from their need to rely upon grossly deceptive ideas such as 'tacit consent', the very basis of their position is unsound.[67]

Representative government

'Representative' government cannot, from a Christian standpoint, claim divine sanction. Representation is indeed a mare's nest. Perhaps Rousseau's most valuable contribution to political thinking was his critique of representation – of the idea that one will can be represented by another.[68]

In a sophisticated but vain attempt to rescue the concept of representation, Hanna Pitkin acknowledges that it is impossible to represent another person's will or desire. She suggests rather that representation involves acting in the interests of the public represented. But, recognising that benevolent despotism may claim to do this, she adds that representative government must also remain 'responsive to the people'.[69] She thus assumes there is such a thing as a public interest, or a common good – a matter to which I shall return – and that 'the people' is an entity having wishes to which a government may respond. The population of a modern state cannot, however, legitimately be said to have the kind of coherence and organic structure that is assumed in talking about its wishes. Certain voluntary human groups may, like individual persons, develop sufficient of a common life and purpose to justify speaking of their wishes or decisions, but the modern state is not one of them, and attempts to make it into such will succeed only at the cost of freedom, individual and corporate. Rousseau's assault on group life within his state was integral to his totalitarian aims. The kind of unity he sought, where 'the will of all' is replaced by a 'general will', is possible only when intermediate groups are eliminated and individuals identify themselves unambiguously and totally with the state.

Furthermore, representative government may be seen to encourage a subtle form of irresponsibility. Millions of adults hand over to a few hundred so-called representatives the right to make decisions on their behalf, while for the following four or five years these millions pursue in good conscience their own interests and pleasures. In any case, serious attempts to challenge decisions of the elected mandarins are denounced as undemocratic. 'Representative government' is perhaps the most effective disincentive there is to constructive social action at the local, regional or functional levels.

If talk of representation is nonsense, proportional representation is (to borrow a phrase of Bentham) 'rhetorical nonsense, nonsense upon stilts'. Such a system would merely give counterfeit validity to a regime on the grounds that it fully embodies 'the will of the people'. Depriving electors of any say in the person who is to 'represent' them, it removes the last vestige of power from local parties, handing it over to huge centralised party machines. This is the system of government which in 1976 the Church of England General Synod thought fit to urge as desirable for introduction in this country.[70] Like many Christian pronouncements on political issues it assumes (and in assuming gives a kind of approval to) a whole set of institutions and principles which are, to say the least, of questionable validity. In advocating proportional representation the Synod assumed that the notion of representation itself is meaningful and practicable.

When challenged on controversial issues of the moment, Jesus – as portrayed in the Gospels – frequently refused to answer in the terms proposed; rather he contested the assumptions of the questioner. Asked to adjudicate in a dispute between brothers about property, Luke has him calling into question the covetousness which constituted the basis of the whole property system and of the acquisitive society of his day (Luke 12: 13–20).[71] When asked whether taxes should be paid to the state, Jesus challenged his questioners with the absolute claims of God: 'Render to Caesar the things that are Caesar's and to God the things that are God's' (Matt. 22: 21). His reply carefully avoids giving a general legitimacy to the state.

Moral and political principles

Christianity does not then provide justification for the claim that obedience to rulers is the first duty of citizens, nor does it supply principles and ideals which limit the authority of the state or legitimise resistance. Behind the model of Christian politics I have been examining lies the belief that 'principles' can be derived from theological propositions in some kind of a political vacuum and subsequently be 'applied' to concrete situations. All we need to do is to get our theology straight, deduce our moral principles and, by means of middle axioms, apply them to the political world. The relationship between Christianity and politics is that of 'implication'. The report *Faith in the City* is rightly critical of an excessively 'deductive and academic' tendency in theology. Yet in its discussion of the connection between Christianity and politics it assumes this very model, referring to the 'social and political implications' of a gospel which is essentially concerned with 'personal relationships and individual responses'.[72] On this assumption the cosmic and social dimensions of Christian faith become matters of secondary importance, being deduced from the individual and personal kernel of the gospel.

In response to this view of the relation between Christianity and politics, it must be insisted that theology is always developed in a particular cultural, economic and political situation and that the very terms and images used in theological discourse are affected by these social factors. How Christians think of God's authority – his 'government of the universe', to use a phrase popular in the eighteenth century – will inevitably be affected by their experience of earthly structures of domination. Either consciously or subconsciously they will draw from this experience in their theological endeavours. If their only experience of human authority has been autocratic they are likely to conceive of God's relation to his people in similar terms. Thinking about God cannot therefore be done in a political vacuum.

A further aspect of this model that needs questioning is the role played by 'principles' in the process of political judgment. I believe

W.G. Ward was right in his insistence that Christian moral judgment is made in the particular case rather than in the general principle. We do not judge the rightness of actions by referring upwards to principles; rather we assess the adequacy of principles by examining the moral status of the particular consequences they entail. As Ward argued, a man does not first come to see that murder is wrong and then deduce that the murder he has just committed must have been bad. 'It is', he maintained, 'with indefinitely more keenness manifest to me that my past act was base, than that those general propositions are true.'[73]

In trying to discover what is right in a particular situation, rather than referring upwards to general principles it is perhaps better to look sideways to situations which are similar in relevant respects. Much legal argument, particularly when appealing to the common law, proceeds by looking for close analogies rather than by invoking general rules. The appeal 'sideways' will not assuredly solve all problems, for there remains the vexed question of which cases are relevant. This difficulty is, however, shared by those who attempt to make such judgments by subsuming particular cases under general rules. A misconceived belief in the priority of moral principles is partly responsible for the insistence by many that Christian pronouncements on political issues should be restricted to the enunciation of generalities rather than the making of particular judgments.

I am by no means suggesting that general rules have no proper role in moral judgment. They may be useful guides to action, but are merely summaries of moral experience on the issue in question. Logically the experience and the particular judgments made on the basis of this experience are prior to the general rule, whose truth rests on the validity of the experience and the soundness of the judgment. How such validity and soundness are to be assessed is a question to which I shall return in the Conclusion.

Nor am I arguing that Scripture and tradition provide anything like a theological justification for anarchism as a positive theory, but rather that they cannot properly be used as a basis for theories of political obligation. It may, however, be worth bearing in mind the words of Pierre-Joseph Proudhon, who echoed Rousseau, in observing that 'Government is either of divine right or it is nothing.'[74]

The analogy between divine and political government has frequently been employed to strengthen the claims of the state. In the ancient Near East kings were thought to be themselves gods, in the most literal sense.[75] Christians could not assent to this position and they replaced it with the associated doctrines of the divine right of kings and the divine analogy. When in the seventeenth century the former came increasingly under fire the analogy was retained, even among contract theorists like Hobbes and Locke. Ideas of divine authority have since that time provided legitimation for structures of civil authority in a way which the following chapters will call into question.

What, then, can properly be said about the relationship between images and concepts used of God and of the state? It often seems that God is pictured as doing more perfectly what the state is failing to achieve. In an age of civil disturbance he was 'the author of peace and lover of concord' who is able to establish 'that peace which the world cannot give'. For Hobbes he was the perfect sovereign, whose omnipotence created an unqualified obligation to obey, an obligation which the *earthly* sovereign could secure only by the consent of the people. Leibniz pictured God as the creator of the best of possible worlds – where, by a sort of cost-benefit approach, evil was minimised and welfare maximised – anticipating in certain respects the bureaucratically benevolent deity of twentieth-century liberalism. Today God is thought of by many people in the North Atlantic nations as the celestial grandmother, indulgently handing out benefits and performing more satisfactorily the role which an under-financed welfare state tries vainly to fulfil.

2

Welfare God and paternal state I

> Some men seem to think the only character of the Author of Nature to be that of simple absolute benevolence. . . . And supposing this to be the only character of God, veracity and justice in him would be nothing but benevolence conducted by wisdom. Now surely this ought not to be asserted, unless it can be proved.[1]

So wrote Joseph Butler, eighteenth-century Bishop of Durham, anticipating a tendency which was to become predominant in later years. Benevolence and welfare are undoubtedly characteristic features of western ideas of both God and the state in the twentieth century. While it is true that these concepts have often in past ages been applied both to divine and political authority, they have rarely been seen as the *principal* attributes of God and the state. In an age when 'courtesy and consideration' are regarded more highly than truth or honesty in public controversy and 'caring and concern' are thought to be the most pressing of social duties, it is not surprising that ideas of welfare emerge as predominant in our thinking about God and the state. Both are seen as all powerful and sovereign within their own spheres, but as using their power benevolently by handing out benefits. As the monolithic and bureaucratic God of Protestantism has increasingly taken over the protective and entrepreneurial functions of saints and angels, so the perennial social institutions of patronage and charity have been centralised and rationalised in the modern welfare state.

Throughout the nineteenth century, in Britain and in other countries of western Europe, the effects of the industrial revolution were making themselves felt in social life. Massive movements of population, leading to the rapid growth of slum dwellings in the larger industrial cities, had reduced the relative importance of the small country towns, where the established church and the gentry, with their paternalistic traditions, were most at home. Working-class discontent was evident; the Chartist movement of the 1840s had sounded a warning. Some regulation of the situation was urgently required in order to prevent revolution. Setting theory aside, piecemeal legislation had been passed to regulate child labour and to compel employers to introduce minimum standards of safety. Reports issued by health and sanitary inspectors, factory inspectors and education inspectors called for changes. Statutory boards were set up to supervise and regulate. While paying lip-service to ideas of *laissez-faire*, mid-nineteenth-century governments made no consistent attempts to follow it.

The growth of welfare legislation in the mid-nineteenth century was due not to the power of some overarching theory but to 'the revelation of intolerable evils', and to a recognition that amelioration was the only alternative to revolution.[2] Practice, as normally happens, preceded a coherent theory and the new legislation was defended on a number of conflicting and incompatible grounds. Certainly extensive governmental action could be justified by the utilitarian principle of the general happiness, and David Roberts rightly points to the fact that many utilitarians believed in strong, centralised benevolent government.[3] Bentham himself, however, had been suspicious of governmental action, believing that all legislation constitutes a restriction on liberty. He had set utilitarianism in the context of two individualist principles: first, that each person is generally speaking the best judge of his own happiness and, second, that the general happiness of a community is nothing more than the sum of the happiness of its members. Curiously J.B. Brebner criticises Dicey in the following terms: 'In using Bentham as the archetype of British individualism he was conveying the exact opposite of the truth. Jeremy Bentham was the archetype of British collectivism.'[4] It is surely Brebner who has misconceived the position, for collectivism is but a corollary of individualism, a belief that a social whole is ultimately nothing more than a collection of individuals.

Even J.S. Mill's modifications of utilitarianism left it implacably opposed to all sorts of paternalism. No government is justified in coercing individuals for their own good. Mill insisted that 'there is a circle around every individual human being, which no government, be it that of one, of a few, or of the many, ought to be permitted to overstep'.[5] While agreeing that all actions are likely to affect others in some degree, Mill insisted that a government has the right to interfere with individuals only when their actions affect others directly and in the first instance, or break some assignable obligation which they may have.[6] While it is true that towards the end of his life Mill was able to justify a considerable degree of governmental regulation, a basic individualism made his theory inappropriate as the ideology of a welfare state.

While it is undoubtedly true that 'utilitarian liberal-democratic individualism'[7] was a major feature of nineteenth-century Britain, at no time did theories of *laissez-faire* achieve total domination of the ideological stage. A paternalistic 'Tory' view of the state continued to be asserted or assumed by many politicians and churchmen. It had found expression in the essays and lay sermons of Coleridge; it is present in Sewell, Maurice, Kingsley and Ludlow, in Disraeli, Matthew Arnold, Ruskin and Carlyle. Arnold's designation of the state in 1869 as 'the appointed frame and prepared vessel of our best self . . . powerful, beneficent and sacred expression and organ', strikingly anticipates the language of the British idealists.[8] This tradition was closely related to liberal theology and frequently to Erastian tendencies.

In these two chapters we shall see how the concept of welfare has come to dominate much contemporary thinking in religion and politics, and I shall examine the roots of this tendency. After a brief and somewhat impressionistic discussion of the present situation I shall consider the thought of William Temple, in whose writings the theme of benevolence plays a major role. In his early years Temple owed much to British idealism as taught by Edward Caird of Balliol College. Also influenced by the Scottish philosopher was William Beveridge, another key figure in the growth of the welfare state. Caird was, of course, part of a whole movement of thought which can be traced back to Thomas Hill Green and Benjamin Jowett. This movement had importance both in religion and politics; later sections will examine how ideas of welfare and benevolence featured as central in both fields.

The 'new liberals' around the turn of the century thus owed much to Balliol College, as did the pioneers of the university settlements in east London. The incarnational emphasis of the *Lux Mundi* school of theologians and the Christian Social Union contributed substantially to this way of thinking. Among liberal Christians of the period, a persistent theme is that of 'personality', human and divine, which played a crucial role, especially in the context of a theology of the atonement. Those chiefly responsible for introducing the social legislation of the Asquith government looked to developments in state welfare which had already occurred in Germany, and we shall note some similarities in the theological and political climate of the two countries.

Confirmation of the relationship between the welfare God and the paternal state comes from the pen of a perceptive agnostic. What occurred, wrote Beatrice Webb, was that 'the impulse of self-subordinating service was transferred consciously and overtly from God to man'.[9] The idea of 'service' will recur frequently in the following pages. It has become a commonplace that the church exists to 'serve society' and that the supreme Christian virtue is 'service'. This is enunciated clearly in the 1980 *Alternative Service Book*, where we pray, at Morning Prayer, that we may 'give ourselves in love and service to one another'; in the marriage office we pray that God may give to the couple 'grace to minister to others'. On Maundy Thursday we ask that we may be given 'the will to be the servants of others' and in the Ordination of Bishops we note that the first duty of a bishop to be listed is 'to lead in serving and caring', and only later is it noted that he has obligations to teach, preach and defend the faith. It is somehow assumed in all this that Christians are in the superior position of offering service to others rather than needing it themselves. Too often we assume that, in the story of the Good Samaritan, we are in the role of the priest, the Levite or (optimistically) the Samaritan, rather than being the victim in need of assistance.

THE WELFARE STATE TODAY

The predominant image of the state held by individuals and shared by groups will depend to some degree upon their position in the social structure and dynamics of a nation and upon their perception of this position. While the white upper-middle-class property owner of Cheltenham or Tunbridge Wells sees the state as protector and guardian, the unemployed black youth of south London sees it as prison warder. Clearly it is not simply a matter of economic class in a crudely objective sense. In the recent conflicts over the miners' strike, undoubtedly many respectable workers, the 'angels in marble',[10] saw Mrs Thatcher's government as holding back the forces of 'anarchy', while a good number of academics, clergy and civil servants looked with some alarm on the use of the police in the explicitly political role of strike breakers. One concept or image of the state which is fairly universally held, however, is that of the sovereign provider of benefits. While no group is entirely happy with the way in which welfare services are distributed, there has been until recently such broad agreement on the general idea of a welfare state that the small minority in the Conservative Party who would like to see it dismantled have been able to exercise a very limited influence even on the policy of the present government. In its third term of office, however, it seems that the Thatcher regime will take more definite steps to reduce welfare services.

The principal welfare services, such as education and the National Health Service, have been popular across a wide social and political spectrum and it would be difficult for a government entirely to dismantle these. The present government has announced major reviews in these areas. The cuts which have taken place in recent years have tended to affect only the very poorest. Peter Taylor-Gooby writes, 'It is those services which cater mainly for the weakest groups of consumers rather than the mass services which have done worst in the cuts of the past decade.'[11]

Industries and services

Welfare is, of course, only one of the functions performed by the state in western capitalist democracies. Principally by means of the device of the public corporation, central and local government play a major part as suppliers of services – such as electricity, water, transport – and as manufacturers (through financial interest in companies like BP and Austin–Rover). Those who were undergraduates at the London School of Economics in the mid-fifties will remember the hymns of praise to the public corporation sung by Professor W.A. Robson in his lectures on British government. It combined, so we were told, the entrepreneurial flexibility of the private company with the public accountability of the government department. As we have learned since then, it also frequently combines the hierarchical attitudes towards the workforce of private enterprise with the bureaucratic ineptitude popularly ascribed to the civil service. Furthermore, while there is at least the possibility of a government maintaining some kind of impartiality in a dispute between workers and management in a private industry, this is hardly possible in a nationalised industry where the government is itself responsible for broad policy decisions and for appointing the board chairman. It nevertheless continues to pose as impartial.

The policy of privatising state-owned services and industries has done something to counteract these tendencies, but brings new problems with it. Central government has less control of and responsibility for the detailed operation of these industries, though it retains sufficient powers to determine general policy directions. The notion that these corporations have been 'returned to the people' is of course an illusion; control is effectively handed over to huge financial conglomerates in the City of London.

Central government, through its control of public corporations and by means of the fiscal and monetary powers of the Treasury, is a major determinant of economic and social developments in western European countries like Britain. The other principal groups whose decisions affect the interests of the people in these countries are the private financial institutions – such as banks and insurance companies – and the senior directors of large private industries. A widely held belief that trade-union leaders have powers which rival those of private finance and industry is mistaken. While they do have certain 'negative' powers, in preventing changes which they believe to be against the interests of their members or of the working class in general, they have very limited powers in positively determining the future course of events. This is largely because, within the present structure of British industry, they possess neither the information nor the resources to influence major decisions. At the level of the individual company, trade-union leaders and shop stewards are rarely consulted on future policy and are only informed on matters which will immediately affect the interests of their members. Consumer associations and other similar bodies have even less influence on industrial policy.

In certain respects the post-war period has seen a decline in the power of the 'nation-state' as it is misleadingly called. In western Europe many defence decisions are taken by supra-national bodies, like NATO, and the power of the bureaucracy at Brussels continues to grow, regulating such things as road transport and the temperature at which beer should be stored in EEC countries. Furthermore governments today find it impossible to control the activities of the huge transnational corporations operating within their borders.

The corporate state

One of the great tragedies of the present century is the way in which trade unions have abdicated from whole areas of their legitimate concern. Much of their energy has quite properly been devoted to improving – at the micro-level – the wages and working conditions of their members. Also, at what might be called the macro-level, great efforts have been made to ensure the election of a Labour government, which it was hoped would act in the interests of the trade-union movement and of the working class in general. Again, in more recent years trade unions have become involved in national tripartite bodies, such as the Manpower Services Commission, with government and the Confederation of British Industry. But very little has been done, in areas between these two levels, towards securing a powerful voice in the policy of the particular industry in which the union operates. Whereas the slogan 'self-help not state help' may be misleading when applied to individuals, there is a great deal that could have been done in the way of co-operative developments by the unions in conjunction with the old friendly societies. Certainly this would be no substitute for political action at the national level, but it might have provided a solid base upon which a truly socialist government could build.

In the post-1945 programme of nationalisation, most trade unions resisted involvement in management by refusing representation on the boards of the state enterprises, because they had a shrewd suspicion that they were likely to be blamed for decisions over which they would have no ultimate control and because of a traditional unwillingness to become involved in policy decisions affecting the industries in which they worked. Unions were, however, lured in the sixties into partnership with government and private industry. This culminated in the so-called 'social contract' and in such dubious institutions as the National Enterprise Board,[12] which was uncritically celebrated in a pamphlet issued by the Church of England Board for Social Responsibility as marking a hopeful sign that there are no basic conflicts of interests and that with a little common sense all will be well.[13]

The malaise in local government

Although there has been, over the past few decades, an enormous growth in local government bureaucracies, the effective power of elected councillors has almost certainly declined. Discussing the staggering shift of investment and employment from productive industry to service industries, R. Bacon and W. Eltis note that between 1961 and 1974 there was an increase of 54 per cent in the number employed by local authorities in contrast to a rise of only 9 per cent in central government.[14] Many welfare services are now managed by local government, but the finance needed for these operations is largely derived from grants by the Treasury and the ultimate control over policy is in the hands of central government. Although local government in Britain has not been self-supporting for many years, it has come to depend more and more on central financing and has thus gradually lost much of its autonomy. By rate-capping and by threatening to withhold grants, central government is able to determine in a quite detailed way the policies pursued by county and borough councils. Two writers refer to 'the overwhelming constitutional, political and financial domination of local by central government'.[15] Proposed legislation will further reduce the independence of local authorities.

Another aspect of these developments is a shift of power away from elected representatives to paid officials. The recommendations of the Bains Report of 1972 that such a change should take place have been widely adopted.[16] It would, of course, be wrong to suggest that such officials are necessarily more reactionary than city councillors, but they tend to mix more readily with other members of local elites, adopting the assumptions of these groups, and are less responsive to local working-class opinion. Kenneth Newton has demonstrated the links which have existed in Birmingham between established business and professional groups and council officials, while another author notes that in Wolverhampton the town clerk, city treasurer, chief constable, medical officer of health and director of education all belonged to the Round Table or Rotary Clubs.[17] Furthermore, paid officials are less likely than elected representatives to question or challenge the policy of central government as their jobs depend upon a smooth working relationship between these authorities; the strengthening of their relative position in local government thus marks a further stage in the centralisation of power in Westminster and Whitehall.

Law enforcement, executive discretion and the treatment of deviants

In western capitalist democracies, then, the government continues to play a major part in determining social and economic developments. As we shall see, its welfare role is of great significance, but it is worth mentioning also the less benign aspects of the modern state. The police, the lawcourts and the prisons exist in order to deal with actions which are thought to be anti-social – normally involving attacks on the person or the property of citizens. Although these institutions are in certain respects reasonably impartial, there are other ways in which the law is administered unfairly. Judges maintain an impartial attitude with respect to the government of the day, but are generally conservative and suspicious of almost any change. Their educational background is public school and Oxbridge and in social life they tend to mix with other members of the upper classes.[18]

It is undoubtedly the case that police and magistrates deal more gently with whites than with blacks, with the upper or middle class than with the poor. Actions which are envisaged as posing a general threat to the property system are dealt with most severely. The police keep a close watch on individuals and groups who are thought to challenge the present social arrangements and at least one Labour minister had her telephone tapped while in office. There is evidence to suggest that British intelligence agencies – or elements within these bodies – actively attempted to destabilise at least one British Labour government in recent years. In the background are the armed forces, who are expected to support the police in cases of crisis, as in Northern Ireland, and who will intervene in labour disputes to maintain 'essential services'.[19] As we shall see, the legal system and more generally the agencies of law enforcement have, over the past few decades, increasingly incorporated welfare elements into their operations.

One of the most alarming features of our present welfare state is the increasing power of government officials to impose certain kinds of treatment on deviants. Although it is true that judges are notoriously inconsistent in the severity of sentences they impose, at least they act publicly and are able to be criticised for their delinquencies. More alarming is the power which resides in parole boards effectively to reduce the sentences of long-term prisoners by as much as one-third. These boards include among their members one psychiatrist, social worker, criminologist and a person who holds or has held judicial office. The board does not meet the prisoner, who is unrepresented at a hearing. On the argument that parole is not a right but a 'privilege', a prisoner whose application is rejected is given no reasons and has no right of appeal. The power which prison officers have in influencing the decision is considerable and the criteria which the boards use are various. 'The outline criteria for granting parole', writes Professor Terence Morris, 'suggest that those most likely to get it will include those whose behaviour has not merely been exemplary, but indicates a willingness to comply with the expectations of the prison system with regard to behavioural change and personal "improvement".'[20]

Another area in which executive discretion blurs the distinction between justice and an attempt to modify or improve human character is delineated by the Children and Young Persons Act of 1969, under which children who have committed no criminal offence may be taken from their families into 'care'. The enormous power social workers have in influencing the decision whether a child should be so treated against the wishes of its parents is no doubt normally exercised with responsibility. Nevertheless the relevant question is whether they should have this power when no offence has been committed.

Lawcourts ought in the first instance to be concerned with the conviction of offenders and the just imposition of appropriate penalties. The idea that punishment should be concerned more with the future of the offenders than with the past act which they have committed is partly responsible for these developments. In certain extraordinary circumstances it may be proper for governments to impose sanctions on a person who has not been convicted of breaking a law, but this should not be done under the cover of the judicial system. Even if the forms of treatment used could be shown to be successful in preventing crime, the system would be unjust as it stands. In fact few if any studies have shown that the forms of therapy employed have had the intended consequences. Perhaps the most vivid portrayal of this approach to punishment is to be seen in the life story of George Jackson, recorded in *Soledad Brother*. Jackson was, at the age of 18, committed to prison on a sentence of one year to life, dependent on good conduct, for driving the getaway car in a robbery in which 70 dollars were stolen and in which no violence was used. His determined refusal to accept a process of degradation imposed by his captors led to parole being continually refused. After having spent ten years in prison, seven and a half of them in solitary confinement, he was accused of killing a prison guard.[21]

It is not difficult to find the origins of the notion of punishment which has inspired these developments. In rejecting all forms of retribution in favour of utilitarianism, liberal theorists like Hastings Rashdall, whose ideas we shall be considering in a later section, opened the way for the gradual replacement of justice by social conditioning. A sovereign but paternal state has become the counterpart of a bureaucratic and benevolent God.

Welfare services and the plight of the poorest

It is important to see the growth of public welfare in western countries in the context of the more general role of the state in maintaining social order. The state today through its family allowances, educational system and health services makes a major contribution to what Marxists call 'the reproduction of labour power', so that private industry has a moderately educated and healthy labour force on which to call, provided at no direct cost to itself. The welfare state's other role is to care for the temporarily or permanently non-working population – the young, old, sick, injured or unemployed.[22]

While it is true to say that there are few who would wish to abolish the welfare state, the reasons why different groups continue to support it are various. Speaking of those nineteenth-century developments which led to the growth of the welfare state, Danish Socialminister Ritt Bjerregaard declared:

Social policy is – historically – the very opposite of socialism; it arose as a way to combat socialism by mitigating some of the most conspicuous excesses of capitalism and thus removing the mobilization basis of the Social Democrats.[23]

State welfare indeed plays an ambivalent role in our social dynamics today. As Richard Titmuss pointed out, it 'can serve different masters' and can be used as an important means of 'social control'.[24] Perhaps the most glaring example of this is to be found in Puerto Rico, where a large proportion of the population depends on food stamps and other handouts, and where support for a continuation of some close association with the USA is consequently widespread. Governor Carlos Romero has recently declared: 'In the past there has been too much dependence on the accustomed government paternalism. Citizens and entrepreneurs turn to the government to solve their problems or difficulties of their own making. This practice must now end.'[25] More generally in western liberal democracies welfare benefits cushion large numbers from the worst effects of the economic system, enabling them to put up with a situation which would otherwise become intolerable.

The welfare state as we know it in Britain today really dates from the Second World War. It is interesting to note how war, in the present century, has been a principal stimulus to the growth of state welfare. The increase in public expenditure has not been a gradual phenomenon, but has made two great leaps forward during the two world wars.[26] For example, the most important Education Acts of the century were passed during or just after a major war. After the Boer War the physical and mental unpreparedness of the working class to fight for their country led to urgent enquiry and action. Also the destruction of houses through bombing, together with wartime experience of tight control on the production and distribution of goods, facilitated an acceptance of state regulation in the ensuing peacetime. The celebrated 'Beveridge Report' of 1942 declared war on the giants of want, disease, ignorance, squalor and idleness and made proposals for their abolition.[27] The Education Act of 1944 laid the basis for developments in the school system and, with the Family Allowances Act of 1945, the National Insurance Act of 1946 and the National Health Service inaugurated in 1948, changed the face of Britain. The fifties and sixties saw the development of new forms of welfare, particularly in the field of personal services. Only in the mid-seventies (under a Labour government) was there a check in the growth rate of government spending on social services. Government expenditure, as a proportion of gross national product, bears little relationship to the political complexion of the party in power. The Swedish conservatives, for example, presided over a huge increase in public spending on coming to power after forty-four years of social-democratic rule.

Government expenditure in Britain has continued to grow, as has the proportion of the workforce employed by central and local government. As a percentage of GNP, government expenditure increased from 16.6 per cent in 1961 to 22.3 per cent in 1981, to become the highest among the major western countries.[28] The trend continues; but it should not be forgotten that welfare is only one item. The British sometimes assume that their own welfare state leads that in other countries, but in 1981 the British government spent a lower percentage of its total expenditure on welfare than the USA, Japan, France, Italy or West Germany.[29]

In recent years there have also been changes in the general structure of the welfare state in the capitalist democracies. Some countries, including France and Germany, started with government-sponsored insurance schemes and later developed systems of national assistance, while others, like Britain and the Scandinavian countries, began with a policy of public assistance and have incorporated the insurance principle by introducing an 'earnings-related' element into welfare provisions.[30]

As early as 1958 doubts were expressed in Britain about whether the welfare state was in fact helping those who needed it most, the very poor. Brian Abel-Smith wrote, 'the middle classes receive good standards of welfare while working people receive a spartan minimum'. From a very different standpoint, authors in a book edited by Rhodes Boyson in 1971 mounted a spirited attack on the welfare state, maintaining that it is not the poor who benefit most.[31] Yet the changes made by the present government over the past decade have made things worse in this respect. Although total government expenditure on welfare increased from £67.9 billion in 1979–80 to £78.9 billion in 1986–7, benefits to the worst-off declined.[32] John Atherton has recently written, 'the Welfare State as it now operates is so implicated in the creation and maintenance of poverty that it must be regarded as a major cause of deprivation'. Further criticisms of this kind have been made both from 'right' and 'left'.[33]

The middle and upper classes are normally in a better position than the poor to benefit from state welfare provisions, particularly in education. Also in assessing which sectors benefit most from the present structure of the welfare state it is important (as Frank Field has argued) to consider who pays. In the post-war period there have been three significant shifts in the incidence of tax: from the rich to the poor, from the single and childless to families with children, and from direct to indirect taxation.[34] As a recent Church of England report observes, there has been a change over the past decades in the way that welfare services have been financed. Income tax, which is a progressive tax, hitting the rich more than the poor, provides only 27 per cent of the revenue spent on welfare, while in 1948 the figure was 32 per cent. Indirect taxes, which hit the poor and rich alike, and national insurance contributions have provided proportionately more. The unemployed contribute £600 million annually from the taxing of their unemployment benefit.[35]

Some critics of the welfare state argue that the prejudice against employing a 'means test' in order to ensure that only the needy receive certain kinds of benefits is another reason why the poor do not profit more from the system. This is related to the theoretical controversy on whether welfare benefits should be considered as rights or more in terms of a 'gift relationship'.[36] Many of the post-1945 advocates of the welfare state, who 'strapped on their armour and declared a holy war on its critics',[37] insisted that there should be none of the old stigma of receiving charity in the new order of things. In so far as certain forms of national insurance involve the payment of regular contributions, the pension and unemployment or sickness benefit can be said to be a right. Yet even here strict actuarial principles have not been applied and the fund from which benefits have been paid has been supplemented by other sources of public income. Also assuming we consider the welfare payments as a right, someone has to determine whether an applicant is entitled to particular benefits and social workers can easily adopt a posture of condescension which leads to friction with their clients. As Marshall has pointed out, with 'the imbalance of authority between the providers and the recipients of the service' there is a danger of paternalism.[38]

Christians played an important role in the development of the welfare state in Britain. Their wholly admirable concern to alleviate suffering and destitution has been a major factor in influencing the course of events. At times Christians deduced moral principles from their theology and self-consciously applied them in issues of social policy in a manner of which E.R. Norman would approve. At other times an instinctive reaction to perceived evils was the most important motive force. It is the argument of this chapter, however, that analogies drawn from theology have played a significant part in affecting Christian social action. The benevolence and welfare functions of a divine ruler became a model – semi-consciously adopted – for a paternal state. It is of course also true that this way of thinking about God was itself related to the social context in which these men found themselves, to the tradition of Tory paternalism which they inherited from their parents and from their public schools. In no single Christian figure do these factors come together more clearly and powerfully than in William Temple.

WILLIAM TEMPLE: GOD AND THE WELFARE STATE

'A meeting of well-known reformers' was how the local paper recorded the marriage, in June 1909, of R.H. Tawney to Jeanette, the sister of William Beveridge. William Temple officiated and the sermon was preached by the celebrated Canon Samuel Barnett of Toynbee Hall.[39]

Temple was probably the first person to use the term 'welfare state' in print[40] and he embodied many of the assumptions and tendencies of his generation, playing – in turn – a unique role in reinforcing and popularising them. More through the force of his personality than the originality or profundity of his ideas, he has had an enormous influence on the political and religious assumptions of our day. Many of the pronouncements of episcopal spokesmen and of church commissions in recent years – characterised as they are by a somewhat uncritical 'left-of-centre' statism – take their tone from the writings of Temple. But his influence extended far beyond the Church of England. It has been said that, after Winston Churchill, the two men who contributed most to the spirit of Britain during the Second World War were the comedian, Tommy Handley, and Temple, the archbishop. A well-known column writer in the *Daily Herald* could even ascribe the Labour victory of 1945 largely to Temple's influence.[41]

Temple: the man and his work

Temple was born in 1881, son of the then Bishop of Exeter, Frederick Temple, who later became Archbishop of Canterbury.[42] He was educated at Rugby School and Balliol College, Oxford, where he came under the powerful influence of Edward Caird. In 1904 he became a philosophy fellow of the Queen's College, Oxford, and was headmaster of Repton School from 1910 to 1914. At this time he published two essays in the celebrated volume, *Foundations* (1912). Three years as rector of St James's Piccadilly were followed by two years working for the Life and Liberty Movement, which was concerned to achieve a greater degree of freedom for the Church of England in determining its worship and doctrine. In 1919 he became Canon of Westminster, remaining for just two years before being consecrated Bishop of Manchester. In 1929 he was enthroned as Archbishop of York and was translated to Canterbury in 1942. He died two years later. Temple was a prolific writer and speaker. His best books were *Mens Creatrix* (1917), *Christus Veritas* (1924) and the Gifford Lectures published under the title *Nature, Man and God* (1934). His meditational *Readings in St John's Gospel* (1939–40) reached a wide audience. Temple also published a number of small books on political and social issues.

The principal philosophical influences upon Temple were those of English idealism of the school of T.H. Green and later the 'process' philosophy of Samuel Alexander and A.N. Whitehead. Evolutionary ideas are evident in his later works, where he referred increasingly to 'the World-Process', rather than to 'the World-Principle', a term which appears in *Foundations*.[43] Philosophically he claimed that he had moved from idealism to a critical realism and developed a growing appreciation for Thomism.[44] This philosophical development was accompanied by a greater willingness to accept the miraculous and supernatural aspects of orthodox Christianity. Nevertheless, even in his early writings, Temple was insistent upon the centrality of the incarnation and on the particularity of God's revelation in Christ, always maintaining that salvation must be seen as a gift of God rather than a human achievement.

Temple's social thought is characterised throughout, however, by a strongly moralistic approach and by a general optimism. 'To deny the reality of moral progress', he declared in 1934, 'is wanton'.[45] On the political events of his day Temple usually adopted a moderate position generally calculated to reinforce the status quo. He gave unhesitating support to the war effort in both world wars, he condemned the general strike of 1926 'unreservedly' and advocated a Bradlean ethic of 'my station and its duties'.[46] Even the Life and Liberty Movement was designed to maintain the established church in its special relationship with the state.

One of his last books clearly reflects this generally conservative position. In his widely read 'Penguin Special', *Christianity and Social Order* (the title is significant), Temple insisted on the church's duty to 'inculcate Christian principles and the power of the Christian spirit'. Earlier he had been optimistic about the role of these principles in solving social problems. 'A religion which offers no solution to world-problems', he wrote in 1920, 'fails to satisfy.'[47] By the 1940s, however, he believed that, while Christianity cannot supply the answers to concrete political problems, it can 'lift the parties to a level of thought and feeling at which the problem disappears'. The role of the Christian religion is to supply ethical principles which can in turn be related to the complex problems of social life.[48]

'The concern of Christians as such', he told the Malvern Conference of 1941, 'is with principles and not with policies. . . . The constant proclamation of principles is the only way, and a genuinely effective way, of fulfilling this responsibility.'[49] Ethics is erroneously seen as the only significant link between religion and politics or economics.[50] Such principles as 'the sanctity of personality' should be seen as the basis from which individual Christians should work out 'middle axioms' which would mediate between these general ethical principles and particular political policies.[51] By insisting that Christians, as such, should be concerned with principles rather than with policies he ensured that nothing they said, as such, would be likely to have much immediate effect.

Like many British philosophers, Temple had almost no historical sense and saw past events as a storehouse of exemplary models which might guide present action, and past writings as being more or less satisfactory answers to a set of timeless problems. Consequently he hardly recognised the importance of the historical context within which Christian faith is practised and formulated. He assumed that if only Christians could get their theology straight they could then deduce universally valid ethical principles which could be applied to social problems. It may be, however, that the social and political commitments of the Christian industrialists and businessmen to whom he appealed were such that their understanding of Christianity was very different from that of Christians from less privileged classes.

God and the state

For Temple both God and the state were in the first instance characterised by 'sovereignty' in their respective realms. God is the one who commands. In contrast to philosophy, religion says that 'God has issued orders, and man's duty is therefore to obey.'[52] Failing to do one's duty is seen by the religious man as 'disloyalty to a king'. He insisted on 'the Majesty of God' and rightly rejected any attempt to describe God simply in terms of love; power too must be ascribed to the deity.[53]

With respect to the state, Temple insisted, in his later writings, that it must be distinguished from 'society', though it is not at all clear to what entity the latter term refers. He spoke of the 'sovereign state' without making explicit how this sovereignty accords with the claims made by groups within and how it relates to the state's international obligations which he recognised. 'The corporate persons', he wrote, 'need freedom just as much as the individual; hence the need, the vital and absolute need, for political sovereignty in any State, which is conscious of itself as a person, that is as having spiritual life.'[54] It is difficult to make sense of Temple's ideas on state sovereignty and it would not be unfair to say that his political theory is generally a somewhat incoherent amalgam of notions inherited from his undergraduate days.

Power and sovereignty are, then, attributes of both God and the state; so are benevolence and welfare. Although God is seen as monarch he has personal and paternal relations with men and women. The heart of religion, Temple claimed, is 'a personal relationship with God' and the closest analogy is to be found 'in our relation to a person whom we trust and love'. He asserted that the ends of life include 'religion, art and science', but 'above all happy human relationships'.[55] He criticised Whitehead for failing to assert the personality of God and, with the philosopher Lotze,[56] maintained that the idea of personality was realised fully in God and in human beings only partially and imperfectly. This emphasis on personality was characteristic of the period and is embodied in the writings of R.C. Moberly, C.C.J. Webb, Hastings Rashdall and the school of 'personal idealists'.[57] The tendency to reduce all important issues to questions of personal relationships reached its nadir, however, at Cambridge, with E.M. Forster and the Bloomsbury Circle: 'only connect'!

If God is personal then God may be seen as 'our fellow-sufferer', who 'suffers as men suffer'.[58] The incarnation of the Son of God and his identification with the pain of the world is seen by Temple as being an indication of the eternal nature of God. God, then, is involved in his creation: he is not the transcendent God of the deists – the monarch who set up a system of laws which never can be broken and then retired; such inflexibility would not be majestic but mulish. Rather God is to be seen as the concerned bureaucrat continually adjusting his rules for the welfare of his constituents; he is 'the all-comprehending Mind'. God, he told the boys of Repton, 'desires the welfare of all His children, and if we love him we shall labour for the welfare of all His children'.[59] The call to service is a constant theme of these sermons. 'The only true dignity', he wrote in an early tract, is 'the dignity of service'.[60]

Conciliation and the common good

The state too must be concerned with welfare, with forwarding the common good of its members. This idea of a general interest or common good, a substantive social good encompassing the good of all citizens, which it should be the object of public policy to realise, was imbibed while Temple studied with Edward Caird at Balliol. 'All classes in the nation', the master had declared in his lay sermon on the occasion of the death of Queen Victoria, 'are bound together by common memories of the past, common interests of the present, and common hopes of the future.' William Temple was probably among the crowd of undergraduates who gathered in the hall and heard these words. The notion of a common good had, of course, been at the centre of the political teaching of T.H. Green, whose influence still lingered among Balliol men.[61]

That such an identifiable common interest exists, Temple never doubted. Before casting his vote a church member should always ask not what is best for himself but 'What will be best for the country?' The criterion of right social action is the 'welfare of society'.[62] Like Dr Thomas Arnold he saw the public school of which he was headmaster as a microcosm of the state. 'Our interests here', he told the boys of Repton in one of his Sunday sermons, 'are altogether dependent on the welfare of our House and School. . . . The life of the school is more important to us than our own lives; there is no conflict of interest.' The preacher voiced the somewhat unlikely proposition that no boy could possibly suppose that anything could be good for himself which was bad for the school and went on to assure the boys that by analogy 'there is one welfare of England which includes the welfare of all classes'.[63] At other times Temple recognised that 'We are still "Two Nations", in Disraeli's phrase', but made no attempt to relate this to the bland assumption of a common interest. He viewed with alarm 'the rapid growth of militant class consciousness' and asserted (without argument) that national loyalty is 'morally superior to class-loyalty'.[64]

Temple believed that on occasions when social conflicts arise ecclesiastical leaders should contribute to a solution by urging 'the spirit and method of conciliation' and by admonishing the parties in a conflict to return to proposals made by royal commissions and other supposedly impartial bodies. The assumption throughout is that there are no basic conflicts of interest and that with a bit of good sense and Christian charity adjustments can be made which will satisfy all parties.[65] In a series of broadcasts in 1940, entitled 'The Hope of a New World', Temple naïvely suggested that 'Christian industrialists and business men should get together, along with some economists and one or two theologians, to work out what is really involved for their own part of the nation's life.'[66]

In *The Education of Citizens*, Temple reflected the influence of the idealist political philosophy of Caird and Green. A man, he wrote, 'has no right to have his talents developed apart from his intention to devote them to the state. . . . The man is essentially *and before all else* a member of the state.'[67] A citizen owes loyalty to the state, or at least to the nation (he normally failed to make a clear distinction between them), 'not because it is his country, but because he is its citizen – not because in some sense it belongs to him, but because in a far deeper sense he belongs to it'. Yet duty to the state ought never to involve neglecting the general interests of mankind; the Christian should check the narrower loyalty by the wider and remember that ultimately 'only to God is an absolute allegiance due'.[68]

Politics and welfare

On the basis of ideas about human personality, brotherhood, service and self-sacrifice Temple outlined a Christian approach to politics. He saw the role of the state as working in a positive way to increase substantive human freedom, to embody and to realise the common good. This was the foundation of the 'Welfare-State', which in 1929 he distinguished from the 'Power-State'. He claimed that the First World War had in fact been fought over which of these conceptions of the state should predominate.

> The war was a struggle between the idea of the State as essentially Power – Power over its own community and against other communities – and of the State as the organ of community, maintaining its solidarity by law designed to safeguard the interests of the community. The Power-State might have yielded to sheer pressure of circumstances in course of time; but it is contrary to the psychology of the Power-State to suffer conversion; it was likely to fight before it let a Welfare-State take its place.[69]

It is the job of the government to ensure decent housing, general education, a minimum income for all, workers' participation in the decisions of the industry in which they labour, adequate leisure and freedom of worship, speech, assembly and association.[70] In an appendix to *Christianity and Social Order* Temple put forward suggestions on how these aims might be achieved.

Temple and Beveridge

Born in 1879, William Beveridge went to Balliol in 1897, where he met Temple and R.H. Tawney, who were fellow undergraduates. Like them he came under the powerful influence of British idealist philosophy. 'Almost certainly', writes José Harris, 'it was from Caird, and from the philosophical tradition of which Caird was an exponent, that Beveridge derived his conception of society as an "organism" which was to be an important feature of his ideas on social reform.'[71]

Beveridge was clearly imbued with the spirit of the reformer from an early age and became sub-warden of Toynbee Hall, under Canon Samuel Barnett, in 1903. Aware, however, of the stigma which settlement work imparted, of 'a gentleman come to do good', he soon left to work in the civil service. Beveridge was in certain ways a paradoxical figure. Described by his biographer as a 'typical example of the classic Weberian bureaucrat', with respect to the reforms he advocated, he himself disliked bureaucratic methods, adopting somewhat autocratic and personal methods.[72] His theoretical admiration for a rational and scientific approach to social problems led him to admire the Webbs and to form an association with the Fabians, though he never became a socialist. A liberal critic of excessive state intervention, Beveridge emerged – during the Second World War – as one of the leading prophets of the modern welfare state. As early as 1904, in criticism of Sir John Gorst's proposals for a school meals service, he wrote, 'Really I don't want anything done at all by the State . . . the remedy is not to remove the responsibility [of parents] but to give them power.'[73] Though a supporter of the voluntary action of such groups as friendly societies he was an advocate of compulsory state insurance and therefore critical of the 1908 Old Age Pensions Act which was voluntary and selective.[74] Beveridge was instrumental in the setting up of labour exchanges and his later work in educational administration – as Director of the London School of Economics and as Master of University College, Oxford – was of considerable importance.

Despite many of his better instincts – or perhaps because of them – Beveridge, through his reports in the early forties, contributed in a major way to a growth in the power of central government. Full employment, he believed, was possible under conditions of private enterprise, but would involve 'a great extension of the responsibilities and powers of the State'.[75] This he was prepared to accept in order to avoid the greater evil of chronic unemployment and to combat the five giants of want, disease, ignorance, squalor and idleness.[76] As a Liberal, Beveridge was concerned to recognise the limits of legitimate state action, but he tended to see these limits as constituted principally by criteria of efficiency. Although he acknowledged an important role for voluntary societies, he believed that they should work in partnership with the state under a minister responsible for voluntary action.

Like Max Weber, Beveridge professed no religious beliefs, but he had clearly been influenced by the liberal Christianity of his day. In an address to the Rochester Diocesan Conference in 1942 he declared, 'Only as men come to see themselves as part of a larger whole, as children of one Father, can the selfishness and the strife which lead to self destruction be banished from the world.'[77]

The conception of God and the state in terms of a conjunction of sovereignty and benevolence or welfare is, then, a feature of the liberal capitalism of many western countries in our day. It would, of course, be inaccurate to attribute these political developments entirely or even principally to the way Christians conceived of God. Secular humanists, like J.M. Keynes, made major contributions to the growth of the welfare state. Yet there was much in common between liberal Christians and many secular humanists, in the emphasis they placed upon personal relationships as constituting the object of ultimate concern. The rhetoric of personal relationships played an analogical role in the politics and religion of many who were influential in the growth of welfare thinking.

In these countries class conflict has been contained by paternalistic legislation, mitigating the harsher consequences of the capitalist system, combined with a subtle manipulation of political and cultural institutions.[78] In situations where this prescription has failed and harsher measures have been adopted, images of God and of the state are rather different and I deal with some of these in chapter 4. William Temple and William Beveridge played an important part in the development of the welfare state, but it is necessary to look deeper into the liberal political and theological climate in which these two men grew up and flourished.

INCARNATION, ATONEMENT AND PERSONALITY

British theology in the decades prior to the First World War was generally dominated by a liberal and optimistic temper. It was widely believed that the progress which had occurred in the past would continue and that it was one of the principal functions of Christian faith to provide the idealism which would inspire this forward movement. Voices like those of J.N. Figgis, P.T. Forsyth and George Tyrrell questioned these assumptions but with little effect until the outbreak of war shattered the dream of inevitable progress. Even Christians of an incarnationalist tendency, however, were somewhat more realistic than many of their humanist contemporaries. E.S. Talbot, in his opening essay in *Foundations* (1912), echoed Figgis in claiming that the optimistic assumption of an inevitable progress, characteristic of the mid-Victorian era, had passed. 'The skies have darkened and men's minds have become more sombre.'[79]

In this section I consider the concepts and images of God which pre-1914 British liberal theologians assumed, and relate these to their ideas about the welfare role of the state. I shall trace the story back from the activities and theology of the Christian Social Union to thinkers like Hastings Rashdall, on the liberal Protestant side, and R.C. Moberly, Charles Gore, Henry Scott Holland and the *Lux*

Mundi school of liberal Catholics. In all these writers the notion of 'personality' – human and divine – played a central role. This emphasis is clearly related to the part played by 'personal relationships' in the dominant ideologies of the time and to the development of the novel in Victorian England. F.W. Bussell, in his Bampton Lectures of 1905, reflected this concern with welfare and personality. 'It is my aim to show', he wrote in his preface, 'how general welfare is bound up with the faith and hopes of Christian belief; and again how the general welfare can only rightly be secured by justice to the particular, by respecting the units which make up the whole.' Put more simply, 'Christian belief and the welfare of society are one.'[80]

The Christian Social Union

It was the Christian Social Union, founded in 1889, which brought together central churchmen like Brooke Foss Westcott, liberal Protestants like Hastings Rashdall and liberal Catholics of the *Lux Mundi* school. The Union was founded as a result of some lectures given earlier in that year by Wilfrid Richmond at Sion College in London, on the theme of 'Economic Morals'. Some of his audience advocated joining the Guild of St Matthew, but most thought that its politics were too radical and its churchmanship too flamboyant. Scott Holland used to refer to its two leaders, Stewart Headlam and H.C. Shuttleworth, as 'Headlong and Shuttlecock'! In contrast, the CSU was rather non-dogmatic, both theologically and politically, and was thus able to encompass a wide cross-section of opinion. It grew rapidly and within five years it had 2,600 members, with affiliated groups in other parts of the English-speaking world. By 1910 its membership had reached over 6,000.

Most members of the CSU held a strongly incarnational theology and a belief in 'a divine order and a divine government of the world', which owed much to Frederick Denison Maurice.[81] It was, however, their conviction that the Christian faith has implications for social life that bound them together. The Union's aim was 'To study in common how to apply the moral truths and principles of Christianity to the social and economic difficulties of the present time'.[82] For some this meant merely the founding and support of 'settlements' in the East End of London, where young unemployed gentlemen, as one member put it, would be given some understanding of how a large proportion of the population of the country lived. Toynbee Hall and Oxford House had both been founded in 1884. Other, more radical members of the CSU insisted that 'the problem of the present age is that of social reconstruction'.[83] The Oxford University branch produced a journal, *The Economic Review*, and drew up lists of tailors and other merchants who, paying decent wages to their employees, could be recommended to members for their patronage. The generally moderate and academic tone of the CSU was parodied by its critics, particularly from the Guild of St Matthew: 'Here is a glaring social evil, let us read a paper on the subject.'[84]

Hastings Rashdall

Among the members of the Oxford branch was a young philosophy don, Hastings Rashdall. Born in 1858 and educated at Harrow and New College, he taught in Oxford from 1888 to 1917 when he became Dean of Carlisle. He died in 1924. He wrote a classical history of the medieval universities, a two-volume work on *The Theory of Good and Evil* and delivered the Bampton Lectures in 1915 on *The Idea of Atonement in Christian Theology*. Rashdall was for some years co-editor of *The Economic Review* and contributed articles on political issues. His sharp mind and his clear expression of it in writing contrast starkly with the sloppy thinking of many members of the CSU and his works still repay attention today.

Rashdall's philosophical position was that of 'personal idealism' and he was critical of the absolute idealism of Caird, Bradley and Bosanquet – an 'imposing rhetoric in which an essentially irreligious and unChristian conception of God is sometimes so skilfully disguised as to deceive the very elect'.[85] Attempts to identify God with 'the Absolute', he insisted, undermine the idea of a personal God, as the more clear-sighted of the absolute idealists recognised. 'God is not God, till he has become all in all', wrote F.H. Bradley, 'and ... a God which is all in all is not the God of religion.'[86] Rashdall was prepared to accept the consequences of his position. 'Of course our God is anthropomorphic', he proclaimed, 'and so must be every God whom the mind of man can really conceive.' Those who pour scorn on anthropomorphism usually end in fetishism, thinking of God in terms of force or matter.[87] Rashdall was even willing to suggest that there is a sense in which God is finite, in so far as everything real is limited, though in the case of God any limitation springs from his own nature and his own creative work.[88] He defined a person largely in psychological terms, as a conscious, permanent, self-distinguishing, active individual, and believed that God alone fully realises the idea of personality. Seeing personality as a matter of degree he asserted that 'Socrates was more of a person than a savage.' It was no doubt this notion which enabled him to defend his virulent racialism.[89] 'Sooner or later', he declared with macabre prognostication, 'the lower well-being – it may be the very existence – of countless Chinamen or negroes must be sacrificed that a higher life may be possible for a much smaller number of white men.'[90]

As with German liberal Protestants, like Harnack, the essence of Christianity – for Rashdall – is contained in the notion of God as Father and fellow men as brothers. Although Christianity does not consist solely in the moral teachings of Christ, it is a religion rooted and grounded in ethics.[91] Christian worship and sacraments are to be seen essentially as means whereby the ideas and the teaching of Jesus are communicated to Christians.[92] In his doctrine of the atonement Rashdall laid great emphasis upon Christ the teacher, as the foundation of his Christology.[93] Reconciliation between God and humans was achieved, not by making any objective change in the situation, but by showing them, through the life and death of Jesus, the effects of their sin and revealing to them the forgiving love of God. Sin was seen, in the first instance, not as the breaking of a law, nor as an offence against the dignity of a king or lord, but rather on the model of a rupture in personal relationships. Any idea that a debt or a ransom had to be paid by the human race for reconciliation to be secured was firmly rejected. Forgiveness is freely granted by God; there is no place for retribution.

In his ethical works Rashdall elaborated a broadly utilitarian critique of retributive theories of punishment, insisting that the only legitimate reason for inflicting punishment on the guilty is that it will do good either to them or to others. In answer to the accusation that non-retributive theories fail to respect the personal dignity of the guilty by not treating them as an end in themselves, Rashdall stated:

> It is the retributive theory which shows a disrespect for human personality by proposing to sacrifice human life and human Well-being to a lifeless fetish styled the Moral Law, which apparently, though unconscious, has a sense of dignity and demands the immolation of victims to avenge its injured *amour propre*.[94]

Just as any punishment of the guilty which God might inflict or permit will be for the person's own good, so punishment inflicted by the state must have a moral end. The state exists for the sake of the good life, 'to make men better'.[95] Yet this does not mean that the state must necessarily take direct action to achieve this end. 'It is quite consistent', he observed, 'to maintain that the State exists to promote morality, but that at the same time it promotes it best by leaving it alone.'[96] The state cannot therefore be indifferent to anything which involves the moral interests of its members and any clear separation between the concerns of church and state was thus rejected.

Rashdall believed that the state should pursue justice, and he distinguished two principal meanings of the term, both having a certain validity. Justice is generally thought to involve, in the first place, equal treatment for all the members of the state and, second, some notion of a proper recompense or reward. In a rigorous examination of these two ideas Rashdall concluded, with respect to the first, that the only absolute right is to equality of consideration, and with respect to the second that what a person 'deserves' is impossible to estimate, as each person owes so much to inheritance and environment. A just distribution should therefore be concerned more with the capacity or needs of individual recipients than with some supposed notion of deserts. In an early version of his position he insisted on 'the necessity of not making justice, even as an ideal, our primary object, but rather general well-being'. Later, however, he modified this by substituting for 'justice' the words 'any actual equality of good', and defining justice in such a way that it is necessarily compatible with the general welfare.[97]

In Rashdall's writings we thus find a strong emphasis on personality, a belief in human welfare as the proper concern both of God and of the state, and an explicit recognition that welfare must take precedence over other social values. These ideas Rashdall shared with other members of the CSU.

Scott Holland and Lux Mundi

Bishop Westcott of Durham was chairman of the CSU and gave a certain respectability to the movement. But although Westcott was generally regarded as the senior member of the CSU its most dynamic propagandist was Henry Scott Holland. Born in 1847, he was educated at Eton; he then went to Balliol, where he was taught by Thomas Hill Green. After fourteen years as a Senior Student of Christ Church he became Canon of St Paul's from 1884 to 1910, when he returned from Amen Court to Tom Quad as Regius Professor of Divinity; he died in 1918. Scott Holland was, observed George Russell, 'the most agreeable man in London'. 'He was never curt or rude', wrote the Honourable Edward Lyttelton, 'and it is

impossible to imagine him ever giving pain.'[98] His published works
are rhetorical and verbose partly because they are often the written
text of sermons or lectures. It was said that Holland would never use
one word when five would do. Although his writings contain
occasional flashes of brilliance, the considerable influence which he
exercised was due to other factors. Like William Temple, Holland
must have been very much more impressive in person than in print
and those who knew him witness to the influence he exercised in
England at the turn of the century. Perhaps, however, it is less a
question of influence than of making explicit the intuitions and
assumptions already held by many of his contemporaries. In a
generally sympathetic study of Holland's social theology, J.H. Heidt
observes, 'Holland's popularity was partially due to the fact that he
reflected all the popular movements of his day.'[99]

Scott Holland, like many of his generation, was optimistic about
human progress and he generally underestimated the power and
pervasiveness of sin and evil. While it is only fair to say that, in his
later writings, he recognised that the kingdom of heaven would not
be realised on earth by a gradual development from within, but
'arrives from afar',[100] his earlier work is characterised by a belief in
the kingdom's 'gradual conquest of the world'. As part of this slow
Christianising process he saw the continued establishment of the
Church of England as 'at once obvious, intelligible, natural,
justifiable'.[101]

Holland's theology was indeed – in contrast to that of the
Tractarians of a previous generation – liberal, but his insistence on
the particularity of the Christian revelation and on the centrality of
church and sacraments distinguishes him sharply from the liberal
Protestantism of his teacher Green. Although he sometimes
expressed his religious beliefs in the language of idealist philosophy
he never accepted the *religion* of the English idealists.[102] The same is
generally true of other contributors to the volume of essays *Lux
Mundi*, particularly of Gore, whose less sanguine disposition was
more in tune with Plato than with Hegel. J.R. Illingworth and the
young Walter Moberly were, however, somewhat less critical of the
idealist framework within which they worked. It is now time to look
at certain features of the doctrine of God which these thinkers
asserted or assumed and to point to analogies in their understanding
of the role of the state.

God as father and friend

Traditional images of God such as king and judge were occasionally employed by these writers. God was indeed:

> Judge eternal throned in splendour,
> Lord of lords and King of kings.[103]

Although R.C. Moberly, in his classic study *Personality and Atonement*, took the analogy of parent and child in his discussion of forgiveness, he insisted that 'the parent has complete command over the child' and that 'the parent's forgiveness is something which only is possible to one who is absolutely ruler and judge and teacher and example all in one'.[104] The image is patriarchal rather than paternal. The author's son, however, writing some years afterwards, was less happy with these authoritarian family models. 'The metaphor of Ruler or Sovereign', he stated in his essay on the atonement in *Foundations*, 'describes the relation of God to man less truly than the metaphor of Father or loving Friend.'[105] Reconciliation was seen in terms of 'the full restoration of delicate personal relations between friends or between parent and child'.[106] In his writings on the theory of punishment, Walter Moberly rejected the conventional retributivist position, maintaining that retribution should be thought of as the natural consequence of wrongdoing as it affects the character of the offender. He agreed with the general approach adopted by McTaggart (in his essay on Hegel's theory of punishment) that penalties imposed on offenders are for the purpose of encouraging their own repentance and internal reformation.[107]

J.R. Illingworth pointed out that sin must be seen not only as breach of a law but as disobedience to a person and that it is more terrible to realise that we have offended our father or our lover than a master or a judge.[108] Scott Holland used the model of 'a spiritual intimacy, a living friendship' with God, no doubt seeing man's relationship with God as the perfect instance of that 'exceptional and beautiful intimacy' which existed between himself and Gore.[109] This emphasis on personality, human and divine, reaches its apotheosis in the US theologian Gordon Kaufman, for whom 'God' is merely 'the supreme symbol for a life-policy of humanizing and personalizing the world'.[110]

The images of father and friend imply divine personality and these liberal Catholics saw the incarnation as 'the adequate and final revelation of the personality of God'. Personality is necessarily social and he is thus 'a social God'.[111] God realises his personality in a divine fellowship which begins within the life of the Trinity and embraces the whole created order.[112] As with earlier Anglican writers like John Donne, the Holy Trinity was also seen as a model for human communities, because humans are made in the divine image.[113] This brings us to a discussion of how these liberal Catholics conceived of the state on the analogy of God's relationship to his people.

The state as grandmother

The social and political ideas of Scott Holland and the *Lux Mundi* theologians were more influenced by T.H. Green than was their theology, though they were prepared to go further than he in advocating state action. 'The State which imposes the Law', wrote Holland, 'is our social self; and in obeying the Law, we obey ourself.' The state, he declared, is 'a sacred thing'. To be sure the author was speaking of the state in its idea – as it ought to be – yet he does not provide sufficient criteria for determining how far the actual state realises its idea and how far the citizen is therefore obliged to obey its laws.[114] While defending private property, Holland and Gore insisted that the rights of property may be justified only in so far as they contribute to the general welfare and common good of the community.[115]

In an extraordinary article in the magazine *Goodwill*, under the title 'Every Man his own Grandmother', Holland defended paternalistic legislation on the ground that now the state is democratic each person has a share in determining the laws. 'Legislation is now made by the people for themselves,' he wrote. 'They themselves pass the laws, not their grandmother for them.'[116] The more democratic a state is the more it can legitimately multiply laws.[117] Here, blinded by a Rousseauesque conception of the general will, he failed to respect a necessary distinction, made some years earlier by J.S. Mill in his essay *On Liberty*, between the government of each by himself and the government of each by all the rest.[118] He thus opened the way to the justification of all kinds of paternalism and even to totalitarian democracy.

Holland believed that people are bound together by a common good. London he saw as 'an immense community, with a common interest and a common welfare'.[119] One of the principal ways by which the state is able to realise the common good is, of course, the legal system. Holland observed that the law cannot go far ahead of public opinion but it can and should embody the conscience of 'the better half of a people', in order to force the rest up to a standard which they would not otherwise attain. He claimed that over the past half-century it had become clear that the only way the individual could survive was by state protection. The state was indeed the home of the citizen. 'What the home once was', he declared, 'now the State is.' It is not entirely clear whether he saw the state as *actually* playing the role of a home, or whether this was an ideal, for later in the same chapter he wrote of the people of London: 'The State, in some far golden day yet to come, may be to them as a home. . . . Its eye will be on them, its arm about them; its friendly co-operation will ensure them consideration.'[120] The paternal role of the state reminds citizens of a heavenly Father 'whose eye is ever on them'.[121] He saw an analogy between divine and human law, with the latter reflecting 'that higher Moral Law which imposes its irresistible authority upon the conscience, as the voice of an Eternal Father demanding absolute surrender of will'.[122]

From what has been said, it will be clear that these theologians and preachers contributed much to the atmosphere in which the 'new liberalism' of the pre-1914 years was able to flourish and it is to the words and works of the new liberals that I now turn.

3

Welfare God and paternal state II

WELFARE, THE NEW LIBERALS AND THE STATE

While it is true that the present structure of the welfare state dates from the Second World War, the roots can be traced back much further. The inter-war years saw extensions in a number of the social services, which built upon already existing institutions. The Lloyd George budget of 1909 and the social legislation of the Asquith government, however, mark a major step in the development of the welfare state in Britain. The legislation of the pre-First World War period was pioneered by a determined group of politicians and civil servants who were dedicated to the notion of the state as playing a positive role in social developments. The 'new liberals', as they were called, were reacting against the nineteenth-century belief in a minimal state, insisting that legislation, so far from merely restricting freedom, can actually be the means of its extension.

Leading figures among the new liberals included such philosophers as L.T. Hobhouse, D.G. Ritchie, Henry Jones and R.B. Haldane, budding sociologists like Graham Wallas, civil servants like Hubert Llewellyn Smith and William Beveridge, economists such as J.A. Hobson, and practising politicians and journalists including H.H. Asquith, Herbert Samuel, Winston Churchill, C.F.G. Masterman and H.W. Massingham. Many of these men, including Wallas, Hobson and Hobhouse, had come from evangelical families and, although they rejected the specifically Christian elements in their upbringing, they carried into their social and political activities that moral earnestness which characterised the evangelical movement of the period.[1] The other principal ideological influence on the new liberalism was the idealist philosophy of T.H. Green and his followers, combined in some cases with an organic model of social relationships, derived in part from T.H. Huxley.

Social legislation

Winston Churchill and David Lloyd George played a decisive role in the introduction of social legislation. Though they were in the first place instinctive politicians, seeing political theories as moderately useful weapons in their armoury, they had certain preconceptions about the role of the modern state. They had a feel for the way things were going and sensed the need for some amelioration in the conditions of the working classes. The researches of B.S. Rowntree and Charles Booth had revealed large areas of destitution in Britain and their reports had had a considerable impact on more sensitive members of the ruling classes. Churchill declared that reading Rowntree's study of poverty in York made his hair stand on end. 'I see little glory', he told a Birmingham politician, 'in an Empire which can rule the waves, and is unable to flush its sewers.'[2] In his celebrated visit to Germany in August 1908, Lloyd George had been impressed by the schemes of social insurance which had been in operation for several decades and he claimed, somewhat extravagantly, that by enacting social legislation the Liberals were 'doing the work of Nazareth'. In the preface to his protégé Winston Churchill's *Liberalism and the Social Problem*, H.W. Massingham echoed Bismarck in pronouncing the aims of the new liberalism to be 'practical Christianity'.[3]

It is impossible to discuss here in detail the social legislation of this period and the process of its formulation and enactment. A non-contributory system of old age pensions was introduced in 1908 for persons over 70. The National Insurance Act of 1911, covering most manual workers, provided small cash grants in case of sickness, with the free provision of medical treatment and drugs; there was, however, no general cover for dependants. A limited scheme for unemployment insurance was also enacted. Labour exchanges had already been introduced, largely on the initiative of William Beveridge.[4]

As late as mid-1908, Asquith had declared that the German system of *compulsory* social insurance was unacceptable in Britain,[5] yet – under the influence of Lloyd George – a compulsory system was in fact introduced within a very short while. The principal difference between the two systems was that in Britain a flat rate of contributions was matched by a flat rate of benefits, while in Germany a graduated system had been introduced. The British legislation was aimed at benefiting a poorer class of worker while Bismarck's aim had evidently been to lure away the better-paid worker from the social democratic camp.

Generally the British legislation was paternalistic in tone and tended to undermine the role which the friendly societies had been playing up to that time. It was probably Lloyd George's original intention to base the insurance schemes on the notion of extending to all citizens the benefits provided by friendly societies, but intervention by commercial insurance companies and by the British Medical Association forced him to change his plans. It has been estimated that by 1891 there were as many as 6 million members of these friendly societies, representing over three-quarters of male adults over 24.[6] Much was made at the time of the self-governing and non-bureaucratic character of the British scheme, but, as one recent writer has remarked, 'as far as self-government was concerned, this was now no more than a form of deception'.[7] The original bill was drawn up by W.J. Braithwaite and a number of Treasury officials, but owing to pressure from various interests it was modified out of all recognition in the course of its passage through Parliament. Those insured were deprived of the choice of doctor and the commercial insurance companies largely got their way. 'I regarded the whole transaction', commented Braithwaite, 'as a betrayal of the spirit of the Bill.'[8]

After a brief but penetrating study of this welfare legislation, in relation to the friendly societies, David Green concludes:

> The state scheme abandoned this fraternal morality. The individual was no longer seen as a morally autonomous being capable of resolving a moral conflict in common action and discussion with his brothers; rather he was a person who could not be trusted to behave unselfishly in the absence of some superior authority.[9]

Positive liberty, citizenship and the common good

In arguing the case for positive state action, the new liberals appealed to a notion of freedom or liberty (the terms are used here interchangeably) which was significantly different from the classical negative idea of liberty as the mere absence of external impediments to action, represented in the mid-nineteenth century in its most radical form by Herbert Spencer. They asserted that freedom to act, in any meaningful sense, involves having the power or the means to do so. Legislation could thus, by restricting the actions of a few, increase the freedom of the many. Some went further and accepted what I have called elsewhere a 'realist' notion of freedom, which was taught by T.H. Green and accepted by some of his followers.[10] According to this view people are truly free only when they are actually doing what is worth while, or when they are in a position to do so. Thus to increase people's opportunity to do evil or to waste their time is not to enlarge their freedom. This realist notion of freedom clearly has possible totalitarian implications.[11] Yet even those, like Green himself and Henry Jones, who held a definitely realist conception of freedom insisted that the state must not take on responsibilities which the individual or the voluntary group could shoulder. 'The civilised state does more for its citizens than the barbarous state', Jones observed, 'and at the same time enables them to do more for themselves.'[12] These liberals were also eager to defend the rights of private property, though their belief in the organic nature of the state required seeing property rights, like all rights, as subordinate to the claims of the common good.[13]

The new liberals thus attempted to redefine the term 'liberty' and so to legitimate their claim truly to be within the traditions of the Liberal Party. Stefan Collini is, however, correct in asserting that this redefinition did not originate with them and is present in some writings of the mid-nineteenth century. 'Every limitation of power is an abridgement of positive liberty,' wrote Cliffe Leslie in 1861.[14] Collini further suggests, quite properly, that any attempt to organise an account of the debate between the new liberals and their critics solely on the basis of this idea of positive liberty would be a mistake. The issues were larger and the conceptual distinction was part of a social philosophy which, as I have maintained elsewhere, grew up as a response to changes taking place in social relationships and in the role of the state.[15]

H.H. Asquith went up to Balliol in 1870 and became a disciple and admirer of Green, though more with respect to the latter's social teaching and actions than to his philosophy, which remained something of a mystery to him. Asquith claimed that, though he never worshipped 'at the temple's inner shrine', he owed to Green more than he could say and in an obituary wrote of his 'commanding influence' over the intellectual and moral life of Oxford. Following the master he insisted that a mere freedom from compulsion does not make men free. 'To be really free', wrote the future prime minister, 'they must be able to make the best use of faculty, opportunity, energy, life.'[16] Asquith had based his election address of 1892 upon this positive notion of freedom; it was this which justified the Liberal Party's insistence on more state intervention. 'I am one of those', he declared,

> who believe that the collective action of the community may and ought to be employed positively as well as negatively; to raise as well as to level; to equalise opportunities no less than to curtail privileges; to make the freedom of the individual a reality and not a pretence.[17]

Asquith was for some time Member of Parliament for the Fifeshire Burghs, where St Andrews University was located. Its professor of philosophy at this time was Henry Jones, who gave his support to Asquith's liberalism. Jones was a true disciple of the Balliol idealists; not only did he teach but he practised what he taught by involving himself in all kinds of social and civic work. 'I was born', he wrote, 'in Llangernyw in 1852, and born again in 1876 in Edward Caird's classroom.' With others of this school he joined city councils and lectured to businessmen on social and civic ethics.[18] As two authors have recently pointed out, the notion of citizenship, of civic responsibility, was central to the thinking of these men. Jones played a major part in the founding of a lectureship in citizenship at Glasgow University and wrote a textbook on the principles of citizenship for British troops stationed in France.[19]

The idea of citizenship became almost a religion for some of these men. Like the German liberal Protestants, they saw the essence of the Christian gospel as a belief in the fatherhood of God and the brotherhood of man. This had for them clear ethical implications. Jones emphasised the immanence of God and, following Green, saw the notion of God's fatherhood as involving 'a nearness of God to man'. Elsewhere he defined religion as being the secular 'devoted to the best we know'.[20] As Vincent and Plant have recently reminded us, idealist philosophers were deeply involved in the ethical societies of the day and some saw their work with the Charity Organisation Society as the practical expression of their Christian humanism. This liberal interpretation of religion was generally consonant with an analogous view of the state. Others went further, effectively reducing religion to benevolent social and political action.

Another element in the political theory of the new liberals was the notion of a common good which embraces the true interests of all citizens. Even those, like Hobhouse and Hobson, who found aspects of idealist philosophy unacceptable, saw the common good as the ultimate criterion of social and political action. The idea of a common good was, according to a recent writer, 'the keystone of Hobhouse's political philosophy'.[21] Yet he saw this as the sum of individual goods, which were – to the greatest possible extent – freely chosen.

Hobhouse, Hobson and the social Darwinists

Freedom of the individual was for L.T. Hobhouse and J.A. Hobson the principal criterion of valid state action. 'In the main', Hobhouse wrote, 'the extension of control does not impair liberty, but on the contrary is the means of extending liberty and may and should be conceived with that very object in view.'[22] Hobhouse agreed with idealist philosophers that it is ultimately for a moral end – for the sake of the development of human personality, of the 'self-government' of the individual – that liberalism strives.[23] Unlike Jones, Haldane and Ritchie, however, he and Hobson were critical of the idealist philosophy; their notion of liberty in particular owed more to the empiricist tradition. As we have seen they accepted a positive understanding of freedom as implying the means or power to act, but they rejected the realist approach.

Although Hobhouse saw no antithesis between law and liberty when talking of the state as a whole, there may indeed be a conflict in the case of a single individual. 'Law', he observed, 'of course restrains the individual; it is therefore opposed to his liberty at a given moment and in a given direction.'[24] Criticising what he believed to be the idealist conception of freedom, he pointed out that Hegel 'saw that freedom involved restraint on something but did not see that it was restraint on something else, that which is free being in the respect in which it is free necessarily unconstrained'.[25] Hobhouse assailed idealist philosophy, blaming it for the outbreak of the First World War. Its effect was to weaken the brain, to undermine morality by blurring the distinction between right and wrong and 'to throw a gloss over stupidity, and prejudice, and caste, and tradition'.[26]

The state can, then, intervene in the social process in order to increase human freedom. How did Hobhouse envisage the practical application of this principle? In the first place it implied for him a considerable degree of equality and a consequent reorganisation of social relationships. The so-called freedom of contract was a dangerously misleading myth; economic necessity may drive men into slavery.[27] Full freedom of consent implies some kind of equality on the part of the bargaining parties.[28] Both Hobson and Hobhouse argued that a general extension of state education could also be justified in terms of enlarging freedom.[29]

A number of the new liberals, including Ritchie, Hobson and Beveridge, had been influenced by developments in the field of biology. Herbert Spencer and others of his ilk had incorporated notions of natural selection and social evolution into their *laissez-faire* theories of the state. Widespread governmental interference in social life to protect the weak would lead to degeneration.[30] Progress is achieved by the survival of the strongest. It is therefore a mistake to intervene in the course of nature.[31] Spencer's political theory was riddled with inconsistencies and contradictions. He recognised in some contexts that the physically fit were not necessarily the most valuable or advanced elements in the state, but continued to apply crude ideas of natural selection to politics. He talked about the danger of protecting the weak but defended a concept of the state – as the policeman protecting private property – in which its job was to do little else. He believed that state welfare would lead to the perpetuation of weak strains, but he accepted private benevolence, which would have precisely the same result. He conceived of 'society' as organic, but insisted on representing government action as a mechanical intervention in the life of the organism, rather than as a part of the organism's self-regulating agency.

T.H. Huxley was critical of attempts to apply biological theories to politics in this way,[32] and, in a number of important works, D.G. Ritchie pointed out that evolution is not identical with progress. Rational selection must take the place of natural selection, which is a cruel and wasteful process.[33] Ritchie in fact employed the idea of the state as an organism to justify collective action and to oppose individualist ideas of absolute natural rights. Hobson too saw the organic state as being capable of growing and adapting to its new obligations in a way which could not be expected if one envisaged it as a mechanism.[34]

New liberals or 'New Tories'?

From what has been said it will be clear that there was a good deal in common between the new liberals and Fabians like Sidney and Beatrice Webb. Sidney had in 1891 remarked on the individualists' inability to recognise the possibility of 'the expansion of the sphere of government in the interests of liberty itself',[35] and the Fabian prospectus proclaimed that its socialist programme would result in much less interference with personal freedom than was the case under the prevailing system.[36] Also a number of the new liberals were closely associated with the Fabians and with the development of the Labour Party; these included Graham Wallas, D.G. Ritchie, R.B. Haldane and Charles Trevelyan.[37] As early as 1902 Hobhouse had hoped for a union between new liberals and the growing labour movement and in his later classification of political positions linked 'ordinary labour' with 'good liberal', claiming that the distinction between them had become obsolete.[38] Nevertheless he remained critical of certain tendencies in socialism, particularly what he saw to be an excessive concentration of power in the state at the expense of individual freedom. Hobson saw the same danger.[39]

What, then, was the significance of the new liberalism and what accounts for its rise? How should we interpret the wave of social legislation in the years prior to the First World War? A number of hypotheses have been suggested. Was it fear of the rising working class, or the hope of capturing its votes by undermining the position of the nascent Labour Party? How far was it due to a genuine humanitarianism on the part of an elite which had become sensitive to the plight of the poor, through involvement in such institutions as the university settlements in the East End of London, like Toynbee Hall, and by reading the reports of such men as Rowntree and Booth? How important was philosophy in affecting the institutional changes that were taking place? In discussing these issues Vincent and Plant tend to confuse the significance of these political movements with the motives and intentions of the actors themselves. They furthermore assert that 'It is through understanding the intellectual concerns of the elite that we can understand the New Liberalism.'[40] Certainly this is part of the story, but it should also be clear that this philosophy grew up in response to a growing crisis in the social and economic life of the country and to the piecemeal legislation of the mid-century.

With respect to the argument that welfare legislation of the period must be seen principally as a result of pressure from below, Henry Pelling and others[41] have argued that the working-class leaders themselves were not particularly enthusiastic in their support of social legislation, though José Harris rightly observes that many politicians of both major parties certainly *thought* that social policy was a matter of electoral significance.[42] Harris criticises what she calls 'a pure class analysis' of the welfare legislation of the pre-1914 period, whatever this might be,[43] and generally assumes that the explicit intentions of the principal actors are the sole explanatory factors to be considered. Looking back, however, it is sometimes possible to see what was happening as part of a more general movement of which the actors were hardly aware. The significance of what they were doing cannot therefore be reduced to an account of their conscious motives and intentions, though any explanation which ignored these factors would be worthless. What Harris says about the shift of emphasis from local to central government and the crucial role of public finance policies is very much to the point in explaining the course of social legislation at this time.

Michael Freeden has argued that around the turn of the century liberalism was transformed 'from a decaying creed under attack from all sides to an aggressive, modernized set of ideas serving as a springboard for political action'.[44] He claims that this transformation can be explained with reference to the internal dynamics of liberalism and that 'the philosophical school of idealism was not an essential link in the transformation of liberal thought'.[45] His argument is based on a peculiar 'reification' of liberalism, which he imagines to be composed of the essential and the incidental. The *laissez-faire* dogmas of Cobden and the Manchester school were incidental to true liberalism, for they 'turned out to be dispensable'. Fear and distrust of the state, 'it transpired, had not been a true characteristic of liberals'.[46] 'The moment the social problem came to the fore, liberal principles moved by their own logic into the vacuum.'[47] But this begs the real questions. In what respects did the new liberals modify the traditional liberalism of Gladstone and Mill? Did their conception of positive liberty and their advocacy of positive state intervention not place them in a radically different position from that occupied by their party in the mid-nineteenth century, when *laissez-faire* was 'the main article of liberalism's intellectual creed'?[48] Was not their position better summarised prophetically by Herbert Spencer as a 'New Toryism'?[49] These are questions which Freeden's essentialist method makes it difficult for him to confront.

It is, as we shall see, undoubtedly the case that T.H. Green can in certain respects properly be seen as an heir to the British liberal tradition. His social philosophy was by no means a direct and unadulterated importation from Germany. Nevertheless his position is fundamentally idealist and, if anything, he is somewhat less 'empirical' than was Hegel himself. It is also the case, as I have tried to show above, that two of the leading intellectual figures among the new liberals, Hobhouse and Hobson, were sharply critical of certain tendencies in idealism. Even so, Freeden undoubtedly misconceives the relationship between idealism and the new liberalism, as has effectively been demonstrated by Vincent and Plant.

The state which emerged as a result of the activities of the new liberals was positive and paternalistic, despite the intentions of their leading theorists. The role which they played is in certain respects clearer to posterity than it was to these men themselves.

THE OXFORD SETTLERS

One of the striking features of social life in the late nineteenth century was the growth of 'settlements' established by groups of upper-class men and women in urban working-class areas, particularly in the East End of London. Parish churches had of course existed in these areas, and the century had seen the building of many mission churches and mission houses, specifically designed to proclaim the Christian gospel among the poor. Many of the priests who worked in these areas, like Fathers Lowder, Headlam and Stanton, also came from elite families. The settlement movement differed from the urban missions in so far as it was less explicitly religious, though many of the settlers were inspired by their Christian faith.

The Barnetts of Toynbee Hall

A key figure in the growth of the settlements was Samuel Barnett, a young priest who had graduated from Oxford, where he had come under the influence of T.H. Green. In 1873 he was asked by the Bishop of London to work in the parish of St Jude's, Whitechapel. 'It is the worst parish in my diocese', wrote Bishop Jackson, 'inhabited mainly by a criminal population.'[50] Barnett accepted the job and with his wife developed the church as a centre of social work, actively engaging in local government politics in the area. He maintained contact with Oxford University and encouraged undergraduates to come and live in the parish for short periods. As a result of a lecture which Barnett gave in St John's College in 1883 a house was founded where a permanent community of university men might live in the East End and share the life of the local people. 'In 1883', reflected Barnett in later years, 'there was a stirring in the waters of benevolence.'[51]

Although Barnett and others fully recognised the dangers of a patronising attitude on the part of the upper-class settlers, he believed that a genuine attempt could be made 'to see, to know and to serve' less privileged sectors of the population.[52] He distinguished settlements from missions as being concerned more with 'mutual knowledge' than with conversion and conducted by 'personal influence' and 'human contact' rather than by creating institutions and organisations. He also saw the role of settlements as different from the Charity Organisation Society, which he had helped to found in 1869. The act of coming to live among the under-privileged, almost seen in 'kenotic' terms, was of the essence of his movement. Barnett also became increasingly critical of the COS's refusal to recognise the positive role which the state could play in social improvement. While he agreed that dependence may demoralise, there is no reason to think that dependence on a state pension, for example, is more demoralising than dependence on a private pension.[53]

In 1884 Toynbee Hall was founded in memory of the young Arnold Toynbee, who had died in the previous year. In the following years many Oxford and Cambridge colleges founded houses and settlements in the poorer parts of British cities and by 1911 there were forty-five in existence.[54] Many of those responsible for formulating and implementing the social legislation of the Liberal government of 1906, including R.B. Morant, Ernest Aves, W.J. Braithwaite, Llewellyn Smith and William Beveridge, had spent time in the settlements, as had later Labour Party men R.H. Tawney and Clement Attlee.[55]

Samuel Barnett had a very particular understanding of God, religion and the church, reflecting the liberal Protestant theology of T.H. Green. Religion, for him, was 'the Power which is the highest within our knowledge expressed in a form which awakens our feeling of dependence, and thus brings us into oneness with our Highest'.[56] He adopted a highly Erastian view of the relations of church and state, seeing the former as a department of state and comparing it to a government post-office, as an organisation whose employees are paid by the state and which exists to serve the interests of the nation. The purpose of the church is 'to make men friends, to unite all classes in common aims, to give them open minds'. Elsewhere he spoke of the nation as a church, whose religion is citizenship.[57] Each nation, with its peculiar national character, has something special to contribute to 'the establishment of a perfect humanity'. It was Britain's role to bring into this movement the idea of liberty – not in the vulgar sense of people doing as they wish, but in Green's words 'a positive power or capacity'.[58]

Central to Barnett's religion were the ideas of friendship, service and reconciliation. He accepted the existence of different classes, of the poor and of the rich – 'There is nothing wrong in the existence of classes', he declared – but, he went on, 'there is the greatest wrong in their antagonism'.[59] He believed classes could live together in concord if certain conditions were fulfilled. Like Coleridge, he emphasised the high moral responsibility that rests on the shoulders of the privileged classes to protect and to befriend the deprived and saw religion as 'the one force which can turn the various and often antagonistic classes into fellow-workers'.[60] He warned that unless something positive were done to improve the conditions of the very poor and to 'mitigate class suspicion' conflict would break out. Of the working man he wrote, 'His wrath is gathering at the power of the ignorant rich over trade. . . . He has learnt, moreover, to doubt the arguments by which property justifies its rights to exceptional regard.'[61] The settlement movement would play an important role in reducing conflict and Barnett was generally optimistic. 'Class barriers, which have defied fierce blows of revolutions', he wrote, 'are falling before the still small voice of friendship.'[62] He proclaimed an increase in kindness and goodwill, and the growth of a government which is more and more efficient, with ever more conscientious civil servants.

The Barnetts believed that religion in general and a people's conception of God in particular have important social implications. 'Among the Hebrews', they observed,

> a new revelation of the Divine character preceded each develop-
> ment in their social life, and in Christian ages a new thought about
> God has gone before the great revolutions of society. Religion
> always directs the strongest current of progress.[63]

They therefore called for 'a new presentiment of God', which could relate to contemporary experience.

Scott Lidgett

Doctor J. Scott Lidgett, a Methodist who was warden of the Bermondsey Settlement, was rather more aware of the dialectical character of the relationship between concepts of God and social experience. In his treatise *The Fatherhood of God*, published in 1902, Lidgett traced the fortunes of this image in Christian history. 'No doctrine of the relationship of God to men', he proclaimed, has assumed such prominence during the last half-century as that of His Fatherhood. ... It has been the inspiring motive of a philanthropic service, ever widening in its range, becoming profounder in its ultimate principles, and more strenuous in its methods.[64]

In contrast to the Old Testament, where God was portrayed more in terms of sovereignty, the New Testament taught of a fatherly God. Nevertheless in the course of Christian history images of political domination returned, and Lidgett pointed to St Augustine as one of the prime culprits. Owing to his peculiar religious experience, to his understanding of divine will, to legal conceptions inherited from some of the Latin fathers and 'to the political analogies which were suggested to him by Catholic organisation, Roman imperialism, and Old Testament history as idealised in the New Testament', Augustine allowed images of sovereignty to take precedence over those of fatherhood.[65] Lidgett noted how in the Middle Ages human authority was strengthened by being seen as delegated from God and how 'the prevalence of the imperial analogies reacted upon the conception of the relation of God to men'.[66] With Luther and Calvin there was a new emphasis of the fatherhood of God, but two factors inhibited the development of the fatherly image: the Augustinian influences in their thinking and the rise of nationalism with the prominence given to the kingly office. 'The concentration of attention upon sovereignty as the supreme human relationship inevitably tended to bring about a similar prominence for sovereignty as the supreme relationship of God to mankind.'[67]

Scott Lidgett saw the nineteenth century as the period when the New Testament doctrine of the fatherhood of God was restored to its rightful predominance – in the writings of Erskine of Linlathen, M'Leod Campbell, Maurice and Kingsley. Lidgett, like R.C. Moberly,[68] tended to picture fatherhood in patriarchal as well as in paternal form. 'Among men', he wrote, 'no authority is so perfect and absolute as that of the typical fatherhood.' It was characterised by a love which 'promotes the well-being of the child' and by 'the practical omnipotence by which the father secures respect for his commands'. He saw this conception of fatherhood as supplying 'the principles upon which social work should be based'.[69]

What organ could perform this work better than that all-powerful but benevolent public institution known today as the welfare state? By an emphasis on fatherhood, he observed, social and political practices will be changed, but 'Authority will be strengthened rather than weakened, while it will be exercised in full regard to the humane ends which it is intended to serve.'[70] Looking back, in 1938, he argued that the social legislation of the twentieth century could be ascribed as largely due 'to the ascendancy of the religious Idea of the Fatherhood of God'.[71]

There can be no doubt that the settlement movement at the turn of the century represents a significant step in the development of welfare ideas in Britain and provided, together with civic activism, one of the principal institutional links between the political ideas of Green and the social legislation of the Asquith government. The liberal theology asserted or assumed by these leading figures in the settlement movement was closely associated with their social activity; the image of a powerful but benevolent deity is dialectically related to emerging ideas of a welfare state in the context of a clearly perceived danger of class antagonism.

THE BALLIOL IDEALISTS

In the sixties and seventies Benjamin Jowett had gathered around himself at Balliol College, Oxford, a number of young and brilliant tutors. Well known as a theological liberal and contributor to the controversial volume *Essays and Reviews* (1860), Jowett became master of the college in 1870.[72] Among the most influential of these young men were Thomas Hill Green, Richard Lewis Nettleship and Arnold Toynbee. The reputation of Balliol as a centre of advanced thinking – liberal both in politics and in theology – attracted such undergraduates as Edward Caird, Herbert Asquith, Herbert Samuel, Alfred Milner, Edward Grey, Charles Gore, Henry Scott Holland and later Beveridge, Tawney and Temple.

T.H. Green is generally acknowledged to have been the inspiration of this intellectual movement. Born in 1836, he went to Rugby School and entered Balliol College in 1855. He was elected fellow of the college in 1860 and became Professor of Moral Philosophy at Oxford in 1878. He died in 1882. Green attempted to incorporate a typically English middle-class radicalism into the framework of an idealist philosophy which owed much to Kant and Hegel. Green and his disciples believed that ultimately only thought is real and that the notion of an external world, wholly divorced from thought, is meaningless. Writing of their mutual friend Arnold Toynbee, Lord Milner observed that, for him, 'The world of sense was but a dream fabric. The only true reality lay in the world of ideas.'[73] Edward Caird insisted that philosophy, on the basis of its recognition of self-consciousness, proceeds to vindicate the validity of religious experience – the consciousness of the infinite – and to assert 'the idea of the unity of man as spiritual with an absolute Spirit'. It is here, in this unity, that Caird found a 'principle of universal synthesis'.[74]

The moral life and the image of God

Green and his idealist colleagues rejected a utilitarian ethic, and the individualism which accompanied it, in favour of a notion of the state as an organism into which each individual is incorporated as a limb or cell. Nevertheless they insisted that the development of personal character is integral to – or rather identical with – that spiritual progress of mankind for which they strove.[75] The whole is a moral entity bound together by a common good which includes the good of all its members. Individuals can have no rights *against* the state, but only as members of a state and in relation to the common good. While valuing human freedom and insisting that morality presupposes intentional and therefore voluntary action, Green rejected the simple empiricist notion of freedom as doing as one likes. True freedom is the ability to make the best of oneself.

Green, Caird and Toynbee were generally optimistic about the possibilities of human development, believing that progress had in fact occurred and that moral effort would ensure continued improvement. 'The world has always seemed very good to me', wrote Green. Caird saw the spirit of Christianity 'slowly and gradually overcoming and transforming the life of men'.[76] These were deeply religious men and would certainly have called themselves Christians. Yet they saw Christianity as part of a universal spiritual quest for the infinite and tended to identify religion with morality.[77] The vocation of the political reformer was therefore essentially religious and was inspired by 'the passion for improving mankind'.[78] Caird saw the evolution of Christianity as a gradual liberation from alien, external elements with which it had become mixed; this involved a realisation that 'the service of humanity is the true and the only service of God'.[79] Like Kant, Caird thought of religious institutions, such as regular times of worship, as necessary owing to the frailty of our nature, but envisaged a danger that people would make of these an end, thinking of them as specially sacred and failing to recognise as holy 'the simple duties of our station'.[80]

The liberal Christianity which these men preached tended therefore to be anti-dogmatic and vigorously anti-sacerdotal. They saw outward institutions as liable to divert people from the spiritual centre of religion. Of Toynbee, Lord Milner wrote, 'Incredulous of miracle and indifferent to dogma, he was yet intensely conscious of the all-pervading presence of the Divine.'[81] Green's understanding of the role of dogma in the early church is similar to that which was later to be popularised by Adolf Harnack. It was, declared Green, 'a necessary result of the impotence of the human spirit to sustain itself at the level to which it had been raised in Christ'. The solidification of Christianity into dogmatic form to some degree both presupposed and was a precondition of the growth of a religious society which saw itself as coextensive with, yet distinct from, the world. Orthodox dogma was a salutary defence against a gnosticism which evaporated the moral content of Christianity, on the one hand, and against an Arianism, which undermined the metaphysical, on the other. Unlike Harnack, however, Green concluded that Christianity cannot divest itself of the husk and retain a kernel. Christian dogma 'must be retained in its completeness, but it must be transformed into a philosophy'.[82]

Stressing that God is immanent in the world, Caird rejected the 'subtle tendency to divide the secular and the sacred', insisting that all things are sacred, or at least capable of being sacralised. This is, of course, a familiar feature of much liberal theology, and had found radical expression in the writings of Thomas Arnold. This denial of a distinction between sacred and secular carries with it certain totalitarian corollaries which are not always discerned by those who eagerly embrace it.[83] Green in turn criticised the monastic ideal as resting on a wrong principle: an antithesis between church and world, between religious and secular. He saw in Catholicism a sectarianism which undervalued and despiritualised civic life. 'Jesuitry' was for him 'the ruin of all public spirit'. Later J.N. Figgis was to point to the important role played by the early Jesuits in the growth of a secular state, though he – unlike Green – regarded this as a salutary development.[84] Green and his fellow idealists consequently maintained a 'high' view of the state, and refused to draw a clear distinction between church and state. He opposed the disestablishment of the Church of England for a number of reasons. In the words of Nettleship he believed that 'it would make the clergyman of the future either a mere priest or a mere preacher, instead of the leader in useful social work and in the administration of such public business as is not directly administered by the state'. Arnold Toynbee also saw the establishment as a remedy against 'sacerdotalism'.[85] Later writers like Rashdall and Henson also viewed the establishment in this light.

The governing concept of God in the writing of these idealist thinkers is, then, that of an immanent spirit, manifesting himself in the life of the world. Caird saw the basis of religion in a human consciousness of the distinction between a self and a not-self, which are related within a higher unity, which is God. For Green, God is the final cause of the individual's moral life and is thus identified with the ideal of the moral self; 'God', he wrote, 'is identical with the self of every man in the sense of being the realisation of its determinate possibilities.' He thus wrote of 'an immanent God, a God present *in* the believing love of him and the brethren, a Christ within us'.[86] Although it is right to think of God in terms of personality, he is not to be conceived as a transcendent being, external to the world; rather we should entertain

the thought of God, not as 'far off' but 'nigh', not as a master, but as a father, not as a terrible outward power, forcing us we know not whither, but as one of whom we may say, that we are reason of his reason and spirit of his spirit.[87]

Caird similarly criticised the deism of Voltaire and Rousseau which involved belief in an external Being who attaches happiness to goodness, rather than 'a Spirit who transcends and embraces all things and beings'.[88]

The pantheistic tendency evident in these ideas of God is consonant with the image of the state – and of social relations generally – entertained by these idealists. Caird saw the national state as 'the highest organised whole, the great ethical unity to which our services are immediately owing'.[89] As Green identified God with the moral potential of the individual, so he saw heaven as the realised ideal of social life: 'a society . . . which shares in and carries further every measure of perfection attained by man under the conditions of life that we know'. It is not surprising to find him telling the young Henry Scott Holland that citizenship is to be reckoned higher than saintliness.[90]

The concept and role of the state

Believing that it is only in social life that people are able to realise their potential as moral beings, these writers insisted that the state thus has a moral end, that of the good life. Green developed a notion of the common good, or the public interest, which it is the proper function of a government to realise and of all citizens to pursue. Accepting this idea of a common good, Toynbee maintained that it

was one of the principal functions of religion to instil into its
adherents 'the consciousness of an ideal self which includes the good
of all'.[91]

While he saw this common good as a substantive good which a
government must pursue, Green was clear that it could never be
realised by direct means alone. Morality cannot be imposed by
legislation. He insisted that

> those acts only should be matter of legal injunction or prohibition
> of which the performance or omission, irrespectively of the motive
> from which it proceeds, is so necessary to the existence of a society
> in which the moral end stated can be realised, that it is better for
> them to be done or omitted from that unworthy motive which
> consists in fear or hope of legal consequences than not to be done
> at all.[92]

Nevertheless Green staunchly defended the right – or rather duty
– of a government to interfere with what was called freedom of
contract, in order to protect the weaker party, and he rejected any
notion of the absolute right of private property. Although governments could not impose morality by legislation it is possible for
them to remove certain hindrances to the good life. Yet in some
respects Green retained the prejudices of an earlier liberalism and
attacked 'paternal government'. In his celebrated 'Lectures on the
Principles of Political Obligation', Green argued that laws which are
unnecessary, on the basis of the principle quoted above, and which
inhibit the growth of self-reliance or take away the occasion for the
exercise of moral virtues such as parental forethought or neighbourly
kindness, ought not to be enacted. They undermine the moral end of
the state by securing compliance by legal sanction and thus remove
the occasion for truly virtuous actions.[93] Yet elsewhere, in a lecture
given just before his death, he seems to have departed from this
principle:

> the man who, of his own right feeling, saves his wife from
> overwork and sends his children to school, suffers no moral
> degradation from a law which, if he did not do this for himself,
> would seek to make him do it. Such a man does not feel the law as
> constraint at all.[94]

In a later section of his 'Principles' he also denied that laws on
compulsory education removed the occasion for responsible and
virtuous action by parents, for 'a law of compulsory education . . . is
from the beginning only felt as compulsion by those in whom . . .

there is no spontaneity to be interfered with'.[95] But this would surely be true in all cases of legal compulsion and seems to remove the apparent check on paternal legislation which Green had earlier enunciated. He might rather have admitted the negative aspects of such legislation while insisting that such interference with the freedom of one group may be justified as a necessary means for realising the good (and indeed freedom) of a succeeding generation; but this was not the line of defence he took.

Positive action by the state can thus be justified by an appeal to the idea of a common good but also by a claim that such action enhances the true freedom of citizens. The notion of positive liberty employed by Green has been of considerable importance in the development of a welfare-state ideology and it is worth some further enquiry. Green criticised the negative idea of liberty, put forward in its purest form by Thomas Hobbes and assumed by many nineteenth-century liberals. A man is said to be free to do something when there is no external impediment placed on his action by human agency. In this view the freedom to do something does not imply the *power* or *means* to do it, but merely the absence of external restraint. A man who cannot visit the beach because he is locked in prison is unfree, but a man who cannot visit the beach because he has no money to pay the fare is not unfree. Green argued that this was an empty freedom and that to be effective freedom must include the power to act. Legislation which restricted the freedom of parents could thus increase the freedom of children; legislation which inhibited the freedom of a handful of factory owners might enhance the effective freedom of a million artisans. This point was taken up and extended by a large number of late nineteenth-century liberals, as we have already seen.

Green, however, went further than this; he not only extended the notion of freedom to include the power to act, but restricted it, by denying that 'the mere removal of compulsion, the mere enabling a man to do as he likes', is a contribution to true freedom, which is 'a positive power or capacity of doing or enjoying something worth doing or enjoying, and that, too, something that we do or enjoy in common with others'. Again he stated that freedom was the power for members of a society 'to make the best of themselves'.[96] The obvious question which will arise is: who decides what is 'worth doing' and what this 'best' involves? This definition of freedom would seem to open the door to all sorts of paternalist legislation as extensions of true freedom.

Other liberals of the period were unwilling to accept this 'realist' notion of freedom. Toynbee defined freedom as 'the power to do what we like' and he rejected Plato's idea of the state, whose function was to put every man in his place; 'to us', he went on, 'it is freedom – to enable every man to *find* his place'.[97] The modern state secures freedom by compulsion; that is by compelling some to respect the freedom of others. In a rather happy phrase, Toynbee spoke of *fraternal* rather than paternal government as the ideal to be realised.[98]

Although the principles he put forward would justify a considerable degree of social action, Green was clearly in favour of as much of this being voluntary as possible. When compulsory action was called for, it could often be better managed by municipal than by central government. Many of the objections to state interference by old-fashioned liberals were, Green maintained, objections to centralisation. 'Most of us would agree', he went on, 'that of late there has been a dangerous tendency to override municipal discretion by the hard and fast rules of London "departments".'[99] As Melvin Richter insists, Green was not a 'collectivist' in the sense of advocating extensive governmental action.[100] Nor indeed was Toynbee, who laid considerable stress upon the importance of friendly societies, co-operatives and trade unions.[101] As we have seen, Green's principles were used by a number of his disciples to justify wide compulsory powers of central government, but Green's own preference was for voluntary and local action.

The Balliol idealists thus assumed a close analogy between God and the state, seen in terms of an almost mystical relationship with their respective subjects. On the one hand there was a benevolent and fatherly God, immanent in the world and wholly identified with the true moral end of his children, and on the other a state embodying a common good within which the true good of its citizens is totally embraced. Lord Milner recalled how Green and his disciples had played an important part in changing the whole political and economic assumptions of Oxford. 'When I went up', he wrote, 'the *laissez-faire* theory still held the field. All the recognised authorities were "orthodox" economists of the old school', but within ten years all had changed. Furthermore this change 'has subsequently reproduced itself on the larger stage of the world'.[102] Milner naturally assumed that the Oxford idealists took the lead, but looking back it is fairly clear that these intellectuals were themselves responding to a changing situation in the country. Owing to the growing power of the working class some amelioration in the condition of the poor was becoming a necessary condition of social order. The intuitions of politicians like Benjamin Disraeli and Joseph Chamberlain may be seen as anticipations of the social and political theory which were later developed.

GERMAN THEOLOGY AND SOCIAL LEGISLATION

It is well known that in the years prior to the First World War, some of the principal architects of social legislation in Britain looked to the German situation for guidance. David Lloyd George himself visited Germany in 1908 as did civil servants Beveridge and Braithwaite. There was considerable agreement that in general a scheme of state-run insurance for workers was a possible and desirable development, though, as we have seen, the details were matters of bitter controversy. It is less well known that in the mid-nineteenth century many Germans had been looking at the British phenomenon of voluntary friendly societies with an eye to encouraging their growth at home and to supplementing their activities by state schemes.[103] The German legislation of the 1880s was not an entirely new development; laws controlling child labour and other social legislation went back to 1839.[104] A recent writer has in fact claimed that the laws passed by Bismarck were 'but a return to the old principle of state interference applied to a new economic background'.[105]

The idea of welfare as one of the principal characteristics of the state was of growing importance in Germany during the last quarter of the nineteenth century. Among socialists the notion of a catastrophic end to the bourgeois state, culminating in a proletarian state which would soon wither away, was generally minimised. The revisionist movement among German Marxists stressed the evolutionary path by which the bourgeois state would be imperceptibly transformed into a benevolent and socialist state. A parallel movement among German Protestant theologians is evident.[106] The idea of an apocalyptic return of Christ on the clouds of heaven to inaugurate his kingdom was discarded and replaced by a conception of salvation as an inward state of blessedness, which would manifest itself in the world by a determination to improve the moral and material life of mankind. The fatherhood of a benevolent God was emphasised with the attendant belief in the brotherhood of man. Even theologians, like Johannes Weiss and later Albert Schweitzer, who proclaimed the message of Jesus to have been essentially apocalyptic, argued that this gospel must be reinterpreted in moral and existential terms if it were to be relevant to the Europe of their day.

Protestant paternalism

The Iron Chancellor himself, rejecting the idea of 'a natural harmony of interests', defended state action and insisted that the idea of a state-sponsored system of national insurance was part of a long-standing paternalistic attitude.[107] 'It is the tradition of the dynasty which I serve', he declared, 'that it takes the part of the weaker ones in the economic struggle.'[108] In a conversation with W.H. Dawson he put the point more bluntly; the purpose of the laws was 'to bribe the working classes, or, if you like, to win them over'.[109] This legislation has thus to be seen in the context of the rapid growth of the labour movement and a fear on the part of the ruling classes that, unless something was done to win over important sections of the working class, revolution would ensue. Kaiser Wilhelm I stated that a remedy for social discontent cannot be sought merely in the repression of socialism – 'but must be sought simultaneously through the positive promotion of the workers' welfare'.[10]

As was later to happen in Britain, the government proposals had a rough ride through the legislature, being criticised from both left and right. Many socialists attacked the proposals as tying the worker to the 'state welfare chain'.[111] Some liberals favoured the alternative policy of increasing employers' liability, but this was opposed by Bismarck on the ground that it would impose unfair burdens on employers and, more significantly, that it would make workers dependent upon agencies other than the state. Bismarck observed how in France huge numbers had become dependent upon state pensions and had therefore a vested interest in political stability. 'I will consider it a great advantage', he declared, 'when we have 700,000 small pensioners drawing their annuities from the state, especially if they belong to those classes who otherwise do not have much to lose by an upheaval.'[112] During the decade of the 1880s schemes were introduced for accident, sickness and old age pensions, each financed differently. The system was, however, incomplete in so far as many workers were outside the scheme. As late as 1895 only half the workforce was covered by sickness benefits. It tended, moreover, to be the poorer workers who were excluded from the state schemes.

Bismarck himself, Schleiermacher's most distinguished confirmation candidate, frequently referred to this social legislation as 'practical Christianity'[113] and the prologue to the 1881 Insurance Bill stated that the 'modern idea of the state . . . is the result of Christian ethics, according to which the state should discharge besides the defensive duty of protecting existing rights, the positive duty of promoting the welfare of all its members'.[14]

Protestant images of God

Perhaps the most influential German theologian of this period was Albrecht Ritschl.[115] Born in Berlin in 1822, the son of a Protestant pastor, he came under the influence of F.C. Baur and others of the so-called Tübingen School in his student days. He soon rejected Hegelian rationalism and became a fierce critic of all forms of metaphysical theology. Religious statements must, he insisted, be seen above all as value-judgments made from the standpoint of faith, rather than assertions about the 'real' nature of things. Yet these statements are made by members of a living community, rather than by isolated individuals. As his son and biographer insisted, it was upon 'the concrete realities of Christian praxis' that he built his understanding of the Christian faith.[116]

Ritschl stressed the ethical content of Christianity and attacked as 'heathen' all attempts to subordinate ethics to cosmology. This ethical emphasis has certain features in common with the thought of Kant, though it may be misleading to refer to him as 'neo-Kantian'.[117] Ritschlian theology became a major strand in what is usually called liberal Protestantism, and through his disciples, Adolf Harnack and Wilhelm Herrmann, Ritschl's influence extended far beyond the academic public to which most of his own writings were addressed.[118]

For Ritschl and his followers 'faith in the fatherly providence of God' was the essence of the Christian world-view. Although he did not see God's kingdom as coming on earth, he did believe that, in striving after the good, Christians could improve conditions in this world. It is with the purpose of serving 'the common good' that every Christian vocation should be undertaken.[119]

In his work on the atonement Ritschl defended Reformation ideas of God as 'the moral power which satisfies the highest human interests with an orderly system of ends', in contrast to medieval conceptions which pictured atonement in terms of 'arbitrary compensation for a personal injury'.[120] He saw this latter under-standing of God developing through Duns Scotus to reach its apotheosis in Socinianism.[121] Yet, despite his references to a retributive element in punishment, Ritschl maintained that the right of civil punishment 'is only a means of upholding the public well-being', just as divine punishment is effected for 'the purpose of perfecting the salvation of the righteous and maintaining their cause in the world'.[122] It is perhaps worth contrasting Ritschl's understanding of God's role in the redemptive process with that assumed by British liberals of the early twentieth century. While the latter thought much more in terms of the restoration of personal relationships – a reconciliation of two estranged friends – as the model of atonement, the German professor gave greater emphasis to the idea of sin as the transgression of a law. Pardon need not be seen as contradictory to law if it is granted in order to encourage obedience to the law.[123]

Paul Tillich states that Ritschlianism was 'a theology which could fortify the strong development of the bourgeois personality'.[124] By this he presumably meant that the generally individualistic and moralistic emphasis strengthened the notion of the responsible self as the basic unit of the state, nourishing, as Herrmann put it, 'the spirit to gain independence in the inward man'.[125] While fiercely critical of pietism and mysticism, Ritschl and his closest followers insisted on the importance of 'the communion of the Christian with God'.[126] Yet this was to be found not by mystical contemplation, lifting the devotee above the world, but by prayerful action in the world. The kingdom of heaven was seen by Harnack as the reign of God in the individual heart and, although this by no means ruled out social action in religion or politics, the ultimate criterion was the welfare of the individual and the integrity of the individual personality.[127]

Max Weber

Max Weber, born in 1864, came in direct contact from an early age with the world of political and social action. His father was involved in the National Liberal Party and his mother was engaged in social work. Traditionally the Liberals were, of course, suspicious of the state, but things in Germany were changing. Looking back from the late 1880s the young Max Weber noted how his contemporaries, even among the Liberals, had come to see a more positive role for the state in social matters.[128] The escalating power of the state and of the bureaucratic caste which administered it fascinated Weber, and some of his most significant academic work was concerned with the study of bureaucracy. He examined how traditional and charismatic forms of authority tended to become 'routinised' and rationalised. While he acknowledged that this extension of state power was needed to regulate an increasingly complex social and economic system, he regarded the development with some unease. His attitude towards bureaucracy has been compared to Marx's ambivalent assessment of the bourgeoisie.

Weber, with Friedrich Meinecke[129] and so many of his generation, followed the teaching of their master Treitschke that 'the essence of the state is power'.[130] Politics is about the distribution, maintenance and transfer of power, and the state is defined as that body which successfully claims the monopoly of the legitimate use of physical force within a given territory.[131] As the large capitalist enterprise expropriates the small producer, so the modern state expropriates all autonomous centres of power within its territory, so that it 'controls the total means of political organization, which actually come together under a single head'.[132] We might add that the 'absolutely transcendent God' of Protestantism,[133] in analogous manner, expropriates the semi-autonomous roles of saints and angels in popular Catholicism. 'The gods', Weber wrote, 'are conceived by analogy to earthly rulers: mighty beings whose power differs only in degree, at least at first.'[134] But he was equally aware that images of God influence, in turn, human thinking about political authority.

Weber was at times critical of the authoritarian ethos of German politics, seeing it as a legacy of Bismarck, who 'left a nation accustomed to submit, under the label of constitutional monarchy, to anything that was decided for it'.[135] This tendency was reinforced by elements in Lutheran piety and by a militarism that pervaded social life. He noted how real power was increasingly concentrated in the hands of a military and civil bureaucracy which controlled the 'everyday administration', rather than being exercised in royal pronouncements or parliamentary speeches.[136] Weber became highly critical of the role of the Kaiser and, with Germany's defeat in 1918, believed that a plebiscitary presidency combined with an active parliament could be a counter-balance to bureaucratic power. He believed in strong leadership. When challenged in a celebrated conversation with Ludendorff, effective head of the German military, he defended his conception of democracy thus:

In a democracy the people choose a leader in whom they trust. Then the chosen leader says, 'Now shut up and obey me.' People and party are then no longer free to interfere in his business. . . .

Later the people can sit in judgment. If the leader has made mistakes – to the gallows with him![137]

In his emphasis on 'the power state' and his belief in the *Führerprinzip* Weber clearly anticipated the populist 'decisionism' soon to be elaborated by Carl Schmitt.

Unlike William Temple, who opposed the power state to the welfare state, Weber saw no conflict between them. One of the reasons he became critical of the National Liberals was that they increasingly ignored the general welfare for the interests of a particular class. His long association with the Verein für Sozialpolitik was partly due to their emphasis upon a politics of welfare, with positive state action to control industry, banking and commerce in the interests of the majority.[138]

Like Ritschl, Weber believed in a scientific approach to the material he studied, drawing a clear distinction between value-judgments and scientific observations. Both men clearly believed that scientific objectivity is possible in the study of human culture and that the value-judgments are added almost as a matter of arbitrary commitment or choice. These can be explained in terms of social and particularly religious upbringing, but cannot be defended or criticised rationally.

Though Weber's own religious beliefs bordered on agnosticism, he assumed a generally liberal Protestant world-view. In his discussion of Calvinism he recognised that belief in the sovereign and all-powerful God by no means excludes a belief in his providence and protection.[139] His own conception of God was that of the powerful but benevolent bureaucrat. In contrast to the Calvinist picture of a 'transcendental being, beyond the reach of human understanding', Weber placed 'the Father in heaven of the New Testament, so human and understanding, who rejoices over the repentance of a sinner as a woman over the lost piece of silver she has found'.[140] This is, of course, a blatantly selective picture of the New Testament image of God and betrays in a quite startling way Weber's own assumptions. As he perceived in his academic work and exemplified in his life, the image of God which is predominant among a certain social group in a given period is often closely related to its understanding of the state.

This brief glance at the ideological background to social legislation in late nineteenth-century Germany provides a further instance of the way in which images and conceptions of divinity appear related to ideas about the proper role of the state. The dislocations produced by industrialisation in the earlier part of the century involved the dramatic growth of an urban proletariat. The development of labour organisations and the demand for improvements in housing, sanitation and working conditions made by these organisations led successive governments to recognise that suppression was not the only means of dealing with unrest. Much of the wind could be taken out of the sails of working-class 'agitators' by introducing legislation to enforce better conditions and to ensure an improved standard of life. These were steps which working-class leaders who had a real concern for the interests of their class could hardly oppose. The changes led in turn to a crisis in social democracy and to the rise of revisionism in Germany. I am not, of course, suggesting that the conscious motives of all those who pioneered such improvements was a cynical desire to sedate the masses. On the contrary, many were deeply moved by the appalling conditions in which huge numbers of their fellow men and women lived.

These two chapters have, I hope, shown the close relationship which has existed between Christian theology and the development of the welfare state. It was not of course the case that theologians borrowed a quite novel image of a benevolent and paternal God from the political rhetoric of their day. These images have been part of a Christian understanding of God from earliest times. Nevertheless they were given a prominence which was new; indeed at times these welfare images of God seem almost to have claimed exclusive validity. 'Hell was dismissed with costs' and a religion developed where, in the celebrated words of H. Richard Niebuhr, 'A God without wrath brought men without sin into a kingdom without judgment through the ministrations of a Christ without a cross.'[141] All this was possible in a situation where welfare provisions and the strong arm of the law were able to hold in strain the incipient discontent of the masses. In Germany, defeated and humiliated at Versailles, with an unstable government and an economic crisis of proportions not experienced in Britain, it proved impossible to contain the discontent and harsher methods which were required to preserve a capitalist structure. In this context other images of God became current among Christians attempting to come to terms with the crisis.

4

No king but Caesar: sovereign God and total state

Totalitarianism may be seen theologically as a modern form of 'henotheism' – or the worship of tribal gods.[1] It transforms an earthly, finite institution or set of institutions into the object of 'ultimate concern', to use Paul Tillich's terminology. Totalitarianism involves giving unconditional love and devotion to something other than the true God: to nation, state, race or movement. The ancient Hebrews called it the sin of idolatry. Totalitarianism collapses the analogical relationship frequently asserted between God and the civil power into an identity. The social unit is regarded as divine or at least it takes the place of God in the life of the militant.

Totalitarianism is a political corollary of immanentism – the belief that God is wholly identified with all or part of the universe. A thoroughgoing immanentism denies that God – the symbol of the ultimate – is in any sense 'beyond' or 'above' the universe. God equals the universe, in so far as it manifests or moves towards some ideal state, usually thought of in terms of unity or harmony. Totalitarianism is the attempt to institutionalise this unity, to legislate this harmony. While it can (as some Hegelian idealists have shown) accommodate a limited 'orchestrated' pluralism, it can find no place for the unscripted action, human or divine – for what Berdyaev called 'the catastrophic interrupting moment'.[2] There is no effective freedom; there are no new beginnings.

We may see twentieth-century totalitarianism as a variety of authoritarian government, though there are also totalitarian aspects to much welfare state thinking. The regimes of Mussolini, Hitler and the Bolsheviks emerged in periods of acute political and social instability. In such times people look to groups which seem able to provide strong leadership and to have the power necessary to impose order in a situation of impending chaos. Lenin's emphasis on the need for a small disciplined party – dating from his celebrated essay of 1902, *What is to be Done* – and his elaboration of the Marxist notion of the dictatorship of the proletariat, culminating in *The State and Revolution*, set the scene for later developments in Soviet 'democratic centralism'. In the context of the chronic instability of the tsarist regime, which was made manifest in the Revolution of 1905, the Bolsheviks consolidated their position and in the confused months which followed the February 1917 Revolution they emerged as the party which knew what it wanted and seemed able to impose it. The same was clearly true in the case of the fascist and Nazi movements. In the ideology of all three there was a strongly 'decisionist' element. This was true particularly in the case of the latter two; Lenin was writing within the framework of a more rationalist tradition. Yet he too laid great emphasis upon Marxism as a 'guide to action' and his quoting of Napoleon, 'on s'engage et puis . . . on voit', indicates more than a hint of decisionism.[3]

Writing to a German friend in 1871, the great historian Burckhardt uttered this ominous oracle:

I have a premonition, which sounds like utter folly and yet which positively will not leave me: the military state must become one great factory. Those hordes of men in the great industrial centers will not be left indefinitely to their greed and want. . . . Long voluntary subjection under individual *Führers* and usurpers is in prospect. People no longer believe in principles but will, periodically, believe in saviors. . . . For this reason authority will again raise its head in the pleasant twentieth century, and a terrible head.[4]

Totalitarianism constituted a challenge to the Christian churches. By their very nature they had to reject the claims being made on behalf of the state or the movement. The regimes of Mussolini, Hitler and Stalin posed a problem for the three great divisions of Christianity, Catholicism, Protestantism and Orthodoxy. The 'German Christians' on the one hand and Karl Barth on the other exemplify two Protestant responses to the Nazi phenomenon. Carl Schmitt, a jurist and political theorist, represents a fascinating but eccentric and atypical Catholic response to Hitler's regime.

Both Italian Fascism and German Nazism claimed to be Christian movements. The situation of the Soviet regime was quite different, being officially committed to an atheist philosophy; its seductive power for Christians was correspondingly less. There have been relatively few Christians who have given positive allegiance and ideological support to the Soviet regime, though at times – both under Stalin and since – it has wooed the Orthodox Church, which has in certain crises given limited support to the government and has generally avoided confrontation. Speaking generally, Christians who claim to be Marxists have adhered to other than Bolshevik forms of communism – as found, for example, in Latin America or western Europe. Yet a number of Russian Orthodox Christians did engage in a dialogue with Bolshevism in the inter-war years. The conception of God developed by Nicolas Berdyaev is particularly interesting from the standpoint of our present enquiry. Though his thought shares certain perspectives with that of Barth – a critique of rationalism in theology, an existentialist tone and a basic Trinitarianism – it contrasts strikingly at other points, drawing on a quite different theological tradition.

TOTALITARIANISM IN THEORY AND PRACTICE

The terms 'totalitarianism' and 'totalitarian state' became popular during the 1920s, having been first applied to the Italian Fascist regime of Mussolini. They were used by Giovanni Gentile, one of the principal theorists of Fascism, and were adopted by *Il Duce* himself, notably in the notorious article on the doctrine of Fascism, which appeared in the *Enciclopedia Italiana* of 1932 under his name. In contrast to liberal democratic ideas of the state as 'night-watchman', maintaining order and interested only in the external actions of its citizens, Mussolini asserted that for the Fascist

everything is in the State, and nothing human or spiritual exists, much less has value outside the State. In this sense Fascism is totalitarian, and the Fascist State, the synthesis and unity of all values, interprets, develops and gives strength to the whole life of the people.[5]

In the 1930s the term was also frequently applied to Nazi Germany and to the Soviet Union. Although these three regimes had much in common, particularly their opposition to liberal democratic systems, there were material differences between them and doubt has consequently been cast upon the fruitfulness of the concept of totalitarianism as an analytical tool.

Use of the term 'totalitarianism' became an important ideological issue in the post-1945 years, when it was employed as a weapon in the cold war. In applying the term to the Soviet Union, certain United States publicists were – according to their critics – able to suggest a greater similarity between Bolshevism and Nazism than in fact obtained. In 1956 Carl Friedrich and Zbigniew Brzezinski defended their use of the term quite explicitly on the grounds that 'Fascist and communist dictatorships are basically alike, or at any rate more nearly like each other than like any other system of government.'[6] For these authors, furthermore, totalitarian dictatorship was a distinctively twentieth-century phenomenon and should therefore clearly be distinguished from earlier forms of autocracy and dictatorship.

Traditional autocracies share many features with totalitarian regimes. They employ terror to ensure compliance and they demand that every individual, group and institution conform to some organic end. Examples of the former were Franco's Spain and Salazar's Portugal, which can hardly be called totalitarian; yet they were not entirely dissimilar to Nazi Germany and Fascist Italy. The principal difference was that they were less radical and dynamic; they were more concerned to preserve or restore a traditional way of life which had recently been challenged than to create a new order. They were thus less messianic, less ideological and laid comparatively little emphasis upon the role of the leader.

This distinction between autocratic and totalitarian regimes has later been employed by the Reagan administration to justify the sympathetic treatment accorded to Cuban or Nicaraguan refugees (said to come from 'totalitarian' states) in contrast to the harsh policy adopted towards other Latin American fugitives (whose governments were merely 'autocratic'). Although the conceptual distinction may be defended, the use to which it has here been put is wholly unwarranted, for the government of an autocracy – like Pinochet's Chile or Duvalier's Haiti – could be at least as ruthless in pursuing its ends and harassing or killing its opponents as a totalitarian government is in pursuing its more comprehensive ends.

While there are thus good grounds for concluding that the term 'totalitarian' has been employed in an ideological manner, there may still be a justification for its use as an analytical tool. A totalitarian regime may for our purposes be characterised as one in which the total life of the individual and of the community becomes the direct concern of the state or of the movement. It becomes the aim of the totalitarian to integrate into a coherent and dynamic whole all aspects of social life. In so far as corporations and groups are permitted, they are absorbed into a greater unity and enjoy no real autonomous existence. It is thus the case that certain forms of corporatism or pluralism are compatible with totalitarianism, so long as the component groups are entirely subsumed under the umbrella of the whole. Thus it may well be that the social pluralism characteristic of Hegel, Bosanquet, Follett and Gierke, unlike the pluralism of English thinkers such as Laski and Figgis, is consonant with a type of totalitarianism.[7] In fact such German theorists as Othmar Spann and Carl Schmitt looked to the corporatism of Gierke, Preuss and Hauriou as a theoretical foundation for the Nazi state.

Other features of totalitarian systems include

1 the manipulation by state or by party of the instruments of communication such as the press, television, radio and more generally the educational curriculum;
2 the employment of terror not simply as deterrence but as a means for isolating individuals and generally causing anxiety;
3 the concern for theoretical purity among party members and the fanatical pursuit of ideological ends, even when these conflict with practical considerations. Hannah Arendt points to the numerous complaints by military commanders about the deportations of Jews and Poles which disregarded 'all military and economic necessities'.[8]

A further aspect of twentieth-century totalitarianism is the so-called leadership principle, or 'the cult of personality'. The leader is seen to embody the will of the masses in a way that parliamentary democracy and representative government fail to do.[9] This notion was institutionalised in the form of the plebiscite. As we shall see, the leadership principle was also applied in Germany to church government.

It is important to distinguish between the theory and practice of totalitarianism. Although modern techniques have made the creation of a system which approaches the ideal type of totalitarianism more possible, it may still be legitimate to apply the term to political theories of the past. In so far as the concept involves the existence of some kind of mass movement, it may be said to be modern, but this kind of popular involvement can already be seen in the English and French revolutions of the seventeenth and eighteenth centuries. One writer has indeed spoken of the theories of Rousseau and the policies of the Jacobins as constituting the origins of totalitarian democracy.[10]

Fascist Italy, Nazi Germany and Stalinist Russia have been seen as the classic examples of totalitarian states, but it should be noted that in no case has a thoroughly totalitarian system been realised in practice. Italian Fascism, which in theory was perhaps the most totalitarian, was in fact the state which least exemplified the idea. The entrenched power of the church, the monarchy, the army and even the police prescribed material limits to the power and scope of the Fascist state. Even in the Soviet Union and in Nazi Germany, where Christians constituted less of a unified body and where the national church had been traditionally subordinate to the state, the government was never able to gain complete control of the churches nor to eliminate Christian belief and practice among the population. Other institutions, including the army and elements in the civil service, also resisted absorption into the system.

Leading US political theorists, like Robert Dahl, Carl Friedrich and Edward Shils, have outlined theories of liberal democracy, pluralism or polyarchism, as representing the polar opposite of totalitarianism.[11] In these, it is alleged, much of the life of the community is beyond the direct concern of government and certain individual and group rights are secured against state contravention. A clear distinction between the two types of regime has, however, been challenged both from the 'right' and from the 'left'.

Fascists and their sympathisers have claimed that in liberal democratic systems real power is held by a small governing elite and that the much vaunted freedom of expression is in practice limited by the control over information exercised by a plutocracy.[12] These criticisms were reinforced from the 'left' by C. Wright Mills in his book *The Power Elite*. Furthermore, Herbert Marcuse and others have denounced the 'one-dimensional' aspect of pluralist democracies, and have argued that totalitarianism 'is not only a terroristic political coordination of society, but also a non-terroristic economic-technical coordination which operates through the manipulation of needs by vested interests', observing that toleration is restricted to those groups which are thought to be 'moderate' and which accept the general consensus.[13] While there is much truth in these criticisms, and it is important to recognise that there are no pure instances of either totalitarian or of liberal democratic regimes, we are not forced to conclude that the distinction between them is illegitimate, either in theory or in practice. The fact that these criticisms by Marcuse and others can freely be propagated in western countries suggests that there is at least some difference.

I have stated that totalitarianism is for the Christian a heresy because it makes 'religious' claims for the state or for the movement. It is, however, worth observing that liberalism or democracy can also become religious and Jürgen Moltmann is being somewhat naïve in quoting John Quincey Adams to the effect that 'democracy has no monuments'. The very phrase 'vox populi vox dei', the extraordinary ideas of a writer like Thomas Davidson (discussed in chapter 5) and the quasi-religious manner in which some US politicians speak of 'the American way of life' suggest otherwise.[14] Yet there is something in the very nature of totalitarianism, unlike liberal democracy, which involves a religious dimension.

RELIGION AND THE NAZI MOVEMENT

The National Socialist German Workers' Party (NSDAP), whose leader Adolf Hitler became German chancellor in January 1933, contained many different tendencies and ideological positions. While some Nazis clearly assumed the Italian ideal of a total state, the leadership manifested a certain hostility to the notion. Hans Buchheim reflected this position when he wrote that 'the bearer of political power is not the state, as an impersonal unit, but this is given to the Führer as the executor of common *völkisch* will'. Alfred Rosenberg, a leading ideologist and longstanding member of the party, maintained that the state must be seen as an instrument at the disposal of the movement. 'It behoves National Socialists not to speak any more of the total state,' he declared in 1934.[15] Hitler himself asserted that 'The *Volk* is primary. Party, state, army, economy, law, etc., are secondary manifestations and methods for the purpose of preserving this *Volk*.'[16] This reflected the suspicion, nurtured by many committed Nazis, of the civil servants, army officers and big businessmen, who frequently appeared to inhibit the implementation of Nazi policies.

There was in the NSDAP also an ambiguity about the question of religion. Evidently in practice the party encouraged a quasi-religious dedication to the cause and devotion to the Führer. Hitler declared that Nazism is 'a form of conversion, a new faith'.[17] Though the Hitler cult was developed by his followers, he himself appears to have accepted the notion of his providential and messianic role by the late 1920s. However, the origins of the notion of the heroic leader who incarnates the spirit of the nation in a quasi-supernatural way go back to nineteenth-century *völkisch* nationalism. By 1920 one nationalist could write of the idea of the leader who 'carries out the will of God which he embodies in himself' and is the 'bearer of godly power, destiny and grace'. Thus the Nazis did not invent the Führer concept, but rather used an already existing idea to promote the claims of Hitler.[18]

Despite these quasi-religious aspects of the movement, the official position of the NSDAP was that 'The Party, as such, stands for a positive Christianity, but does not bind itself in the matter of creed to any particular confession.'[19] However, the term 'positive' was variously interpreted. Christians within the movement understood it to mean a sort of highest common factor shared by the mainline churches, while anti-Christians, like Rosenberg, suggested that positive Christianity was opposed to the negative Christianity of the Roman Catholic and, to a lesser extent, the Protestant churches, and was a faith which 'calls to life the forces of the nordic blood'.[20]

By the end of the 1920s the Nazi movement enjoyed considerable support from Protestant churchmen, lay and ordained. It has been estimated that, by 1930, over half the seminary students were followers of Hitler, and in one theology faculty 90 per cent of the students were Nazi supporters or sympathisers.[21] Even Pastor Martin Niemoller, soon to become a leader of the so-called Confessing Church, welcomed Hitler's rise to power and draped his church in swastikas. In 1932 the Faith Movement of German Christians had been formed by a union of two smaller groups, under Pastor Joachim Hossenfelder; their slogan was 'the swastika on our breasts and the cross in our hearts'.[22] A Swedish press report records in 1933 the extraordinary sight of '200 clergymen dressed in brown uniforms, riding boots, body and shoulder straps', at a synod in Brandenburg.[23]

The 'German Christians'

The 'Deutsche Christen' were not merely Christians who gave political support to the Nazi Party but Germans who generally portrayed the rise of Nazism in religious terms. The Führer was 'the redeemer in the history of the Germans'. Pastor Julius Leutheuser declared: 'Christ has come to us through Adolf Hitler. . . . We know today the Saviour has come.'[24] It was perhaps the idea of a spiritual unity among Germans which attracted these Protestants, many of them coming from the liberal cultural-Protestant tradition, in which the church was seen as the religious aspect of the life of the *Volk*.[25] The church must 'be co-ordinated into the rhythm of the National Revolution, it must be fashioned by the ideas of Nazism, lest it remain a foreign body in the unified German Nazi community'.[26] The activities of the 'Deutsche Christen' in the early years of Hitler's regime led to opposition from a number of quarters.

In the Nazi Party itself there was an element, led by Rosenberg, which was vigorously anti-clerical and wished to dissociate the movement from all forms of institutional Christianity. These men believed in a kind of pantheistic Nordic religion. Rosenberg criticised

> The remote and fearful God, enthroned over all; this is Jahweh of the so-called Old Testament, a God to whom one prays in fear and praises in trembling. He created all of us out of nothing and if it suits Him He decrees magical miracles and constructs a world for His own glorification.[27]

Other Nazis, including Himmler, Schirach and Bormann, joined Rosenberg in opposing Christianity from various standpoints. Bormann, insisting that National Socialism – based on scientific foundations – is incompatible with Christianity, wrote of 'Almighty God' as a 'world force', the immanent power that 'moves all these bodies in the universe'.[28] However, most leaders of the Nazi movement, including Hitler himself, were prepared, as a matter of expediency, to see religion as a private affair with which the party should not interfere. 'Faith', declared Rudolf Hesse, 'is a very personal matter'; or – put more bluntly by Goebbels – 'For the Church there is only one solution: Back into the sacristy. Let the Church serve God; we serve the people.'[29] The struggle continued within the party, with Cajus Fabricius attacking the pagan beliefs of some members and arguing that Nazism 'is a movement determined by Christianity'.[30] He was, however, expelled from the party and arrested.

The Nazi government was clearly concerned to prevent the churches from exercising any social or political influence in the new Germany and Hitler appears to have cherished the secret hope of eventually destroying the Christian faith altogether. From the practical standpoint, however, he wished to avoid a head-on collision with the churches, partly because of the influence they had among army officers and in the higher ranks of the state bureaucracy. Despite the propaganda of Rosenberg and others, over 95 per cent of the German people registered as church members in 1939.

The 'Deutsche Christen' were also opposed by important groups in the Protestant Church itself. Their more bizarre pronouncements, including their denunciation of the Old Testament 'with its Jewish morality of rewards and its stories of cattle-dealers and concubines', met with opposition even from Nazi sympathisers in the church.[31] It was largely in opposition to the 'Deutsche Christen' that the so-called

Confessing Church was formed. Their position was summarised in the celebrated Barmen Declaration of 1934, which was largely written by Karl Barth, Professor of Theology at Bonn. Article 5 stated: 'We reject the false doctrine that the State, over and above its special commission, should and could become the single and totalitarian order of human life, thus fulfilling the church's vocation as well.' The declaration also condemned a false view of the church as 'an organ of the state'.

Two issues particularly concerned the Confessing Church in these early years: the extension of the 'leadership principle' to church government resulting in the creation of a *Reichsbischof*, with a highly orchestrated campaign for the election of Nazi sympathiser Ludwig Müller; and second, the attempt by the government to extend the ban on Jews in government employment to the pastors of the church. On these two matters the opposition of these Christians was theological and conservative rather than explicitly political; this was emphasised by Barth and others.[32] Thus a clear distinction is to be drawn between the position of the Confessing Christians and the resistance to Nazism. The former objected

> not because they were in disagreement with the policy of the Third Reich ... but only and quite exclusively because they saw the Confession of Faith of the Church attacked and out of their loyalty to Christ wanted to protect it, even if doing so meant risking their lives.[33]

Dietrich Bonhoeffer voiced a deep Lutheran conviction when he wrote:

> Without doubt, the Church of the Reformation has no right to address the state directly in its specifically political actions. It has neither to praise nor to censure the laws of the state, but must rather affirm the state to be God's order of preservation in a godless world.[34]

Leading sympathisers of the Confessing Church, like Bishop Marahrens of Hanover, were perfectly happy with much of Hitler's policy and gave public thanks to God for the conquest of Poland, as did the Catholic hierarchy. The latter were also concerned principally with defending the interests and privileges of the institutional church and avoided any criticism of Hitler's policies, except when it seemed likely to affect the church. 'At no time', writes G. Zahn, 'was the individual German Catholic led to believe that the regime was an evil unworthy of his support.'[35]

Hirsch and Althaus

While most of the 'Deutsche Christen' came from a liberal theological background, this was not so in the case of two outstanding Protestant theologians who joined the Nazi movement, Emanuel Hirsch and Paul Althaus. Hirsch was born in 1888 and studied theology in Berlin under Adolf Harnack and Karl Holl. The latter's interpretation of Luther's 'two kingdoms' theology and his belief in the 'hidden and mysterious purposes' of the sovereign creator manifesting themselves in human history made a considerable impression on the young Hirsch. He believed that God reveals himself not only in the person of Jesus Christ but also in the history of great peoples, particularly in German history. He taught that the *Volk* is, like the state and the family, a divinely created 'order'. He thus endowed Herder's conception of the *Volk* with theological significance. A recent writer has pointed to the way 'Hirsch was determined to give history a theological meaning'.[36] He embraced the nationalist dogma of Schleiermacher and Fichte that the frontiers of the state should follow the boundaries of the nation to form a *Volksstaat* which would embody the cultural life of the racial community. The hidden sovereignty of the divine ruler was replicated in the hidden sovereignty of the *Volk* and its Führer. Into his political theology of nationalism Hirsch imported decisionist modes of thinking derived principally from Kierkegaard.

This theological historicism brought Hirsch into conflict with Karl Barth and other dialectical theologians, including particularly Friedrich Gogarten, in the early 1920s. They believed that he was endangering the transcendence of God by allowing for a 'continuum' between divine and human existence. A lively debate continued for more than a decade, until Hirsch's manifest support for Hitler and the Nazi movement led to a decisive break between them. In 1937 Hirsch joined the NSDAP and became a supporting member of the SS. He believed that the Nazi movement had brought a much needed unity of spirit into German social and political life and attacked the liberal and pluralist ideal where 'public life restricts itself to ordering external things and the common spirit becomes a religiously and morally neutral characterlessness'.[37] Hirsch was denounced by his former friend Paul Tillich for converting the concept of *kairos*, which is essentially a prophetic and eschatological idea, into 'a priestly-sacramental consecration of contemporary events', thereby sanctifying the political programme of the Nazis.[38]

Paul Althaus, in contrast to Hirsch and the 'Deutsche Christen', was careful to distinguish his political support for Hitler from his religious faith. 'Belief in the success of the German task', he maintained, 'has nothing to do with belief in the victory of the Kingdom of God.' He attacked the 'delirious words' of the Thuringian 'Deutsche Christen', insisting that the Hitler movement was concerned solely with national life; 'we are not saviours of the world'. A conservative Lutheran in theology, Althaus adhered to the concept of 'orders' of creation (*Ordnungen*) – institutions each with its own autonomous criteria for action, each having a divine sanction for operating within its respective sphere.[39] On the question of totalitarianism he was ambiguous. In 1935 he defended the idea of a total state, 'laying claim to all individuals, all areas of life through the state for the necessities of life of the *Volk*'.[40] Later – in common with official Nazi ideology – he distinguished between totalitarianism and the totalitarian state, rejecting the latter. 'A state which knows itself as a servant to the life of its *Volk*', he wrote,

> will not rob the other associations and orders in the *Volk* . . . of their self-reliant, spontaneous life. It will embody totalitarianism . . . it will call forth the free spirit of totality, i.e., the spirit of responsibility for all forms and spheres of life in the presence of the duty to be the *Volk*.[41]

Althaus believed that the Nazis had been justified in subverting the Weimar Republic because, like the Napoleonic occupation of Germany in 1813, the regime was undermining the life of the *Volk*. He defended the *Führerprinzip* as reflecting the need for leadership and authority, and saw in the Führer the embodiment of the *Volksgeist*.[42] Althaus recognised his indebtedness to Herder and the early German Romantics for his *völkisch* emphasis.

CARL SCHMITT

Unlike Hirsch and Althaus, Carl Schmitt was a Catholic, passionately critical of the Romantic thinkers of the early nineteenth century. Born in 1888 of a lower-middle-class family in the predominantly Protestant town of Plettenburg (Sauerland), he originally intended to become a priest but eventually decided to study law and pursue an academic career. He taught at Strassburg, Munich, Greifswald and Bonn from 1916 to 1928, when he moved to the Graduate School of Business Administration in Berlin. After a short spell at Cologne, he returned to take a chair in law at the University of Berlin from 1933 to 1945.

Schmitt defended – on his own terms – the Weimar Republic and in 1932 had urged President Hindenberg to take emergency powers and suppress the Nazi and Communist parties. After Hitler's accession to power, however, he joined the Nazi Party and for a few years acted as the unofficial *Kronjurist* (constitutional adviser) to the new regime, until some of his former colleagues – now in exile – exposed his opportunistic conversion to Nazism, pointing out that he had in the past opposed the rise of Hitler and had dedicated books to Jewish friends. This led Schmitt to introduce anti-Semitic phrases into second editions of his works to show his loyalty to the new order, but to no avail. These attacks on him from abroad were reiterated by his opponents in the party; he was investigated by the SD (the security branch of the SS) and in 1936, despite his relationship with Hans Frank and Hermann Goering, was relieved of party positions and was lucky not to be arrested. From this time onwards he restricted himself to academic activities, though even in the field of international law he managed to alienate party zealots. After the war Schmitt was detained by Allied forces, but it was eventually decided not to proceed against him. He continued to publish works on legal and political theory and died in 1985 at the age of 97.[43]

Weimar and parliamentarism

Carl Schmitt believed that human nature – being evil – demands an authoritarian system of government and he was a great admirer of nineteenth-century Catholics like de Maistre, Bonald and the Spaniard Donoso Cortés, 'whose contempt for man knew no limits'. 'If men were good', the German theorist observed, 'my views would be wicked; but men are not good.'[44] Despite this low view of human nature he paradoxically held the quasi-Rousseauite idea that the will of the people is supreme. Despite all its weaknesses he saw the Weimar constitution as having been accepted by the popular will and therefore binding on all political activists; he also believed that such a constitutional regime must embody certain apparently undemocratic provisions if it is to survive. In particular there must be some way to cope with the 'exceptional case' and with groups opposed to the constitution itself, who may properly be denied an 'equal right' to compete for power. The republican government must draw a clear line between its internal friends and enemies and act accordingly.

In the first place there must be in every system of government some provision for the exceptional case, which does not fall clearly under any single general rule. The only kind of provision that can be made is in terms of *who* makes the decision that such an exceptional situation exists. By very definition such situations cannot be covered by legal and constitutional norms. 'The most guidance the constitution can provide is to indicate who can act in such a case.'[45] Schmitt defined the sovereign as the person who makes the decision on such occasions, and he linked this notion to his defence of 'commissarial' dictatorship.[46] This he distinguished from 'sovereign' dictatorship, in that it was a short-term expedient to deal with an emergency situation. Although the dictator should be able temporarily to suspend the operation of laws he would have no power to change them or to introduce new laws. Schmitt interpreted article 48 of the Weimar constitution in this context and argued that it was a necessary provision which gave wide powers to the president in a state of emergency. Citing some words of Kierkegaard for support, Schmitt argued that a study of the exceptional case is significant not only intrinsically, but also because it sheds light on the nature of the rule. 'The exception is more interesting than the rule,' he observed. 'The rule proves nothing; the exception proves everything.'[47]

The notion of 'equal chance' was developed in the context of the growing power, during the Weimar Republic, of political movements explicitly opposed to the constitution, both from right and left. Schmitt insisted that a political system must have power to protect itself and that this applies as much to a constitutional system as to any other. He thus denied the right of these groups to participate on equal terms with parties which accepted the constitution and, as we have seen, he advocated the president's duty to use his emergency powers to prevent their coming to power. He would have appreciated the observation of the odious but perceptive Portuguese dictator Salazar that the weakness of liberal regimes results primarily from the fact that 'they are constrained by their principles to act as if they had none, and so are driven to act inconsistently in order to exist'.[48]

Liberalism, according to Schmitt, undermines the very notion of the state and of the political, reducing social life to a matter of economics and ethics. The political battle between friend and enemy 'becomes competition in the domain of economics and discussion in the intellectual realm'.[49] Thus, in the mythology of liberalism, economic theory goes hand in hand with ethical theory: unrestrained competition results in economic harmony, while free competition of opinions (inspired by that 'romantic conception of unending conversation') results in the discovery of truth.[50] He characterised nineteenth-century developments by relating the cultural, institutional and constitutional aspects in the following manner:[51]

freedom, progress, reason	v.	feudalism, reaction, force
in alliance with		*in alliance with*
economy, industry, technology	v.	state, war, politics
as		*as*
parliamentarism	v.	dictatorship

This conflict had resulted in the supremacy of industrialism and parliamentarism – a victory for liberalism over feudalism – but new tensions immediately arose; politics had not been abolished but had simply been disguised. Economic liberalism does not necessarily lead to freedom, and technical progress may result not merely in increased comfort but in the production of destructive instruments. 'A system of mutual contracts finally deteriorates into a system of the worst exploitation and repression.'[52] Karl Marx therefore pursued liberals into their own economic stronghold, challenging them on their home ground with their own weapons.[53] The effort to transform the state into a market-place failed; decisions needed to be made, friends and enemies needed to be defined. Politics, according to Schmitt, is and will remain not a clash of opinions about truth in the market-place of ideas, but a conflict of wills about what decisions should be taken. He portrayed the parties of his day facing each other 'as social or economic power-groups calculating their mutual interests and opportunities for power'.[54]

I have said that Schmitt defended Weimar 'on his own terms', for he was highly critical of the parliamentary system and at times appears to have advocated a 'sovereign' rather than a merely 'commissarial' dictatorship. He claimed that parliamentarism had arisen as the result of the adventitious alliance of liberalism and democracy in the nineteenth century and ascribed its crisis to the fact that the two had fallen apart. There is, he maintained, no necessary incompatibility between democracy and dictatorship; 'the will of the people' (the essence of democracy) can be secured at least as well by acclamation and plebiscite, as by representative government. In an age of mass democracy, parliament had become 'a gigantic antechamber in front of the bureaux or committees of invisible rulers'. Real decisions were made elsewhere.[55] Parliamentarism reflects the liberal assumption that 'political conflict can be transformed into a matter of opinion' and can be resolved by free and rational discussion.[56]

In Schmitt's essay on *The Crisis of Parliamentary Democracy*, it is not at all clear where the argument leads. In so far as it was a criticism of the theoretical foundations of the Weimar Republic, its critics replied that the argument misfired, because Weimar's ideological basis is not to be found in the classical liberalism of J.S. Mill and Guizot, but in the much more hard-headed social and legal theories of such men as Max Weber, Friedrich Naumann and Hugo Preuss.[57] If Schmitt's argument was that the practice did not conform to the classical theories of representative government, and that many important decisions were taken not in open parliament – as that theory requires – but behind the scenes, his critics replied that this may not necessarily be a bad thing. As Richard Thoma pointed out, 'The worth and vitality of a political institution in no way depends on the quality and persuasiveness of the ideologies advanced for its justification.'[58] Nevertheless unfulfilled ideological expectations may lead to unease and discontent, and Schmitt's essay may well be interpreted as an attempt to explain the contemporary crisis in these terms.

In the preface to the second edition, Schmitt defended his critique of the classical liberals on the ground that discussion and openness remain essential to any notion of parliamentarism and that it is in their works that the clearest defence of these institutions is to be found. In answer to the 'elite theory of democracy' as it has come to be called, proposed in Britain by such writers as James Fitzjames Stephen and Arthur Balfour and later by Italian and German theorists[59] – that parliamentary government leads to the emergence of competing political elites of high calibre or at least of reasonable competence – Schmitt expressed scepticism, observing that in many parliamentary systems politics 'has become the despised business of a rather dubious class of persons'.[60]

Schmitt allowed himself to 'pass over in silence' the 'utterly fantastic political aims' that Thoma imputed to him, of favouring a nationalistic dictatorship allied to the Catholic Church which would restore 'order, discipline and hierarchy'.[61] Yet if this essay is read in the context of his other works of the period such an interpretation of his intentions is not entirely inappropriate. His authoritarian propensities emerged in his admiration for de Maistre and other Catholic reactionary writers of the previous century and his work entitled *Römischer Katholizismus und politische Form* (1923) proclaimed that 'the Church embodies the sublime conception of authority in its complete purity'.[62] This book was translated into French and admired by such Catholic intellectuals as Jacques Maritain; it appeared in English as one of a series entitled 'Essays in

Order', with an introduction by Christopher Dawson. Schmitt was fascinated, as was Hitler himself, with the power of the Roman Church as manifested, for example, in its defeat of 'Der grosse Bismarck' during the *Kulturkampf* of the previous century.[63] He openly admired the Fascism of Mussolini, celebrating his 'heroic attempt to preserve and assert the dignity of the State and national unity'.[64] Such was Schmitt's admiration for authority and power that he was prepared – conceptually at least – to ally Catholicism with Marxism against Bakunin's libertarian position.[65]

Decisionism

Despite his identification in the early years with Catholicism, Carl Schmitt had no time for traditional natural-law theories. Law is constituted by command rather than by moral right and, with Hobbes, he proclaimed: 'autoritas non veritas facit legem' ('authority not truth makes law'). With the English theorist he also believed that authority is dependent upon the power to protect and that citizens implicitly consent to obey that power which is able to offer them security. It is on this ground that his recognition of Hitler's regime may partially be explained.[66] In his legal theory he not only rejected natural-law positions but also attacked 'pure' theories of law, which portray the legal order as an artificial and autonomous system of norms, with no essential basis in social fact. Hans Kelsen's identification of the state with the legal order, rather than seeing it as the source of this order, disposes of the idea of sovereignty and reiterates, in effect, 'the old liberal negation of the state'.[67] This is the basis of Schmitt's rejection of the liberal *Rechtsstaat* (rule of law) in favour of 'the just state' of National Socialism, which does not close its eyes, as the former does, to social and political realities. This terminology was, however, repudiated by party leaders, who wished for tactical reasons to retain the notion of *Rechtsstaat*. Nevertheless Schmitt's decisionist model was adopted by Nazi lawyers like Hans Frank, who declared, 'Constitutional Law in the Third Reich is the legal formulation of the historic will of the Führer, but the historical will of the Führer is not the fulfilment of legal preconditions for his activity.'[68]

Schmitt's insistence on the *political* role of the state, as the body which must make decisions and defend the interests of its 'friends' against assaults from the 'enemy', led him to reject ideas of state neutrality. He pointed to the gradual 'neutralisation' of institutions which had occurred since the Enlightenment; from the substantive political function of decision-making they had been relegated to a purely instrumental role. First God, in eighteenth-century deism, had been neutralised and removed from having any effective say in the running of the universe. Then, with Hegel, the monarch is reduced to the role of merely crossing the t's and dotting the i's. Increasingly the market and the state were seen either as neutral arenas or as arbitrating institutions with no significant positive role.[69] He warned against the depoliticising of the state and argued that some decision-making centre is absolutely necessary for an ordered polity. 'The modern state', he lamented, 'seems to have actually become what Max Weber envisioned: a huge industrial plant.' Schmitt here anticipated a critical trend later taken up by the Frankfurt School and by Jürgen Habermas.[70]

In his critique of English political pluralism, Schmitt insisted on the peculiar role of the state as the body which draws the line between friend and enemy – which can demand of citizens the sacrifice of their lives in its defence. 'The political entity is something specifically different and, *vis-à-vis* other associations, something decisive.'[71] When a group other than the state becomes the body which is able to make such decisions and to protect the lives of its members, it takes on the nature of the state and the old political order has dissolved.

Schmitt – a theorist of totalitarianism?

George Schwab, a present-day interpreter and apologist of Schmitt, states that he 'never entertained the thought of a totalitarian state'.[72] He certainly denied that his conception of politics requires the state to determine every aspect of a person's life 'or that a centralized system should destroy every other organization or corporation'.[73] He even adopted the idea of *Ordnungen*. 'Luther', he declared in 1934, 'defended vigorously and knew how to preserve . . . the natural orders of marriage, family, order, person and office.'[74] Though he was undoubtedly an authoritarian, who recognised that any matter – religious, cultural, racial – may become political, this does not amount to totalitarianism. Furthermore, in 1933 Schmitt denounced those contemporary parties which 'attempt to lay hold of the people and accompany them from the cradle to the grave . . . in order to instill in their adherents the correct *Weltanschauung*' and thereby 'totally politicize' the German people.[75]

Yet this is not the end of the story, for Schmitt attempted to distinguish between a qualitative and a quantitative total state. The latter, where the state is pressured by numerous groups and parties into meddling in all departments of life, was exemplified for him in the Weimar system. The former, involving the notion of an organic unity, was to be found in Fascist Italy. In his defence of the so-called Enabling Act of March 1933 which gave wide powers to Hitler, he extolled the idea of the leader who embodies in his person the will of the people – a homogeneous people, excluding communists, liberals and other heterogeneous elements. There was to be a real equality between the Führer and his people, who must come from 'a similar racial stock'. It was suggested that this would prevent, in some mysterious way, the leader's power from becoming tyrannical. In the early years he saw the church as providing the inspiration for this organic structure but he later looked to the state; after the Nazis took power he moved on to a racial emphasis, which had been absent from his former writings. While Schmitt was under pressure from the SS in the mid-thirties, one of his students maintained that he, like Hitler himself, had moved from Catholicism through statism to a devotion to the movement and the *Volk*. Thus although he may be absolved from advocating the total state he did in his Nazi years move to belief in a totalitarian *völkisch* community, based on 'the racial similarity of the German people in process of unification'.[76]

Political theology

From the standpoint of our present concerns, one of Schmitt's most significant contributions was in the realm of political theology. He argued, in his essay of 1922, that all the most important concepts of modern political and legal theory were 'secularized theological concepts', not only in the sense that they were historically derived but because they bear close structural resemblances. Religious ideas of God's omnipotence lead to political theories of the sovereign lawgiver, and (as Francis Bacon had noted) 'the exception in jurisprudence is analogous to the miracle in theology'.[77] Furthermore, the idea of the modern constitutional state, in which all eventualities are covered by some law, 'triumphed together with deism, a theology and metaphysics that banished the miracle from the world'. It was from their standpoint of dogmatic theism that such reactionary theorists as de Maistre were able with the aid of analogies from theology to reassert the need for personal sovereignty in the political sphere.[78]

Schmitt rejected the kind of reductionism which dismisses a person's theories as mere products of their social role, such as the characterising of Hegel's system as the outcome of his professorial position which enabled him, with contemplative superiority, to postulate an absolute consciousness. These approaches he relegated to the level of *belles-lettres*.[79] He nevertheless advocated 'a sociology of the concept', which recognises and explains how political and juristic concepts in a given time and place correspond to 'the general state of consciousness' and manifest a similar structure to that found in current metaphysical or theological systems. 'The metaphysical image that a definite epoch forges of the world', he declared, 'has the same structure as what the world immediately understands to be appropriate as a form of its political organization.'[80]

Applying this to the course of modern post-Enlightenment history Schmitt saw a declining belief in a transcendent God being replaced by either a positivist indifference to all metaphysics or an immanent-pantheistic philosophy exemplified in the Hegelian system, which many of its radical followers pushed one step further into atheism. Earlier, in his essay on political romanticism, Schmitt had argued that metaphysical developments from the seventeenth century on had effectively eliminated the transcendent God and that his functions were taken over by 'humanity' and 'history' in the Enlightenment. Consequently for Rousseau and the Jacobins 'politics becomes a religious matter', the enemy becomes an atheist, denying the secular deity.[81] Curiously in these passages he outlined what was to become his own personal journey from religious authoritarianism to political totalitarianism.

Partly in reply to criticisms made by Hans Blumenberg in the first edition of his *Die Legitimität der Neuzeit*, Schmitt wrote in 1970 his *Politische Theologie II: Die Legende von der Erledigung jeder politischen Theologie*. There he distinguished his position from that of other writers attacked by Blumenberg and maintained that 'All my statements on the subject of political theology have been the assertions of a legal scholar about a systematic structural kinship between theological and juristic concepts that obtrudes itself both in legal theory and in legal practice.'[82] Blumenberg comments in later editions of his work that this does not imply any assertion about the derivation of one structure from the other or of both from a common source.[83] While this is so, it does not exclude the possibility of such derivations in particular cases, and it is the role of the historian to specify the nature of the relationship in the concrete instance. It is, in fact, a purpose of the present work to do precisely this.

Although Schmitt was not a typical militant Nazi, he is representative of a large section of the German population who were willing to accept Hitler as the lesser of two evils and to compromise their integrity by conforming to Nazi ideology. Yet even in his early years he was no mere reactionary. He was, like Thomas Hobbes and Donoso Cortés, an authoritarian who endeavoured to re-establish authoritarianism on a new foundation. As Hobbes had abandoned divine-right theories in favour of popular consent as the basis of the sovereign's legitimacy, Schmitt saw in plebiscitary populism the means of salvaging decisionism in an age of universal suffrage.

KARL BARTH

Arriving in Bonn two years after Carl Schmitt had left for Berlin was the celebrated Swiss theologian, Karl Barth, at the height of his powers. Barth was born in Basel in 1886, and after studying in Bern, Berlin, Tübingen and Marburg was ordained in the Swiss Reformed Church in 1908. After a short while in a Geneva parish, from 1911 he served for ten years as pastor in the industrial town of Safenwil, where he published the first edition of his celebrated commentary on Romans in 1919. He moved from Switzerland and from parish life in 1921 to teach at Göttingen and then Münster; in 1930 he was appointed to a chair in Bonn. With Hitler's rise to power Barth was largely responsible for composing the famous 'Barmen Declaration' of 1934, where the Confessing Church stated its theological basis for resisting tendencies within the German church and certain actions of the Nazi government. A member of the Swiss Social Democratic Party (SPD) from 1915, he later joined the German SPD. Retaining his membership after 1933, he was dismissed from his post for refusing to take the oath of allegiance to the Führer. He was reinstated on appeal, but was then pensioned off by the Reich Minister of Education in June 1935, when he returned to his native country to teach at the University of Basel, where he continued work on his massive *Church Dogmatics*. He died in 1968.

If Schmitt's position represents a striking exemplification of political and legal decisionism, that of Karl Barth marks a radical revival of theological and ethical decisionism. The sovereignty of the state in the former is replicated at the theological level in Barth's conception of divine sovereignty, and Schmitt's rejection of natural-law theories is paralleled in Barth by a passionate denunciation of natural theology. Most of the serious political and theological errors of his day were ascribed by Barth to the *analogia entis* (the analogy of being, which he described as 'the invention of Antichrist'[84]) and to the concomitant belief that any truth about God can be discovered by human reason. Divine revelation is, for him, the sole source of our knowledge of God.

While it would be disingenuous to suggest that Barth's theology is a mere product of the social and political crisis of his day, it would be less than generous if we refused to recognise in his theology a considered response to this crisis. This is indeed Barth's own perception of the situation and he later told how his onslaught on contemporary liberalism was stimulated by his horror at the statement in 1914 by German professors, including many of his own teachers, in support of the Kaiser. A heated controversy has raged for some years about the precise relationship between politics and theology in the writings of the Swiss prophet. While any serious commentator must agree with his lifelong friend and collaborator Eduard Thurneysen that 'Karl Barth's word was from the beginning a "political word" ',[85] the precise relationship is a matter of dispute. Was his theology in any way a function of his political commitments, as F.-W. Marquardt argues, or is Eberhard Jüngel right in maintaining that 'for Barth the political is surely a predicate of theology, but theology is never a predicate of the political'?[86] Even if this remarkably undialectical formula accurately conveyed the great theologian's perceptions of what he was doing, which is doubtful, it would not necessarily be the whole truth about the situation.

More important, from our standpoint, than the role played by political commitment in the formulation and development of Barth's theology, is the fact that the enthusiastic *reception* of Barth's theology among significant groups of Christians, especially in Germany,[87] is partially to be explained by the political climate of the period. In the Barthian system, churchmen found what seemed to be a solid basis upon which to stand in the face of the shifting sands of Weimar liberalism and later against the total claims being made by the Nazis. These churchmen were in search of some sovereign authority with which to confront the totalitarianism of Hitler. The theological liberalism and rationalism of the previous century and a half had, Barth claimed, issued in the political religion of the 'Deutsche Christen' which was the apotheosis of *Kulturprotestantismus*. Only by appealing to a transcendent God, revealing himself uniquely in the person of Christ, can the church stand against such political idolatry. With Tertullian he cried, 'What has Jerusalem in common with Athens?'

God and the state

Although I shall be concerned less with Barth's explicit theology of
the state than with the political aspects of his conception of God, the
two issues are connected and a brief look at his understanding of
politics and the state is relevant to our concerns in this book.[88]

In his early years Barth was an enthusiastic 'religious socialist',
perceiving a close affinity between his Christian faith and the political
and economic policies of socialism. Although remaining on the
political left, he later repudiated religious socialism, postulating a
radical discontinuity between the Christian hope and all political
programmes. In the first edition of the *Römerbrief* this led to a kind
of revolutionary anarchism, which effectively undermined all claims
to legitimacy made on behalf of the state. 'An individual,
conservative or revolutionary, who deals seriously with the state', he
thundered, 'will be overcome by evil.'[89] After reflecting upon the
events in Russia, however, he drew back from this position in his
second edition, published in 1921, where he voiced an almost
Burkean suspicion of revolutionary movements, which frequently
restore old tyrannies in a new and more powerful form. The
Christian, in submitting to civil authorities, deprives them of their
power and pathos; but 'stir up revolution against them and their
pathos is provided with fresh fodder', their mythological power is
strengthened. Standing behind the existing order is God, and civil
disobedience is insubordination to him.[90]

Nevertheless Barth continued to maintain the basically Augustinian thesis that the state is not part of the order of creation but of sin
and redemption. It is a consequence of human sin and a partial
remedy for the evils following from sin; as such it is able to deliver
the human race from total chaos, preserving a 'space' within which
the gospel can be proclaimed.[91] From 1928 to 1931 Barth lectured
on ethics, but never published the texts because they assumed the
Lutheran notion of 'orders of creation' (*Ordnungen*), which he was
soon to reject.[92] This idea of 'orders' involved a belief that the family,
the state and other social institutions are part of God's creation and
as such form a hierarchy of authority having divine sanction. He
believed that Althaus's idea that the material principle of ethics is
found in the reality of the human condition in relationship to its
environment undermines the sovereignty of the divine command. He
also noted this tendency in the ethics of Emil Brunner, whose volume
Das Gebot und die Ordnungen appeared in 1932. It was in this
context that Barth rejected the theology of 'orders' – which he

dubbed 'the most evil of all theological doctrines'.[93] Yet at times he is found referring to the state as 'one of the "powers" *created through Him and in Him*', 'one of the constants of the divine Providence and government of the world' and 'an instrument of divine grace'.[94] This sounds quite similar to the 'evil' Lutheran doctrine of *Ordnungen* against which he had fulminated in earlier years.

It is indeed impossible to distil from Barth's writings, even at a particular stage in his pilgrimage, a coherent idea of the state and its relationship to the heavenly kingdom or the rule of God. He defined 'natural law' as 'the embodiment of what man is alleged to regard as universally right and wrong, as necessary, permissible and forbidden "by nature"', but suggested that for the church to base its political stance upon such natural law would mean that it 'was sharing in human illusions and confusions'. Yet in the same lecture he spoke of the state as knowing – at its best – of 'the various ideals based on natural law'.[95] Ought the church, then, to take no cognisance of this standard of right and wrong?

At times Barth seems to have advocated an autonomy for the state; he was clear that the state is by its nature secular and cannot become the church or the kingdom of God, and that the formation of Christian political parties is 'a disastrous enterprise'. It is, nevertheless, possible to distinguish between better and worse states and Christians can give the state 'an impulse in the Christian direction'. However, on the criteria for determining this direction he was silent. He distinguished between power in the service of law (*potestas*) and power which operates independently of law (*potentia*) but it is unclear whether he meant civil or moral law and, if the latter, how this relates to the natural law which he seems to have regarded with such disfavour.[96] Barth branded the state as 'spiritually blind and ignorant' and yet attempted to distinguish between a just and an unjust state without explaining how the pursuit of justice by such a chronically handicapped institution is possible at all.[97]

Barth and the Nazis

The rise of the Nazi movement and its accession to political power in January 1933 was the context within which much of Barth's most constructive theological work was done. We have noted how his opposition to the claims of Hitler lost him his chair at Bonn in 1934–5 and how he gave unhesitating support to the Confessing Church. Nevertheless, in these years he maintained that the church had no right to condemn the Nazi movement as such, for this was a political matter and therefore beyond the proper sphere of church pronouncements. He had rejected Paul Tillich's appeal to campaign against the Nazis prior to 1933 and he refused Dietrich Bonhoeffer's demand for a statement on the Nazi challenge in 1931, arguing that the church had no mandate to pronounce on the political programme of the Nazis.[98] There was nothing in Christianity, he wrote defiantly in 1939, which would of necessity have driven believers 'in principle and at once to disavow the new political experiment'.[99] Yet the NSDAP had been openly committed since 1920, in their own words, to 'the dismissal of all Jews . . . from all responsible positions in public life' with their possible deportation and the seizure of their land; furthermore the regime had in July 1933 banned all opposition parties. This 'new political experiment' had also resulted in campaigns of terror against the Jews in a number of cities. In the light of all this, it is astonishing to read the complacent remarks of Barth.

Barth indeed opposed the 'Deutsche Christen' but on theological grounds, seeing them as part of the much larger movement of *Kulturprotestantismus*. 'I am withstanding a *theology*', he declared in December 1933, 'which today seeks refuge in National Socialism, not the National Socialist ordering of State and Society.'[100] In part 1 of his second volume of the *Church Dogmatics*, published in 1940, Barth defended the position he took in these years. The 'German Christians', in identifying their political hopes with their Christian faith and interpreting the latter in the idiom of the former, were merely repeating what had been done by liberal Protestants for centuries. Humanists of the eighteenth century, Hegelians and Romantics of the nineteenth century and religious socialists of the twentieth century had done the same thing. All these movements were founded on a belief in some kind of natural revelation alongside the revelation of God in Christ.

If such a combination of divine and human is possible, who – he demanded – is to say that the 'German Christians' erred? No one outside Germany should cast a stone at these men, for their position had merely involved the combination of Christianity 'with a race nationalism which happened to be rather uncongenial to the rest of the world'.[101] Uncongenial, one might add, to the Jewish people in particular! Barth claimed that in assailing natural theology and in defending the rights of the church he and the theologians of Barmen had been cutting at the very roots of the 'German Christian' heresy – though as one recent commentator unkindly remarked: 'We have little to learn from any church or any prophet who cannot recognize murder until it is murder in the cathedral.'[102]

As the thirties proceeded, Barth's position on the Nazi movement itself changed. Even by 1934, defending his decision not to take the oath of allegiance, he told a friend that in the eyes of the regime Hitler was 'an incarnate God'. No longer did he see Nazism as merely a new political experiment; he now saw it as constituting a quasi-religious and fundamentally anti-Christian dogma, a 'new Islam'. What had emerged in Germany was a 'totalitarian and radical dictatorship' which could no longer claim to carry out a divine commission and could not therefore in the strictest sense be called a 'state' at all. German National Socialism was, for the Christian, '*the* political problem of our day' and the fight against it effectively assumed the character of a crusade (though he rejected the term).[103] Barth went so far as to declare that Czechs, in fighting against the German invasion of their country, would be fighting in the cause of Jesus Christ, and he was attacked by the German Confessing Church for speaking here as politician and not as theologian.[104]

Divine decisionism

'The word of God', we read in the first volume of the *Church Dogmatics*, 'is understood primarily as a decision or it is not understood at all.'[105] Karl Barth's doctrine of God may be seen as a transposition into theological idiom of the political decisionism asserted in its most uncompromising form in the writings of Carl Schmitt. The latter – according to his celebrated dictum 'All significant concepts of the modern theory of the state are secularised theological concepts'[106] – would no doubt say that Barth's notion of divine sovereignty represents a *re*transposition. In any case the two theorists had much in common and were, as we shall see, faced with analogous problems.

In his early period Barth, with Gogarten and their associates in 'dialectic theology', had laid great emphasis upon God as the 'wholly other' – the transcendent deity, isolated, abstracted and absolutised – who cannot be comprehended by humans, and the nature of whose being can find no analogy on earth. Reflecting on these writings in 1956, Barth noted how they had portrayed God's relationship to humanity almost exclusively in terms of 'domination', leading to a denigration of man – 'this miserable wretch'. Although these theologians were hostile to metaphysical systems, they painted a picture of God which had more in common with 'the God of the philosophers' than with the living God of Abraham, Isaac and

Jacob.[107] Despite their insistence on the otherness of God, these dialectic theologians were perfectly prepared to ascribe to him such political attributes as might, majesty, dominion and power. Human beings stand before God as their 'sovereign Lord', the omnipresent one who possesses 'infinite and irresistible power', and Barth proclaimed 'the absolute lordship of God'.[108]

Even in his later work, God was frequently seen as 'ruler of all things'. Barth observed that throughout his life his 'theological thinking centers and has centered in its emphasis upon the majesty of God'.[109]

> He is sovereign, He is majesty. He is the omnipotent God. He has aseity, as the old theologians used to say: He is sufficient unto Himself and He needs no other. . . . He looks down – even more, He steps down from the unsearchable heights of His godliness into the depths of an existence eternally different from Him.[110]

Not only is God sovereign, but his grace is spoken of as 'totalitarian' – as all-embracing. In Barth's thinking, God and the total state are potential rivals in a single enterprise, fighting for the same ground. This was the case with National Socialism. Yet he distinguished between kinds of totalitarianism and saw Soviet and East European communism in a different light. In this case the total state was seen as playing an *analogous* role to the totalitarian claims of God; this is why Barth was able to say that 'to a degree the Communist state might be interpreted and understood as an image of grace – to be sure, a grossly distorted and darkened image'.[111] The Swiss theologian's distinction between communist and Nazi totalitarian regimes met with fierce criticism from Emil Brunner, Reinhold Niebuhr and others.[112]

The ethics of divine command

Barth's emphasis upon the power and sovereignty of God led him to view Christian ethics in terms of divine commands. In volume 2, part 2, of the *Church Dogmatics*, published in 1942, Barth spoke of ethics as 'a command, directed to man and absolutely supreme and decisive'.[113] The pattern of Christian life must be found in the obedience of Christ to his heavenly Father. Any attempt to judge or to justify the command of God according to some higher criterion was said to undermine Christian ethics, 'for the man who obediently hears the command of God is not in any position to consider why he must obey it'.[114] I am confronted by 'the sovereign decision of God', by 'the divine command' which comes to me 'as something alien', challenging me to respond in obedience. God is described as a 'transcendent Commander' (*überlegener Gebieter*).[115] The human response, however, is not one of passive acceptance but is active and decisive. In the section on 'The Sovereignty of the Divine Decision', the Swiss theologian, clearly under the influence of contemporary existentialist anthropologies, insisted that human life 'consists in a continuous series of decisions which we have to make and execute'. The human being, made in God's image, is defined as 'that essence which is constantly realizing its existence in acts of free determination and decision'.[116] Yet these human decisions take place always within the context of a divine decisionism.

Rightly wishing to get away from the Kantian notion that persons can be morally obligated only by a law which they impose upon themselves, Barth declared, 'If there is an *ought* it must not be the product of my own will.'[117] Nevertheless he believed that it must be the product of some will – of the divine will. In Christ, he maintained, all human autonomy is put to death; 'all the places where man might hide from God and arrogantly try to make his own decisions, all the refuges and strongholds of our ethical neutrality, are destroyed and dismantled'.[118] In the later editions of the *Römerbrief* he had already opposed the incommensurable pre-eminence of God to all human endeavours which 'not merely cannot be successful, but ought not to be so'.[119]

There is at times a kind of antinomianism in Barth which would be more congenial to Lutheran than to Calvinist tradition. 'I am already choosing wrong', he asserted in one of the later volumes of the *Church Dogmatics*,

> when I think that I know and ought to decide what is right, and I am doing wrong when I try to accomplish that which I have chosen as right. I am already putting myself in the wrong with others, and doing them wrong, when ... I confront them as the one who is right.[120]

The practical implications of such a position suggest that Barth's determination to stand out from most of his colleagues by refusing to take the oath of allegiance to Hitler was wrong and that he ought to have conformed.

Barth insisted that the divine command which constitutes Christian ethics must be seen as part of a whole ethos, rather than as a collection of universally applicable principles. The Ten Commandments (like the Sermon on the Mount), which have frequently been misunderstood as propounding general rules of conduct, are in fact addressed to a particular group in a specific historical context. The Mosaic commands are to be read as part of a whole legal and social system and ought not to be abstracted from this system.[121] God's commands are given in the concrete and particular rather than in the abstract and general, and are to be regarded as unconditional. In discussing the plot to assassinate Hitler, Barth stated that Stauffenberg – a Catholic who had taken his stand on the basis of natural law – had 'no clear and categorical command from God to do it', otherwise he would have been willing to die in the attempt.[122]

This ethic of divine decisionism led critics to attack Barth's picture of God as indiscriminate and irrational. He denied the accusation: 'What this God determines is not a whim, and what He presents to man to do or not to do is not the product of the fickle caprices of a tyrant whose right consists in his might.'[123] He rejected the idea that divine arbitrariness implies caprice. God's will is consistent and his choices are good. Barth rejected the nominalist position that God, having created by his will the present universe, could equally well have chosen to create a universe which operated on quite different principles, 'as if God could exercise a different choice and action and capacity from what He has done'.[124] God, the commander, is also the creator and redeemer of humankind – he is no strange and alien dictator, but the One who is gracious to us in Jesus Christ.[125] This is very similar to Schmitt's justification of the *Führerprinzip* on the grounds of a familial relationship between the leader and his people. Discussing the theology of Quenstedt, Barth denied that God could properly be thought of as 'a tyrant'; his will, which obeys his own law, 'shows itself to be a good will, worthy of Himself and therefore really righteous'.[126] How this is compatible with what he said on ethical decisionism in part 2 of the same volume is not at all clear. If, as quoted above, he insisted that there could be no criterion by which to judge divine commands, how can God's will *show itself* to be good? Barth could consistently have asserted its goodness as an act of faith, but how could it possibly be shown?

Barth also rejected the Thomist and Leibnizian notion of God's will being limited by what is 'possible in itself', as though he must be thought of as working within certain external constraints. Rather he appealed to the notion of auto-limitation, familiar to theorists of constitutional law. 'The real and effective limit of the possible is the one which God has imposed on Himself.'[127] Yet he refused to carry this principle into Christology, rejecting the 'kenotic' understanding of the incarnation as involving a renunciation by God the Son of his sovereign power when he took human flesh.[128]

Barth's response

Barth was, of course, fully aware of the ambivalence of power and the problems about God's supposed omnipotence. The term 'Almighty' (*Allmächtige*), he observed, has more to do with a 'revolutionary and tyrannical spirit' than with God. In a post-war lecture, given in his old university of Bonn and surrounded by rubble and ruin – visible consequences of human destructive power – he noted how Hitler had normally used the term 'the Almighty' when referring to the deity. Unqualified, the term represents 'Chaos, Evil, the Devil', the opposite of God, whose might never precedes right but is always accompanied by it. God's omnipotence ought not to be identified with omnicausality but rather is an aspect of his freedom 'to be true to Himself'.[129]

Remaining sensitive to the accusation that his doctrine of God implies a dictatorial or tyrannical deity,[130] the Swiss theologian introduced a somewhat different emphasis in his later works. Undoubtedly aware that his earlier divine decisionism had functioned not only as a ground upon which to stand against Nazism, but also as a model which reinforced an autocratic conception of political power, he insisted that God's freedom does not imply 'naked sovereignty' or 'unconditioned power', and even that it involves 'absolute obedience'. Manifestly unwilling to abandon the language of power and sovereignty, he remained vague about limitations hinted at and gave no idea of what is involved in the 'obedience' of God. The deity of the Gospels is 'no lonely God, self-sufficient and self-contained', he affirmed.[131] These later writings stressed the 'omnipotence of love' in God and the 'partnership' between God and the human race.[132]

The strongly Trinitarian emphasis of Barth's theology from the early days might have provided him with a model to undercut the authoritarian emphasis of his decisionism.[133] In the first volume of his *Church Dogmatics* he criticised a conception of God which did not recognise a variety in the Godhead. Later in the same work he stressed the 'dynamic and living unity' of the Trinity.[134] Yet orthodox Trinitarianism does not necessarily undermine monarch- ism, as is proved by the case of Tertullian, whose treatise *Against Praxeas* vigorously rebutted any suggestion that the divine monarchy is impaired by Trinitarian orthodoxy. In these days of military juntas, and remembering the Soviet *troika*, we should readily understand how this can be so. If, however, our Trinitarianism takes seriously the incorporation of the humanity of Christ into the life of the Godhead, then a conception of God's relationship to the universe and to humankind in particular might be drawn out which would provide an alternative model to the hierarchical and authoritarian model which Barth appears to have accepted in his early and middle period.

In Barth's post-1945 writings, as I have already suggested, a new prominence is given to 'the humanity of God', with stress being laid upon a kind of partnership and participation in the relationship between God and those creatures made in his image. These ideas were, however, developed more fully and consistently by a Christian from a quite different theological tradition who was also reacting to the political and cultural events of his day, the Russian writer Nicolas Berdyaev, whose ideas will be the subject of our next section.

NICOLAS BERDYAEV

The first two decades of the twentieth century in Russia were years of remarkable intellectual ferment. With the declining power of the tsarist autocracy, numerous groups of radicals – Marxists, socialists, anarchists, liberals and others – had become increasingly vocal. The existence of various sects of Marxism at this time is well known in the west, in particular the struggle for hegemony between Bolsheviks and Mensheviks. Less known is the role played by religion in these political movements. Christopher Read has done something to remedy the situation in his fascinating survey of the Russian intelligentsia of this period.[135] Some Marxists moved away from what was seen as the crude materialism of Plekhanov and Axelrod towards philosophical idealism and even towards the Christian religion.

Among these Marxists-on-the-move was an outstanding thinker who was to exercise considerable influence – particularly in western Europe – in the coming years, Nikolai Alexandrovich Berdyaev.[136] He was born in Kiev in 1874 of an aristocratic military family and educated in a military academy. Expelled from university for his socialist opinions, he was exiled to the north of the country. In 1917 he became Professor of Philosophy at Moscow University, where he remained until he was expelled from the Soviet Union in 1922. By this time he had become an outspoken critic of autocratic tendencies in Bolshevism and had linked his concern for freedom with belief in God, in the form of a Christian personalism. 'While still a Marxist', he later wrote, 'I saw elements in Marxism which were bound to lead to despotism and the betrayal of freedom.'[137] In the post-1905 years he came under the influence of the 'mystical anarchism' of G.I. Chulkov (1879–1939) and V. Ivanov (1866–1949) but, dissatisfied with the effete and unrealistic conception of freedom and an apparent lack of concern for truth which characterised many anarchists of the time, he turned increasingly to Russian Orthodox traditions. Nevertheless he could hardly be called 'orthodox' in his theology. His emphasis upon freedom as the centrepoint of philosophy led him to criticise monarchical and patriarchal images of deity, developing a notion of God as interdependent with the universe, in many ways similar to the 'process' theology associated with followers of A.N. Whitehead, though without the metaphysical paraphernalia of that school.

Berdyaev's exile began in Berlin and later he moved to Paris where he joined a large Russian *émigré* population. Retaining his radical and almost anarchistic ideas about God and the state, he was critical of the deeply reactionary position of most *émigrés*. He shared certain beliefs with another exiled Christian, Sergius Bulgakov (1871–1944), also a former Marxist who had returned to Orthodoxy.[138] Bulgakov had been Professor of Political Economy in Kiev from 1901 until 1906 when he moved to a chair in Moscow. He wrote extensively on the agrarian question in Russia, engaging in controversy with Lenin and others. While at Kiev he had, however, already begun to move away from Marxism, and partly under the influence of nineteenth-century Christian thinkers, particularly Dostoevsky, Solovyov and Feodorov,[139] he became a Christian. He was eventually reconciled to the Russian Orthodox Church and ordained priest in 1918. Expelled in 1923, he became an intellectual leader of the more enlightened of the Christian exiles. Berdyaev – as a libertarian – remained somewhat critical of this socialist cleric, with his more authoritarian beliefs.

As we have noted, Berdyaev saw Soviet communism as exemplifying the denial of freedom and embodying the idea of a totalitarian state. In his lectures on *The Meaning of History*, originally given in Moscow at the Liberal Academy of Spiritual Culture in 1919–20, he explained Marxist and other positivist notions of inevitable progress – either gradual or catastrophic – towards utopia, as the secularis-ation of Jewish and Christian eschatology. 'The messianic idea of the Jews as God's chosen people', he declared, 'is transferred to a class. ... The working class becomes the new Israel, God's chosen people, destined to emancipate and save the world.'[140] He saw this as part of a much longer process of secularisation beginning with the Renaissance, when science, art, economics, politics and other aspects of human culture became autonomous. Even religion was secularised and 'the bonds holding together the various spheres of social and cultural life now become relaxed, and these spheres become independent'.[141] This account of Marxism in particular and of modern history in general – as a secularisation of Jewish-Christian theology and eschatology – became a commonplace in the 1930s among Christian intellectuals, being adopted by such influential figures as William Temple.[142]

Berdyaev saw the growth of totalitarianism as a religious tragedy, revealing the human need for 'an integral relation to life', which the process of secularisation had undermined in the modern world.[143] Not only was the Soviet state obliterating freedom, but 'the very taste for freedom is disappearing, even the comprehension of what freedom really is'. This development of totalitarianism he ascribed to the utopian desire to impose an integration in the social and political order – in the realm of Caesar – which is appropriate only in the realm of spirit. 'Only the Kingdom of God, the realm of Spirit', he declared, 'can be perfect and harmonious, not the realm of Caesar. Such a perfect realm is conceivable only eschatologically. A perfect and harmonious order in the realm of Caesar would annihilate freedom.'[144]

In contrast to Karl Barth, who – in the face of the total and sovereign claims made by the Nazi movement – set forth the total and sovereign claims of a divine commander, Berdyaev questioned the very conception of authority which the totalitarian movements of his day assumed. His attack on state sovereignty went hand in hand with a rejection of a divine sovereign. His passion for freedom led him on the one hand to a kind of anarchist position in politics and on the other to belief in a God who is characterised by a loving and suffering involvement in the tribulations of the world and who inspires and liberates rather than dominates humankind.

In making the categories of freedom and spirit central to his understanding of life, Berdyaev rejected the priority which most philosophers had given to 'being'. He believed that traditional metaphysics and ontology were incompatible with a true understanding of human experience. Having read Kant, he 'arrived at the position which compelled me to reject ontology, or the science of Being, altogether'.[145] This had significance both for his politics and his religion which we shall now consider.

The God of freedom

It was, he wrote in his autobiography, as a religion of emancipation 'that Christianity presented itself to me and called upon my allegiance'.[146] Yet he found in the Christian religion traces of bondage which went back to certain aspects of Greek ontology and to a system of slavery. 'It is a matter of regret', he lamented, 'that Christians have expressed their piety in bows, fawnings and prostrations – gestures that are symbolic of servility and humiliatior.'[147] In his doctrine of God he was critical in the first place of all abstract, conceptual language about God. 'The knowledge of the divine life', he declared in his Moscow lectures,

> is not attainable by means of abstract philosophical thought based upon the principles of formalist or rationalistic logic, but only by means of a concrete myth which conceives the divine life as a passionate destiny of concrete active persons, the divine Hypostases.[148]

Berdyaev linked the adoption of a slavish posture towards God to the tendency in rationalist thought to objectivise God and define him in abstract conceptual categories. Following Feuerbach, he saw the objectivised God as 'a god alienated from man and lord over him'. The slavish social relations experienced by humans have thereby served as a model for relations between humans and God. The concept of God, in cosmomorphic terms, as the cause of the world, acting as a force in time and space, is a reflection of the sovereign and total state: 'What is determinism in nature is domination in society.'[149] God should be seen, rather, as a mystery to be spoken of only indirectly, in the language of myth and symbol. Yet this language reflects not merely the subjective experience or sentiment of individuals but 'the very heart of existence and the deepest mysteries of life'.[150] The Russian philosopher anticipated Tillich's warning against identifying the symbols with reality and failing to see them as pointers to some reality which is beyond them.[151]

Berdyaev was also critical of talk about an immobile, inert and impassive God. Such abstract monotheism implies a kind of idolatry.[152] It was in the idea of the Holy Trinity that he found the antidote. His belief in the triune God involved the assertion of a dynamic interrelationship between the divine persons:

> The destiny of the Crucified Son of God constitutes the deepest mystery of Christianity. For the tragic passionate mystery experienced by the Divine Being presupposes the transposition of the principle of mobility and of interior tragic conflict into the nature of the inner divine life.[153]

He insisted that Christianity is not a 'monistic and monarchical religion', but that it is centred on the Trinitarian notion of 'God-manhood'.[154] This latter term, which implies a co-operation between God and the human race in the creative and redemptive process, he derived from Solovyov.

Berdyaev's Trinitarianism served to undermine not only an abstract monotheism but also much of the political language frequently used of God. 'The pure monotheism upon which Judaism set so high a value', he wrote,

> was still a monarchical despotic understanding of God. It is only the God who reveals Himself in His Son, in the God-Man, Who ceases to be God the despotic monarch, and becomes the God of love and freedom. . . . The divine Trinity marks the triumph over the monarchical ideas about God.[155]

The critical approach which Berdyaev adopted towards all ontological conceptions of God was thus extended to a condemnation of most sociomorphic images. These he believed were normally images of despotism and domination. 'I cannot admit the conception of an almighty, omniscient, punitive deity beholding this stricken world of ours,' he wrote. 'I can consent to and understand only the image of a loving, suffering, crucified God: I can, that is to say, only accept God through his Son.' God suffers with the world and with the human race and through his identification with human tragedy becomes the liberator.[156]

In a discussion of the relationship between freedom and authority, Berdyaev called for a 'theonomy', which would transcend autonomy and heteronomy.[157] Autonomy is manifested in the arbitrary decisions of the individual will; while heteronomy is seen in the idea of a despotic God who issues commands which must be blindly obeyed, and in the notion that sin is first and foremost disobedience to the divine will. He believed rather that:

> we are no longer slaves but sons possessing freedom which has been bought for us at a great cost. In the Son the Father is revealed as infinite love. We can no longer regard God as a sovereign exacting obedience to His will and a formal submission to His power, since such a conception is due entirely to the oppression exercised by sin upon the natural man.[158]

Sin should be understood more as a loss of freedom than as disobedience to divine commands.

Berdyaev was not entirely consistent in his use of terms, and his writings in general give the impression of a certain looseness of thought. This is evident in his discussion of the question of divine power. God is not to be thought of as master; the idea of domination is not appropriate to him: 'no power is inherent in God. The will to power is not a property of his.'[159] Yet a few years earlier he had maintained that 'Sovereign power is God's alone. . . . God is power rather than authority.' By this he seems to have meant that God, unlike human political authorities, makes no attempt to dominate. Rather he possesses a true spiritual power. Berdyaev went on to say that this power is characterised by freedom and incarnated only in the form of love.[160]

In a previous section we have seen how Karl Barth modified his conception of God by introducing the notion of 'the humanity of God', concluding that Christians should not attempt to elevate God by lowering humankind. The idea of God's 'humanity' fits much more comfortably into the theology of Berdyaev. 'Any doctrine which is degrading to man also degrades God,' he wrote in 1940.[161] He argued that 'man as we know him is to but a small extent human; he is even inhuman. It is not man who is human but God.' He denied that a secular and autonomous conception of humanity can be postulated apart from God. In order to have the human image man must have the divine. In the Christian doctrine of the incarnation 'the humanity of God is revealed'. Anthropology must be based upon Christology. So the Russian philosopher developed his critique of secular humanism as inadequately based; without a belief in the humanity of God it slips into inhumanism. Left to himself man reflects the image of the brute. Manhood is either God-manhood or brute-manhood.[162]

The vigorous rejection of God as a transcendent monarch ruling over his realm and issuing commands to his servile creatures, and the insistence on seeing him as participating in the suffering and in the tragedy of existence, might be thought to imply a kind of pantheism. Berdyaev rebutted the suggestion. The image of God as wholly immanent in the world, identified with the evolutionary process, is one which negates human freedom and personality as much as does that of the divine despot. It undercuts any possibility of human initiative and of a genuine newness; everything is seen as the unfolding of some predetermined order.[163] Pantheism is not in the first place a heresy which concerns God but one which invades human personality and freedom. He saw the totalitarian systems of Nazism and Bolshevism as 'special types of mysticism', embodying a pantheism which abolishes the transcendent and identifies divinity with historical movements of race and class.[164]

While pantheism is often thought of as the polar opposite of transcendentalism, the relationship is in reality more complicated. A transcendentalism which exalts God and debases humankind, which makes God everything and humans nothing, is ultimately little different from a doctrine which makes the universe into God. Both tend to monism. Berdyaev indeed recognised that in the history of religious thought a pantheistic emphasis, reacting against an undialectical transcendentalism, has sometimes been an emancipating force. Examples can be found in early Quakerism and other movements of the seventeenth century. Yet in unmitigated form – eliminating everything unscheduled and covering all eventualities in an organic totality – it soon becomes an enslaving system. A dualism between God and the world is necessary if human freedom is to be a reality. The notion of God as an all-inclusive unity, so attractive to the rationalist philosopher, is ultimately disastrous politically and religiously.[165] A false immanentism which identifies God with the universe, and a false transcendentalism which makes him responsible – as absolute ruler or as absolute cause – for everything that happens, lead ultimately to atheism. 'Men first of all rationalize divine Providence and adapt it to their own level, and then they rise in revolt against their own false ideas and become atheists.'[166] In a similar way, having made excessive claims for the state, they are driven to anarchism. It is to this aspect of Berdyaev's thought that I now turn.

Freedom and anarchy

'When I was a small boy', Berdyaev wrote, 'the sight of a government building or state institution filled me with abhorrence, and I desired its immediate destruction. ... The state appeared to my youthful imagination as a Leviathan, embodying all that is monstrous, cruel, suppressive and inquisitorial, and its representatives as the torturers of men.'[167] Yet in his Moscow lectures on *The Meaning of History*, he was critical of anarchism as affirming a 'freedom which inwardly devours and consumes itself' and which ultimately ends in collectivism or communism.[168] Clearly he was thinking principally of the doctrines of Bakunin and his Russian followers. In later life, however, he called himself an anarchist, by which he meant that claims made by states to 'sovereignty' and the assertion of an obligation on the part of subjects to obey their laws are based on false arguments and analogies. In particular he attacked all ideas of the sovereignty of the state. He spoke of the idea of sovereignty as the result of a 'hypnosis'; it is a slavish idea founded on the idolatrous ascription of a sacred status to worldly institutions.[169] The ascription of sovereignty to the state is parallel to the invention of a 'God of might and authority'.[170]

Berdyaev was equally critical of the notion of a general obligation upon people to obey the dictates of the state. He insisted, as indeed Barth had done in his celebrated commentary, that Paul's Epistle to the Romans by no means implies a general obligation to obey all governments. Discussing Paul's statement that 'there is no power but of God', he maintained that 'the Apostle Paul's words have no religious meaning whatever: they are purely historical and relative, called forth by the position of Christians in the Roman Empire'.[171] Berdyaev was clear that the claims made for the sovereignty of the people and for the sovereignty of democratic governments based on ideas of consent were equally invalid. The inclination to deify governments is manifested in different ways, but 'Christianity cannot be reconciled to the sovereignty of any kind of earthly authority – not the sovereignty of a monarch, not that of a people or of a class.'[172]

Anarchists were right when they protested against 'the idealization and exaltation of the state' and against 'despotic centralization'; when they denied that the state has the right 'to set "great" ends before itself and sacrifice men and women . . . for the sake of these supposedly great ends'. Any attempt by political authorities to 'enforce communion' must be tyrannical.[173] Following Tolstoy he taught that political power is 'bound up with sin and evil' and that 'the Kingdom of God is anarchy'.[174] Nevertheless, some kind of state is necessary in this fallen world, but it should operate as a co-operative association rather than a quasi-divine centre of command.

The attraction which Berdyaev, as a young man, had felt in Marxism was its message of liberation to the oppressed but, as we have seen, he soon came to believe that it would lead to a new form of oppression. Revolutions he thought to be inevitable; they tear down structures of oppression which have become intolerable. While he therefore depicted the October Revolution as 'richly deserved', he foresaw dangers to human liberty.[175] When the masses claim sovereignty, freedom is threatened. For a love of freedom is aristocratic and not democratic. 'The majority of men do not in the least love freedom and do not seek after it.'[176] A mass democratic movement does not seek to establish freedom but has other ends in view.[177] In a brief discussion in 1934, Berdyaev perceived, as Carl Schmitt had done from his quite opposite standpoint, that fascism, in making the state into a direct expression of the popular will, 'is more opposed to an aristocratic and liberal system of government than to a democratic one'.[178] With Proudhon he saw the French revolutionary declaration of rights as easily degenerating into 'a charter of protection for *bourgeois* interests'.[179] Thus Berdyaev was never uncritical in his welcome for revolutionary change. In early writings, he argued that 'revolution and reaction are of one nature – twins' and pointed out that the nihilism of the left was but the child of the nihilism of the Russian autocracy. 'In revolutionary Jacobinism', he asserted, 'the spirit of political autocracy and despotism is always to be found.'[180]

Like some other thinkers in the anarchist tradition, Berdyaev carried his criticism of political authoritarianism not only into the sphere of theology but into that of family structure. He claimed that the 'patriarchal conception of God depends upon the social relationships that exist in the family and reflects them'.[181] Proudhon had also observed this, but the Frenchman believed that such patriarchalism was perfectly appropriate to the family and was illegitimately extended into cosmic and political discourse. Berdyaev, however, like the aristocratic Shelley and Bakunin, extended his critique of authoritarian structures into the domestic sphere. 'Family', he wrote in his autobiography, 'has been, and still is in a large measure, a means of enslavement; it is a hierarchical institution based on domination and submission.'[182]

Berdyaev rejected the popular empiricist notion of freedom as simply absence of external restraint. It is a spiritual phenomenon in which human personality is recognised as of incalculable worth, developing in the context of community or *soborny*.[183] This Russian word can find no simple translation in English, but connotes co-operation, community, participation and fellowship. It is frequently used by Orthodox theologians to characterise the life and worship of the eastern churches, in contrast to Roman Catholic authoritarianism and Protestant individualism.

Berdyaev thus distinguished between individualism and personalism, and ascribed many of the evils of his day to a false, atomising individualism, which forms the sand on which collectivist autocracies are constructed. While totalitarianism represents the model towards which states naturally tend and should not therefore be seen as a temporary and distinctively modern phenomenon, its fuller realisation in the twentieth century can partly be ascribed to the breakdown of community and the triumph of individualism. He saw state socialism, which brings to an end the creative life of the individual, as the consequence of this atomisation – the attempt to compensate for the destruction of true community by the creation of 'communal and compulsory life' centred on the state.[184] A further modern contribution to the growth of totalitarianism is the unprecedented development of technical instruments which, so far from being merely neutral means for achieving specified ends, have changed organic communities into organisations.[185] Totalitarianism is ultimately a religious tragedy, for it reveals the human search for spiritual realisation in the realm of Caesar, and gives religious legitimation to social structures and institutions in the form of a political pantheism.

In this chapter we have seen how two Christian thinkers, Barth and Berdyaev, reacted differently to the growth of totalitarianism in Europe in developing quite different conceptions of God. There is an interesting parallel in the post-Reformation period, also a time of instability and conflict. As Barthians returned to ideas of a sovereign God to combat the inordinate claims of the state and the Christian ideological backing given to those claims by the 'Deutsche Christen', so many Puritan parliamentarians maintained that the kingship of God implies that all people, including kings, are his subjects. Their resort to an authoritarian image of God to oppose the authoritarian state was perhaps effective while they were in a minority, but it had the result of confirming, by analogy, the *concepts* of authority and domination which they were contending against. The Cromwellian state manifested some of the worst features of royalist autocracy, and the Protestant churches in post-Second World War Germany, dominated by Christians of the Confessing Church, provided scant theological foundation for a free and participatory politics. In challenging the prevailing authoritarian model, Berdyaev – like Winstanley and some of the more radical Christians of the seventeenth century – may have made a more lasting contribution to human freedom and to the undermining of political autocracy.

GOD, TOTALITARIANISM AND THE BUGBEAR OF 'SOCIETY'

Deploring man's 'evil servile dependence upon the state', Berdyaev suggested that 'he himself creates that dependence by hypostatizing society and creating myths about it'.[186] The discipline of sociology must indeed bear some responsibility for nourishing the growth of totalitarian theories, in so far as it is committed to the notion of 'society'. The assumption made by many sociologists and anthropologists – that over and above the individuals, groups and institutions existing in a given legally and politically defined territory (a 'state') there is such a thing as 'society', which embraces and encompasses them all – has had disastrous consequences. To be sure the existence of the family and other groups is recognised, but they are located 'in society'.

It is sometimes suggested that totalitarian theories depend upon the failure to distinguish 'state' from 'society', but precisely the opposite is true. The very assertion that there is, transcending the empirically defined state, a mystical entity which in some way comprehends and engulfs the social units within it provides a foundation for totalitarian theories.

Anthropologist M.G. Smith proclaims that society is 'a self-sufficient, self-perpetuating, and internally autonomous system of social relations'.[187] But where is such a system to be found? What are its boundaries? Do they coincide with the legally defined borders of the state? Do the social relationships which subsist in England (or Britain or the EEC) constitute anything remotely resembling a 'self-sufficient . . . system'? Merely to ask these questions exposes the absurdity of 'society' as a descriptive or analytical term. Although such an autonomous total system does not exist it might well be the policy of some group or movement to bring it into being. This was indeed the explicit aim of Mussolini and Hitler. Instead of restricting themselves to the study of social relationships, many sociologists have 'reified' these relationships and invented a mythological and mystical entity called 'society', which has played the sinister role of providing a basis for modern developments in totalitarian theory.

In analysing the meaning of such expressions as 'sanctions imposed by society', Ralf Dahrendorf asks, 'Does "society" in such expressions mean all people in a given society?'[188] In the very asking of the question he betrays the sociological fallacy, treating as unproblematic the expression 'in a given society'. Elsewhere he recognises that it is a mistake to relate the noun 'society' to a single agency or collectivity. What, then, does 'a given society' stand for? While acknowledging the 'vexatious' nature of 'society', he believes that sociologists have to 'identify the agency responsible for social rules'. Despite his warnings, Dahrendorf soon drifts back into talking of 'society as a whole with its legal system', 'the encounter of the individual and society', 'the prescriptions of society' and even 'the point of view of society'.[189]

The authors of a recent work entitled *Society* – after exposing some of the confusions and contradictions in the various uses of the term 'society' – conclude that the study of sociology has progressed when its practitioners have turned from 'fruitless speculation on society as such'. 'Sociology', the authors proclaim, 'can apparently get by perfectly well without society.' Then, quite inexplicably, on the very same page they succumb to the mystic lure, urging their sociological colleagues to reopen the question 'What is society?' as 'arguably the central analytic issue of sociology – its object of inquiry'.[190]

The fallacies with which I am here concerned are most evident in the writings of Emile Durkheim. I am not referring to his insistence that human groups and communities are really existing entities, *sui generis*, and that statements about them cannot be reduced to statements about their individual members, but rather to his assumption that over and above the individuals and groups in a given, politically defined, territory there is such a total entity as 'society'. Durkheim attempted to explain religious phenomena as functions of this entity and contended that the term 'God' is merely 'a figurative expression of the society' and that 'in the Divine I can only see society transfigured and thought of symbolically'.[191] Not only is religion explained in terms of 'society' but, much more seriously, 'society' is portrayed as divine. Indeed he went so far as to assert that this total entity performs divine functions: 'Kant postulated God, since without this hypothesis morality is unintelligible. We postulate a society specifically distinct from individuals, since otherwise morality has no object and duty no roots.'[192] Gillian Rose comments that for Durkheim society has become 'the transcendental precondition' of the possibility of moral experience.[193] As the ultimate norm, by which moral judgments are validated, society is thus transformed into a quasi-divine entity and a major contribution was made to the further development of totalitarian dogma.

The structural-functionalist theories, with their conception of groups or institutions which are 'dysfunctional' to the social system and the notion of ethnic minorities lying 'outside the system', have definite totalitarian implications.[194] It is only a short step in the same direction to recommend that these dysfunctional groups should be eliminated or that these extra-systemic minorities should be deported.

The suggestion of Friedrich von Hayek that it is methodological holism (the assertion of the objective existence of human groups as such) which must bear responsibility for totalitarianism and kindred evils is fundamentally misconceived. Groups, associations, families and societies (like the Society for the Prevention of Cruelty to

Animals, or the Society of Jesus) exist as real units and the attempt to analyse their life and activities simply in terms of the individuals who compose them is a mistake.[195] It is rather in the concept of 'society' itself – as some mystical entity over and above these groups – that the evil is to be located.

Hayek, after having attacked in his early writings the notion of 'society' as an objectively existing entity, has spent the rest of his life singing hymns of praise to 'a free society'.[196] In his 1945 lecture on 'Individualism: True and False', he maintained that individualism is a 'theory of society', and suggested that it starts from 'men whose whole nature and character is determined by their existence *in society*'.[197] He went on to speak of 'the forces of society' and of 'society' as an 'organism', which has 'common purposes'.[198] Hayek's later work, such as *The Constitution of Liberty*, is similarly marred by an uncritical use of the concept of 'society', with all its total implications. Phrases like 'the cultural heritage of society', 'the economic policy of a free society', and so on, assume the existence of some mystical entity with a consciousness and a purpose of its own.[199]

Georg Simmel made valiant attempts to escape from the tyranny of 'society', but only at the cost of adopting a methodological individualism which held that 'society merely is the name for a number of individuals, connected by interaction'.[200] Yet even he was unable to escape from language which suggests the existence of some overarching totality called 'society' which 'transcends the individual and lives its own life which follows its own laws; it, too, confronts the individual with a historical imperative firmness'.[201]

Time would fail us to speak of Mannheim and Merton, of Horkheimer and Adorno. In their continued use of the term 'society', social scientists are unwittingly fortifying totalitarian modes of thought, even if it is only the one-dimensional liberal-bureaucratic system, of which Max Weber was the prophet and which Marcuse referred to in the passage quoted earlier in this chapter. Furthermore the notion of society today provides the 'new right' with a convenient concept for expressing its cultural xenophobia, for it is 'society' which must have common values, a single culture and an ethnic identity.

5

Federal politics and finite God: images of God in United States theology

From his Harvard University chair, A.N. Whitehead assailed the notion of God found in the Hebrew Psalms and current· among Christians of his day: 'This worship of glory arising from power is not only dangerous: it arises from a barbaric conception of God.'[1] Much twentieth-century theology emanating from the United States is marked by a criticism of traditional images of God, particularly those which suggest omnipotence and autarky. The political and social experience of Americans and the ideologies growing out of this experience have been related, often quite explicitly, to their theological critique.

This chapter examines two interconnected themes: the attack on autarky as a characteristic of God and the state, and the rejection of monarchical images of God in favour of some kind of 'democratic conception' of God. The influential philosophers William James and John Dewey set the stage for many of the distinctive developments in twentieth-century US thinking on these matters. Their attack on philosophical monism led those influenced by them to criticise centralised political power and to question the images of God as an all-powerful ruler. Traditional respect for a federal constitution – involving interdependence among the states of the union – reinforced by a pluralist ideology find analogies in the assault upon the autarkic and impassible God by 'process' philosophers from Whitehead to Hartshorne. Furthermore American concerns for equality and democracy resulted, in the early decades of the twentieth century, in an attack on monarchical language about God and in the search for alternative images and concepts from three groups of liberal

131

Protestant thinkers: first, theologians of the Chicago school (Shailer Mathews and his colleagues); second, popular philosophical writers, George Howison and Harry Overstreet; third, Walter Rauschenbusch, with other writers of the 'social gospel' movement. Gordon D. Kaufman's recent attempts to suggest 'a conception of God more in accord with the modern notion of a unified ecological order'[2] take up some of the loose threads left by these earlier American writers.

MONARCHY AND AUTARKY ASSAILED

The two themes of this chapter – the critiques of monarchy and of autarky – are connected; for, as Alexis de Tocqueville observed, it is democracy which requires an artificial division of power, formalised in the federal system and guaranteed (at least in theory) by a plurality of interdependent social groups. 'There are no countries', he wrote in 1835, 'in which associations are more needed, to prevent the despotism of faction or the arbitrary power of a prince, than those which are democratically constituted.'[3] The artificially created federal system might do for the USA what traditional associations and aristocracies had done for Europe in constituting a bulwark against centralisation and tyranny. So too the democratic images of God, suggested by the Chicago school of theologians, have much in common with conceptions of a God in certain respects interdependent with the universe, as propounded by 'process' thinkers. Nor should it be assumed that the influence flows only one way – from political experience to religious conceptualisation – for the very political system which evolved from colonial days was moulded by such religious ideas as that of the covenant made by the God of Israel with his people, which functioned as a model for social and political relationships in and among the Puritan settlements of New England.

There were indeed other religious and political tendencies in twentieth-century America. I say nothing, for example, of Roman Catholic or fundamentalist religious thinking, nor of radically individualist trends in social and political theory. Nevertheless the movements discussed here represent significant elements in the political and religious life of the country in the modern era. Likewise the pragmatic and pluralistic tendency at this time was not restricted to the USA; it was part of a wider movement (encompassing such European writers as Bergson, Eucken and the British philosophers James Ward and F.C.S. Schiller) that was critical of rationalism and emphasised the importance of action and involvement in the process of understanding. Yet in no other country did this movement attain such an influential position as in the United States.

The connection between political and religious symbolism is widely recognised, not least in the contemporary American context. Henry B. Parkes sees the political and religious evolution of the American people as manifesting 'the same psychic tendencies': a repudiation of external authority, confidence in the average person and an optimistic belief that evil can be overcome by determination.[4] Sociologists, anthropologists and other observers of American culture have in recent years rejected a somewhat facile theory of 'secularisation' and devoted attention to the phenomenon of 'civil religion' – which appears to function as ideological protection for political and social institutions.[5] It has even been suggested that the hegemony enjoyed by the USA in the post-1945 world has been positively related to the flourishing of 'establishment' religion, just as the decline in Britain's international role during the present century was accompanied by a withering of this form of religion. Unlike the prophets of ancient Israel, however, the author of this thesis assumes that the decline in religious practice is the consequence rather than the cause of political deterioration! Whether a general co-relation between establishment religion and international hegemony can be maintained is, however, debatable.[6]

The triumphalist tone of much present-day American religion (particularly noticeable in Washington) seems, however, to reflect the role played by the White House, Capitol Hill and the Pentagon in the drama of world politics. The somewhat bombastic tenor of the Anglican liturgy as performed in many Episcopal churches today is reminiscent of the great Anglo-Catholic Congress rallies of the 1920s in London, when the British Empire was still a reality; it presents a striking contrast to the rather modest and less confident ethos of most English parish churches today.[7]

James and Dewey

Two of the most popular – and in certain ways most typical – American philosophers of the early twentieth century were William James (1842–1910) and John Dewey (1859–1954). Both linked their understanding of the universe, in its relationship to God, to the federal democracy in which they lived. Dewey was in fact one of the first American thinkers to emphasise the social context of ideas, insisting that the development of even the natural sciences must be seen against the background of the social situation in which they are practised. Knowing, he argued – in the natural sciences as much as in other fields – is not outside and above social activity, but must be seen as itself a social activity, like agriculture or transport. Classical scientific theories assumed a feudally arranged hierarchy of classes, with events being 'governed' by laws. This way of thinking, he went on, 'is a survival of reading social relationships into nature – not necessarily a feudal relationship, but the relation of ruler and ruled, sovereign and subject'. Modern images of nature and of the natural sciences assume, in contrast, 'the substitution of a democracy of individual facts equal in rank'.[8]

Dewey and James were pragmatists, claiming that the truth of a belief should be judged by its usefulness, by whether it contributes to the realising of some tangible human end. James wrote of 'the will to believe' and Dewey insisted that 'there is no knowledge except as our desires, our interests, our purposes, in short the whole bent of our moral nature is concerned'.[9] They continually appealed to the supposed facts of human experience rather than to grand meta-physical systems. James, in his celebrated Gifford Lectures of 1901–2 on *The Varieties of Religious Experience*, concentrated his attention on the analysis of individual religious experiences as recorded by their subjects. Dogmatic assertions which went beyond the evidence he called 'over-beliefs', which could not claim the same scientific status as could the strict conclusions of empirical investigation. Nevertheless religious over-beliefs are valuable, as attempts to account for the phenomena discovered, and they involve the assertion of a real difference in the constitution of things from that accepted by materialists.[10]

James envisaged a 'pluralistic universe', presided over by a finite God – who makes the best of a difficult job by bringing some coherence into a situation of potential chaos. The universe is 'more like a federal republic than an empire or a kingdom', where there is no 'final solution' (a striking premonition of a later and more sinister usage), and where there will always remain self-governed elements resisting a reduction to monolithic unity. James linked 'the rising tide of social democracy' with a decline in the 'older monarchical theism'.[11] Vehemently opposing the tendency in idealist philosophy to identify God with 'the Absolute', he insisted that the God of the Bible and of religious experience is a finite being, who symbolises 'the ideal tendency in things'. He is not a God who issues commands which must be obeyed unthinkingly, but one who calls men and women to co-operate with him.[12]

In his early writings Dewey maintained that the social and political relationships in which people live 'must set the form and sound the keynote to the understanding of Christianity' but equally insisted that it is belief in an 'actually working God' which gives meaning to social organisation. This God he pictured as incarnate in human beings and reflected in a democratic order.[13] In his later work Dewey used religious language less frequently, but when he spoke of 'God' it continued to signify those forces in the world which lead to the unification and realisation of ideal values. God may thus be seen as analogous to the state as 'regulator' of the groups within it, 'defining the limits of their actions, preventing and settling conflicts'. He pictured the state as a conductor who, though not making music himself, co-ordinates the various sections of an orchestra.[14]

For both James and Dewey the concept of 'process' was crucial. The latter insisted that the idea of a static, final and ultimate good – an intellectual product of feudalism – was disappearing along with the related concept of a 'bounded, ordered cosmos, wherein rest is higher than motion'. James too saw the universe as 'incomplete' and in the process of development.[15] This was seen as an integrated biological, psychological and cultural tendency with profound religious significance. Process for them meant that the whole of existence is social and dynamic, that perfection is found not in a fixed state but in a movement towards coherence and integration. James and Dewey were taking up an earlier tradition of American liberal Protestantism, represented in the mid-nineteenth century by such men as Bushnell, Emerson and Channing. Of this tradition H.R. Niebuhr wrote:

> Whether conceived in political or ecclesiastical or economic or cultural terms, the coming kingdom is never regarded as involving both death and resurrection, both crisis and promise, but only as the completion of tendencies now established.[16]

Process and pluralism

Dewey's friend and close collaborator Arthur Fisher Bentley (1870–1957) applied the idea of process to the political sphere. His purpose was to direct the attention of political scientists away from the formal, legal and institutional aspects of their subject towards the real forces which operate in politics. Instead of talking of ideas, feelings and myths, they should examine actual human behaviour. Bentley insisted that, when this is done, politics is seen to be a 'process' in which numerous groups contend for power. These groups reflect human interests which are essentially plural and competitive; he could find no place in his understanding of politics for a national interest or a common good. These concepts must be seen as nothing more than weapons, used to forward the interests of those who use them. Unlike many of his successors Bentley saw this process at work not only in so-called democracies, but in tsarist Russia and in primitive societies, though taking a somewhat different form. The government's role is to contain the conflicts between groups and to facilitate a temporary equilibrium, though Bentley warned that it should not be seen as above the conflict but as itself the leader of a group or set of groups.[17]

Bentley was one of a number of US social scientists who in this period stressed the concept of process – moving, as A.J. Balfour had advocated, from an 'anatomical' or structural emphasis to a 'physiological' or functional approach to the study of social and political relations. Balfour had claimed that the organs discussed in constitutional textbooks are among the least interesting social institutions: 'from the point of view of politics Function is more important than Structure'.[18] Discussing such American scholars as Charles Beard, James Robinson, Oliver Wendell Holmes, John Dewey and Thorstein Veblen, Morton White writes:

All of them insist on coming to grips with life, experience, process growth, context, function. They are all products of the historical and cultural emphases of the nineteenth century, following, being influenced by, reacting from its great philosophers of change and process.[19]

Albion Small had already anticipated Bentley's emphasis on process in his *General Sociology* of 1905, and others, including Mary Parker Follett, were to develop these ideas in the following decades.[20]

The influence of Bentley's *The Governmental Process* has, in fact, grown with the years. Its general theme was taken up by David Truman, in *The Process of Government*, and by a whole school of pluralist writers from the 1950s onwards. Many, however, differ from Bentley in maintaining that this competitive system – in which numerous groups contend for power – is particularly characteristic of the United States and that it is good. The popular writer Walter Lippmann had maintained in 1929 that each American citizen belongs to many different groups and that there is a criss-crossing of loyalties which guarantees that people 'behave moderately' and that power 'is distributed and qualified so that power is exerted not by command but by interaction'.[21] Gradually what was a descriptive theory thus gained prescriptive force.

These developments in pluralist theory went hand in hand with theories about totalitarianism; their popularity in the post-1945 period is partly due to their use as weapons in the cold war. In contrast to the totalitarian systems of the eastern bloc, a pluralist system was said to prevent the emergence of a single power elite, ensuring that all elements of the population are able to make their voices heard in the political process. The idea was applied by Robert Dahl and N.W. Polsby to local political decision making in the city of New Haven, where no single elite could be identified and where numerous groups were able to influence the outcome of political struggles. More recently the notion of a corporate state has been extensively canvassed.[22]

Pluralist theory in the USA has had its critics. Some, like the Marxist C. Wright Mills, deny that the description is accurate and assert that real power is held by a relatively small and coherent 'power elite' of military, economic and political leaders. Others accept the pluralist analysis and claim that the United States is indeed controlled by 'a plurality of entrenched oligarchies' which derive their power from private interest, paying no attention to the common good. They thus call for more government regulation and the revival of some notion of a common good. Robert Paul Wolff in particular has argued for restoring a conception of community in which a general will might be realised. Other critics observe that the degree of plurality is severely limited, excluding those groups which might constitute a challenge to the prevailing system – that pluralism in the USA is a 'one-dimensional' phenomenon, to use a phrase of Herbert Marcuse. Others again criticise the assumption of some pluralists that political power can be assessed simply in terms of decision-making processes. The one who sets the agenda, thereby excluding certain matters from coming up for decision, also has significant power.[23]

Despite extensive criticism, the idea that the United States is a pluralist democracy, in which a multitude of cross-cutting groups ensure an interdependence of the various interests, and where everyone has an equal right to join like-minded persons and make their influence felt, remains powerful. These notions of inter-dependence, equality and democracy provide the backdrop against which ideas of God's relationship to the universe have been developed by American writers of the present century.

PROCESS PHILOSOPHY AND GOD

Whitehead

Many ideas pioneered by James and Dewey were taken up by Alfred North Whitehead (1861–1947) and incorporated into his very different metaphysical framework. In 1924 the famous British mathematician and co-author with Bertrand Russell of *Principia Mathematica* left England for a chair in philosophy at Harvard University. His three books *Science and the Modern World* (1925), *Religion in the Making* (1926) and *Process and Reality* (1929) have had a considerable influence on the development of American philosophical theology. Although he was not a theologian himself, this did not prevent Whitehead from making magisterial pronouncements on the subject.

Whitehead's complex metaphysic, expounded in his Gifford Lectures, *Process and Reality*, rejected any notion of a static underlying substance to the cosmos. Rather he posited actual entities dynamically related as part of a developing universe. God should not be viewed as the unmoved mover who created the universe by his fiat, nor 'in the image of an imperial ruler'. He should be seen as that being who continually brings order out of primordial chaos; he is therefore not *before* but *with* all creation. Looked at from one standpoint God may be thought of as complete, but from another he is in a dynamic interdependence with the universe. He is thus – like all entities – 'dipolar', having a 'primordial' and a 'consequent' nature.[24] Unfortunately neither Whitehead nor his followers have succeeded in showing how these two poles relate to each other. Both God and the world manifest a multiplicity in unity, but they 'move conversely to each other'. God is primordially one, acquiring a multiplicity in the creative process; the world, on the other hand, is primordially many, and acquires a consequent unity.[25] In his earlier writings Whitehead had pictured God almost entirely in terms of his primordial nature, but later came to believe that God, like all entities, has this dipolar character. Yet he never followed through the consequences of his later recognition of God as an actual entity by acknowledging that as such he could become an agent of efficient causality in the world.

The consequent nature of God is characterised by a patience and a tenderness 'which loses nothing that can be saved'.[26] Whitehead contrasted the 'Galilean vision' of a humble God with the official religion of post-Constantinian Christendom. 'The code of Justinian and the theology of Justinian are two volumes expressing one movement of the human spirit. . . . The Church gave unto God the attributes which belonged exclusively to Caesar.'[27] He is here echoing what he earlier stated in his Lowell Lectures of 1926, quoted at the beginning of this chapter. This view of the universe, 'in the guise of an Eastern empire ruled by a glorious tyrant', may have marked a necessary stage in the progress of religion towards a universal faith, but it is inappropriate for the modern world. Love, rather than fear, should be the keynote of religion, and God should be regarded as 'the ideal companion' of human beings in their solitariness or – in a celebrated phrase – 'the fellow-sufferer who understands'.[28]

Whitehead and his followers among process theologians picture God's power in terms of attraction rather than compulsion, tracing the 'persuasive' power of God back to some themes found in Plato. 'The power of God', he wrote in 1931, 'is the worship he inspires.'[29] As Daniel Day Williams observes, this God does not drive the world but 'lures it through the power of the vision he inspires'. Williams links Whitehead's notion of divine persuasion with his admiration for the non-violent political tactics of Mahatma Gandhi.[30] This 'persuasive' power of God emphasised by Whiteheadians has been the object of some cogent philosophical and theological criticism,[31] but from our standpoint it may be seen as analogical to the role which education and reformative notions of punishment play in their liberal social theory.[32] Compliance is secured not by compulsion but by persuasion, conditioning and manipulation.

Whitehead himself claimed that there were certain social and political consequences of his metaphysical position. He saw the philosophy of Descartes as 'very concordant with the individualism which had issued from the moral discipline of the Middle Ages'. Although Cartesian philosophy had swept away barbaric superstitions it led, in the nineteenth century, to an individualism which was destructive of moral and aesthetic values and a failure to recognise the 'intrinsic worth of the environment'.[33] A true understanding of evolution and of God's relation to the universe implies adaptation, interdependence and co-operation rather than antagonism and competition. This, he believed, should be reflected in social and political life and it is in this context that he stressed the role of 'self-governing institutions' within the larger national state.[34] One of his followers has in fact argued that his metaphysical system provides a philosophical basis for the 'democratic way of life'.[35]

Insisting that metaphysics furnishes a criterion by which to assess the validity of traditional conceptions of God, Whitehead also recognised that metaphysics itself depends for its substance on 'those elements which may roughly be classed together as religious and moral intuitions'. He also explicitly acknowledged the role of 'value-judgments' in this process, but was preserved from a simple relativism by his persistent belief in what Williams described as 'an evolutionary development integral to the nature of the universe'.[36] These value-judgments are not, therefore, arbitrary preferences but in some way reflect the nature of reality. Yet *theology*, for Whitehead, was manifestly beholden to philosophy in a fundamental way – Christianity is a religion in search of a metaphysic.

Whether Whitehead is right in claiming that Christianity must find a basis in metaphysics, and whether his own system adequately provides such a basis, is questionable.[37] Undoubtedly some of his strictures on traditional theology are legitimate and his critique of imperial images of God has much validity. Yet his alternative image of God as a constitutional ruler – passive rather than active, who listens rather than speaks (except, like Bagehot's monarch, with the right to be consulted, to warn and to advise!) – is unsatisfactory. It assumes that passivity and even weakness are in some way admirable in themselves. There may, however, be a legitimate role for constraint and even force in cosmic as well as in civic life. The notion of God as in certain respects affected by, and therefore dependent on, the universe clearly challenges orthodox belief in the impassibility of God. This aspect of his thought has been most coherently developed by Charles Hartshorne.

Hartshorne

The widespread assumption, derived from classical philosophy, that perfection implies changelessness and self-sufficiency, is one which Charles Hartshorne (1897–) has made the object of a sustained assault. He finds this idea of God philosophically unsatisfactory, religiously unsatisfying and politically dangerous. In the first place, the idea of God as the absolute knowing subject logically requires that he is 'internally' related to the objects of his knowledge and that therefore he is affected by them. Hartshorne further attempts to show that 'excellence or value has a dimension of dependence as well as of independence'.[38] A person, and in particular a sensitive person, is more dependent on his or her surroundings than an animal, who in turn is more dependent than a cabbage and a cabbage more than a stone. If we thus think in terms of a hierarchy of being, then surely God must, in certain respects, be supremely dependent. If God is a loving God he will respond to what happens in the universe. But this does not mean that he is tossed hither and yon by events over which he has no control.

When considering the question of God's autarky it is important to ask whether we refer to his nature, will, knowledge or feelings. Following Whitehead's notion of a dipolar God, Hartshorne maintains that there are two sides to God's *nature*, an enduring and a developing aspect. God is both absolute and relative (related to the whole universe); he is both necessary and contingent, perfect and in the process of becoming. If God is truly personal by nature he must have real relationships beyond himself and be affected by these relationships. If God is personal he must be social.

Again, it is possible to conceive of God's *will* as being wholly and immutably directed towards the good, while at the same time changing its specific content in the light of the free actions of humans. One rather unsatisfactory way of attempting to preserve his impassibility is by maintaining that God knows all possible courses of human action and the consequent situations which might occur and has a prearranged response. Thus, although God cannot know whether I will – at time t – do x, y or z, his fixed will is that if I do x then he will respond by bringing about q.[39] It is not, however, necessary to assume this kind of bureaucratic model in order to safeguard moral consistency in God. We can simply assert that whatever situations God is faced with he responds in a way which is for the best.

With respect to his *knowledge*, if we believe that human actions, being free, are therefore not strictly predictable, and that God's perfect knowledge (omniscience) means that he knows only what it is possible to know, then as the future is not knowable God cannot be said to know it. Thus his knowledge increases with each new human action which occurs and may in this sense be called dependent.

Classical theology, it is argued by Hartshorne and others, including recently John Macquarrie,[40] has seen God as impassive and changeless and is thereby inconsistent with the Christian revelation of a personal God. Hartshorne makes it clear that he is not attacking the Christian religion, but rather is calling for it to be 'judged in its own terms, not in terms of its borrowed Greek garments'.[41] Whether God can be said to have *feelings* or passions – positive (e.g. joy) or negative (e.g. pain) – has been a contentious issue in Christian theology. Many of the biblical writers spoke as though God has passions, such as anger, jealousy, sadness and so on. Early Christian thinkers, under the influence of Greek philosophy, attempted to explain this language away and maintained the notion of God's autarky.

To say that God cannot suffer pain might, however, be said to constitute a limit on his omniscience, for to know pain it is necessary to experience it. Furthermore, it is suggested, to speak of the love of God necessarily implies that, when his people suffer, God suffers in sympathy with them. So far as the cross of Christ is a revelation of God's eternal character, then he must be seen as a God who can and does suffer. A further reason for maintaining the impassibility of God has been due to a belief that passions impair judgment; but this is so only in the case of fallen human beings and not with God, whose passions can properly be said to strengthen his judgment.

Some traditional theology has, of course, insisted it was only in his human nature that Jesus suffered. In his divine nature, which he shared with the Father, he could not suffer, for this would suggest divine dependence which is an imperfection. In the twentieth century, however, an increasing number of theologians have been willing to question the condemnation of 'patripassianism', and have been prepared to speak of the suffering of God the Father. The passion of Jesus is pictured as a revelation of the eternal nature of God, as one who loves even to the point of pain. Such a position is represented imaginatively in the poems of G.A. Studdert Kennedy, in some of William Temple's writings, and more recently in the work of Japanese theologian Kazoh Kitamori and in that of the popular German writer Jürgen Moltmann.

> How can it be that God can reign in glory,
> Calmly content with what his Love has done,
> Reading unmoved the piteous shameful story,
> All the vile deeds men do beneath the sun?
>
> Are there no tears in the heart of the Eternal?
> Is there no pain to pierce the heart of God?
> Then must He be a fiend of Hell infernal,
> Beating the earth to pieces with his rod.[42]

The idea of the suffering God is also to be found in many of the religions of the oppressed.[43]

As already noted, Hartshorne explicitly relates his critique of the classical images of a transcendent and autarkic being to the political and social world. 'Those who profit most by social injustices', he wrote,

> have only to recall that since God's in his heaven, all must be right with the world. Those who have reasons of their own for opposing social change have only to reflect that the Orderer of all things is above time and change, and that all possible value is realized – despite the seeming evils of the world – in the eternal perfection of the Creator.[44]

Hartshorne, with William James and the political pluralists, pictures God – like the cosmos itself – as 'the inclusive Society of societies'. He links his censure of the tendency to worship the coercive power of God to the need for the nations of the world to search for accommodation rather than confrontation, claiming that the dissociation between power and sensitivity, found in much popular religion, has been carried over, with disastrous consequences, into the world of international politics.[45] Hartshorne does not, however, reject the ascription of power to God. The problem with much popular thinking on the subject is not in ascribing too much power to God, but 'in an over simple or too mechanical conception of the nature of power in general'.

Hartshorne would presumably welcome some recent developments in social theory which emphasise the way power is often exercised by limiting the viable options in a given situation and by influencing the unstated presuppositions. In response to an overemphasis on power as the ability to affect the decision-making process, which marked the theories of such writers as Robert Dahl and Nelson Polsby, there was a renewed stress on power as the ability to determine the agenda and to mould the assumptions of a community. In their remarkable study of *Power and Poverty*, Bachrach and Baratz drew attention to the fact that many of the most significant issues in a community are never actually decided on. Accepted values and practices 'operate systematically and consistently to the benefit of certain persons and groups at the expense of others', and those who are able to determine these values and practices wield great power. From a Marxist standpoint the Italian theorist Antonio Gramsci has similarly pointed to the way ruling classes are able to establish a hegemony in the cultural and ideological field and thereby maintain their economic and political superiority.[46]

While he emphasises the importance of political freedom and participation, as analogous to the relationship which he envisages between God and the universe,[47] Hartshorne recognises a legitimate use of force in international politics in order to prevent gross injustice. Coercion should not become a monopoly of the wicked. He illustrates his position with reference to the divine analogy:

> the best expression of belief in God is an attitude of social awareness which treats all problems in the spirit of mutuality except where others insist upon treating them in another spirit, at which point we must in our local way, like God in his cosmic way, set limits by constraint to the destruction of mutuality.[48]

Yet he also writes of the 'gentle passivity of God' and reduces all power to influence.[49]

There is thus, for Hartshorne and for other process thinkers, an analogy between human and divine government. In both cases the 'governor' should be seen not as imposing some total, preconceived plan but as responding to the free decisions of his or her subjects. Neither should be seen as having absolute control but as being faced with 'recalcitrant' material, which must be respected: bringing order out of potential chaos. Hartshorne thus rejects the 'God of power and might' which he finds in traditional theistic belief.

Apologists of classical theism, particularly of the Thomist variety, have been quick to reply to the accusations of Hartshorne, Macquarrie and other critics. In the first place they have pointed to certain inadequacies in the God of process theology. As Eric Mascall observed, if God is seen simply as a fellow sufferer our attitude towards him should be one of sympathy rather than adoration![50] The criticism is, however, misconceived, as Whitehead, Hartshorne and other process thinkers insist that God as 'fellow sufferer' is only one of the images legitimately used when considering one 'pole' of the dipolar God. God must also be seen as exercising a persuasive power or influence in the world, which they claim to be quite as effective as the coercive use of power which many traditional images of God assume. As we have noted, what is perhaps more problematic is the relationship which these process thinkers wish to assert between the two 'poles' – or aspects – in God. They appear to be poles apart.

Secondly these apologists have insisted that the 'classical' position attacked by process writers has not in fact been held by the best classical philosophers. In particular they have maintained that when Aquinas, for example, spoke of God as 'unchangeable' he was not attempting to describe God, but rather denying that the concept of change can properly be applied to God, who transcends such categories. He was, in other words, offering a statement of what cannot properly be said about God, rather than a doctrinal description of God.[51] Even though this point may be valid, it is nevertheless the case that the concepts and images which process theologians have attacked have been widely used as positive 'descriptions' of God both in popular theology and in the worship of the Christian Church, and therefore merit much of the condemnation which Hartshorne and his colleagues pronounce.

A further criticism which might be made of Whitehead and his followers is that, having ostentatiously ushered out the ghost of classical metaphysics through the front door, they have welcomed several equally wicked neo-classical spirits through the windows and that the consequent state of theology – shackled to a new ontology – is worse than the first. It is worse because the ontology is apparently more plausible, though in fact equally untenable.

Wieman

Henry Nelson Wieman (1884–1975) played an important part in popularising Whiteheadian philosophy among American theologians of the 1930s and 1940s and was in some respects a bridge between process philosophers and the Chicago school. He was appointed to the University of Chicago as Professor of Philosophy in 1927, being seen as a Whiteheadian who could translate the complex thought of the master into language comprehensible to ordinary mortals.

Wieman argued for the immanence of God in the universe, as 'an actual, existing, operative reality in our midst bringing forth all that is highest and best in existence, far beyond the scope of our specific understanding'. Anticipating Paul Tillich, he defined God as the symbol for that which 'rightfully commands the supreme devotion of man'.[52] While he strongly asserted the reality of God ('the actual God', he wrote, 'is a fact like a stone wall or a toothache'[53]), he denied that God could properly be thought of in personal terms, except in a highly metaphorical manner, for persons are moulded by creative processes which are logically prior to them; a personal God would thus be dependent upon these processes. God is not dependent on existence, but 'existence is dependent upon him for all the great good it contains or may ever hope to attain'.[54] This is a curiously un-Whiteheadian argument, for, as we have seen, the British philosopher was perfectly prepared to deny that God should be thought of as creator and thus to allow a kind of dependence in the deity.

Wieman drew attention to the importance of growth – in religion as in the natural world. He maintained that growth, as distinct from mere incrementation, involves an organic development which forms or strengthens bonds of mutual support between diverse activities. It is in fact the work of love, if by love we mean the formation of bonds between individuals, 'whereby each works to conserve the system as a whole'. Wieman here seems to preclude the role of love as a force which may in certain circumstances work towards the disruption or dissolution of 'the system'.[55]

In asserting the reality of God, Wieman was critical of humanistic idealism and attacked a pragmatic conception of God as the symbol for our chosen ideals. No doubt with some of his future Chicago colleagues in mind, Wieman asked in 1926, 'Is religion preeminently a device for glorifying social cooperation and arousing utmost devotion to those goals of endeavor which society holds to be the highest. . . . [or] Is it the experience of that from which new ideals may be derived?'[56] Wieman clearly held to the second alternative, pointing out that if religion simply reflects our ideals it cannot deliver us from the limitations of these ideals. Wieman therefore pictured God as the actually existing reality in our midst which continually elicits 'all that is highest and best in existence'. Though functioning through human conscious purpose, he brings forth 'values over and above all human power of control and conscious interest'.[57]

As God is conceived as facilitating growth through the cultivation of co-operative bonds between distinct elements in the universe, government – by analogy – should perform the same role in social life. If freedom is to prevail, governments must provide conditions favourable to 'creative interchange between individuals and peoples'. Wieman consequently called for greater international co-operation. 'No government and people', he maintained, 'can stand and grow strong without close connection and mutual support with other governments and people.'[58] Unlike many liberal theologians of his day, Wieman was, however, no naïve optimist and did not fail to recognise the power of evil in the world. 'This is not a nice world', he strikingly observed, 'and God is not a nice God. God is too awful and terrible, too destructive to our foolish little plans to be nice.'[59]

Shailer Mathews and the Chicago school

Theology in the University of Chicago, at the time Wieman arrived, had been dominated for many years by a number of outstanding teachers of a liberal Protestant tendency. Their concern was not simply with academic theology, but with influencing the life of the church by bridging the gulf between scientific theology and parish life. Their mission was seen by Dean Shailer Mathews as 'the democratization of an idea'.[60] Leading members of the school in its early period included Gerald Birney Smith (1868–1929), Shailer Mathews (1863–1941), Shirley Jackson Case (1872–1947) and Edward Scribner Ames (1870–1958). While they differed in many respects, these men all insisted that the Christian faith must be understood in the context of 'the total surroundings in which its adherents lived'.[61] They believed that history, sociology and psychology, rather than philosophy, provide the idioms for theological discourse, that 'The character of God will be found in the experienced reciprocity between man and his environment rather than in the realm of metaphysical causation.'[62] Christian doctrines have not sprung up as isolated and independent systems of truth, but rather in response to social and religious needs and tensions, at particular periods of history. Mathews thus likened them more to the structure of common law than to philosophical systems.[63]

Thus the pragmatic and behavioural emphasis which we have already noted among philosophers and political scientists in the early decades of the present century manifestly had parallels in contemporary theology. 'If we wish to understand religion', declared Mathews, 'we must examine the individual and social behavior of men. . . . Behavior has preceded definition.'[64]

With some of these writers a stress on the social context of belief led to an assertion of social determinism, at least with respect to *dominant* theological systems. The Christian religion has remained historically significant, declared Edward Ames, 'in just the measure to which it has embodied the emotional, moral and intellectual realities of successive generations of adherents'.[65] For Shailer Mathews, the important question to ask is not whether a doctrine is 'true' but whether it successfully co-ordinates religious experience and unquestioned beliefs in a manner which satisfies. Only as religion 'aids in personal adjustment to forces in the cosmos' can it survive. Yet Mathews was clear that religious practices and patterns often outlive the social structures from which they have sprung, acquiring new social functions.[66] He defined God as 'our conception, born of social experience, of the personality-evolving and personally responsive elements of our cosmic environment with which we are organically related'. Elsewhere he spoke of God as a symbol for the personality-producing activities of the universe.[67]

Mathews believed that attempts to define an 'essence' of Christianity in terms of some set of basic doctrines were misconceived. 'It must be viewed as a genetic social and religious movement rather than as a system of truth.' The identity of Christianity is to be found in a continuity of life which lies behind 'the variant practices and theologies'. Thus Christianity is simply that collection of beliefs and practices accepted by people who call themselves Christians. Yet even he could not refrain from some characterisation of Christianity, in terms of its content, as being that phase of the total life of Christians 'which expresses loyalty and trust in Jesus Christ as a Savior'.[68]

Mathews paid particular attention to the political context in which theology develops and to that analogy between structures of divine and civil authority which is the principal theme of the present volume. Theology is a 'super-politics', theories of the atonement represent a 'transcendental penology', and the Calvinist conception of God is the theological parallel of absolute monarchy. 'If we study the relations of a monarch and his subjects in any social order', he wrote, 'we shall find analogies which have been used to set forth the idea of the relation of the divine and the human.' Mathews himself believed that theology is a mere 'function' of religious life, which in turn is 'the expression of a social order' conditioned by economic and political forces, in addition to more general cultural factors.[69] He nevertheless assumed that his own social and religious beliefs had some kind of validity and confidently set them forth in his Harvard lectures of 1916, *The Spiritual Interpretation of History*.

In his important work, *The Psychology of Religious Experience*, Edward Ames emphasised the role played by democratic conceptions in his day. He attributed the church's loss of influence among the industrial classes partly to its failure to adapt the gospel to the democratic spirit of the age. 'It continues to maintain ideas of God drawn from patriarchal and monarchical types of life', he wrote,

> consequently it interprets spiritual relations in terms of princely favors which are bestowed upon men through grace as free gifts. But the laborer and the voter have come to prefer to think of themselves as earning what they get. They are event more anxious to receive what they believe they deserve than to gain favors through charitable benevolence, even if it be represented as divine.[70]

Democracy meant for Ames an emphasis upon freedom, participation and imaginative co-operation among individuals; God should be seen as an immanent presence in the world, embodying these social ideals.[71] The moralistic and optimistic tone of Ames's theology represents something of an extreme position among the writers whom we are here considering and it was this idealism which was the target of Wieman's attack, noted above.

Two philosophers: Howison and Overstreet

Some of the principal themes developed by theologians of the Chicago school were anticipated in the writings of George Holmes Howison (1834–1916), Professor of Philosophy in the University of California from 1884 on. John Macquarrie follows John Passmore in linking his name with that of the eminent British idealist J.M.E. McTaggart, under the heading 'Pluralistic Personal Idealism'.[72] Howison was critical of the absolute idealism of Hegel and his disciples as undermining the fundamental importance of human personality. In a celebrated controversy with Josiah Royce and others, he outlined his idea of God in contrast to the monistic conception which, he claimed, leads to a pantheism 'at war with the characteristic interests of human nature'.[73] God should be thought of not as a transcendent being who creates a universe *ex nihilo*, but as the first among equals in a community of minds, to whom the others 'spontaneously make reference'.

Howison denounced a 'magisterial and monarchical conception of God, which left men nothing but the submissive subjects of a Lord', appealing to the teaching of Jesus which presented God as 'Friend and moral Father of men'. With Jesus, religion was thus transformed from the worship of an exalted and unapproachable sovereign into 'a joyful communion in all goodness and nobility with a perfect Guide and Friend'. Rather than rejecting the idea of divine grace, Howison reinterpreted it in the light of this notion of God. The grace of God grants to its objects the prospect of equality with him, and 'intends to confer companionship – yes, partnership – in every power and gift'.[74]

The ideas of Howison were popularised by Harry Overstreet in a number of works written over more than half a century. In an early article on 'The Democratic Conception of God', he claimed that the modern age was distinguished by democratic assumptions where there is no place for 'an eternally perfect being', for

the society, democratic from end to end, can brook no such radical class distinction as that between a supreme being favored with eternal and absolute perfection and the mass of beings doomed to the lower ways of imperfect struggle.

Rather he proposes a God who

> is in the making, growing with the growth of the world; suffering and sinning and conquering with it; a God, in short, that *is* the world in the spiritual unity of its mass life . . . a God in and of the total world-process.[75]

Curiously he appears to end up with just that kind of pantheism which his mentor abhorred.

In a later work Overstreet not only rejected imperial and monarchical images of God but concluded that even belief in God 'as a Heavenly Father who orders our welfare and expects from us adoration and obedience, is, from the modern point of view, inadequate'.[76] It is a mistake to think of God as an individual over ourselves; rather he is a symbol for the immanent principle in the universe which tends towards integration. 'To love God', he declared in a memorable phrase, 'is to love the processes of bringing life into a more vital integration'; wherever there is a 'passionate love of integrating' there is the love of God.[77] This whimsical notion has something in common with the ideas of Whitehead and Wieman on the role played by God in the universe and is closely related in many of these writers to a strong emphasis upon God as the 'personality-producing' tendency at work in the cosmos. Overstreet continued to maintain this position into the 1950s and posited a struggle between those who adopt models of domination and 'create gods and social systems in their own image' and those 'whose liking is for equality, and who yet may be destined to create a religion, a politics, an educational system, and an economic order in their own image'.[78]

Walter Rauschenbusch and the social gospel

The theology of Walter Rauschenbusch was more in line with traditional Christianity than were most of the foregoing ideas. He was born in 1861 at Rochester in New York State, the son of a German pastor who had emigrated in 1854. He became a Baptist minister and after a period of teaching he worked as pastor in the notorious New York slum district known as Hell's Kitchen. This practical experience of church life distinguished him from many contemporary theologians and undoubtedly prevented his theology from becoming a mere academic flight of fancy. He later returned as professor to Rochester Theological Seminary.[79] In the early decades of the twentieth century Rauschenbusch had a great influence among Protestant clergy of the United States; his book *Christianity and the*

Social Crisis, published in 1907, sold over 50,000 copies. Though frequently criticised for his supposedly liberal and optimistic religion, he had – unlike many of those liberals discussed above – a profound belief in the reality of sin and evil and in the need for redemption. Yet his belief that the social and international order can and should be 'Christianized', and that 'under the warm breath of religious faith, all social institutions become plastic',[80] suggests that he failed to acknowledge the relative autonomy of the secular.

Rauschenbusch was critical of despotic images of God, as found among the Hebrews and other ancient peoples, and maintained that 'when Jesus spoke of God as our Father, he democratized God himself'.[81] People's conception of God is affected by the social and political relations which they experience. Under a political tyranny God becomes cruel and arbitrary:

> The conflict of the religion of Jesus with autocratic conceptions of God is therefore part of the struggle of humanity with autocratic economic and political conditions. . . . The triumph of the Christian idea of God will never be complete as long as economic and political despotism prevail.[82]

Ideas of sin as disobedience to the commands of a ruler, of merit as offsetting delinquencies committed against a feudal lord and of the intercession of the saints as favours which a noble patron could secure for his clients were clearly developed under the influence of particular social formations.[83] Democratic conceptions of God demand a revision in the notion of sin. No longer should it be seen as rebellion against a divine autocrat – as treason – but rather as an offence against the principle of brotherly love and co-operation.

The new democratic images which must be adopted view God as immanent in the world, as man's 'chief fellow-worker', a God who 'has always suffered with and for mankind'.[84] In a book of *Prayers of the Social Awakening*, Rauschenbusch addressed God, in a 'Prayer for Working-men', as 'Thou mightiest worker of the universe, source of all strength and author of all unity'. Again, a prayer for immigrants begins: 'O Thou, great Champion of the outcast and the weak'.[85] These themes are a striking anticipation of certain tendencies in the liberation theology of the present day, as was his call for a rejuvenated eschatology. Eccentric fundamentalist interpretations in this field had frightened Christians away from eschatology, and they fail to see that the Apocalypse 'expounds the old social hope of Israel'.[86] He wanted to revive 'the millennial hope, which the Catholic Church dropped out of eschatology' – the idea of a just social order 'in which the brotherhood of man will be expressed in the common possession of the economic resources of society'. He nevertheless saw this coming about partly as the result of a gradual development rather than catastrophic intervention. Unlike some of his optimistic contemporaries Rauschenbusch was, however, clear that this process would not be without conflict. 'We should estimate the power of sin too lightly if we forecast a smooth road.'[87]

Rauschenbusch depicted the kingdom of heaven or the reign of God as a commonwealth based upon the principle of co-operation – between God and humans and among humans themselves. His emphasis upon the role of co-operation led him to recognise the importance of the principle of solidarity among the working class and also the increasingly vital role played by corporations and other social groups in a capitalist state. The corporation, he observed, had become a state within the state and 'is steadily superseding the old-fashioned private business in all the large and distinctively modern forms of undertaking'.[88] As we shall see, this emphasis on co-operation and integration led, in Rauschenbusch as in some other writers of the period, to a theology of the natural world, and to a concern with ecology.

Walter Rauschenbusch was but one among a number of theologians generally classed as the 'social gospel' school. His predecessors, including Josiah Strong (1847–1916) and Washington Gladden (1836–1918), insisted that the Christian gospel is concerned not merely with the salvation of the individual soul but with the redemption of the social and natural order. They emphasised the central importance of the kingdom of God in the teaching of Jesus and saw the kingdom coming into being through the 'Christianization of all life'.[89] Strong founded the League for Social Service to forward these ideals on a practical level.

One of the most influential among writers of the social gospel school was Robert Archey Woods (1865–1925), who was warden of South End House (formerly Andover House) in Boston, which was modelled on the university settlements in the East End of London. As a young man he had been deeply influenced by Canon Samuel Barnett and had stayed in Toynbee Hall for some months. Democracy was for these social gospel writers more than a system of government; it was seen as a spirit which must pervade the whole of life, including industry, education, social relationships and, naturally, religion. In the political realm it is manifested in the federal system of government – as found in the USA – where a huge and diverse nation has been held together in liberty. 'By the complete establishment of a federal union . . .', Woods declared, 'it has been demonstrated to the world that such a democratic nation can exist.'[90] Woods claimed that the old monarchical image of God 'will fade into the darkness with the social system which gave it rise', and that a new understanding of deity will emerge:

> society as a federal union, in which each individual and every form of human association shall find free and full scope for a more abundant life, will be the large figure from which is projected the conception of the God in whom we live and move and have our being.[91]

Divine democracy and civil religion

The theological developments we have been discussing can partly be seen as the reaction to a challenge by the growing secular movement in the USA. Religious traditions and images, claimed the secular humanists, are totally opposed to the social and political principles upon which the country is founded. While the latter are based on reason and human welfare, the former appeal to irrational authority of one kind or another. Some secularists wished to turn American democracy itself into a religion which would replace Christianity. 'We must', cried Thomas Davidson in an extraordinary article, 'find a religion in our civic principles and aims.'[92] The framers of the US constitution not only laid the basis for a free government but were sweeping away the very foundations of old religions. This new religion of democracy was, he claimed, fully in line with the evolutionary theories of Herbert Spencer and others. Religion is that which 'places us in such harmony with our environment that we attain the highest possible development or satisfaction, – development in knowledge, love, and will. But surely', he went on, 'no institution was ever better calculated for this than our republic.'[93] Davidson linked this henotheistic belief in the nation as a religious symbol quite closely with foreign policy issues and asserted that the benevolent treatment of Cuba by the USA vindicated his claim,

> not only that Americanism is a religion, but that it is the noblest of all religions, that which best insures the realization of the highest manhood and womanhood and points them to the highest goal. . . . In teaching children to lead the life of true Americans, we shall be leading them in the paths of eternal life.[94]

While this position of Davidson seems to take a nationalistic form, he would have claimed that it is of universal application. It clearly illustrates the way things go when God becomes a mere function of human ends or ideals – a symbol for personal development.

THEOLOGICAL IMAGINATION

The theologian in our own day who has been most concerned about developing a set of images and conceptions of God 'suitable for orienting contemporary human existence with its unique problems' has been the American theologian Gordon Kaufman.[95] Flawed though many of his arguments are, we should be grateful to him for raising these central issues, which are too rarely approached by English-speaking theologians today. In an early book he recognises that human welfare cannot properly become the sole criterion of good and evil and attempts to outline a conception of 'God' as the ultimate 'limit' which all humans experience. Sometimes he defines God as 'the Limit' and sometimes as an 'agent' – 'the dynamic acting reality beyond the Limit'. This ambiguity renders his early position incoherent. By introducing the notion of a 'world' which is beyond the limit he falls into the very metaphysical–cosmological dualism which, he asserts, makes Christianity irrelevant in the modern world.[96]

In later works Kaufman abandons this metaphysical position, adopting a frankly pragmatic understanding of 'God' as the symbol for liberal humanitarian ideals. The adequacy of any system of beliefs is to be judged by whether they satisfy human ends. 'Their ultimate *raison d'être* is to serve certain human needs or intentions.'[97] Images and concepts which will lead to a humanising and a relativising of contemporary existence must be evolved. The concept of God can survive only if it is seen as contributing to our struggle to 'humanize' the world. This is the criterion by which our images and concepts of God must be judged. Kaufman argues that old authoritarian images of God which nourished imperialism, colonialism, slavery and genocide 'are no longer tolerable'. Critics may ask whether they were ever tolerable. Why the 'no longer'? Perhaps because, in a nuclear age, they might involve our own destruction too.

Answering the criticism that his own position, which takes human welfare as the criterion of an adequate conception of God, is just one more ideology competing with others, Kaufman asserts that this criterion is in fact implicit in all religions. Every religious tradition is concerned with human salvation or fulfilment and religions can thus be compared in terms of their contribution to human welfare. While agreeing that each religion might have a different conception of what constitutes welfare, he arbitrarily rules out appeals to supernatural or otherworldly sanctions. Yet the differing notions about what constitutes true human welfare are relevant here. Traditional Christianity has never maintained that human welfare or fulfilment *in this order of things* is the end which may unambiguously be pursued. 'If your hand offends you cut it off . . .' In his later work Kaufman is manifestly calling for a God who will legitimate the liberal universalism to which he is committed.

Kaufman sees it as the specific task of theology to 'think through and make explicit the criteria for an adequate understanding of God and then to reconstruct traditional images and ideas on the basis of these criteria'.[98] This might appear to be a somewhat ambitious manifesto, for such reconstruction of images has in the past normally stemmed from the devotional and liturgical life of the church, rather than from the speculations of academic theologians. A modern writer has suggested that a convenient test of the adequacy of images and concepts used of God is whether we can employ them in prayer and worship. Applying this test to Kaufman's reconstructive endeavours, the parish priest might find himself leading his congregation: 'Glory be to the complex configuration of factors, powers and processes (physical, vital and historico-cultural) . . .' or 'O thou focal term of an overarching conceptual framework . . .'[99] Not even Anselm could convincingly continue the prayer!

Works whose titles begin with the word 'Towards' are not calculated to inspire confidence in the authors' ability to reach their appointed goal. Kaufman's chapter in *Theology for a Nuclear Age*, 'Towards the Reconception of God', although containing many perceptive criticisms of traditional language, makes few positive suggestions for new concepts and images of God, nor does he point to where we might look for such developments. He does, however, call for a conception of God 'more in accord with the modern notion of a fundamentally unified ecological order',[100] taking up a theme upon which earlier American theologians had dwelt. As we have noted, members of the Chicago school envisaged God as symbolising the reciprocity between man and his environment. Gerald Birney Smith had asked himself what conception of God would emerge in the future:

We cannot yet tell. But it will express the experience of kinship between man and that quality in environment which supports and enriches humanity in its spiritual quest. . . . The experience of God will take the form of comradeship with that aspect of our non-human environment which is found to reinforce and to enrich our life.[101]

Rauschenbusch, in one of his prayers, asked God to 'enlarge within us the sense of fellowship with all the living things, our little brothers, to whom thou hast given the earth as their home in common with us'. The prayer goes on to recognise the sin of having ruthlessly exercised dominion over the natural world and asks that we may not leave anything behind 'ravished with our greed or spoiled by our ignorance'.[102]

This is clearly a large subject which cannot fully be dealt with here. Nevertheless, as Kaufman rightly argues, irresponsible exploitation of the natural world may well have been legitimated by an unbalanced use of divine analogies drawn from the world of political domination. Unfortunately he does not go on to suggest the kind of co-operative images which might be appropriate in an ecologically conscious religion. Kaufman, like Fichte, fully recognises the problem of relating his humanism to an understanding of the 'natural world'. Are human beings to be seen as *part of* nature or as transcending and possibly modifying it by intentional action?[103]

The humanistic religion proposed by Kaufman as a substitute for traditional versions of Christianity might well serve as a basis for revamping the civil religion to which some US sociologists have drawn attention in recent decades. If, following Parsonian dogma, no 'society' can exist without a set of common 'values', and if religion provides a foundation for these values, then such a religion performs a useful if not essential function in perpetuating a society. 'It is of the nature of a republic', declares Robert Bellah, 'that its citizens must love it, not merely obey it.'[104] In a book dedicated to Parsons, Bellah reiterates this position, pronouncing civil religion to be 'indispensable' to republican forms of government.[105] Similarly Richard Neuhaus, an ecumenically minded Lutheran, points to the inadequacy of the secularist assumption that the state has no religious basis. He appears to favour some kind of highest common factor of Judaeo-Christian beliefs, which might form a basis for a national religion.[106]

It is undoubtedly the case that religion has been a powerful factor throughout history in reinforcing the outrageous claims to obedience made by governments. Those who – following Rousseau – wish to reinforce these claims will naturally seek to invent some sort of henotheistic religion for the purpose. Whether a religion whose early disciples were accused of turning the world upside-down (Acts 17: 6) and who declared, 'we ought to obey God rather than men' (Acts 5: 29), will function in this way is, to say the very least, questionable.

Although the writers we have discussed wrote from different philosophical traditions, their theology has common features. The pragmatic and anti-metaphysical position of most Chicago theologians stands in stark contrast to the ontology of Whitehead and his followers. Yet they shared an emphasis on evolution, process and 'integration'; they also placed a high value on the 'personality-producing' influences in the universe. These are the considerations, closely linked to their political and social beliefs, which led them to criticise monarchical images of God and call for new democratic and ecological conceptions of God. It would, however, be wrong to suggest that theology is simply to be regarded as a consequence of social dynamics. There are occasions when theology plays an active role in influencing political developments. The social situation in the early 1930s which made it possible for Roosevelt to introduce the New Deal legislation, for example, was partly determined by the liberal theology of earlier decades. Images of God become *dominant* in a given social situation when they are consonant with widespread assumptions about political authority.

We must be grateful to these theologians for their critique of traditional language about God and for pointing to the perilous political consequences of monarchical imagery; but it should also be emphasised that there is a danger in the glorifying of weakness and passivity and in the wish to avoid all traces of conflict in religion as well as in politics. Older monarchical images should be balanced by new ones rather than being discarded. Perhaps in the present day it is to the liturgies of the non-European world we might look for such images, like the Nicaraguan mass which proclaims: 'You are a working God, a God with a weather-beaten face.'

6

Impassible God and autarkic state

'Pantheism', wrote Heinrich Heine in 1835,

> is the open secret of Germany. We have, in fact, outgrown deism.
> We are free and we want no thundering tyrants; we have reached
> majority and can dispense with paternal care. Neither are we the
> work of a great mechanician. Deism is a religion for slaves, for
> children, for Genovese, for watchmakers.[1]

Heine clearly perceived a close analogy between divine and political
authority, seeing the rejection of deism in the late eighteenth century
as linked to a revolt against political tyranny. As the despotic king
had fallen in France, the God of deism had fallen in Germany. In a
prophetic passage he foresaw an attempt to preserve theism by
moving in the direction of the benevolent God of liberal Protestantism and the welfare state. Of God, he wrote, 'Growing still more
spiritualised, he becomes a loving father, a universal friend of man, a
benefactor of the world, a philanthropist; but all this could avail him
nothing. Hear ye not the bells resounding,' he concluded in a
memorable passage. 'Kneel down. They are bringing the sacraments
to a dying god!'[2] It should, however, be noted in this context that
the God of eighteenth-century deism was, in contrast to the Socinian
God of an earlier century, no thundering tyrant but an enlightened
and constitutional monarch, ruling according to established laws.

ROMANTICS AND NATIONALISTS

I shall examine the assumption of early German nationalists that perfection implies self-sufficiency and investigate the analogy between divine and political autarky. While, as in Aristotle, a totally transcendent God, unconcerned with and even ignorant of the cosmos, may be autarkic, another way of securing divine autarky is to identify God with all that is, so that there is nothing beyond or outside him upon which he might be thought to depend. In the modern world these two tendencies – transcendence without immanence and immanence without transcendence – go back to Hobbes and Spinoza respectively; their political corollaries are indeed remarkably similar.

The theme of divine immanence was elaborated by J.G. Herder (1744–1803), who has been called, somewhat misleadingly, the father of German nationalism.[3] Writing towards the end of the eighteenth century, Herder was in full revolt against the rationalism of Enlightenment thinkers, though he shared with them a certain cosmopolitanism (or rather Europeanism) and a belief that the medieval age was a time of darkness. In Germany the Enlightenment philosophy was embodied most eminently in the writings of Immanuel Kant (1724–1804) and at this time it was necessary for any thinker wishing to make his mark to engage with Kant. Some, like J.G. Fichte (1762–1814) and Friedrich Schiller (1759–1805), saw their position as a development of Kantian thought.[4] Others were prepared to challenge the sage of Königsberg. Herder was one of these, emphasising the importance of non-rational elements in human life and pointing to the unique character of each people, with its legends, myths and poetic imagination. What sets a people apart as a distinct entity is its peculiar language, for it is language which expresses the collective identity and experience of a human group.[5] He attacked those who thought it superior to speak French and who despised their native tongue. In his third (unpublished) draft of the *Ideen*, Herder referred scornfully to the German princes who are mostly 'Frenchmen' and 'neither read nor understand the barbarous language in which I write'.[6]

Herder saw God as the universal spiritual power which underlies all cosmic forces. He urged a reassessment of the philosophy of Spinoza. Discussing the Jewish philosopher's dictum, 'There is but one Substance, and that is God. All things are but modifications of it', one of the characters in Herder's 'Conversations' (1787) demanded, 'What is Substance but a thing which is self-dependent,

which has the cause of its existence in itself?' He went on to insist
that 'all things must depend upon one self-dependent nature'.[7] The
autarky of God reappears throughout the 'Conversations', and clearly
Herder believed such self-sufficiency to be an aspect of his
perfection.

The influence of the pietist tradition is manifest in the work of
Herder and in later German Romantics, like Schleiermacher. Koppel
Pinson has indeed suggested that certain elements in this religious
tradition were transposed into the political realm – that nationalism
is pietism politicised. He draws attention to the pietist belief in the
mystical and inward relationship between the one and the many,
which forms a harmonic whole. As the believer is brought into
interior communion with the divine, so the citizen's nationality is
essentially an internal, spiritual relationship. The anti-intellectualism
of the pietist movement led also to a kind of religious populism
which was adopted by many German nationalists.[8]

The Romantic movement was closely linked to the growth of
German nationalism but not all the Romantics were nationalists.
Herder was himself no nationalist, in the sense of believing in the
nation-state; he showed little enthusiasm for the movement which
demanded that the political boundaries of the state must follow
those of the nation. His patriotism was more cultural than economic
or political and it was left to a later generation to extend his ideas
into these realms and develop the full doctrine of nationalism.
Herder had in fact no great interest in German unity – in the
creation of a German state encompassing the whole nation.

The position of Goethe and Schiller was similar to that of Herder,
since they believed that the German national spirit is expressed in a
cultural and spiritual supremacy rather than in political forms.[9]
'Sundered from politics', wrote Schiller, 'the German had founded a
value of his own. . . . It is an ethical greatness, it dwells in the culture
and character of the nation, which are independent of any political
destiny.'[10] The young Romantic poet Novalis (Friedrich von
Hardenberg) can hardly be called a nationalist either. It was to the
notion of Christendom, in its medieval form, that he turned for
inspiration. He emphasised the miraculous and otherworldly aspects
of religion and was bitterly opposed to the spirit of the Enlightenment. Like Hegel, he was, however, less concerned with the nation
than with the state, which he believed should be all-embracing and
total in its demands on the citizen.[11]

Fully fledged nationalism was the doctrine of the next generation
of writers, represented by Schleiermacher, Fichte and Adam Müller

(1779–1829). These men believed that the political boundaries of Europe needed redrawing to express the reality of the nation. Yet they were not entirely agreed about what this implied. Some thought in terms of state boundaries following the natural, physical divisions, which were somehow assumed to coincide with cultural divisions. Fichte, as we shall see, insisted that the state must be an entirely self-sufficient unit, economically closed off from other states. Müller, who at first rejected this position, came round to accepting it in his later writings, though unlike Fichte – who had argued for autarky partly on the ground that international trade leads to war – the younger man defended autarky as a means of strengthening the state to conduct war more successfully. 'In the war of one national power against another', he wrote, '... the essence and the beauty of national existence, that is, the idea of the nation, becomes particularly clear to all those who participate in its fate.'[12] Müller's economic nationalism also led him to follow Fichte in a hostility towards coined money and a preference for paper money which has no value beyond the national frontier.[13]

Some of these nationalists saw the state as playing a dynamic role in strengthening, if not creating, the nation. Discussing the ideas of the celebrated historian, Franz Leopold Ranke (1795–1886), R.A. Pois writes: 'A people might have a sense of national identity, but it was only through the "moral energy" (*moralische Energie*) of the state that this people could be infused with a sophisticated awareness of its own being and purpose.'[14] Ranke believed that nations have a natural tendency to become states, but that in his day there was hardly a single example of a true nation-state.[15] This idea of the nation as being created by the state has become a feature of modern African nationalism. German nationalists of the period also disagreed about the internal structure of the nation-states of the future. While agreeing that they should be independent and self-sufficient, some desired a strong and all-embracing central government, while others were liberals – or rather pluralists – who believed in a devolution of power to regional authorities and functional bodies. Schleiermacher, like Hegel, welcomed local loyalties within a state. Though he insisted on a strong central government able to defend the state and to maintain order, he asserted that 'In its internal constitution, however, it should allow a great deal of freedom to the individual states and their rulers and allow them to develop and govern themselves according to their own peculiar characteristics.'[16]

The writings of Fichte, Schleiermacher and Hegel, for all their differences, manifest a common belief in self-sufficiency as an aspect of freedom and therefore of perfection, relating this belief to conceptions of God and the state. All tried to unite an idealist metaphysic to a Christian understanding of God, though without conspicuous success. Their insistence on autonomy and autarky must be seen in the context of the contemporary crisis in the relationship between the multiplicity of German states and the unity of the nation. The Napoleonic invasions had brought the issue to a head, when it became clear that a divided Germany was unable to resist the political humiliation of defeat and occupation. Pictured putting the final touches to his *Phänomenologie*, with apparent indifference to the battle of Jena raging outside his window, Hegel too lamented the political disarray of Germany and in his later writings assumed that the borders of the state should coincide with those of the nation to form a self-sufficient whole.

FICHTE

Of all the post-Kantian German writers, it is Fichte whose thought reflects most clearly the analogy between the self-sufficient state and the autarkic God. The idea of self-sufficiency as an essential aspect of perfection emerges particularly in his later works. In the political sphere Fichte's ideal of a 'closed commercial state', set forth in 1800 in his tract of that title, and his subsequent espousal of German unity and the nationalist cause embody the autarkic principle, while his religious writings increasingly portray God as an absolute, unchanging and impassible being. The two principal influences upon Fichte were – in the sphere of thought – the Enlightenment as seen from the Kantian viewpoint and – in the sphere of events – the French Revolution and the Napoleonic invasions of Germany.

Fichte's life and work

Johann Gottlieb Fichte was born in Saxony in 1762, the son of a poor seller of linen ribbons. His early education was financed by a local landlord and he was thus able to study at the universities of Jena and Leipzig. Being refused financial support for further theological studies by the Saxon Protestant Church in 1787, he took work as private tutor to a succession of rich families. He became a fervent disciple of Immanuel Kant, seeing in his philosophy a possible way of resolving the conflict between a determinism which he had learned from Spinoza and a profound conviction of human free will. Fichte moved to Königsberg to sit at the feet of the master and his early work, *An Attempt at a Critique of all Revelation*, published anonymously in 1792, was widely believed to be by Kant himself, so closely did it follow his ideas.

Fichte here saw religion as based upon practical reason and he regarded God as the postulate which makes sense of our moral experience rather than as a being whose existence explains the origin of this experience.[17] He firmly rejected a heteronomous ethic which derives moral judgments from divine commands, insisting that the content of divine law is precisely the same as that of practical reason. The fact that a duty is also seen as being commanded by God adds gravity and strengthens the efficacy of the moral law by providing an additional (but preliminary) motive for acting rightly, without making that duty in any way more binding.[18] This motive must, indeed, soon be replaced by the autonomous desire of duty for duty's sake. With the deist writers of the earlier part of the century, he thus believed that divine revelation merely reissues information which can be derived by human reason.

In 1794 Fichte was appointed to a chair in Jena. Unhappy with the Kantian distinction between a knowable world of phenomena and an unknowable world of reality, Fichte rejected the notion of an external world of objects over against the experiencing self. Such 'realism' could not, he believed, account for the self-conscious ego, nor for the fact of human freedom. A world of objects exists only in so far as these objects are posited by the ego. The ego is thus the transcendental principle of subjectivity, which can never be objectified or causally determined, for it is itself the presupposition of all objectifications. It was this priority of the ego which guaranteed for Fichte the principle of human freedom. He developed this position in his abstruse *Wissenschaftslehre* (1794) and in more popular writings such as *The Vocation of Man* (1800). Though rejecting Kant's conclusions, he developed his own early philosophy within the broad parameters of the transcendental method.

While at Jena Fichte also published in 1796 his treatise on *The Science of Rights* (1796) and *The System of Ethics* (1798). The influence of both Kant and Rousseau is apparent. In the former work Fichte attempted to found an organically conceived state upon the basis of a contract between individuals. In his later writings, however, he placed greater emphasis on the organic nature of the whole and less upon the individualist basis.[19] After five years in Jena he was dismissed on a charge of atheism. In his essay on 'Our Belief in a Divine Government of the Universe', he had in fact identified God with the moral order and concluded that 'we do not and cannot grasp any other God'.[20] There can be no rational justification, he argued, for inferring the existence of a separate entity as the cause of the world order. Fichte was keen, however, to distinguish his position from that of many Romantics, whose attempt to unite idealism with pantheism he rejected. He saw the tendency to divinise nature as undermining human freedom.

On leaving Jena, Fichte moved first to Berlin and eventually secured a post at the University of Erlangen. This was the era of Napoleon's defeat of Prussia and the French occupation of Germany. Fichte continued to lecture widely and in 1807 gave his celebrated 'Addresses to the German Nation', which called for a national regeneration in the face of the Napoleonic invasions of Germany. In 1811 he became rector of the new University of Berlin, at which Schleiermacher held a chair of theology. He died in 1814.

As Fichte moved away from Kant's philosophy, he began to adopt different political positions. In place of the Kantian notion of an interdependent community of states, he defended the idea of self-sufficient states based upon natural geographical boundaries or, in his later writings, upon linguistic and cultural divisions. In his religious thinking, however, the influence of Kant remained and he continued to interpret and judge religious statements by the criterion of their moral effect. Nevertheless on the one hand he attributed to speculative reason a more important role in religion than Kant would have allowed, moving in his later writings towards a form of theism, or at least absolute idealism. On the other hand there are in his popular religious works definite traces of a pietism somewhat similar to that of Schleiermacher. Throughout these writings a tension is evident between the God of speculative philosophy and the God of moral and religious experience. Willing to follow neither the path of Hegel nor that of Schleiermacher, he never succeeded in resolving this tension.

The self-sufficient state

Fichte's 'Addresses to the German Nation' established his reputation as a leading theorist of German Romantic nationalism, yet some of his ideas were anticipated in his tract on 'The Closed Commercial State' seven years earlier. In this work he had put forward the ideal of a state which is wholly self-sufficient with respect to basic economic needs and which is thus able to cease from all foreign commerce. 'The state', he insisted, 'should shut itself off from all commerce with foreign countries and form a separate commercial body as it has already formed separate legal and political bodies.'[21] Fichte maintained that states are natural units, whose borders are geographically determined by rivers, mountains and seas. These borders are more significant from the standpoint of economic self-sufficiency than from that of military defence. When the borders of states defy nature and cut across geographical boundaries war is the consequence. The British Isles, for example, are naturally a part of France and the political separation between them has led to endless conflict.

Fichte claimed that international commerce leads states to seek hegemony in the world market and to expand their territory beyond their natural boundaries. The closed commercial state on the other hand will be content with its natural borders and will have no incentive to expand beyond them. The only kind of foreign commerce permitted would be of goods which cannot be grown in a country owing to climate; in this case there would be a direct exchange of goods between one country and another. Fichte opposed foreign travel undertaken for idle curiosity and believed that it should be restricted to artists and scholars like himself, who should be sent abroad at public expense.

While his earlier tract is concerned largely with the state, seeing its borders determined by physical factors, his 'Addresses' echo Herder in speaking rather of the nation; here he envisaged its borders as constituted by cultural and particularly by linguistic factors: 'the inner frontier drawn by the spiritual nature of man'. The mere fact that a group of men and women live together protected by rivers or mountains does not make them a nation; this is the product of 'a far higher law of nature'.[22] Prior to accepting this nationalist position Fichte appears to have passed through a brief 'Europeanist' phase when, in 1804–5, he argued that Europeans are essentially one people and that the continent should be seen as 'the one true fatherland'.[23] Soon, however, he moved on in his first dialogue on patriotism to a belief in the principle of national unity based upon a notion of linguistic identity and national character:

B. – You are a German, are you not?

A. – No. I'm not a German. I am a Prussian. More than that I am a patriotic Prussian.

B. – Understand me rightly. The separation of Prussians from the rest of the Germans is purely artificial. . . . The separation of the Germans from the other European nations is based on Nature. Through a common language and through national characteristics which unite the Germans, they are separated from the others.[24]

This dialogue, written prior to the Prussian defeat at Jena, was followed by a second dialogue. Here he advocated the creation of a national church, committed to a minimum of dogmatic beliefs but calculated to strengthen national sentiment. In an extraordinary passage he pictured the congregation gathering outside the church building in the early morning. The doors being opened they would file in to the accompaniment of soft music. When all were seated, curtains at the altar would be drawn aside to reveal the parish armoury of cannons, muskets and other weaponry. The Justice of the Peace would then unfurl the national flag and the service would begin. This somewhat anticipated the *Catéchisme de la révolution* printed by the state press of Haiti in 1964, which defined the Duvalierist sacrament of extreme unction as 'a sacrament instituted by the popular army, the civil militia and the Haitian people . . . to crush with grenades, mortars, mausers, bazookas and flame throwers' the enemies of the revolution.

Fichte's 'Addresses' appear to have made little impact at the time. His disciples later speculated why it was that the occupying French forces permitted such stirring exhortations to continue. The unflattering truth is that, as not infrequently happens with visiting lecturers, the audience was small and the authorities were unaware of their being given. In these addresses the philosopher reminded his hearers that the German people had been advised some years earlier to form a closed commercial state but had ignored the call, principally because of 'our idolatrous veneration of coined metals'. The nation had in fact become more and more dependent 'upon the unnecessary wares produced in foreign lands'. It had adopted words of Latin origin, rather than retaining a German vocabulary. Why speak of *Humanität* rather than *Menschenfreundlichkeit*?[25] Such was the plight of Germany, 'sunk into this state of dependence', that deliverance could come by no normal means.

Fichte called for a 'higher patriotism, which embraces the nation as the vesture of the eternal', and for a moral regeneration of the German people: 'The means of salvation which I promise to indicate consists in the fashioning of an entirely new self.'[26] K.S. Pinson has noted how the philosopher here used religious terminology. 'The national *Wiedergeburt* (regeneration) of Fichte's *Reden* and of the Prussian War of Liberation', he observes, 'is but a transfer of an idea from the realm of religious experience to that of national activity.'[27]

This notion of a new self has also been characteristic of some recent nationalist movements in post-colonial states.[28] It is through education that this new self is to be born; 'education alone . . . can save us from all the ills that oppress us.'[29] Fichte saw in the educational theories of Pestalozzi a means of achieving this end and, anticipating Thomas Arnold and William Temple, he saw the school as a microcosm of the ideal state. The school is, he declared, 'a little economic state' where 'no article of food, clothing, etc., and, so far as this is possible, no tool is to be used, which is not produced and made there'.[30]

In his later writings Fichte thus believed, like all nationalists, that the political borders of the state should follow the cultural boundaries of the nation, but that – as happened in ancient Greece – nation and state had become separated in Germany. Political borders must therefore be redrawn. Yet he also maintained that it was wrong for a state to attempt to incorporate foreign nations within it. Now when the state's borders are determined by physical factors (incorporating the idea that the state should be large and diverse enough to permit economic autarky) this anti-expansionist principle makes sense. More problematic is the situation of the nation delineated by cultural and linguistic factors. What guarantee is there that the territory it occupies will form a militarily defensible and economically viable unit (let alone one capable of autarky)? Such a nation-state will surely be tempted to pursue an aggressive policy in order to achieve that degree of autarky which is necessary for its integrity. Fichte seems to have recognised this danger and he saw a balance of power among these states as the sole means of restricting such expansionist tendencies.

In its idea, nationalism is necessarily opposed to imperialism, yet in practice frequently leads to it. In the search either for economic self-sufficiency or for defensible natural boundaries, imperial expansion follows inexorably. This tendency is reinforced by the belief, frequently entertained by nationalists, that their own nation has a universal mission – it exists not just for itself but for the benefit of the whole human race. Fichte's assertion that only Germans really understand the science of knowledge (*Wissenschaft*) and that their vocation is to develop it, sharing its benefits with others, has clear imperialistic implications.

Following Rousseau, Fichte attempted to found an organic and total state on the basis of an individualistic conception of consent. 'In our own Age', he declared, 'more than at any previous time, every Citizen with all his powers, is subjected to the purpose of the State, is thoroughly penetrated by it and so has become its instrument.' He saw the state as a microcosm which 'must regard itself as a completed whole'.[31] To suggest, with a modern writer, that he swung violently between an 'almost insanely individualist' and 'a ruthlessly authoritarian' position is somewhat misleading.[32] For individualism and authoritarianism ought not to be seen as opposite poles; individualism has frequently provided the basis upon which authoritarian regimes have been built. Being a disciple of Rousseau, Fichte had little conception of the importance and legitimacy of groups intermediate between the state and the citizen, and it is perhaps this weakness which partially accounts for his authoritarianism.[33]

The autarkic God

In his tract on the closed commercial state Fichte had argued against all forms of dependence upon foreign countries; in the following year he characterised God, the Absolute, as 'reposing within and upon itself, without change or alteration, firm and complete of itself . . . without any foreign influence; for every thing foreign must vanish when we speak of the Absolute'.[34]

In attempting to understand Fichte's conception of God it is necessary to distinguish three periods. His Kantian phase continued until the mid-1790s; this was followed by a post-Kantian period lasting to the turn of the century; a final phase was characterised by a move towards absolute idealism. Throughout his life, however, he recognised a tension between the God of piety and religion – the God of the heart – and the God of the philosophers, the immutable first cause, which he had noted in his 'Aphorisms on Religion and Deism' (1790).

In his early writings he had denied that anything can be said about God as he really is – in himself he is unknowable. God may be considered only as he has relations with humans; 'concerning his objective existence all further investigations are completely impossible.' The 'sensuous presentations of divine attributes' are not to be taken as descriptive of God but rather to be seen as regulative ideas. Any suggestion that God can be affected by human 'whining and contrition' was rejected as incompatible with the divine impassibility.[35] Yet even in these early writings he was tempted to go further and wrote of certain properties being ascribed to God as the first steps towards a speculative knowledge. 'These properties', he went on, 'show God as an unchanging, never suffering, omnipotent Being.'[36]

Manifestly dissatisfied with Kantian dualism, Fichte began to identify God with the moral order as a super-sensible ordering reality. This was his position by the turn of the century. 'Every belief in a divine being which contains more than this concept of the moral order is, to that extent, imagination and superstition.'[37] It was this reductionism which had led to Fichte's dismissal from Jena on a charge of atheism. Though he vigorously defended his position, his ideas were soon on the move once again and in his popular lectures on *The Vocation of Man* he referred to God as infinite will, and began to develop a form of absolute idealism.

In later life Fichte was more prepared to elaborate on the true nature of God, whom he identified with the absolute. In his popular lectures of 1805 on 'The Nature of the Scholar' he spoke of God as 'absolute, self-comprehending unity, without change or variableness'.[38] Again in his 'Way Towards the Blessed Life' he attacked the idea of an 'arbitrary and capricious God' and spoke of him in terms of a 'self-comprehending, self-sufficient and absolutely unchangeable unity'. He asserted that this God can be approached only by pure thought, that

> only through a systematic study of philosophy is it possible for man to elevate himself to Religion and its blessings, and that everyone who is not a philosopher must remain for ever shut out from God and his kingdom. . . . True God and the True Religion are to be approached and comprehended only by pure Thought.

Fichte did, however, maintain – somewhat unconvincingly – that it is possible for the fruits of such a philosophical understanding to be communicated, 'in a generally comprehensible form', to those who are without the benefit of university education.[39]

In his early writings Fichte clearly believed that the religious nature of man requires a God 'who permits him to petition, who feels suffering and friendship', one who may be pictured in frankly anthropomorphic terms as 'the supreme world sovereign . . . judge of rational spirits . . . subordinated to no one, hence also the lawgiver'.[40] Yet he saw this as regulative rather than speculative language and rejected, in the words of Xavier Léon, a God who 'wears the mask of the human figure and the mark of finitude', as an idol.[41] The Christian faith is, in his view, related more to the feelings than to the speculative thought of mankind – 'determined more for the heart than for the understanding' – and he thus used anthropomorphic language 'until the reason of man arose to a consequential concept of deity'.[42]

Like Hegel, Fichte thus appears to have believed that a conceptual knowledge of God, achieved by pure thought, is superior to speaking of him in terms of images. I say 'appears', because in some places he declaimed in an almost existentialist way about life, action and commitment as the means by which humans truly know. In his *Science of Rights* he insisted that the ego should not be thought of as some essential substance which *possesses* certain powers to act in this way or that; rather it must be seen as action itself: 'it is what it acts, and when it does not act it is not at all.'[43] In *The Vocation of Man* he spoke of a voice loudly proclaiming, 'Not merely to know, but according to thy knowledge to do, is thy vocation . . . for action thou art here; thine action, and thine action alone, determines thy worth.'[44] This voice, he claimed, leads us from mere cognition to something beyond and even opposed to knowledge. The free action of the self-conscious individual transcends all intellectual and reflective thought. It is this commitment – this faith – which 'lends a sanction to knowledge' and 'proceeds from the will, not from the understanding'.[45] The kind of philosophy a person chooses is determined by the sort of person he or she is.[46]

For Fichte, therefore, truth is discovered not by detached, impartial speculation but by a commitment of the conscience. Knowing is achieved by becoming involved with reality, not by mere contemplation. 'My world', he declared, 'is the object and sphere of my duties, and absolutely nothing more. . . . We do not act because we know, but we know because we are called upon to act:– the practical reason is the root of all reason.'[47] Fichte therefore criticised the belief of some Kantians that *a priori* conceptions, or categories, exist in the mind in advance of all experience, 'like empty rows of shelves, waiting to have something put on them'.[48]

It is difficult to reconcile all this with the idea – shared by Hegel – that ultimate reality is known most fully by pure thought and in conceptual form. Perhaps we can interpret what he said about that pure thought, which is necessary for a true knowledge of God, as thought which must stem from action and commitment. In any case the idea of God always involves self-sufficiency. The idea of independence – *Selbständigkeit* – which played such a vital role in Fichte's ethical theory as the necessary condition for free and moral action, becomes the goal of the state, though it is perfectly realised only in God. We are dependent, absolutely dependent upon him; he is in no way dependent upon us. There is a strong Lutheran strain in his thinking. Whatever man does, as man, is worthless:

Only when a foreign power takes possession of him, and urges him forward, and lives within him in room of his own energy, does true and real existence first take up its abode in his life. This foreign power is God.[49]

Fichte believed that the religious attitude involves above all acceptance of what happens in the world as the will of God, for all things work for good for those who love God. There is patently a tension between his piety and his insistence on independence (*Selbständigkeit*) or self-activity (*Selbsttätigkeit*) in his ethical theories.

The story is told of a devoted student of Fichte's who took a copy of the master's 'Way towards a Blessed Life' to the war front with him. During the battle he was shot, but the bullet was stopped by the book. On examining the book, the student observed that the bullet came to rest at the words:

The truly moral and religious man . . . must accept everything just as it happens; for everything that comes to pass is the will of God with him, and therefore the best that can possibly come to pass.[50]

There is, in these sentiments, much in common with the piety of Friedrich Schleiermacher and it is to his life and works that I now turn.

SCHLEIERMACHER

Friedrich Daniel Ernst Schleiermacher was possibly the most influential Protestant theologian since Calvin. Here I consider only one aspect of his thought: his belief that perfection involves self-sufficiency with respect both to political and to religious life. His growing devotion to the cause of German nationalism, during the years of the Napoleonic invasions, is in part a consequence of his conviction that Prussia was unable on her own to achieve the degree of independence appropriate for the existence of a state. His analogous assumption of divine autarky played an important part in the development of his theology and also led to his belief that the life of the individual Christian – in so far as it shares in the life of God – is characterised by a tranquillity which transcends the conflicts of the secular world. Schleiermacher thus made a major contribution to the growth in Germany of an authoritarian nationalism in which the individual Christian plays a generally quietist role, obeying the powers that be and accepting the political arrangements of the time. It should, however, be emphasised that I am here referring to the long-term social consequences of his theology rather than to the actual political positions he advocated or adopted, which – as we shall see – were sometimes hostile to the established order and to the ruling class of his day.

Prophet and preacher

Born in 1768 at Breslau, the son of an army chaplain of the Reformed Church, the young Schleiermacher was sent to school with the Herrnhuter, or Moravian, Brethren. Although he grew critical of some aspects of their pietism, this early experience had a lasting effect on his theology. In 1787 he entered the University of Halle, which had been a centre of pietism for many years. Then, like Fichte, he was for a while private tutor to an aristocratic family. After ordination in the Reformed Church, he became hospital chaplain in Berlin, where he published his celebrated *Speeches on Religion* (1799) and his *Soliloquies* (1800), both characterised by a strongly Romantic emphasis upon personal religious experience. Schleiermacher was appointed Professor of Theology at Halle in 1804. With the Prussian defeat of 1807, he returned to Berlin, where he soon became pastor at Trinity Church and later Professor of Theology in the new University of Berlin, where he remained until his death in 1834.[51]

In times of social unrest or political instability governments tend to take more notice of ecclesiastical affairs than in quieter periods. What were merely *Pfaffengezanken* – parsons' quarrels – for eighteenth-century Prussian governments became of political moment. The clergy were urged by the government to support the national struggle and to give unambiguous allegiance to the autocratic regime of the king. Though he enthusiastically supported patriotic calls to sacrifice in the struggle against Bonaparte, Schleiermacher was critical of what he called the 'caste-spirit' of Prussian conservatism and became something of a spokesman of the rising liberal middle class. In the years following the defeat of the French he was engaged in preaching, teaching and administering the theological faculty in Berlin, and in writing his impressive and influential book on *The Christian Faith* (1821–2).

Although he adopted a moderate and conciliatory approach to the political problems of his day, Schleiermacher's conservative critics, in 1822, made an unsuccessful attempt to have him removed from his chair. As time went on, however, he appears to have become reconciled to the government and was considerably embarrassed when a French newspaper in 1831 included him as one of the leaders of the opposition in Berlin. He replied by claiming, 'I shall always be on the side of the king.'[52] Though a defender of monarchy, he maintained that in the case of a true king – as distinct from a despot – subjects have the right of petition while the king, 'spiritually united with his people', proclaims 'only such acts of will as his subjects will approve of'.[53] Here we find a striking anticipation of the populist decisionism of Carl Schmitt.

Schleiermacher's intellectual development is marked by a gradual move away from a stress on the experience of the individual in the context of family and small community towards a recognition of the larger units – church and nation – to which men and women belong, and which powerfully influence their political and religious lives. In his early *Soliloquies* he wrote of the only realities as being the individual and the 'infinite totality of spiritual beings'.[54] These soliloquies do, however, contain seeds of a later nationalism. The author there made reference to 'the individual character' which each state should possess and to the 'readiness to set one's life at stake rather than see the fatherland perish'; also he was critical of the *laissez-faire* theories being advocated by von Humboldt and others.[55] In his religious writings the emphasis shifted from seeing religion as based on the feelings and personal intuitions of the believer to a notion of the collective experience of the Christian church as the source of Christian doctrines which were for him 'accounts of the Christian religious affections set forth in speech'.[56] This later emphasis is, however, anticipated in the fifth of the *Speeches* where he spoke of the church as 'indispensable for every religious man'.[57]

The German nation

The French invasion of Germany convinced Schleiermacher and many others of the inadequacy of a merely Prussian patriotism and he became a fervent advocate of German unity. Drawing on examples from classical history, in his speech to the Royal Academy of Sciences of 1814, he observed: 'The individual Greek states ended as martyrs to this petty form of political existence, where a loose federative bond could not protect them.'[58] States are not, he insisted, made by deliberate human action but are natural entities. He came to accept the basic dogma of nationalism that the borders of the state should follow those of the nation, for the nation, like the church, is an organic whole, manifesting a national character and sharing a common destiny.[59] It should, however, be emphasised that he opposed any identification of church and state, being critical of

Lutheran positions on this question. Not only must the church be distinguished from the state; it ought ideally to be separated from it.[60]

Schleiermacher defended monarchy as the best form of government, symbolising the unity of the nation, and even suggested that the king must be absolute in order to give liberty to his people. Like God, the monarch must be totally free from dependence; he is omnipresent – and therefore must be free from private interests or business activities, which would tie him to particular places or groups – and eternal, for in a hereditary monarchy the king cannot die.[61] The theologian thus anticipated Hegel's insistence that the king must symbolise the self-sufficiency and independence of the state, by his detachment from private interests and freedom from commercial entanglements. The king is the source of liberties and rights. The people's share in governing is seen as a grant of the monarch.[62]

Echoing Herder, Schleiermacher saw language as playing a central role in constituting German nationality and he defended the conception of the *Volksstaat*.[63] He frequently insisted on the ideal of an independent nation – 'its peculiar nationality should be relieved from the pressure of foreign dominion' – and he affirmed the 'sacred sense of the rights of nations and states'.[64] He also proclaimed, in words which might have been spoken by Enoch Powell, that a nation must be protected from immigration:

> Every nation, my friends, which has developed to a certain height is degraded by receiving into it a foreign element, even though that may be good in itself; for God has imparted to each its own nature, and has therefore marked out bounds and limits for the habitations of the different races of men on the face of the earth.[65]

It is not surprising therefore that Schleiermacher regarded resistance to the Napoleonic invasion as a sacred duty. It must be, not simply the work of kings with their hired armies, but a truly popular movement, 'a struggle that will unite sovereign and people by a more beautiful bond than has existed for centuries'.[66] Despite his importance as one of the fathers of German Romantic nationalism, however, his primary significance is as a theologian.

Schleiermacher's God

Following in the footsteps of Kant, Schleiermacher believed that speculative philosophy, or metaphysics, can make no significant contribution to religion, that is to the knowledge of God. Even the orthodox conception of God as a personal transcendent being, he taught in the *Speeches*, is 'only one way of characterizing God'. To treat this concept as some kind of description of God is 'vain mythology'.[67] 'The usual conception of God', he wrote in a celebrated sentence, 'as one single being outside of the world and behind the world is not the beginning and the end of religion.'[68] To suggest that we can come to know anything significant about God by human reasoning would, he explained, mean that religion is a question of knowledge rather than of feeling and consciousness. Schleiermacher appears at this point radically to diverge from Plato, whose ideas exercised a considerable attraction for him. Anything that can properly be said about God is regulative rather than speculative in its reference. We speak of God as he relates to the world and can say nothing about him as he is in himself.

The tendency to reduce religion to philosophy, to a matter of 'knowing', was thus resisted. Schleiermacher also insisted that it may not be reduced to morality – to 'acting'. Piety is not the craving for 'a mess of metaphysical and ethical crumbs', but is constituted by a quite distinct feeling (*Gefühl*) of absolute or utter dependence.[69] Like Calvin, with whom he shared more than is at first apparent, he was suspicious of speculation, emphasising the practical nature of Christian faith. 'The duty of a Theologian', wrote the Genevan reformer, 'is not to tickle the ear but confirm the conscience, by teaching what is true, certain and useful.'[70]

In *The Christian Faith* Schleiermacher stated that any philosophy is compatible with Christian faith 'so long as it allows an object to which the feeling of absolute dependence can relate itself'.[71] Elsewhere he referred to God as the 'whence' of our pious feelings. He thus seems to have been prepared – with Kant – to talk about the 'existence' of God, but beyond this all we can say relates to 'the being of God in the world'; any attempt to speak of 'God in himself' would be disloyal to the character of the discipline of theology.[72]

Bearing this in mind, what does Schleiermacher say about God, particularly with respect to his self-sufficiency? He insisted that religion consists essentially in a consciousness or feeling of absolute dependence. The question arises whether this feeling in some way reflects reality or whether its sole reference is subjective. When a person feels depressed this says nothing about the state of the world outside. When, in contrast, a hand is plunged into cold water it usually feels cold; the feeling is an indication of what is the case in the world. In his later work at least, it appears that Schleiermacher thought of the feeling of absolute dependence as reflecting something true about a person's relationship to God. He says for example that there can be 'no such thing as a feeling of absolute freedom', on the ground that such *a state* of absolute freedom is impossible rather than because it is psychologically unknown. Some feelings are clearly more valid than others.

For Schleiermacher the attributes of God cannot be derived from his essence, but only from our experience of his action among us. God is thought of as the absolute cause of our existence and must be conceived, in contrast to all relative causes, as omnipotent and eternal, as omnipresent and omniscient.[73] Implicit in the eternity or timelessness of God is the notion of his unchangeability. 'No religious emotion shall be so interpreted, and no statement about God so understood, as to make it necessary to assume an alteration in God of any kind.'[74] Furthermore God must be conceived as independent – not depending upon anything beyond himself. Schleiermacher's rejection of miracle – conceived as a supernatural intervention in the natural order – is supported by an observation that such arbitrary divine action would imply incompetence and lack of true omnipotence in the Creator.[75]

As omnipotent and 'Lord over all', God cannot be obligated. Like the earthly monarch, he must be in a certain respect absolute; he 'can stand under no law'.[76] Schleiermacher furthermore rejected any notion of 'a self-limitation of the divine omnipotence'.[77] While discussing Trinitarian doctrine, Schleiermacher assumed that dependence involves imperfection and implies subordination. Thus he rejected any real distinctions in the godhead, maintaining that such distinctions would imply that 'the Father is superior to the other two Persons', owing to the dependence of the Son on the Father and the 'twofold dependence' of the Spirit (in western theology).[78]

There are two interesting consequences of this notion of God. If he is unchangeable and independent then he cannot suffer; he is impassible. That the divine nature cannot suffer was accepted by him as 'a truth long recognized' and he used it to refute a false view of the atonement which depends upon the sufferings of Christ being infinite. Even with respect to his human nature, there is a suggestion that Schleiermacher's preference for the Johannine accounts of Jesus's life derive partly from an assumption that self-sufficiency is an aspect of his perfection. This emerges particularly in his rejection of the synoptic account of Jesus in the Garden of Gethsemane as implying a weakness 'that is not far from sin'.[79]

The second consequence is Schleiermacher's denial that in prayer human beings can 'exert an influence on God'. Such an idea, involving as it would the failure to recognise that 'there can be no relation of interaction between creature and Creator', is a lapse into magic.[80] If we do lay before God a wish that something might happen in the world, we must be aware 'that we are laying it before the unchangeable' and that true prayer has the result of 'moderating the wish that it expressed, of replacing the eager desire with quiet submission, the anxious expectation with devout calmness'.[81] It is thus a reaffirmation of that consciousness of absolute dependence which is the essence of religion.

Just as God is 'high above all change', knowing neither joy nor pain, so the Christian, participating in the divine being, 'reaches beyond both and constantly draws near to a quiet peace'.[82] As Karl Barth has observed, Schleiermacher's ideal of a Christian life is characterised by peace and tranquillity. Just as Jesus was above the controversies of his day and manifested in his life 'equanimity, the same unshakable calm in all relationships', so must Christians rise above the conflicts and passions of their day and enjoy peace.[83] The final section of the *Soliloquies*, on 'youth and age', proclaims an inner freedom and self-sufficiency which triumphs over the claims of time; towards the end of his life, writing to a friend, he referred to himself as 'your whitehaired but still vigorous and *unchanging* friend'.[84]

The attempt by Robert R. Williams to paint Schleiermacher as a founding father of process theology is ingenious but unconvincing. He writes that, for the German, 'God's immutability is to be understood not in classical terms of self-sufficient power and being, but as eternal love.' Williams claims that, for Schleiermacher, the exercise of God's power in the act of creation is limited by his love, while the omnipotence of divine love is manifested in his redemptive work. But, as we have seen, Schleiermacher explicitly rejected any idea of divine self-limitation. Again, Williams refers to a 'reciprocity between God and the world', asserting that for Schleiermacher 'God takes account of the world, and thus change and alteration are reflected into [*sic*] God. The immutability of divine love *requires* the mutability of divine power.'[85] From what I have already said it should be clear that Schleiermacher would have discounted any such suggestions. What Williams is in fact doing is developing a part of Schleiermacher's position in a way which conflicts with much of what the German theologian explicitly wrote. He comes clean at the end of his book when he writes, 'I admit that I have had to tug and pull a bit to coax a concept of divine mutability out of Schleiermacher', but that this concept is 'required by his overall argument'.[86] Williams's assertions in fact support my position in this chapter that the idea of divine autarky was not arrived at by Schleiermacher simply through employing the theological method he claimed to follow but was derived in part from elsewhere.

The coherence of Schleiermacher

As with Fichte, the assumption that perfection involves self-sufficiency and changelessness played a major part in Schleiermacher's thinking. For one who purported to derive theology from the religious experience – the pious feelings – of believers, it is curious that he took little note of the Old Testament idea of a God who loves and hates, who changes his mind and who suffers with his people. It is, in fact, a feature of his preaching that he paid almost no attention to the Old Testament, regarding the Hebrew experience of God, prior to the advent of the Redeemer, as entirely superseded and of no relevance to the life of the Christian. Again, the parables of Jesus – such as the unjust judge – suggest more of a reciprocal relationship between God and humanity than his theology allows. By excluding all religious experiences that could not be subsumed under the feeling of absolute dependence, Schleiermacher ensured an image of God's sovereign independence which almost makes Calvin look liberal.

In *The Christian Faith* Schleiermacher insisted that love and wisdom are the two principal attributes which reveal God's nature, yet he failed to explain how love can convincingly be portrayed as impassible – how, for example, the lover can be totally unmoved by the self-destructive actions of the beloved. Elsewhere, however, he noted this characteristic of love, which involves the lover being affected by the beloved. This led him to call into question one of the principal images which he used for picturing God's relationship to the world – that of an omnipotent and loving ruler. In *The Christian Faith* he referred frequently to God's government of the world (*Weltregierung*). Nevertheless he regarded the image as defective because of the necessary element of mutability implied in the concept of loving ruler. The notion of the universe as God's work of art (*Kunstwerk*) was, therefore, from this standpoint superior.[87]

Van Harvey has asserted that even, if one accepts the notion of absolute dependence as the essence of religion, our absolute dependence on God does not imply his absolute independence. 'That God is absolutely independent', he writes, 'is not given in the feeling of absolute dependence.' If this were indeed so, Schleier-macher's insistence on the autarky of God must be seen as an illicit importation from idealist philosophy, reinforced by the political analogy, rather than as a legitimate deduction from the religious experience of absolute dependence. If the *feeling* of absolute dependence is a valid indication of an actual *state* of absolute dependence (which I have argued is Schleiermacher's view) then Harvey is wrong. Absolute dependence means ultimate dependence. If God were to depend on anything beyond himself, then we may be *immediately* dependent on God, but we would be absolutely dependent on that upon which God depends. 'It doesn't follow . . . from the fact that we are absolutely dependent on God', asserts Harvey, 'that God is absolutely *in*dependent from us.'[88] The relationship would not then be one of absolute dependence but interdependence, which is precisely the relationship Schleiermacher wished to reject. It may therefore be concluded that God's autarky is a corollary of our absolute dependence. Nevertheless we may still see the importance of idealist philosophy and political experience in his religious thought. The feeling of absolute dependence itself is given such prominence in his system precisely because it does imply divine independence and a rejection of anything approaching a reciprocal relationship between ruler and ruled.

The themes of human dependence on and subjection to divine and political authority – to an alien power – characterise the thought of Schleiermacher. The emphasis upon the 'good pleasure' of an apparently arbitrary God,[89] deriving from his Calvinist background, and his belief in political 'decisionism' are linked. Obedience to orders was clearly reckoned by Schleiermacher to be of the essence of this subordination. A passage in his *Life of Jesus* (1832) reflects this belief. Discussing the question of to whom the saying of Jesus at his crucifixion, 'Father forgive them', was directed, he maintained:

> Nothing had to be forgiven the soldiers, for no judgment of the morality or the legality of the execution could be passed by them. They could have their own personal feelings on the matter, but these could not influence their actions. They acted only in accordance with their profession. They only carried out a mission that they were commanded by their superiors to perform. They had no right to avoid the duty thrust upon them.[90]

The pleas of war criminals that they were merely following orders thus find their basis in a political and theological tradition to which Schleiermacher made a significant contribution.

HEGEL

'A nation which has a false or bad conception of God', declared Hegel in his posthumously published *Lectures on the Philosophy of Religion*, 'has also a bad State, bad government, bad laws.'[91] Hegel's own conception of God is closely related to his political thought. He drew many analogies between divine and civil authority and I shall be particularly concerned with those that involve ideas of autonomy and autarky in the divine and political spheres, showing how his ideas of religion and politics come together in his peculiar understanding of world history.

Georg Wilhelm Friedrich Hegel was born in 1770 at Stuttgart and was raised in a strongly Lutheran environment.[92] He studied theology in Tübingen and worked as a tutor first in Switzerland, then at Frankfurt. He became critical of the 'positivity' of the Christian religion, believing that orthodox supernaturalism leads to belief in an arbitrary deity and an incoherent universe. He later rejected these judgments and his early writings on Christianity remained unpublished until long after his death.[93] In 1801 he moved to Jena, where he lectured to a dozen or so students and wrote his *Phenomenology of Mind*. He left Jena after the famous battle of 1806 and for some time edited a newspaper and taught in a school. In these years he published the *Science of Logic* and the first edition of his *Encyclopaedia*.

In 1818 Hegel succeeded Fichte in the philosophy chair at Berlin, where he wrote his major treatise on politics, *The Philosophy of Right*, and lectured on many other philosophical topics. He retained a profound interest in theology and moved towards a somewhat more orthodox position in his later years, though the relationship between his philosophy and his religious ideas remains a matter of dispute. He became Rector of the University of Berlin in 1830 but died in the following year.

The secret of Hegel

Hegel's style is frequently enigmatic and abstruse and his philosophical system is complex; his followers and expositors have often thought it necessary to emulate him in this. Commenting on James Hutchison Stirling's book, *The Secret of Hegel*, published in 1865, a wit remarked that if the author had discovered the secret he certainly kept it to himself! Though he shared with Romantic writers a critical approach to Enlightenment rationalism, Hegel concurred with

Fichte's belief that the enterprise it represents – the search for a rational knowledge of the universe – should not be rejected out of hand but should be pursued in another idiom. Like the Romantics, however, he was dissatisfied with the agnosticism and duality bequeathed by Kant, and he joined in their search for an ultimate unity. Yet Hegel dismissed their belief that this unity could be found only by turning from conceptual knowledge to an imaginative appreciation based upon feeling or intuition.

Hegel was not, then, a Romantic *tout court*. If we think of nationalism as involving a belief that the political frontiers of the state should follow the 'natural' or cultural boundaries of a nation, it is not obvious that Hegel should be called a nationalist either. As many recent commentators have insisted, Hegel was no German nationalist, in the tradition of Fichte and Schleiermacher. He denied that the German Empire – composed as it was of hundreds of distinct units – constituted a state, for it lacked effective power to defend its political integrity, and he seems to have manifested little concern that it should become one, for he probably did not think of it as even forming a nation. Nevertheless he did believe that Prussia was a nation and possessed the necessary conditions of statehood. Though he cannot be called a German nationalist, he may properly be called a Prussian nationalist.

There is ample evidence from his later writings, particularly the *Philosophy of Right*, first published in 1821, that Hegel assumed states to be what nations are destined to become. A nation does not begin by being a state but, if it is to realise its true end, it will become one, thereby establishing – through common laws and a constitution – its sovereignty.[94] This position he reaffirmed in successive editions of his *Encyclopaedia*, where he stated, 'Back to the very beginnings of national history we see the several nations each possessing a persistent type of its own.' This peculiar national character is destined to be maintained by the institutions of the state. 'In the existence of a *nation*', he wrote, 'the substantial aim is to be a state and to preserve itself as such.'[95] Hegel spoke of the state as 'the mind [*Geist*] of a nation', by which he meant that the constitution of the state embodies the character and consciousness of the nation in tangible form. Each nation is different and therefore must have a constitution which is 'appropriate to it'.[96]

Kedourie and Avineri are thus wrong in concluding that because Hegel was not interested in German unity he was not a nationalist. It is like saying that a Welshman – believing in independence for his native land – is not a nationalist because he has no interest in a

United Kingdom.[97] There is ample evidence to show that Hegel believed in the existence of historically and culturally defined entities, each with its peculiar character and traditions, which should ultimately manifest its life in the form of a state. Though critical of fanatical nationalists, he appears to have adhered to the basic tenet of nationalism that the political frontiers of the state should follow the natural boundaries of the nation.

Autonomy of the nation-state

It is not possible here to enter fully into the intricacies of Hegel's political and theological thought; we can merely look at how he pictured both God and the state in terms of self-sufficiency, and how he thereby contributed to a way of thinking which was to become highly significant in the modern world. What both God and the state have in common is 'spirit' (*Geist*). God, for Hegel, is absolute spirit while the state is objective spirit, that is spirit made concrete in the world. The very essence of spirit is freedom (*Freiheit*), which involves autonomy, or self-sufficiency; the word he frequently used is *Selbständigkeit*, which he effectively equated with freedom.[98] The ancient Stoics had taught that there is in all humans a drive to become autonomous or self-sufficient. The only activity, however, which adequately displays this autonomy is thought, not thought about external objects – for this exhibits a dependence on something beyond itself – but rather contemplation.

For Hegel, following Aristotle, such independence is not possible for individual humans, because it is only in the context of a political community that they can develop their full potential. One who is incapable of communal life or is so self-sufficient that he or she does not need it is either a beast or a god.[99] For the German philosopher, as for the Greek, it is the state which alone may, on earth (objectively), manifest a kind of self-sufficiency. Individual citizens, by seeing themselves as parts of an ethical community, are able to maximise their freedom – wishing and choosing to do what is demanded by the situation, and so uniting what Hegel called 'subjective' and 'objective' freedom. Absolute autarky is to be found only in God – or the absolute – who ultimately embraces the totality of being.

For those unfamiliar with Hegel's conception of the state it is worth saying a few words. When he referred, in his mature writings, to the state he did not mean in the first instance the machinery of government, the civil service or the military forces. The state is an idea, which he believed to be realised more or less adequately in the 'states' of his day. In so far as these 'states' were structured so that the citizens were able to live what he called the ethical life – that is to do what is right, what the situation demands (objectively), but to do it as a matter of choice (subjectively) – the state is concretely manifested. The state must assume the existence of a structure of family life and a system which caters for the needs of people (what he called 'civil society') but it is an idea distinct from these and is symbolised and made objective in a constitution.

Hegel claimed that the relationship between states can in certain respects be compared to that between individuals in civil society. Yet within the structure of civil society the units are interdependent in various ways, while states are 'wholes whose needs are met within their own borders'.[100] Hegel thus assumed the autarkic nature of the state. The rapturous language which he frequently used about the state, as a 'divine idea', 'absolutely rational' and so on, has led to a belief that he defended totalitarian dictatorship and even that he was the direct ancestor of Nazi political theories. In two chapters of misrepresentation and misquotation, Karl Popper set the tone for this jihad against Hegel.[101] As few English philosophers of the 1940s and 1950s had bothered to read Hegel, this diatribe remained virtually unchallenged for several years. Those in Scotland or at Merton College who knew the subject were understandably stunned. When Hegel used such language about the state he was clearly referring not to any particular state, but to what the state stands for – the ethical life or human fulfilment in the context of a just and free community. This is why he could say that 'man must . . . venerate the state as a secular deity'.[102] This language is strikingly similar to that used earlier by Thomas Hobbes, who had referred to the sovereign as a 'mortal God'.[103]

Like Aristotle, Hegel realised that the kind of autarky which is appropriate for the state is possible only when a high degree of plurality and diversity is manifested. He therefore insisted on the importance of classes, estates, corporations and regional governments in what may be called an articulated state.[104] He observed that in the large modern state it is only in the context of these groups that the individual citizen can hope to participate in public life and, in a now celebrated passage, he denounced the belief that the state is a machine with a single spring imparting movement to all the rest – a belief that leads to an 'illiberal jealousy' of all corporations and groups by central governments.[105]

This sociological pluralism of Hegel is, however, largely nullified by an ultimate political monism, whereby the central authority, symbolised by the 'immutably sacrosanct' person of the monarch, delegates, or hands over, powers to these subordinate bodies. The notion that these bodies might have inherent rights not derived from the centre was unknown to Hegel.[106] He insisted on the 'sovereignty of the state', as a principle according to which the particular interests of corporations and other groups 'must be subordinated to the higher interests of the state'.[107] This belief in a higher interest or a general welfare, as a substantive end which governments should pursue, distinguishes Hegel from the political pluralists who denied such a common end, believing that it is the proper role of government to provide a structure within which individuals and groups can pursue substantive ends chosen by themselves.

Hegel laid considerable emphasis on the importance of a constitution and on the distinctive role of the monarch. He believed that all states should have a written constitution and a codified system of laws and he was therefore critical of the British form of government. There is, however, no single pattern of constitution which is right for all countries at all times; rather each should have a system appropriate to its peculiar culture and tradition. Yet he was able to outline certain principles which an ideal constitution would embody.[108] There must be an organ responsible for determining general laws (the legislature) and another which subsumes individual cases under these laws (the executive).

Hegel also insisted that there must be a third element in the constitution which symbolises the positive and subjective aspect of law – which pronounces the 'I will'. This 'ultimate self', in which the will of the state is concentrated, is the monarch, whose existence – like that of God, in the so-called ontological argument – is necessarily implied by the very concept.[109] The actual substantive powers of the monarch are minimal, for it is the legislature which decides what the law should be according to rational criteria, and the executive which puts it into force. The distinctive principle of the crown is that of absolute self-determination; it stands for the unity, independence and sovereignty of the state. Hegel believed in hereditary monarchy, not primarily because it is less likely than elective systems to lead to faction and dispute, but rather because it symbolises the state as self-sufficient – as unmoved mover. Although, as we have seen, Hegel believed that it is possible to distinguish these three aspects of the constitution, they must not be thought of as entirely separate but, as in the case of the 'persons' of the Holy Trinity, each shares in the work of the other.[110]

The state is, for Hegel, the ultimate moral community; there is no such thing as an international community above the state. The nation-state is 'the absolute power on earth', which is sovereign and autonomous against its neighbours.[111] Each state should recognise the sovereignty and independence of other states and not 'meddle with the domestic affairs of another'; it can make treaties and ought to keep them, but disputes between states can ultimately be solved only by war.

God as absolute and self-sufficient spirit

Hegel believed that when theologians speak of God they refer to what philosophers call absolute spirit. What theology says in the language of images or representations (*Vorstellungen*) philosophy says in the language of concepts (*Begriffe*); each supplements the other. While it is true that Hegel believed a conceptual – or rational – knowledge of God (the absolute) was superior to an imaginative appreciation, this conceptual knowledge Hegel saw as ultimately religious and indeed Christian. This is because reason is the region of the spirit in which God reveals himself to the human race.[112] Those who believe in the superiority of a non-conceptual, or non-rational, knowledge of God – the advocates of 'narrative theology' in our own day, for example – hardly inspire confidence in their thesis by writing interminable treatises and commentaries explaining (in conceptual language) the significance of their stories. If non-conceptual knowledge is indeed superior, tell the story, paint the picture, sing the hymn and go home!

Hegel insisted that any language, concrete or conceptual, which portrays God as a being who exists as an object entirely distinct from and over against a universe which he has – some time in the past – created, must be rejected as totally misleading. In so far as God can be said to have created the world, it is by objectifying an aspect of himself. So the relationship between God and the world must ultimately be seen as a 'relationship' between God and himself – as a 'moment' (that is a stage in a dynamic process) in the life of God. Human knowledge of God is not then like knowledge of an external object, but it is God's knowledge of himself taking place in human consciousness. 'Finite consciousness knows God only to the extent to which God knows Himself in it.'[113] This may seem radically different from and opposed to popular religious images of the relationship of man to God in terms of a child speaking to his father. There is, nevertheless, a similarity to the Pauline teaching that Christian prayer is a moment in the life of the Trinity, when the Holy Spirit within us speaks through us to the Father, or again that only the Spirit of God can comprehend the thoughts of God and that humans participate in this knowledge only through the indwelling Spirit.[114]

This dynamic action of a God who objectifies an aspect of himself in the creation of the universe is, for Hegel, anticipated in the life of the godhead itself:

> First of all Father, power, the abstractly universal, as yet incomprehensible. Secondly, he is an object to himself, an other of himself, a self-duplicating, the Son. This other of himself, however, is just as immediately himself; he knows himself and contemplates himself therein – and precisely this self-knowing and self-contemplating is, thirdly, the Spirit himself.[115]

God, in his ultimate being, must not at all events be thought of as a monolithic and static unity, but as a dynamic process of differentiation and unification. His creative activity is something necessary, not in the sense of his being subject to external constraint, but as a manifestation of his very nature as love. Creation is therefore not the arbitrary act of a celestial despot.

Hegel's concern to emphasise that the created universe is not some object entirely distinct (let alone separate) from God is closely related to his characterisation of God, or the absolute, as self-sufficient. If there could be something which exists over and against God, he would not be truly infinite and autonomous; there would be something other than himself which would limit and affect him. It is for the same reason that he defended the traditional notion of creation *ex nihilo*, rejecting any suggestion that creation involves the rearranging of pre-existent matter. For here again there would be some external constraint upon God; his autarky would be endangered. In so far as God may be said to create out of anything, it is out of himself that he creates the universe.[116]

In interpreting Hegel (as has also happened in the case of Hobbes) many political philosophers have studiously ignored what he actually said and wrote about the importance of religion for an understanding of politics; they maintain that it is perfectly possible to appreciate his political ideas without coming to terms with his theology and metaphysics. Some have even suggested that Hegel did not use religious concepts like 'God' with serious intent, to refer to what Christians generally mean by the term, but as an esoteric way of talking about humanity, and that he is therefore to be viewed as a secular humanist. Hegel did indeed attack contemporary theologians for their Kantian denial of the possibility of a rational understanding of God and of the universe, and for their romantic belief that faith can be based upon feelings, but he did not attack the Christian religion. Indeed, as we have seen, he defended such specifically Christian doctrines as the incarnation, the Trinity and the idea of revelation as wholly rational, denouncing theologians of his day for having 'done everything in their power to do away with what is definite in religion, in that they have thrust dogmas into the background'.[117] He saw himself as having produced a Christian philosophy in which, as Karl Barth put it, 'theology seemed to be taken better care of than in theology itself'.[118] Barth, though ultimately denying that human reason is able to comprehend God and the universe, appreciated Hegel's attempt to take seriously the particularity of the Christian faith, with its historical reality, and to face up to the problem of the relationship between Christianity and scientific culture.

God and the state

I have tried to indicate those aspects of Hegel's thought which suggest an analogy between God and the state. Both are essentially spirit: the latter is spirit objectified; the former is absolute spirit. They are both characterised by self-sufficiency, by an autonomy which secures their independence and freedom. God ultimately absorbs the universe, as a 'moment' in the divine process, so the state ultimately absorbs all associations, corporations and groups within it. The total God is the model for the total state.

Hegel saw the process by which God reveals himself as a concrete historical process. Furthermore he pointed not only to the process as such but to particular events as highly significant. It is in this context that he saw the incarnation. The making concrete of the divine in human history is of importance not merely as the illustration of a general truth – the unity of divine and human natures – but as the specific realisation of this truth. While he rejected any idea of a smooth upward progress, insisting on the role played by conflict and tragedy in human history, he did believe that world history manifests a pattern. What appears to be a mere succession of happenings, 'one damn thing after another', is seen as a meaningful story of God's revealing himself as rational and absolute spirit, through the idea of the ethical life made concrete in the state. History is the story of freedom, a story which he tells in his *Phenomenology of Mind* and in his *Lectures on the Philosophy of History*. He distinguished three great epochs – the oriental, where only one was free, the classical, where some were free, and the Germanic or Christian period, when all are to be free. Each aspect of freedom, objective and subjective – referred to above – has asserted itself at different periods and become predominant. It is only in the final epoch that they will cohere into a single political system, in a full realisation of the idea of the state.

The part which philosophers may play in this process is limited to that of understanding and explaining, having no advice to give on what ought to be done next. The latter is the role of men of action, like Napoleon, who make decisions on criteria quite different from those of philosophy. Philosophers conclude that things are as they are, but Hegel went further. In 'The German Constitution', written at the turn of the century, he declared that the only effect of the essay – 'when published' – would be

> that of promoting the understanding of what is, and therefore a calmer outlook and a moderate endurance of it. . . . For it is not what is that makes us irascible and resentful, but the fact that it is not as it ought to be. But if we recognize that it is as it must be, i.e., that it is not arbitrariness and chance that make it what it is, then we also recognize that it is as it ought to be.[119]

Perhaps this is why he never published the essay![120] Despite what Hegel said about the centrality of freedom, it is clear from this passage and from other of his writings that his system ultimately has the effect of stifling human freedom, demanding as it does a kind of coherence and integration in both politics and theology, which is not possible this side of the *eschaton*.

AUTARKY IN POLITICS AND THEOLOGY

The idea that perfection necessarily involves self-sufficiency or 'autarky' has been widely asserted or assumed from early times, with respect both to the state and to God. When a nation in the modern world achieves unity after a long struggle – as in the case of Germany or Italy – and when a nation liberates itself, or is liberated, from colonial domination, it frequently pursues a policy of economic self-sufficiency, seeing this as a necessary condition for an effective political independence. The idea of economic autarky played a prominent role, from time to time, in the ideologies of Fascist Italy and Nazi Germany, though its practical effect is arguable. Selective rhetorical use of the concept did, however, play some part in the attempt to legitimate aggressive expansionism by both countries.[121]

In the case of ex-colonial states the idea of autarky played a more defensive role, being part of a strategy to fend off or at least limit the attempt by North Atlantic powers to effect a continued domination of the newly 'independent' state. In response to the quite explicit efforts by France to regain political control through economic domination of her ex-colony, Saint-Domingue, the Haitian mulatto politician Baron de Vastey wrote in 1817, 'A nation must be able to supply herself with everything she principally wants. If she depends for subsistence on foreign markets, she has no more her independence in her own hands.'[122] Throughout the nineteenth century a succession of Haitian nationalists urged their government to move in the direction of economic self-sufficiency, though with little success.[123] Nevertheless, such objectives are limited by a realisation that autarky can often be achieved only by accepting a substantially lower standard of living than might be enjoyed under less stringent economic policies. Haiti is today the most economically self-sufficient among the island states of the Caribbean, with relatively low import and export coefficients, but it is also the poorest. This self-sufficiency is, however, an incidental consequence of poverty rather than the result of a policy deliberately pursued.

Nationalists have frequently advocated the making of material sacrifices in order to secure the conditions, as they see it, of a truly sovereign and independent state. Louis Joseph Janvier claimed that an effective independence, based on economic autarky, was more important than short-term prosperity, and pointed in horror to British domination of the Egyptian economy.[124] At one stage, Castro's Cuba set out to diversify its economy in such a way that it would be less dependent on sugar exports and a list was made of all items which were imported, with the object of pursuing a radical policy of import substitution. Soon, however, the programme was abandoned and emphasis was once more placed upon sugar exports as the basis of the national economy.[125]

Some early Haitian writers extended the notion of autarky to the cultural sphere, insisting that the country should liberate itself from dependence upon France and develop a literary tradition distinct from that of the former metropolis. As the Napoleonic invasions of Germany had stimulated and popularised the search for an independent cultural and linguistic tradition, so the United States invasion and occupation of Haiti (1915–34) led to a revival of demands for *une littérature indigène* and to respect for the Kréyol language.[126]

Classical doctrines of autarky

Concern with autarky has been a characteristic feature of periods when people have been much exercised by the relation of the local political unit to the wider world, whether it be – in the ancient world – the relation between the *polis* and the rest of Greece, or the demands made in the modern world for national self-determination. It is a notable feature of such periods that the idea of self-sufficiency, being an aspect of perfection, is also ascribed to God.

Plato believed that God is changeless. 'Is it not true, then', demanded Socrates in *The Republic*, 'that things in the most perfect condition are the least affected from outside?' He concluded that the divine nature, being perfect, cannot be subject to transformation. He held that change means decay.[127] The idea of perfection as autarky was applied by the Cynics to the individual. They maintained that the ideal person was the self-sufficient one, for whom all things outside himself were indifferent, including the *polis*. This was not, however, the view of all Greek thinkers, and Aristotle believed that the individual could realise perfection only in the context of the *polis*.

Aristotle agreed with Plato that, of two otherwise similar things, the less dependent is the more perfect, claiming that the higher animals are more self-sufficient than the lower; the final good he asserted is autarkic.[128] As God is a perfect being he must be characterised by autarky. There can be in God no potentiality, but only actuality. Unactualised potentiality would imply change and also a dependence upon something outside himself to initiate the process of actualisation. The only sort of activity which is self-sufficient is contemplation and this is the only activity that can be ascribed to God. He is the unmoved mover, the object of whose knowledge is himself. So keen was Aristotle to represent God as independent and impassible that he portrayed him as not knowing about terrestrial affairs, for a knowledge of what is happening in the universe would imply some kind of dependence. A being who witnesses is a being who is affected by what he witnesses. 'One who is self-sufficient', he wrote,

> can have no need of the service of others, nor of their affection, nor of social life, since he is capable of living alone. This is especially evident in the case of God. Clearly, since he is in need of nothing, God cannot have need of friends, nor will he have any.[129]

Human individuals are able, through practising contemplation, to approach autarky but can, as political beings, never be totally self-sufficient for they will always need something beyond themselves.

Classical Greek political theorists spoke of the *polis* too as autarkic, but it was an ideal which could not fully be realised. As Victor Ehrenberg has pointed out, 'Very few *poleis* ... were in a position to feed their citizens, let alone supply them with all that was required for a civilized life.'[130] Imports of grain, wine, raw materials and commercial products had to be paid for by exports. In the later Hellenistic period the economy was based on larger units than the *polis* and serious efforts to achieve economic autarky were abandoned. Nevertheless the ideal was maintained.

Among classical theorists, then, it was Aristotle who argued most clearly for the autarkic state, because the *polis* is for him the 'final and perfect association'.[131] As the household is more self-sufficient than the individual, the *polis* is more self-sufficient than the household. Autarky is, however, inversely related to the degree of unity manifested by the different kinds of body. The self-sufficiency which the *polis* can achieve is possible only because it is of a greater size and diversity than the family and any attempt to impose upon the former the kind of unity appropriate to the latter is misconceived. Autarky implies pluralism.[132]

Curiously Aristotle did not himself appear to have extended this reasoning to the autarkic God, though some Christian Trinitarians have clearly done so. In answer to the argument that a loving God must *necessarily* have created a universe to be the object of his love, such Trinitarians have replied that the diversity within the self-sufficient divinity enables such love to be manifested among the 'persons' and that God's creation of a universe was a free act.

In some later Greek thinkers the qualities which had been applied to the *polis* were seen as characteristic of the king, who plays an analogical role to God. As a sole and unique being, the king is a reflection of 'the Higher King'. As God governs an ordered universe, so the king should preserve order and harmony in his realm. 'God rules of, and by, Himself, to all the great height of his authority,' wrote Pseudo-Ecphantus the Pythagorean. 'Is it not so with our earthly king, and is he not also, and as much, self-sufficient?'[133] Some of these ideas were later borrowed by Eusebius and applied to the Christian emperor Constantine.[134]

The impassible God

This leads us to a brief consideration of the role played by ideas of divine autarky in the development of Christian doctrine. The concept of impassibility is integrally related to that of autarky. A wholly self-sufficient being cannot be affected in any way by anything outside himself. As God is a perfect being and perfection involves autarky, so he must also be impassible. He can know neither pain nor joy. The fathers of the early church, influenced as they were by classical philosophy, generally accepted the idea that God 'needs nothing and is self-sufficient'.[135] This led to two problems.

In the first place the God portrayed in Scripture, particularly in the Old Testament, is a God who loves and hates, a God who responds to events in the world, one who suffers with his people. Origen led the way in arguing that this language must be taken in an 'allegorical and human manner', rather than being seen as descriptive of God.[136] Metaphysical conceptions of the omnipotence, omniscience and impassibility of God were believed to be more accurate and literal ways of speaking about him. Nevertheless a radical idea of divine self-sufficiency is hardly compatible with basic Christian assumptions about divine providence and the efficacy of petitionary prayer.[137]

The second problem arose from the suffering of Christ, the Son of God. The idea of God's impassibility influenced the formulation of both Christological and Trinitarian doctrines.[138] Orthodox theologians argued that Christ, being of two natures, suffered only in his human and not in his divine nature and that his suffering in no way affected the Father, a distinct person of the Trinity. Monophysites found problems in maintaining the idea of divine impassibility because the sufferings of Christ must have been endured by his single divine/human nature, which he shared with the Father.

The mainstream of Christian theological speculation has generally retained the notion of divine impassibility while vainly attempting to reconcile it with the religious experience of a living and loving God. Sympathy, it has been argued, by no means implies sharing in the suffering of the victim. God's infinite sympathy with human suffering no more implies his own suffering than the sympathy of Father Damien with the lepers necessarily involved his suffering from the disease himself. It has in fact been suggested that God's omniscience enables him to understand and sympathise with those in pain without having to share in it. Others would reply that true omniscience implies a real as well as a notional understanding of suffering, and to say that God cannot feel pain is to say that he cannot know pain, which is to limit his omniscience.[139]

Those who challenge the idea of impassibility do not wish to deny that God is consistent in his purposes. To reject absolute changelessness is to assert not the contrary but merely the contradictory. It is important for those who criticise traditional notions of God's autarky to show in what respects he may be said to change and in what respects he remains the same. This is not always done. David Jenkins, for example, in *Living with Questions* speaks of the 'suffering of God' and states that 'it is God who suffers – the one true, almighty, transcendent, holy and righteous', yet on the previous page he asserts: 'He is God the changeless; he is God the unchangeable; he is God the wholly perfect and the wholly infinite and the wholly independent of everything else.'[140] Jenkins makes not the slightest effort to reconcile these palpably incompatible positions and presumably regards them as questions with which he and we have to live.

In the field of philosophical theology the living God of religion has frequently been sacrificed to the impassible God of philosophical speculation. Mystics, preachers and hymn writers have, however, stubbornly continued to use language which challenges the autarkic model but only the occasional philosophical theologian has attempted to accommodate these insights. As we have seen, even theologians like Schleiermacher, who claimed to base their dogmatic structure upon the conscience and experience of the Christian believer, clung tenaciously to the idea of divine self-sufficiency. It seems that we must wait until the twentieth century for a philosophical theology which endeavours to accommodate the passionate God of Christian experience. Some of the strengths and weaknesses of this movement we have already noted in chapter 5.

That this philosophical movement should have found its most fertile soil in the United States, a country where a federal political structure requires the recognition of a basic interdependence of the units, is perhaps no accident. As I have shown in chapter 5, there is a manifest connection between political and religious thinking in this matter, though there is, of course, no simple or necessary connection here. It is quite possible – as in the case of some isolationist Americans – to see, as Aristotle did, federal diversity as a basis for constructing a self-sufficient union.

In this chapter I have looked at ideas of divine and political autarky in the context of the rise of German nationalism, suggesting that the passionate concern of Fichte, Schleiermacher and their contemporaries for a united, independent and self-sufficient Germany is closely related to their conception of divine perfection. The philosophical theology they inherited – which assumed that divine perfection implies divine self-sufficiency – provided them with a theoretical apparatus with which to interpret the nationalist sentiment of their day, which, strengthened by the Napoleonic invasion and occupation, in turn reinforced the conception of divine autarky. The dialectical relationship between religious and political ideas on the one hand, and between these ideas and the political events (and more generally the social tendencies) of an era on the other, is thus well illustrated by the study of early German nationalism. The malignant effects of the ideology of autarky – both in the role played by nationalism in the modern world and in the alienating of millions of women and men from the idol of an unmoved and impassible God – have become starkly evident in the present century.

7

Atheists and anarchists

A POLITICAL ATHEISM

Much modern atheism is highly political. The rejection of God's existence – in the form of an attack upon the idea of a divine tyrant – by such nineteenth-century writers as Mikhail Bakunin, Pierre-Joseph Proudhon and Percy Bysshe Shelley is closely connected to a more general critique of authority, in the domestic, civil and cosmic spheres. The assertion of an analogical relationship between atheism and anarchism is, however, by no means an exclusively modern phenomenon and was made by a number of writers in the past. In the fourth century, for example, Eusebius of Caesarea, defending the analogy between a monarchical God and an earthly king, concluded that polyarchy is anarchy, that polytheism is in reality atheism and that atheism and anarchism tend to go together.[1] In seventeenth-century England, King James I denounced critics of royal authority as political atheists. 'It is atheism or blasphemy', he wrote, 'to dispute what God can do ... it is presumption and high contempt in a subject to dispute what a king can do, or say that a king cannot do this, or that.'[2] John Locke, whose ideas on kingship were rather different, also perceived an analogy between the rejection of divine and human authority. 'Those only doubt of a Supreme Ruler and a universal law', he warned, 'who would willingly be under no law, accountable to no judge.'[3] The advent of atheism and anarchism as significant movements in the modern world was, however, heralded by the execution of Louis XVI. 'As in France fell the monarchy, the keystone of the old social system,' wrote Heinrich Heine, 'so in Germany fell theism, the keystone of the intellectual *ancien régime*.'[4]

There is, of course, no necessary or logical connection between atheism and anarchism. It is perfectly possible to be a theistic anarchist, like Tolstoy and Berdyaev, or an atheistic authoritarian, like Saint-Simon and Nietzsche. Nevertheless, as I have already observed in previous chapters, analogy often influences the way people think and act. The influence may be unconscious; at other times explicitly analogical 'arguments' are advanced to promote causes which appear to have been adopted for other reasons. Before discussing further the relationship between atheism and anarchism, though, it is necessary to say something about the ambiguity of these terms.

Atheism is a particularly difficult concept to clarify, because an atheist is usually thought to be one who denies the existence of something; but of what? In order meaningfully to deny the existence of something it is necessary to have a fairly clear idea of what that something is like (or rather would be like if it existed). It is frequently the case that the kind of god whose existence many self-proclaimed atheists deny is a god, the existence of whom few self-proclaimed theists would be prepared to assert. All theists deny the existence of certain kinds of god. Early Christians were sometimes called atheists for denying the being and power of the civic gods of the Roman Empire – the dominant conception of deity in their time. Explicit atheism is frequently a legitimate protest against false conceptions of God. The fathers of the second Vatican Council declared that 'believers can have more than a little to do with the birth of atheism', both because of their false images and concepts of God and because of the sinfulness of their lives. More recently a French theologian has argued that the image of God as a powerful guardian of the status quo has led to 'un athéisme politique'.[5]

Another way of dealing with the problem would be to say that atheists are those who have no place for the word 'God' in their vocabulary. But this is hardly satisfactory, for it may be the case that they use another word or phrase which theists would regard as representing what they mean by God. Some would in fact define God in such a way that anyone who thinks seriously about the universe and about the meaning and purpose of human life must be a theist. If 'God' is the symbol for that which is of final significance, the 'object of ultimate concern', or 'the absolute', then only those who refuse to think seriously and consistently can possibly be atheists. Theoretical atheism – contrasted with a practical atheism, which ignores God or treats him as less than of ultimate importance – is thus a contradiction. 'There is', pronounced Paul Tillich, 'no possible atheism.'[6] In his 1910 thesis he noted that for Schelling

> The idea of God is not an object of dispute or discord; all particularity, from which alone there is conflict, disappears within it. The madman who denies it unwittingly expresses it; he is unable to unite two concepts logically except in this idea.[7]

Likewise, McTaggart observed that in Hegelian cosmology the important question is not whether God exists but 'What is God's nature?'[8] This is not, however, an issue I wish to pursue here. I am concerned rather with the denial of – or the attack upon – a particular concept of God, as an omnipotent (or at least very powerful) and arbitrary personal being, who governs the universe as a monarch rules his realm.

The three thinkers I am particularly concerned with in this chapter may perhaps more accurately be called anti-theists than atheists. They attacked a particular image of God. At times they even seem to have assumed his existence, seeing themselves as rebelling against his tyranny, just as did Prometheus or Milton's Satan. They would agree with John Stuart Mill, in his discussion of Mansel's theology, when he wrote:

> I will call no being good, who is not what I mean when I apply that epithet to my fellow-creatures; and if such a being can sentence me to hell for not so calling him, to hell I will go.[9]

Shelley, Proudhon and Bakunin saw themselves as leaders of a moral crusade against a cruel and ruthless heavenly power, the counterpart of an arbitrary and tyrannical government. Their position is summed up by the Russian, when he declared, 'If God existed it would be necessary to abolish him.'[10]

The term 'anarchist' is also problematic. Popularly, anarchism and anarchy imply social chaos, or the violent destruction of a settled order. Even some who are claimed as fathers of anarchism, like William Godwin, used the term in this pejorative way. Literally it means 'no rule', but this idea has been developed in different and contradictory ways.[11] All anarchists agree that the state – or coercive civil authority – should be abolished, though they do not agree on their vision of the social arrangements that should replace it nor on the best means of achieving their end. Anarchists include radical individualists, critical of all types of co-operation, and communists whose ideal is a community of goods in which nothing is individually owned.

Some anarchists have been extreme pacifists, opposed to all forms of violence, while another tradition believed in 'propaganda by the deed'. As one anarchist put it:

> Dynamite! Of all the good stuff, that is the stuff. Stuff several pounds of this sublime stuff into an inch pipe . . . plug up both ends, insert a cap with a fuse attached, place this in the vicinity of a lot of rich loafers who live by the sweat of other people's brows, and light the fuse. A most cheerful and gratifying result will follow.[12]

Writings like this, and the activities therein described, have given anarchism a reputation that is largely undeserved. Most anarchists eschew the kind of violence advocated in this pamphlet.

Marxists are, in a certain respect, anarchists – believing that under communism the state will wither away when the administration of things replaces the government of men. They differ most clearly from communist anarchism in their notion of the dictatorship of the proletariat – the supposed transitional state which will succeed the overthrow of the bourgeois state. Anarchists insist that the revolution must be followed immediately by the abolition of all coercive authority, otherwise a new ruling class will establish itself and the last state will be worse than the first. The emergence of Stalin's dictatorship would have been no wonder to Proudhon and Bakunin, who could already see the dictatorial tendencies inherent in Marxism. Ernst Bloch pours scorn on the warnings which came from these men about the dangers of a combination of socialism and absolutism in which all power would be concentrated in the state. This, however, is not surprising as it comes from one who blindly believed that utopia would be built in the Stalinist regime of East Germany in the 1950s.[13]

These three anarchists agree in relating their critique of civil authority to their assault upon celestial power. Their political writings are saturated with religious language and images, as their attacks upon religion are informed by their political commitments. Shelley and Bakunin, both of aristocratic birth, extended their attack on authority to the domestic sphere, while Proudhon, of working-class background, firmly believed that a paternal – we might almost say patriarchal – structure is a legitimate feature of family life. The link between ideas of authority in family, state and cosmos had already been recognised by Catholic reactionary writers like de

Maistre and Donoso Cortés;[14] in an earlier period Bishop Joseph Butler noted how 'the subordinations, to which they [children] are accustomed in domestic life ... prepare them for subjection and obedience to civil authority'.[15] The link between anarchism, atheism and feminism was also asserted by Emma Goldmann, and by a group associated with the Argentinian anarchist journal *La Voz de la Mujer*.[16]

In attacking divine and civil tyranny, Bakunin, Proudhon and Shelley were inspired by a high moral purpose. The revolution they desired involved no mere change in social institutions, but a moral regeneration which would transform individuals and the communities to which they belonged; they saw the removal of coercive authority as bearing a dialectical relationship to this moral reformation. 'No great political and social transformation', wrote Bakunin, 'has been made in the world without being accompanied, and often preceded, by an analogous movement in religious and philosophical ideas which direct the consciences as much of individuals as of society.'[17] Shelley and Proudhon, too, recognised that some degree of individual moral reform is necessary before government is entirely done away with, yet they also saw government as a cause of individual moral degeneration. Both steps must be taken together.

BAKUNIN

Mikhail Bakunin believed that politics and theology are closely connected, stemming from the same root and pursuing the same aim. 'We are convinced that every State is a terrestrial Church', he declared, 'just as every Church with its Heaven – the abode of the blessed and the immortal gods – is nothing but a celestial State.'[18] He saw God as playing an analogous role in the universe of ideas to that played by the state in the social life of a people. Both represent power and domination and thus lead to restrictions on human freedom. Whoever says political power says domination, and this implies two classes, the oppressed and the oppressors. 'But here Satan steps in, the eternal rebel, the first freethinker and the emancipator of worlds.'[19] Bakunin contrasted the God of the theologians – a serious but evil being – with the God of the metaphysicians, without flesh or bones, will or action, who was nevertheless resuscitated in the modern world to veil the turpitudes of bourgeois materialism and 'the hopeless poverty of their own thought'.[20]

The life of a professional revolutionary

Bakunin is undoubtedly one of the most vigorous and colourful figures in the history of anarchism. Born in 1814, of a landowning family, he was sent at the age of 14 to the artillery school in St Petersburg. He became an officer in 1833, but after only two years left the army and, having interested himself in the philosophy of Kant and Fichte, went to university in Moscow. He became involved in squabbles within his family, taking sides with his sister against their father, who subsequently refused to pay for him to study in Germany. In 1840, the celebrated Russian writer, Alexander Herzen (1812–70), with whom he had been in close contact, lent him the money to leave Russia, at the age of 26. From then onwards Bakunin spent much of his life in exile, living in Germany, Switzerland, France, Belgium, Italy and England. He first became involved with the left Hegelians, including Marx, and then met Proudhon, whose libertarian socialism gave him inspiration.

For a time Bakunin took up the cause of Polish nationalism and Panslavism, seeing it as a means of undermining the power of the tsar. He was arrested for subversive activities in Saxony and extradited to Russia, where he was immediately imprisoned. From 1851 to 1857 he languished in the subterranean dungeons of tsarist Russia. It was during this period that he wrote his extraordinary confession to Tsar Nicholas – more of an *apologia* than an apology! As Eric Voegelin observes, Bakunin retained a certain respect for his enemies when he believed them to stand for some important principle. 'In spite of my democratic convictions', he told the tsar, 'I have worshipped you profoundly in the last year, as it were against my will. . . . You are the only one among the ruling heads of the time who has preserved his faith in his imperial calling.'[21] Being banished to Tomsk in western Siberia, Bakunin managed to escape through Japan to the USA and eventually back to Europe. He had by now become a legendary figure in the revolutionary underworld – in Herzen's words 'a giant with leonine head and tousled mane'.[22] From this time until his death he was restlessly involved in a series of poorly organised and ill-conceived conspiracies. He emerged as leader of the anti-authoritarian socialists in the International, but was expelled from the movement at the Hague conference of 1872. His last years were spent in Lugano, where he died in 1876.[23]

Freedom and the state

Claiming to be 'a fanatical lover of freedom',[24] Bakunin was dedicated to the overthrow of all coercive authority, which restricts human liberty. He distinguished three aspects of freedom. In the first place it involves a full enjoyment by everyone of their human powers, by means of education and the material means to self-fulfilment. It is remarkable that he listed what has later come to be called 'positive liberty' first, insisting that where people lack the basic means to satisfy their needs liberty is impossible. He therefore saw socialism and freedom as linked. Attempts to achieve socialism without freedom lead to slavery and brutality, while freedom without socialism is privilege and injustice.[25] The second aspect of freedom is 'the revolt against the supreme phantom of theology, against God'. This implies, thirdly, 'the revolt against the tyranny of man, against authority, individual as well as collective, represented and legalized by the State'.[26]

Bakunin was implacably opposed to all forms of coercive political authority, claiming that they inevitably lead to slavery. The liberal state is little better than the absolute state. All political power, whatever its origin or form, 'necessarily tends toward despotism' and the best men are easily corrupted by power.[27] He exposed the hollow claims of 'representative government' and attacked the sacred institution of universal suffrage as 'the most refined manifestation of the political charlatanism of the State'. Both Bismarck and Napoleon III had built their power on this dogma, which is 'the surest means of making the masses co-operate in the building of their own prison'.[28] Bakunin denounced all talk of a 'general interest' which governments should seek to further as 'an abstraction, a fiction, a falsehood'. Such notions are a camouflage under which 'the positive interests of the regions, communes, associations and a vast number of individuals' are subordinated to those of a ruling class.[29]

Bakunin's analysis of capitalism owed less to Proudhon than to Marx, to whom he declared in 1868, 'I am your disciple and I am proud to be so.'[30] He accepted with qualifications the Marxist ideas of exploitation and of class struggle and the need for a revolution to overthrow the bourgeois state. Bakunin agreed to dissolve his International Social Democratic Alliance and to incorporate it into the International Working Men's Association, but soon tensions became evident between the Marxists and Bakunin's followers. The latter believed that the movement should campaign for the immediate abolition of hereditary private property, a move which would lead on to revolution. He referred to property as the god of the bourgeoisie, with the 'science' of political economy as its metaphysic. The god must be destroyed. Marxists placed less priority on this matter, believing that such property should be abolished after the revolution. The executive took the Marxist stance, but was defeated at the 1869 Basel congress. This led to a Marxist vendetta against Bakunin, who was subsequently expelled from the movement.

Bakunin's opposition to Marxism was, however, more wide-ranging. 'I detest communism', he had declared in 1868,

> because it is a negation of liberty and because I can conceive nothing human without liberty. I am not a communist because communism concentrates and absorbs all the powers of society into the state; because it necessarily ends in the centralization of property in the hands of the state, while I want the abolition of the state.[31]

He criticised talk about 'educating the masses' as a precondition of revolution. The best education was active participation in the revolutionary process. This led him to take a more positive attitude towards the revolutionary potentiality of two important classes, the peasants and the lumpenproletariat (the very poor, outcasts and unemployed). 'If the workers of the West delay too long', he declared prophetically in 1869, 'it will be the Russian peasant who will set them an example.'[32]

Around this time Bakunin came under the influence of a much younger man, the fanatical Sergei Nechaev, whom he met in Geneva. Together they drafted manifestos which advocated terror as an instrument of revolution. 'We recognise no other activity but the work of extermination', they exclaimed, 'but we admit that the forms in which this activity will show itself will be extremely varied – poison, the knife, the rope etc.'[33] In justifying this position – which is not, however, representative of his general emphasis, which was more pacific – Bakunin asserted that the state itself is an instrument of violence and can be overthrown only by violence. Even when dressed up in liberal and democratic forms, it 'is necessarily based upon domination and violence'.[34] As unrestricted commercial competition leads to small firms being swallowed by huge enterprises, so in the international field small states are absorbed by more powerful ones. Expansion is the only way for nations to survive, and this involves holding in subjection millions of alien peoples by means of a large military force.[35] The only way to check the vicious circle of violence is by the abolition of the state.

Bakunin's analysis of the past and present and his programme for the future were frequently ill conceived. Nevertheless there runs throughout his mature writings a consistent thread – a suspicion of power and of all claims to political authority, a love of liberty and a consequent recognition of the need for a radical transformation of social life involving an abolition of the state. He argued in favour of a federal organisation, based upon workers' associations, city and village communes 'and finally of regions and peoples', and he pointed to the USA as 'the finest political organization that mankind has ever known'.[36] Again he told the League of Peace and Liberty, 'We must reject the politics of the French revolution ... and resolutely adopt the politics of freedom of the North Americans.'[37] Yet the US government too was based upon the oppression of millions of workers and slaves and was destined to pass away. The revolution which would accomplish this must, however, involve a transformation of the human mind, and this meant the abolition of religion – the death of God.

A tyrannical God

Taking his lead from Schleiermacher, Bakunin ascribed religion to a sense of absolute or unqualified dependence by the ephemeral individual upon eternal and omnipotent nature, manifesting itself particularly in a craven fear. 'Consider the tame dog imploring his master for a caress or look', he cried; 'isn't he the image of a man kneeling before his God?'[38] Bakunin noted the lack of reciprocity in traditional ideas about the relations of the autarkic God and dependent humankind. Humans need God, but he has no need of them. 'It would be impious to say that God may feel the need of man's love,' he remarked. 'For to feel any need whatsoever is to lack something essential to the fullness of being.' This makes it impossible for God really to love human beings. Rather the relationship is one of 'absolute overbearing power', of a similar kind, though more formidable, to that exercised by the German emperor over his subjects.[39]

Bakunin believed that it is important to discover the origin of belief in God in order to free men from it. The mere fact that a belief is ancient is no indication of its truth, because man is a progressive being; behind him is animality, before him is humanity. He must therefore look forward, not back. In his essay on 'God and the State', he traced the development of religion from the pagan belief in numerous national gods to monotheism. 'Before the altar of a unique and supreme God was raised on the ruins of the numerous altars of the pagan gods', he wrote,

> the autonomy of the various nations composing the pagan or ancient world had to be destroyed first. This was very brutally done by the Romans who, by conquering the greatest part of the globe known to the ancients, laid the first foundations ... of humanity. A God thus raised above the national differences, material and social, of all countries ... must necessarily be an immaterial and abstract being.[40]

Preparatory work for the acceptance of such divinity had already been done by Greek metaphysicians and by the Jewish people in their development of the idea of a universal but also personal God. The Jews had, long before the birth of Christ, become 'the most international people in the world' and on the basis of this experience evolved the concept of a universal deity. This brutal, selfish and cruel God, Jehovah, made the acquaintance of the impersonal God of Greek metaphysics in Alexandria:

> He married her, and from this marriage was born the spiritualistic – but not spirited – God of the Christians. The neo-Platonists of Alexandria are known to have been the principal creators of the Christian theology.[41]

Jean-Jacques Rousseau had maintained that religion is necessary for the existence of a state and had elaborated the notion of a civic religion, which would give ideological support to human government. Bakunin accepted the empirical judgment of the Genevan theorist, but drew other conclusions. He advocated rather the abolition of both religion and the state.[42] Even the United States, the most democratic country of his day, assumed the existence of a divine providence. 'Whenever a chief of State speaks of God', he wryly observed, 'be sure that he is getting ready to shear once more his people-flock.'[43] Not only is it the case that the idea of God is used to justify political domination, but belief in God reduces the status of the human person. Echoing Ludwig Feuerbach, he wrote of Christianity, 'God being everything, the real world and man are nothing. God being truth, justice, goodness, beauty, power, and life, man is falsehood, iniquity, evil, ugliness, impotence and death. God being master, man is the slave.'[44] He spoke, like Nietzsche, of God as 'a corrosive poison, which destroys and decomposes life, falsifies and kills it'.[45]

Bakunin saw Protestantism as 'the bourgeois religion *par excellence*', in combining celestial aspirations with a healthy respect for earthly prosperity. 'Consequently it is especially in Protestant countries that commerce and industry have been developed.' This was of course a familiar assertion in the period, later to be popularised by Max Weber. Bakunin accounted for the prevalence of deism among French bourgeois leaders as being the nearest they could safely get to Protestantism without wholly alienating themselves from the Catholic routine of the masses.[46]

Furthermore Bakunin denounced God for always siding with the strongest – with the possessing classes against the poor and the weak.[47] Curiously it is on precisely the opposite grounds that Nietzsche – believer in the *Übermensch* and assailant of all notions of human equality – attacked the Christian God. He was, for Nietzsche, the God of the weak and the poor in spirit. Both, from their different standpoints, however, demanded the death of God. Bakunin wrote:

> There is only one way to emancipate those slaves, and that is self-abdication, self-annihilation, and disappearance on the part of God. But that would be too much to demand from this almighty power. He could sacrifice his only son. . . . But to abdicate to commit suicide for the love of men – that he will never do.[48]

God must therefore be killed by scientific criticism. Adapting the analogy used by Charles Kingsley and Karl Marx, he maintained that people resort to church, as to the pot-house, in order to 'stupefy themselves, to forget their misery, to see themselves in their imagination, for a few minutes at least, free and happy'.[49] If they were to be given a truly human existence they would no longer need religion, and it is only a social revolution that can give them this.

A further charge made against God by the Russian anarchist was that the concept of an arbitrary divine ruler negates the idea of law. If God exists then there can be no regularity and order in the universe, for it becomes subject to the arbitrary decrees of an omnipotent despot. 'The theological hypothesis of divine legislation leads to a manifest absurdity and to the negation not only of any order but of Nature itself.'[50] Such a divine figure also reduces man to the status of a slave, whose freedom is destroyed by divine providence; all that remains is privilege – special rights reserved by divine grace to favoured individuals or institutions.[51]

Why was Bakunin so worried about this supposed challenge to human freedom? He himself was a determinist, believing that every human individual is but the product of material causes and that his 'soul' is 'completely determined by the individual physiological quality of his neuro-cerebral system which, like the other parts of his body, absolutely depends upon the more or less fortuitous combination of causes',[52] It is hard to understand why external objects placed by divine or human government in the path of such robots should be seen as any different from those other physical factors which already determine their behaviour. If human beings are like waves which 'rise up for a moment and then vanish in the vast collective ocean of human society'[53] – mere material entities pushed hither and yon by external forces – it is not clear why we should get excited about a certain class of such forces which are ascribed to human or divine agency. For these too are inexorably caused by prior material factors. I remember a cartoon some years ago in which a prisoner was complaining to a judge: 'You cannot punish me, I am a victim of social forces.' 'So am I,' replied the judge. 'Hang him.'

The very structure of Bakunin's libertarian position is thus built upon sand. He claimed to be developing Proudhon's ideas without the metaphysical and idealist baggage. What he in fact did was to deprive Proudhonian theory of its spiritual foundations. A wit once observed that when Marx turned the Hegelian dialectic on its head the brains fell out. Something similar might be said of Bakunin's adaptation of Proudhon's theories. Do we then find in the French writer a more coherent doctrine?

PROUDHON

'Every society is formed, reformed or transformed with the aid of an idea,' wrote Proudhon in 1864.[54] He believed furthermore that these controlling ideas have a theological analogue: 'He who denies his king denies his god.' The French anarchist was himself prepared not merely to deny but to denounce both divine and political authority, ideas which were for him inseparably connected. To his celebrated aphorism 'Property is theft' he was willing to add 'God is evil'.

Always a rebel

Throughout his life, Proudhon recognised a close link between religion and politics. In the early days he thought that a reformed church was possible and that it might provide the necessary religious support for a free state; but as the 1840s progressed he became increasingly hostile to both church and state, though continuing to recognise the important and even beneficial role of religion. By 1848, however, he had become an outspoken critic not only of religion but of God himself. In his *Système des contradictions économiques* of 1846 he had declared war on religion and God in the most uncompromising terms.[55]

This movement from a critical acceptance of Christianity, through a kind of deism to anti-theism, was accompanied by a growing rejection of authority in the political realm, for 'religion is unquestionably the oldest manifestation of government and the highway for authority'.[56] In *De la création de l'ordre* (1843) Proudhon had argued in favour of the centralisation of commerce, agriculture and industry, with the state as regulator of workshops and policeman of markets and as late as 1847 he had seen a considerable role for the state in a post-revolutionary France. But by 1849 he was insisting that social change must come from below 'and not from the initiative of the government' and that anarchy was the condition of developed societies.[57] His essay on the 1848 revolution written from prison in 1851 is a classical text in the history of anarchism. In a well-known diatribe, he denounced all forms of government:

> To be governed is to be watched over, inspected, spied on, directed, legislated at, regulated, docketed, indoctrinated, preached at, controlled, assessed, weighed, censored, ordered about, by men who have neither the right nor the knowledge nor the virtue. To be governed means to be, at each operation, at each transaction, at each movement, noted, registered, controlled, taxed, stamped, measured, valued, assessed, patented, licensed, authorised, endorsed, admonished, hampered, reformed, rebuked, arrested. It is to be, on the pretext of the general interest, taxed, drilled, held to ransom, exploited, monopolised, extorted, squeezed, hoaxed, robbed; then at the least resistance, at the first word of complaint, to be repressed, fined, abused, annoyed, followed, bullied, beaten, disarmed, garotted, imprisoned, machine-gunned, judged, condemned, deported, flayed, sold, betrayed, and finally mocked, ridiculed, insulted, dishonoured. That is government, that is its justice, that is its morality.[58]

Proudhon's later development of a theory of federalism ought not to be seen as a retreat from the ideal of anarchy, but as a realistic proposal for moving in that direction. I shall examine Proudhon's critique of divine and political authority and note how he saw the two as part of a single problem. Unlike Shelley and Bakunin, however, he did not carry his attack on authority into the family, which he conceived to be the legitimate realm of hierarchical rule.

Pierre-Joseph Proudhon was born in Besançon in 1809, the son of a poor cooper and brewer. As a child he looked after cows and did other occasional jobs until, at the age of 11, he was given a scholarship to the local college. In 1826, owing to family poverty, he left college and became a printer's apprentice. The publishing house for which he worked specialised in works of theology; as proof-reader he thus became familiar with academic works and was a diligent reader at the local library. In 1838 he was awarded the Suard fellowship by the Académie de Besançon, which provided him with a small grant to support his academic and journalistic work. The young Proudhon published a number of works in the 1840s, among which was his famous essay *Qu'est-ce que la propriété?* He enthusiastically supported the revolution of 1848 and for a time was a representative in the assembly, where he managed to alienate almost all his fellow deputies of the right and the left. Proudhon edited a series of newspapers and founded a bank, but soon got into trouble with the government of Louis-Napoleon and took refuge in Belgium.

On his return to France in June 1849 he was imprisoned for three years, but continued to produce important works including his massive book *De la justice dans la révolution et dans l'église* and one of his most important books, *Du principe fédératif*. His health declined and he died in 1865. Other works were published posthumously including his notebooks and correspondence.

Central themes running through the writings of Proudhon are those of justice and liberty. Although, like other socialists of his time, he laid considerable emphasis upon equality, it was always in his case related to liberty and justice. This respect for freedom led him to embark upon a sustained assault on every form of coercive authority and a searching criticism of all claims to moral authority.

From deism to anti-theism

Proudhon was fascinated by the idea of God. 'Seized since childhood with that great idea', he wrote 'I felt it overflowing within me and dominating all my faculties.'[59] Much of his social and political critique is couched in theological terms and is frequently consistent with Christian faith. He denounced the idolatry practised by the bourgeois classes of his day. Property he declared to be 'the last of the false gods'. By property he meant not personal and family possessions, which he fiercely defended, but the existence of rented land and accumulated capital. Property reaps without labouring, harvests without sowing, consumes without producing; unlike the idols known to the psalmist who 'have hands and handle not', property has hands and grasps. It has achieved a sacred status in capitalism; as with the ark of old, no alien hands must be laid on it. Property produces wealth for its owner without his working, and can indeed be said, like God, to create *ex nihilo*. Idols were not, however, the exclusive possession of the bourgeoisie; the masses too had their false gods. 'Like Israel in the desert, they improvise gods when no one has taken the trouble to provide them.' Proudhon listed the great revolutionary figures of the past, Danton, Marat, Robespierre, Napoleon, up to his particular *bête noire*, the Italian nationalist Garibaldi. 'Do not touch their anointed, or they will treat you as sacrilegious.'[60]

Proudhon thought the idea of God to be so important that it could not simply be abolished. Like government, it must be replaced with something else or things will fall apart. 'We cannot entirely dislodge God without showing the unknown which is to succeed him in the order of human conceptions and social developments.' Some idea of God is needed as the fixed point to which absolute values must be related.[61] In his *Système des contradictions économiques* of 1846, he spoke of God as 'a being apart, omnipresent, distinct from creation, endowed with imperishable life as well as infinite knowledge and activity, but above all foreseeing and just, punishing vice and rewarding virtue'.[62] God is personal or he is nothing. Yet this transcendent God was also seen as inhuman and monstrous. Human beings must chase him from their consciousness as hostile to their nature. So far from worshipping him as sovereign and guide they must see him as their implacable antagonist. The qualities we ascribe to him 'are constituted otherwise in God than in us' and this makes of him a being 'essentially anti-civilised, anti-liberal, anti-human'.[63] Proudhon saw humans as destined to fight against God; he therefore was less an atheist than an anti-theist – a term he himself used.[64]

Proudhon's principal reason for attacking God was the role that he played in human life, as a providence depriving human beings of freedom and as a tyrant issuing arbitrary commands which divest them of moral responsibility. A further accusation was that he had become a God who maintained an unjust social order. 'The priests have made him . . . the God of the privileged, of the rich and of the bourgeoisie, an exploiting and reactionary god.'[65]

Proudhon saw Christianity as having initiated a critique of destiny and he proclaimed that the French Revolution completed the task of human liberation in its revolt against providence.[66] Humans must take God's place in the chariot of destiny. Proudhon's assault on providence was in fact analogical to his attack on *laissez-faire* liberalism. Where liberals, like Adam Smith and later F. Bastiat, saw 'economic harmonies' (the title of Bastiat's book), Proudhon saw economic contradictions which need to be resolved by social action. Yet, despite his assault upon providence, he continued to speak of a divine order in the world and even referred to the revolutionary movement in the nineteenth century as providential.

A further reason for Proudhon's attack on God was the arbitrary nature of divine commands, which were thought to constitute human duties. Pierre Haubtmann has pointed to the impact made on Proudhon by such writers as Joseph de Maistre, Louis de Bonald and Félicité de Lamennais.[67] In reaction to the Enlightenment and the revolutionary movements of the previous century, these men asserted an authoritarian theory of church and state and a corresponding image of God as a divine despot. With this notion of God, which Proudhon assumed to be the orthodox Christian doctrine, 'moral sanctions come from the throne of God, like lightning: he it is who, according to his own good pleasure, tries us, afflicts or rewards us, pending the final adjustment.'[68] Earlier, in his first published essay, he had ascribed to the Jewish rabbinic tradition the widely accepted belief that, to be meritorious, obedience must be blind.[69] Proudhon believed that theology reverses the proper order of things and makes justice merely the consequence of God's arbitrary decrees. Human experience rather witnesses to the supremacy of justice which points to the divine and is the measure of true religion. 'Justice', he declared, 'is the supreme God.'[70] Religion had become a set of beliefs imposed by authority and his strictures on religious positivism are, as we shall see, paralleled in his condemnation of political sovereignty whether ascribed to monarch or mob.

On the question whether religion is a necessary feature of human life Proudhon was ambivalent. Philosophers and the mass of the people too, he insisted, have need of 'a guide for the reason, a rule for the conscience, a superior standpoint', which is found in religion.[71] Yet elsewhere he wrote of man's destiny as being 'to live without religion' and referred to his anti-theism as involving an exclusion of religion from morality and government.[72] Proudhon was, however, a furious critic of the scepticism – or rather cynicism – of Joseph Ernest Renan, which spelt 'a contempt for everything divine and human'. Commenting on the popularity of Renan's *Vie de Jésus*, he exploded, 'God and men, religion and justice, Christ and the revolution, are equally insulted in this book, and the success it has enjoyed will be our eternal disgrace.'[73]

As we have seen, Proudhon recognised the central role which religion does, and in some respects must, play in human life. It cannot be simply abolished. This recognition led him to take an interest in the ideas of Ludwig Feuerbach which were circulating among the intellectuals of Europe in the early 1840s. Though competent in a number of classical languages, Proudhon could not read German. With assistance from his friends, however, he picked up enough about Feuerbach to know that his answer to the problem of religion was inadequate. 'It is impossible for me to welcome this new religion', he declared, 'by telling me that I am its God.'[74] Humanism he believed to be a false religion; to affirm the deity of man is as dangerous to justice as are the dogmas of traditional theism.[75]

For Proudhon the key to a revised understanding of God and religion is to be found in the economic and political realm. How people will understand 'God' in the future will depend upon the replacement of a political system based on coercive authority by an economic system founded on contract. 'The Supreme Being is to X as the governmental system is to the industrial system.'[76] It is therefore appropriate for us to consider at this point the elements of Proudhon's social doctrine.

Approaching anarchy

Proudhon saw the authoritarian political structures under which people have lived from the earliest times as intimately related to their subjection to false religions. It is as if the human spirit has been shut up in a sealed box of which government is the bottom and religion is the top. In the modern world, however, humans have broken out of the box and now see that 'this God, source of all power, origin of all causality, of which humanity makes its sun, is a lamp in a cavern, and all these governments made in his image are but grains of sand that reflect the faint light'.[77]

Proudhon believed that a notion of authority which is appropriate only in the context of the family has been transferred to the cosmic and to the political orders. The child's legitimate adoration for the father is improperly replicated in a worship of God and the state.[78] Proudhon explicitly defended the idea of the husband as sovereign of his realm, enjoying a kind of divine right to rule his wife and children. His attack upon communism was partly inspired by its tendency to undermine the structure of the family.[79]

Following de Maistre, Proudhon insisted that authority cannot be created artificially; it is a mystical or divine principle. 'Government', he declared, 'is of divine right, or it is nothing.'[80] It was one of Rousseau's principal errors to believe that authority can be created by the will or consent of the interested parties.[81] Authority, like moral duty, is prior to will. Indeed much present-day political theory proceeds on the false assumption that persons can be bound only by some prior consent (or promise) on their part. This idea – going back from Rawls through Green and Kant to the contract theorists of the seventeenth century – is frequently derived from mistaken notions of individual moral autonomy and provides stubble for constructing the mare's nest of 'political obligation'. 'Talk not of tacit consent', wrote the French anarchist in a memorable phrase.[82]

Proudhon in fact turned Rousseau inside out. The eighteenth-century Genevan derived an organic and indeed totalitarian idea of the state from a radically individualistic social theory. Proudhon, on the other hand, asserted the organic nature of human groups, seeing the state as, at best, a mechanical construction for the attainment of limited ends. Rousseau began with 'the false, thievish, murderous supposition' that only individuals are good and that they have been corrupted by social relations. He then has these individual atoms form an association for the mutual protection of the privileged classes. 'It is this contract of hatred', he continued, 'this monument of universal misanthropy, this coalition of the barons of property, commerce and industry against the disinherited lower class . . . which Rousseau calls *Social Contract*.'[83] Human groups should rather be thought of as plants which successful revolutions may straighten and support, but which no human action can arbitrarily reconstruct. They can be trained to grow in new directions but that is all.[84]

For Rousseau the only important units were the individual and the sovereign state. He had denounced all other associations as divisive. This hostility to groups goes back to before the Revolution. Turgot formulated an edict of 1776 outlawing associations of workers, tradesmen or masters, and by 1791 Le Chapelier could claim 'there are no longer any corporations in the State; there is nothing except the particular interest of each individual and the general interest'.[85] It is this tendency in French political theory and practice that led to Proudhon's suspicion of Jacobinism and of ideas of 'community' and 'fraternity'. In the mouths of those who used them, they represented an assault on the family, on the civic community and on the functional group. Community meant for him oppression and servitude; it is contrary to the free exercise of our faculties, violating the principles of conscience and equality.[86] In his essay *De la capacité politique des classes ouvrières*, written in 1864, Proudhon proposed a conception of 'mutualism', which he contrasted with the idea of 'community'. It was characterised by the notion of participation, and would involve a redistribution of land, a specialisation of functions and an emphasis upon individual and collective responsibility; it would minimise the role of central government.[87]

Proudhon denounced theories of sovereignty, whether of the individual or of 'the people', for putting will above reason and passion above right.[88] In one of his early writings he maintained that law should be seen as the expression not of a single will, nor of a general will, but rather as a reflection of the natural relation of things, given by God and discovered and applied by the reason.[89] This notion of a divine order lying at the basis of any valid human order and expressed in law has, of course, much in common with traditional Christian ideas of natural law and was never entirely renounced by Proudhon.

Coming himself from the working class, Proudhon had no illusions about 'the people'. He had a rather low view of human nature in general and distrusted the rootless masses – 'that great beast that is called the public'.[90] A passage of his last great work strangely anticipates the belief of later elitist writers, like Arthur Balfour:

> Left to themselves or led by their tribunes, the masses will never create anything. They set their face towards the past; no tradition forms among them, there is no sense of continuity, no idea which acquires the force of law. . . . The advent of democracy would begin an era of decadence.[91]

The proletariat, he told Beslay in 1861, is 'an evil I want to destroy, not a god to whom I offer incense'.[92] Proudhon dedicated his *Idée générale de la révolution*, with a certain irony, to the bourgeoisie as a revolutionary class. 'Is it possible', he demanded, 'that, after having accomplished so many revolutions, you have yourselves become counter-revolutionaries?'[93]

So far as Proudhon had any place for the notion of authority it was seen as present in the whole of a community, rather than being held by some individual or group or majority. Yet political theories of his day postulated a division of people into classes or castes, subordinate to one another, 'graduated to form a pyramid, at the top of which appears, like the Divinity upon his altar, like the king upon his throne, AUTHORITY'.[94] Indeed the very concept of the state and of government imply subordination and ultimately coercion. The more active the state, the more its members will withdraw from constructive social life and depend upon 'the providence of government', which he saw as a debilitating force playing an analogical role to that of divine providence.[95] He derided the sacred claims made by the state: 'You shall love the Government, your lord and your god, with all your heart, with all your soul, and with all your mind', because the government knows better than you do what is good for you.[96]

Proudhon was therefore critical of the national workshops, proposed by Louis Blanc and other socialists, and instituted in 1848 by the government of the Second Republic. Like many projects initiated by the Manpower Services Commission in our own day, these workshops were generally unproductive, being designed primarily to 'create jobs'. He lamented the existence of half a million civil servants, not to mention a further half-million troops. 'Do you not think', he demanded, 'that complete Anarchy would be better for our peace of mind, our labour and our prosperity, than this million of parasites armed to attack our liberties and our interests?'[97]

In his early tract on property Proudhon had proclaimed himself an anarchist.[98] Anarchy, he told the readers of La Voix du Peuple, is the condition of mature societies, while hierarchy is characteristic of primitive societies. Like Henry Maine, later in the century, he saw a historical movement away from status towards contract (or, as he would call it, anarchy).[99] Even in Du principe fédératif, where he appears to modify some of his anarchist sentiments, he criticised the state ownership of transport and communications and argued that schools should be separated from the state no less strictly than churches.[100] The state should initiate rather than execute.[101] In this essay Proudhon set out some of the practical steps which might be taken in the direction of anarchy. He believed that, in dividing power, separating administrative functions and respecting the independence of groups, people would be protected from tyranny.[102] In a letter to Millet towards the end of his life Proudhon described how he regarded federalism as a step in the direction of eventual anarchy.[103]

A political theology

Proudhon denied he was an atheist. This was partly because of its odious connotation of crass materialism, but also because he believed that human beings cannot know anything about God.[104] At times this agnosticism took on an almost mystical quality. What he called 'methodological atheism' seems to have involved the notion that in order to reach some understanding of the ultimate it was necessary to pass through 'a complete negation of God'.[105] In an unpublished manuscript he wrote of the God, 'hidden, invisible, inaccessible, indefinable, inconceivable by rational means', who stimulates and torments us in our hearts.[106] To the end of his life Proudhon maintained an otherworldly aspect to his thinking and spoke of the human vocation in the following way:

> To be men, to raise ourselves above earthly fatalities, to reproduce in ourselves the image of God, as the Bible has it, and finally to realise on earth the reign of the spirit, that is our end.[107]

Furthermore he never entirely renounced the idea, expressed in his essay on the observance of Sunday, of a divine order which would guide people in deciding how to live. 'To govern men', he had written, 'it is necessary to find the divine order. Everything that returns to this order is good and just, everything that forsakes it is false, tyrannical and bad.'[108] Contemplation of the infinite which frequently leads to quietism may also lead to social action, when it is realised that justice is truly divine. As we reflect this divine image in our lives, by acts of justice, we shall achieve our true happiness.[109] Above all, he concluded, the reign of the spirit may be achieved only 'by sending the Eternal Father back to heaven. His presence among us holds by but a single thread, the budget. Cut that thread, and you will find out what the revolution should put in place of God.'[110]

It will be clear from what has been said that Proudhon's hostility towards God may be called political in its inspiration. He saw the picture of God as a divine despot, issuing arbitrary decrees and depriving humans of all freedom and responsibility, as at once the analogue and the legitimation of the coercive and tyrannical state. Perhaps it would be more accurate to see his hostility to coercive authority in the political and theological spheres as stemming from his basic moral commitment to freedom and justice. 'The critique which I have made of the idea of God', he wrote to a French priest, 'is analogous to all the critiques I have made of authority and of property.'[111] The picture of God he entertained was one popular in his day and one which may be traced back at least to the positivism of the late Middle Ages. It is present in many Calvinist thinkers of the post-Reformation era, in Bodin and in Hobbes. Eighteenth-century rational religion presented a somewhat modified picture of God as operating within the confines of a system of law, but this notion of an arbitrary sovereign re-emerged in the writings of Catholic thinkers during the turbulent years of the French

Revolution and was intimately connected to the authoritarian reaction. In England the authoritarian reaction to the French Revolution occurred earlier than in France and was seen as part of the national struggle against the forces of Bonaparte. It is in this context that the libertarian ideas of Percy Shelley must be understood.

SHELLEY

'I am', wrote Shelley in a letter to the editor of *The Examiner*, 'a devoted enemy to religious, political, and domestic oppression.'[112] Though his aristocratic family background was very different from Proudhon's working-class origin, they shared a dislike of coercive authority and a corresponding passion for liberty. Shelley's principal writings – poetry and prose – are centred on the problem of authority in the family, religion and the state and his attacks on political despotism are closely related to his rejection of a celestial sovereign. His atheism, being an aspect of his libertarian or anarchist convictions, may properly be called political.[113] Shelley's picture of God was analogous to the image of the despotic state, and his attack on both was pungent and unremitting. He also shared with Proudhon a suspicion of democracy and of 'the mob'. Shelley was, however, unlike the Frenchman, prepared to extend his libertarian principles into the life of the family.

The setting

Percy Bysshe Shelley was born in 1792, the eldest son of Sir Timothy Shelley, a Whig Member of Parliament associated with the Duke of Norfolk's faction of the party.[114] Having been twice baptised, he spent his childhood in the family home at Horsham. Percy went to Eton and then to University College, Oxford. After only a few months he was, however, expelled from the college for refusing to state whether he was the author of a tract entitled *The Necessity of Atheism*.

The first two decades of the nineteenth century witnessed perhaps the most repressive government which England had experienced since the seventeenth century. The bloody excesses of the French Revolution and the Napoleonic wars had led to a fear among the ruling classes which bordered on panic. Despite discontent with the grossly unfair system of parliamentary representation which effectively deprived them of political power, large sections of the middle class were prepared to accept a degree of repression rather than risking a popular uprising.

From 1812 the government was presided over by Lord Liverpool, whose principal ministers were determined to repress with considerable brutality all signs of popular discontent. Liverpool himself, a wit observed, was so conservative that had he been present at the creation he would have implored God not to disturb the chaos. 'His mediocrity was his merit', wrote Lord Acton; 'the secret of his policy was that he had none.'[115]

For a young man in revolt against the conventions and institutions of his day it was a depressing period. The intellectual climate was generally conservative or even reactionary. Edmund Burke, who had defended the American colonists, had, in the eyes of many contemporaries, deserted the cause of liberty in launching his bitter attack on the French revolutionaries and their English sympathisers. Coleridge, Wordsworth and Southey, who had welcomed the French Revolution with varying degrees of enthusiasm, had become critical of utopian enterprises and emphasised the importance of traditional institutions, like church and monarchy, defending an authoritarian, structured and paternalistic state. Abroad the Holy Alliance linked the reactionary powers in a determination to resist all popular movements of liberation and the 'privileged gangs of murderers and swindlers, called Sovereigns, look to each other for aid against the common enemy'.[116]

The mass of people for their part suffered from the effects of war and from the dislocation produced by the rapid growth of manufacturing industry. Sporadic outbreaks occurred and the Luddite riots of 1812 shook the country. In the following year a mob attempted to storm the Tower of London, the Prince Regent was shot and the law of habeas corpus was suspended. In 1817 three leaders of an abortive march from Derbyshire were arrested and executed, largely on the evidence of a government *agent provocateur* named Oliver. Shelley's writings reflect his bitter opposition to this repressive government. His 'Address to the People on the Death of the Princess Charlotte' contrasts the death of the princess with the execution of the three Derbyshire leaders. Englishmen should indeed be sad, for 'a Beautiful Princess is dead', but much more should they mourn the departure of freedom. 'Let us follow the corpse of British Liberty slowly and reverentially to its tomb.'[117] Two years later occurred the notorious Peterloo massacre, when troops (mostly the part-time yeomanry) charged a demonstration in St Peter's Fields, Manchester, killing eleven and injuring many hundreds. It seemed that the government almost wished to provoke disorder. From Italy, Shelley composed *The Mask of Anarchy*, in which murder, fraud and hypocrisy appear associated with the names of three leading government ministers, Castlereagh, Eldon and Sidmouth, in a 'ghastly masquerade'.

The French Revolution

As in recent years the United States invasion of Grenada, the victories of the Sandinistas in Nicaragua and the miners' strike in Britain have assumed a symbolic role in the cultural formation of radical youth, so the French Revolution and its aftermath stood as an ensign for Shelley's generation. For the poet himself it represented both a hope and a warning. The revolutionary leaders demonstrated that things could change, that the structure of oppression they inherited was not immutable. And yet the dynamic of destruction carried the movement first to tyranny and then to 'anarchy', his term for a situation of social chaos. Such anarchy provided, in turn, the seedbed for a new authoritarianism. Having overthrown 'the whole of that peculiarly insolent and oppressive system' of which the civil and ecclesiastical system had been part, the revolutionaries failed to deal with 'those passions which are the spirit of these forms' and they employed violent means to achieve their ends. In consequence, a reaction set in, with the advent first of Napoleon and then of the restored monarchy.

> Suddenly fierce confusion fell from heaven
> Among them: there was strife, deceit and fear:
> Tyrants rushed in, and did divide the spoil.

Nevertheless it was a monarchy with 'his teeth drawn and his claws pared'. As with the seventeenth-century revolution in England, 'abuses were abolished which never since have dared to show their face'.[118]

In his preface to *The Revolt of Islam*, written in 1817, Shelley had been able to sound a more hopeful note. While he characterised the period as one of 'gloom and misanthropy', he felt that his generation had 'lived to survive an age of despair' and that it was possible to perceive 'a slow, gradual, silent change'. It was this belief that inspired his epic.[119]

The Revolt of Islam, originally entitled *Laon and Cythna*, is set against the background of a revolution that failed. As P.M.S. Dawson has argued, the poet's aim was not to show how the French

Revolution might have succeeded, but to demonstrate how good may stem even from a revolution which was doomed to fail.[120] It raised the dilemma of whether revolutionary leaders should adopt the methods of their adversaries. Failure to act decisively and even ruthlessly often results in defeat, yet to do so implies another kind of defeat. It was the problem facing Salvador Allende in Chile, whose attempt to act in a constitutional manner, restraining the radicals among his own supporters, has been cited as a reason for his eventual defeat. Yet to have done otherwise would not only have invited immediate military intervention, but would have gone some way to rendering such intervention legitimate in the eyes of many. Shelley would claim that the forces of a true moral revolution were strengthened in the long run and that short cuts lead to a Stalinist outcome.

While critical of the excesses in France, Shelley insisted that the revolution had produced worthy fruit and he denounced the repressive policies of the British government. He linked the love of civil liberty with a rejection of God as a supernatural despot – an image of the deity entertained by many of his religious contemporaries. In his preface to *The Revolt of Islam*, he distinguished this 'erroneous and degrading idea' of God, which is spoken against in the poem, from 'the Supreme Being itself'.

Not only was Shelley in revolt against political and divine despotism but he objected also to social and domestic tyranny. The system of patriarchal domination in the family, as he had experienced it, revolted him. Furthermore he denounced the institution of marriage as 'this most despotic, most unrequired fetter which prejudice has forged to confine its energies',[121] though this did not prevent his twice engaging in its tyrannical regime. The poet found the kind of freedom he sought, at least in domestic affairs, outside his home country, and he spent his last years in Italy, where he died in 1822 by shipwreck, at the age of 29.

Godwin and Shelley on authority

The young Shelley had been an admirer of William Godwin and had accepted many of his principles. Godwin was a radical individualist, who believed that government is 'an usurpation upon the private judgement and individual conscience of mankind'. As government is evil, 'the object principally to be aimed at is that we should have as little of it as the general peace of human society will permit'.[122] Force and not consent is the basis of all government; it may be wise on occasions to obey rulers but it is never right to reverence them. All government is bad, but power centralised in monarchy becomes despotic. 'Monarchy', declared Godwin, 'is founded in imposture.' He believed that human nature is 'perfectible', by which he meant 'susceptible of perpetual improvement', and that there would be a gradual and peaceful progression towards a stateless society, achieved by a reformed educational system and the influence of a free press. The government of men would be replaced by the administration of things. 'Executive power will, comparatively speaking, become everything, and legislative nothing.'[123] While he followed Godwin in his approach to issues of liberty and authority, Shelley became critical of his radical individualism. The poet derided the notion of 'each citizen sitting by his own fireside' having no concern for others and maintained that 'individuals acting singly with whatever energy can never effect so much as a society'.[124]

William Godwin was born in 1756, the son of a dissenting minister, and for a short time followed his father's calling. He had begun as a Calvinist in theology and passed through deism and Socinianism to become 'a complete unbeliever' by 1787.[125] His radicalism thus developed out of a dissenting tradition going back to the sectarian groups of the seventeenth century. Godwin saw religion as an important element in social life and believed its general effect was to strengthen authoritarian systems in his own day. Although, in its idea, religion is a great equaliser – bringing the most powerful king to the same judgment seat as the poorest peasant – its practical consequence was to keep down the weak and the poor.[126] In his earlier writings Godwin had wrestled with the Calvinist idea of God which he had inherited. He spoke of God as 'our master and proprietor', who 'may do what he will with his own', and yet he went on to declare that 'God has not a right to be a tyrant.'[127] His rejection of free will, in both God and man, is due to his dislike of arbitrariness.[128] In later life Godwin stated unequivocally that 'the God of the Christians is a tyrant'. Most prayers are more like 'petitions addressed to an inexorable tyrant ... than the sober and heartfelt emotion of a man who knows that he has recourse to a being of reason and benignity'.[129] He drew an analogy between the perpetual vigilance of an all-seeing God and 'the constant terror of spies and informers' which haunted the subjects of the earthly power.[130] Shelley himself later took up these themes.

Shelley insisted that no moral obligation can stem from the will of a lawgiver, nor from the punishments which he is able to impose on those who transgress. Government is a consequence of human

ignorance and wickedness. 'In proportion as mankind becomes wise
. . . should be the extinction of the unequal system under which they
now subsist. Government is, in fact, the mere badge of their
depravity.'[131] He proclaimed the importance of conscience and
individuality against the claims of rulers.[132] In his *Declaration of
Rights* (1812) the poet maintained that governments have no rights
and exist in order to protect the rights of their members; they have
no power to make law but only to declare as law 'the moral result of
the imperishable relations of things'.[133] Governments which went
beyond this became tyrannical and must be resisted. Shelley likewise
rejected the idea of a divine omnipotent being whose decrees are the
source of moral obligation. 'An all-powerful Demon might, indubit-
ably, annex punishments to virtue and rewards to vice', he told Lord
Ellenborough, 'but could not by these means effect the slightest
change in their abstract and immutable natures.'[134]

Shelley saw a close analogy between political tyranny and popular
conceptions of an omnipotent and despotic God. With Godwin he
regarded Milton's Satan as possessing virtue because of his resistance
to a divine despotism, and it is clear that the poet was considerably
influenced by Milton, particularly in his composition of *Prometheus
Unbound*. He believed Prometheus, however, to be 'a more poetical
character than Satan' (by which he meant more admirable), being
free from the taint of ambition and malice. He represents 'the type of
the highest perfection of moral and intellectual nature'. Jupiter, who
had chained Prometheus to his rock, was pictured as 'our almighty
Tyrant'.[135]

Perhaps Shelley's most spirited attack on what he believed to be a
Christian idea of God is to be found in his notes to *Queen Mab*, first
printed in the summer of 1813. The term 'God' originally stood for
the unknown cause of events which could not otherwise be
explained. Then:

By the vulgar mistake of a metaphor for a real being, a word for a
thing, it became a man, endowed with human qualities and
governing the universe as an earthly monarch governs his
kingdom. Their addresses to this imaginary being, indeed, are
much in the same style as those of subjects to a king. They
acknowledge his benevolence, deprecate his anger, and supplicate
his favour.[136]

Clearly Shelley's objection is not merely to a belief in God but to the
practices associated with such belief, such as prayer and worship

involving, as they do, 'a certain degree of servility analogous to the loyalty demanded by earthly tyrants'.[137]

During his stay in Italy Shelley came across some of the manuscripts of Torquato Tasso, a figure with whom he was considerably fascinated. Discussing the sonnets written by Tasso to his persecutor, which contained a good deal of flattery, he compared them to the prayers a Christian directs to his God, whom he knows to be 'the most remorseless capricious & inflexible of tyrants, but whom he knows also to be omnipotent'.[138]

> Serene in his unconquerable might
> Endued, the Almighty King, his steadfast throne
> Encompassed unapproachably with power
> And darkness and deep solitude and awe
> Stood like a black cloud on some aery cliff
> Embosoming its lightening – in his sight
> Unnumbered glorious spirits trembling stood
> Like slaves before their Lord – prostrate around
> Heaven's multitudes hymned everlasting praise.[139]

In his 'Essay on the Devil and Devils', probably composed in 1819, he returned to the subject, denouncing Christian theologians for acting 'like panic-stricken slaves in the presence of a jealous and suspicious despot' by inventing flattering but contradictory phrases, 'endeavouring to reconcile omnipotence, and benevolence, and equity in the Author of an Universe, where evil and good are inextricably entangled'. The devil is invented in order to extricate them from this difficulty.[140] Shelley went further with the analogy and compared the 'dirty work' done for God by the devil to the role of informers and *agents provocateurs*, like Oliver. 'It is', he continued, 'far from inexplicable that earthly tyrants should employ this kind of agents, or that God should have done so with regard to the Devil and his angels.'[141]

A further aspect of authority, civic and celestial, to which the poet drew attention is the fact that it subsists largely because of the subjects' consent to it. The notion of a despotic God derives its power from the fear and ignorance which lead people to accept it. Similarly the power of a government is to a considerable degree dependent upon a willing subservience of the people. Their liberation will involve throwing off this moral chain. As Dawson has shown, this is clearly illustrated in *Prometheus Unbound*, where the authority of Jupiter is derived from the grant of Prometheus himself. The latter's liberation is greeted with the words of Demogorgon,

'Conquest is dragged captive through the deep', reminding the reader of the verse from Psalm 68, taken by St Paul to refer to the victory of Christ: 'Thou hast gone up on high, thou hast led captivity captive.'[142]

Revolution or reform?

Being opposed to all forms of authoritarianism, Shelley was committed to the extension of an effective freedom to all classes of the population and to a consequent policy of economic equality and respect for civil rights. He believed that this could be achieved by peaceful reform, but that gradualism may be overtaken by events. He feared what he called anarchy or social disorder, but was also critical of all forms of government. How did he relate these principles to the political events of his day?

Despite the apparent victory of oppressive forces in post-Napoleonic Europe, signs of popular unrest and a desire for liberty were manifesting themselves, not only at home and in Ireland, but in Greece, Spain and Germany. In what may have been an early sketch for the 'Ode to Liberty', the poet mentioned these signs of hope and quoted the prophet Isaiah: 'The Lord hath broken the staff of the wicked & the sceptre of the rulers.'[143] Yet Shelley was keen to warn radicals against the dangers of mob rule and of appealing to violence. It was this civil disorder which the actions of Liverpool's government were provoking and which some of his ministers appeared eager to encourage. In the *Mask*, the figures of Murder, Fraud and Hypocrisy were followed by that Anarchy which their actions were conspiring to incite:

> Last came Anarchy: he rode
> On a white horse, splashed with blood;
> He was pale even to the lips,
> Like Death in the Apocalypse. . . .
> Then all cried with one accord,
> 'Thou art King, and God, and Lord;
> Anarchy, to thee we bow,
> Be thy name made holy now!'

Shelley was thus generally critical of appeals to violence on the part of the oppressed and at times he advocated a type of passive resistance later to be adopted by Gandhi. In *The Mask of Anarchy* he imagined a future popular demonstration in which military action would be met by stubborn but non-violent defiance.[144] This line he advised, principally because the consequences of passive resistance would be more advantageous and would sow deep seeds of discontent in the army itself. Violence, on the other hand, leads to further violence in a deadly spiral: 'when man sheds the blood of man, revenge, and hatred, and a long train of executions, and assassinations, and proscriptions is perpetuated to remotest time', he wrote in 1817.[145]

Five years earlier Shelley had already adopted a radically pacifist position and had urged the Irish people to pursue their struggle by peaceful means, insisting that virtue – acquired by the practice of temperance and charity – together with wisdom – achieved by reading, talking, thinking and searching – were necessary before defying the tyrant. In this early tract, Shelley actually maintained that violence is never justified and that 'Force makes the side that employs it directly wrong.'[146] This position was also clearly stated in his *Declaration of Rights*, where he decreed that 'No man has a right to disturb the public peace by personally resisting the execution of a law, however bad. He ought to acquiesce, using at the same time the utmost powers of his reason to promote its repeal.'[147] Despite its decidedly moderate tone, this pamphlet was regarded as subversive and Shelley's Irish servant, Dan Healy, was imprisoned for distributing it.

Shelley's rejection of violence was linked to his suspicion of 'the mob' and of the activity of 'illiterate demagogues'.[148] On a number of occasions he reiterated the view that the masses were unable to initiate a constructive revolution and that popular agitation would end in 'anarchy' and in a new despotism. He expressed doubts about whether the poor were capable of discerning their own true interests and saw the enlightened portion of the educated classes as the group upon whom the burden of reforming activity should fall. The change, he told Thomas Love Peacock in 1819, should commence among the higher orders, or anarchy would lead to despotism.[149] Poets – 'the unacknowledged legislators of mankind' – were to be in the vanguard of this movement.[150]

Like Proudhon, Shelley believed that true revolution involves a moral reformation which would redirect those passions and dispositions which provide the basis of oppressive institutions. He saw conventional religion – with its God of power and might, superior to all moral laws, who issued commands to a fearful humanity – as reinforcing an unjust and tyrannical state. The separation of politics from ethics had been a fatal error in world history and it was foolish to think that evil will produce good or that falsehood may generate truth.[151] So in *Prometheus Unbound* and in *The Revolt of Islam* he emphasised the need for an interior liberation which would accompany institutional changes. In the former we see almost a 'politics of forgiveness', when Prometheus revokes the curse which he had called down on Jupiter. Having summoned the Phantasm of Jupiter to repeat the curse, the chained hero continues:

> *Prometheus.* Were these my words, O Parent?
> *The Earth.* They were thine.
> *Prometheus.* It doth repent me: words are quick and vain;
>   Grief for a while is blind, and so was mine.
> I wish no living thing to suffer pain.

Again in the final speech of Demogorgon we read:

> To suffer woes which Hope thinks infinite;
> To forgive wrongs darker than death or night;
>   To defy Power, which seems omnipotent;
> To love, and bear; to hope till Hope creates
> From its own wreck the thing it contemplates;
>   Neither to change, nor falter, nor repent;
> This, like thy glory, Titan, is to be
> Good, great and joyous, beautiful and free;
> This is alone Life, Joy, Empire and Victory.[152]

A strongly moral understanding of politics frequently results in the kind of fanaticism which rejects all compromise, accepting only the ideal solution to political problems. Surprisingly in Shelley there is a pragmatism which is prepared to settle for the best in the circumstances. 'Nothing is more idle', he wrote, 'than to reject a limited benefit because we cannot without great sacrifices obtain an unlimited one.'[153] During the crisis of 1819 he told Leigh Hunt:

> You know my principles incite me to take all the good I can get in politics, for ever aspiring to something more. I am one of those whom nothing will fully satisfy, but who am ready to be partially satisfied by all that is practicable.[154]

As with Rosa Luxemburg, revolution may thus be combined with reform, by seeing reform as the limited political means towards an ultimate revolutionary end.[155]

In the wake of the Peterloo massacres, however, we note a changing emphasis in Shelley's thinking. Addressing manual workers he exhorts them to revolutionary action:

> The seed ye sow, another reaps;
> The wealth ye find, another keeps;
> The robes ye weave, another wears;
> The arms ye forge, another bears.
>
> Sow seed, – but let no tyrant reap;
> Find wealth, – let no impostor heap;
> Weave robes, – let not the idle wear;
> Forge arms, – in your defence to bear.

A similar theme emerged in his fragment 'What men gain fairly', where he suggested that those who have made unjust or fraudulent gains may properly be despoiled and 'left in the nakedness of infamy'.[156]

In *A Philosophical View of Reform*, written in 1820, Shelley reasserted his clear preference for gradual and peaceful reform. A direct and violent assault on the centres of power might result in the tragedy of civil war.[157] He nevertheless realistically observed that the time for conciliation may have passed and that the masses had been cheated for so long that they may no longer be prepared to wait for the 'slow, gradual, and certain' advent of reform.[158] The situation is closely parallel to that found in parts of contemporary Latin America where radicals are faced with deciding how far to provoke a confrontation with political elites, knowing that this is likely to lead to a violent repression of an already suffering people. Shelley refrained from urging others to follow dangerous paths which he was himself unable to tread.

Liberty and equality

What kind of reform did Shelley demand? What was his concept of freedom for the people? In the first place he clearly thought that political liberty and more specifically parliamentary reform was needed. Although he subscribed to an appeal for the widows and children of the executed Luddites, he thought that the thousand-pound fine imposed upon the Hunts for their radical journalism was 'an affair of more consequence'.[159] Yet in his *Mask of Anarchy* the poet clearly recognised the notion of 'positive liberty', as it later came to be called. In answer to the rhetorical question 'What art thou freedom?' we read:

> Thou art clothes, and fire, and food
> For the trampled multitude –
> No – in countries that are free
> Such starvation cannot be
> As in England now we see.

Liberty for the masses may indeed demand restrictions on the few:

> To the rich thou art a check,
> When his foot is on the neck
> Of his victim.[160]

He saw gross economic inequalities as involving 'flagrant encroach-ments on liberty'.[161]

While a certain elitist emphasis is present in Shelley's writings and there is occasional aristocratic arrogance in his actions, he was deeply committed to an egalitarian policy. 'Am I not', he demanded of Elizabeth Hitchener, a 'worshipper of equality?' Though absolute equality may be impossible of achievement, there must be 'a strenuous tendency towards it'.[162] Political power was determined by wealth; the constitutional forms simply legitimised the situation. He wrote of the power of the rich increasing and of monarchy as 'merely the mask of this power and . . . a kind of stalking-horse used to conceal these "catchers of men", while they lay their nets. Monarchy is only the string which ties the robber's bundle.' The blatantly unjust distribution of wealth and the spirit in which it was defended in Britain made inevitable 'some momentous change in its internal government'.[163] Shelley traced back the idea of equality, strangely, to Plato and its propagation to Jesus and to Christianity 'in its abstract purity'. He saw the gradual abolition of slavery and emancipation of women as part of this movement.

> Never will peace and human nature meet
> Till free and equal man and woman greet
> Domestic peace. . . .
> Can man be free if woman be a slave?[164]

Shelley's religion

Shelley's own metaphysical and religious beliefs are not easy to discern. In his early years he seems to have believed in a rather crude form of materialism, which he soon rejected as unsatisfactory. In 1811 he accepted the Lockean idea that there are no innate ideas and that 'all ideas are derived from the senses'.[165] Angela Leighton has pointed to the way this strict empiricism and a demand for clear and distinct ideas came into conflict with Shelley's conception of poetry. This contradiction centred on the notion of the sublime. His poetic work seems to have involved the 'deceptive and superstitious devices of language' in order to function properly.[166] The idea of inspiration also was difficult to accommodate in a Lockean world-view. Even in his early writing, however, he is found speaking of God as 'the soul of the universe'. The natural world itself points to the fact that 'some vast intellect animates Infinity',[167] and the notes to *Queen Mab* suggest that his denial of God did not imply the rejection of 'a pervading Spirit coeternal with the universe'. In his early correspondence with Elizabeth Hitchener, Shelley wrote of God as 'the existing power of existence' and towards the end of his life he continued to refer to God in terms of that 'Power by which we are surrounded'. In the light of his belief in God as 'another signification for the Universe', Southey told him, he should not call himself an atheist.[168]

Shelley was, however, an atheist in the sense of denying the existence of a supreme personal being, transcending a universe which he had created. He wished to convince Elizabeth Hitchener of the non-existence of such a being on the grounds of truth and also as 'the most summary way of eradicating Christianity'.[169] Despite its title, Shelley's celebrated tract, written while an undergraduate, *The Necessity of Atheism*, merely argued, in a somewhat naïve way, that the arguments put forward by theists were unsatisfactory and that 'there is no proof of the existence of a Deity'.[170] It falls short of asserting an atheist position. Writing to Godwin, however, the young poet declared that he had by this time become 'in the popular sense of the word "God", an Atheist'.[171]

A Refutation of Deism, Shelley's 1814 Humean dialogue, gives a clear, if indirect, indication of his ideas on religion. Eusebes, a sceptical but orthodox believer, effectively disposes of the rational religion of the deist, while Theosophus, in turn, mounts a vigorous attack upon what he conceives to be the immorality and absurdity of supernatural revelation.

In his 'Essay on Christianity', probably written early in 1820, Shelley adopted a more positive approach, contrasting the religion of Jesus with the institutionalised Christianity which had evolved into the repressive religion of his day. In an extended commentary on the saying 'Blessed are the pure in heart for they shall see God', the poet interpreted Jesus as saying that virtue is its own reward. To be of pure heart, honest intentions and a good conscience is what it means to see God. He rejected as idle dreams of the visionary or pernicious representations of impostors the notion that the vision of God is some kind of extrinsic reward for the pure in heart: 'What! After death, shall their awakened eyes behold the King of Heaven? Shall they stand in awe before the golden throne on which He sits, and gaze upon the venerable countenance of the paternal Monarch? Is this the reward of the virtuous and the pure?'[172]

Shelley was keen to reject an ethic of retribution, retaliation and reward in religion and in politics. Punishment may never legitimately be inflicted merely because a person deserves it, but is justified only when it has 'a decisively beneficial result in which he should at least participate'. He thus assailed ideas of eternal punishment. While insisting that justice must be a principal aim in social and political life, he understood justice in terms of the greatest quantity and quality of happiness which will ensue from any action. The distinction between justice and mercy, he asserted, 'was first imagined in the court of tyrants', where freedoms are regarded as a result of grace and favour.[173]

Shelley's early rejection of religion was expressed largely in terms of a philosophy which he soon came to reject and he needed some further criterion for renouncing organised religion while accepting poetry. He found this essentially in terms of the moral effects of the two practices. While he saw the latter as an important weapon in the struggle for human liberation, institutional religion played the role of reinforcing unjust structures of domination in domestic and in civil life.

NI DIEU NI MAÎTRE

The three atheist anarchists discussed in this chapter were reacting to an unbalanced and ideologically determined image of God cultivated by the ruling classes to endorse oppressive political structures; it was an image that encouraged a sense of inferiority and powerlessness among the mass of the people. Shelley, Proudhon and Bakunin made important contributions to political theology, by drawing attention to these features in contemporary Christianity. To be sure, as Thomas Merton observed, 'many who consider themselves atheists are in fact persons who are discontented with a naïve idea of God which makes Him appear to be an "object" or a "thing", or a person in a merely finite and human sense'.[174] Yet in the case of these men the discontent is moral rather than metaphysical in its origin. They regarded traditional ideas of God as an outrage against human freedom and dignity.

Much of what these men wrote about the Christian religion as practised widely in their day was accurate; dominant conceptions and images of God were unbalanced and served to legitimise oppressive structures of political power. We may indeed go further and acknowledge, from a Christian standpoint, the rather profound understanding which is to be found, particularly in some of the works of Proudhon, of a God who is beyond human knowing and who is ultimately a mystery. Nevertheless it would be quite wrong to call them 'Christians'. They would have rejected the idea and we do them no honour by such incongruity. In an address at a memorial service for the agnostic social scientist, R.M. Titmuss, Bishop Trevor Huddleston described him as a 'true Christian', by which he obviously meant 'good chap'. 'I am sure', wrote his daughter, 'this would not have pleased him.'[175]

Today there is also much to be learned from the *political* theories of Bakunin, Proudhon and Shelley. While the structures of domination and control are different in the late-twentieth-century North Atlantic world from the strong-armed tactics these three men had to face, the state is as powerful as ever. Comparing the peaceful Scotland of his day with that 'scene of wild confusion' which existed in the fourteenth century, James Fitzjames Stephen pointed out that force still reigns supreme. 'The reason why it works so quietly is that no one doubts either its existence, or its crushing superiority to any individual resistance which could be offered to it.'[176] The same can be said in comparing the civil order found in the countries of the OECD today with the arbitrary power and civil turmoil these anarchists experienced.

It might be argued that the analogy between atheism and anarchism is imperfect because, while the former denies *the existence* of God, anarchists deny not the existence of the state but its legitimacy. This would indeed be so if one thinks of the state as simply a collection of institutions. What anarchists deny, however, is the existence of the state as an authoritative body with the right to impose its laws by coercive sanctions. Successfully to convince people that kings, queens and prime ministers have no right to order them around is to abolish the state. The state exists because thinking makes it so. As Hobbes observed, 'Reputation of power, is power; because it draweth with it the adherence of those that need protection.'[177]

The belief that the state is 'created by God' or 'sacred' is one which Christians have frequently asserted and have thereby done immense harm in fortifying the claims of oppressive regimes, and it is closely related to authoritarian images of God. The sinister dictum of F.D. Maurice, that 'The State is as much God's creation as the Church', has been widely adopted by subsequent Anglican writers.[178] The dire implications of this theological position can be seen in the activities of the 'Deutsche Christen' discussed in a previous chapter. Those who believe, with the apostle, that 'Where the Spirit of the Lord is, there is liberty',[179] will take care to moderate their enthusiasm for the state, which is essentially an organ of coercion and manipulation, and therefore opposed to the freedom of individuals and voluntary groups.

The critique of God and the state proposed by Bakunin, Proudhon and Shelley was based on a commitment to freedom and responsibility as marks of individual and group life. They feared and opposed democracy as much as autocracy, having no confidence in majorities, which can easily form the basis of new dictatorships. However, they did believe that men and women were naturally good, and they looked forward to a revolution that would liberate them from coercive institutions. Their belief that evil in the world is due to unjust relationships and to corrupt coercive institutions, rather than to innate human corruption, is sometimes contrasted with the Christian belief in 'original sin'.

On this matter two points need to be made. First it is clear that all three acknowledged the need for individual moral reformation, which must accompany an authentic revolution. Secondly Christians too believe that humans are naturally good, in the sense that they are created in God's image. Original sin is not some inherent fault located in the individual soul, but rather that 'body of sin' into which all are born, in which all consequently share. Original sin is fundamentally a dislocation of relationships, between human beings themselves, and with him who is the ground of their being; it is the placing of self in the centre of life and attempting to order the world around one's selfish concerns. As Augustine pointed out, the essence of the 'earthly city' is a disordered love. Therefore baptism is not to be viewed as a spiritual operation performed on an individual (a kind of 'original-sin-ectomy'), but it symbolises and effects the incorporation of the baptised into a new set of relationships, into a new community which recognises God as the centre of life and fellow humans as brothers and sisters.[180]

8

Conclusion

This work could be read as a study in sovereignty: sovereignty asserted as absolute or challenged by appeal to divine sovereignty in the seventeenth century, restricted by law in the eighteenth, reinforced by ideas of autarky among the early German nationalists, rejected by the anarchists and atheists, democratised by writers from the United States and made benevolent by the theorists of welfare. As such it takes up the theme of my earlier book on *The Pluralist State*. Such a reading is legitimate but partial, treating the subject purely in terms of a 'history of ideas', without seeing the close relationship between these ideas and what was happening 'on the ground'.

I have indeed indicated the nature of this relationship in particular cases. The anarchism and atheism of the nineteenth century should be seen as a reaction to authoritarian political structures of the day. Yet anarchism and atheism were always minority movements, reflecting the anxiety of a relatively small number of thinkers whose passionate concern for freedom was not always shared even by those in whose interests they saw themselves acting. The emphasis upon autarky among German nationalists was, I have argued, related to the Napoleonic invasions and occupation of Germany, while the most vigorous challenge to autarkic and monarchic images of God and the state have come from the United States, which perceives itself as an interdependent federation of states and a pluralistic structure of interrelated groups. The welfare and totalitarian images of God and the state must in turn be understood against the background of a crisis in capitalism, in which the state has been recognised as the only organ capable of containing the discontents and potential conflicts between classes. In those countries where a welfare solution was tried and failed to contain the conflicts, or where it was not for various reasons tried, the mailed fist of totalitarian dictatorship was resorted to by a fearful populace.

The logic of analogy

Particular representations of God are frequently related to concepts and images of political authority. We noted a *positive* relationship in the cases of welfare images (in chapters 2 and 3), of autarkic conceptions (in chapter 6) and in the political theology of US writers (in chapter 5). The same positive relationship can be observed in the case of the atheist and anarchist thinkers dealt with in chapter 7, though, of course, in this instance a recognition of the positive relationship led to a denunciation of both. While the link between images of God and the state is sometimes difficult to trace, what emerges from our discussion is that dominant representations used of God are often positively related to the prevailing political rhetoric of the time, which in turn expresses a response to, or a reflection of, political movements and to changes taking place in the social structure.

Images of God and the civil government are sometimes *inversely* related, so that a picture of God becomes current which is in conscious or semi-conscious reaction to prevailing ideas about the state. Many of the religions of the poor and oppressed have seen the true God as identified with, and manifesting the idealised character-istics of, the *victims* of political authority rather than with the wielders of it. He is the suffering, crucified God of Studdert Kennedy, chaplain to British troops in the trenches of the First World War, and of the Japanese theologian Kitamori.[1] A prayer book found on the body of a Haitian guerrilla leader, killed in 1920 during the struggle against the US occupation of his country, included a 'revolutionary prayer to our Saviour Jesus' and also a prayer to 'God who was born; God who died; God who came to life again; God who was crucified; God who was hanged'.[2]

At other times the divine analogy has been explicitly *rejected*. In chapter 4 I noted how total claims being made by Nazi publicists led many German followers of Barth to reject the divine analogy and insist that the kind of ultimacy claimed for the race or the movement is appropriate only to God, whose sovereignty calls all human institutions into question. There is no earthly analogue to God. This is similar to the position taken by many Puritan parliamentary writers in seventeenth-century England.

Images of God frequently strengthen current political arrangements, giving some kind of legitimacy to the established order. This is true with welfare pictures of God and also with the 'democratic' conceptions of God which were popular among liberal Protestants in the USA. In an earlier period, the medieval picture of a God presiding over a feudal court, surrounded by ranks of angels and archangels, characterised by order, law and hierarchy, reflected the prevailing political structure of the day. There are indeed occasions when the divine analogy reinforces the status quo, but the heavenly model may also function as a criterion by which to judge and criticise current political procedures. Peter Brown observes:

> Christian writers did not mindlessly create a mirror in Heaven that reflected, in rosy tints, the hard facts of patronage and *prepotenza* that they had come to take for granted on the late Roman earth. The role of replication in late antiquity was subtly different: it enabled the Christian communities, by projecting a structure of clearly defined relationships onto the unseen world, to ask questions about the quality of relationships in their own society.

These projections, Brown goes on, allowed them to engage in 'muffled debates on the nature of power in their own world, and to examine in the light of ideal relationships with ideal figures, the relation between power, mercy and justice as practised around them'.[3]

The replacement of monarchical by democratic and participatory images proposed by twentieth-century American writers must be perceived as reflecting developments which had already occurred at the political level, and as contributing to their legitimation. The adoption by Berdyaev of a similar range of divine pictures and concepts is, however, to be seen rather as a reaction to totalitarianism and as linked to demands for political changes based upon liberty and popular participation. To borrow Karl Mannheim's distinction, an image which functions as ideology in one context may be utopian in another.[4]

Monotheism and monarchy

It is sometimes asserted that monotheism, whether or not it developed as a reflection of imperialism, has operated as an ideological justification for autocracy and that Trinitarianism, in contrast, is a guarantee of liberal democracy or of some form of political pluralism. Was the link between Arianism and imperialism in the fourth century merely adventitious? A number of writers have suggested otherwise. 'The Arians', declared Conrad Noel (the 'red vicar' of Thaxted) in a pamphlet of 1909, 'held that God was a solitary being remote from the interests of men, a sombre emperor in the Heavens. . . . Now, if this was so, they argued that such a solitary being was best represented upon earth by a solitary tyrant.'[5] A similar position was advanced by Erik Peterson in a more academic and sophisticated form.

The idea of the divine Trinity as a model for political relationships, however, goes back much further. That remarkable Russian writer Nikolai Feodorovich Feodorov is often quoted here, but I find the idea most fruitfully developed in the political theology of John Donne, who used royal images of God to affirm the principle of monarchy but also to expose injustice and corruption at the royal court and in the City of London. Donne, indeed, went further. He modified the unitary emphasis by a robust Trinitarianism which he used as a model for the kind of social pluralism which he wished to see established and preserved in England.[6]

Peterson's theory has been reiterated in the present day by Jürgen Moltmann in a number of his writings. Unfortunately considerable confusion is caused by these writers' adopting a definition of 'monotheism' as belief in God as a monolithic and undifferentiated unity. Such a belief would clearly be incompatible with Trinitarianism, in anything more than an 'economic' form.[7] This is not the traditional understanding of the term monotheism, which refers to belief in one God, rather than to the nature of God's unity. It would be better if we coined the term 'monolithism' for belief in the kind of monolithic, undifferentiated and monarchic deity to which Peterson and Moltmann refer. Some, though probably not all, Muslim ideas of God would qualify. A recent writer refers to the Muslim 'conception of a God who is indivisible, indissociable . . . "solid casting", in modern industrial terminology'.[8] Thus all monolithites (not of course to be confused with monothelites) would be monotheists, though not all monotheists would be monolithites. Again not all philosophical monists nor all theological unitarians would be monolithites, allowing, as many would, a notion of plurality within the unity. Some Hebrew scholars, for example, have argued that Israelite monotheism by no means excludes such differentiation, while Donne saw anticipations of Trinitarianism not only in the Old Testament but also in the Koran.[9]

Does belief in, and worship of, a monolithic God necessarily lead then to autocracy or absolutism in politics? Moltmann states that 'there is no monotheism without theocracy'; he maintains that 'monotheism is monarchism' and that 'the idea of the almighty ruler of the universe everywhere requires abject servitude, because it points to complete dependency in all spheres of life'.[10] To be sure, as we have seen, the analogy between divine and political structures of authority has commonly been used in this manner. Yet belief in a divine sovereign has also been a ground upon which the claims of earthly tyrants were resisted. While James I used celestial monarchy as a justification for royal absolutism, Puritan parliamentarians, with a similar Calvinist belief in a divine sovereign, denied any analogy with the civil power. God is the one and only true king; all people, including earthly rulers, are but his subjects. Calls for unquestioning obedience by earthly rulers were thus rejected.[11]

Twentieth-century Barthians adopted a similar stance in the face of the totalitarian claims of Hitler. It was, they alleged, theological liberalism and the henotheistic image of a tribal God that were being used to support the ideology of the regime. Divine sovereignty, on the other hand, calls into question all earthly claims to absolute authority, constituting a challenge to political theologies which attempt to use Christian faith as a political ideology – to what has been called the 'politicisation' of Christianity. An emphasis upon the transcendence of the sovereign God leads, Barthians would assert, not to a replication of such structures of power in the political realm, but to a questioning of all absolute claims made by earthly rulers. 'We must obey God rather than man.'

No doubt there is truth in all this and yet it too contains a danger. Christians are able to justify a nervous sitting on the political sidelines giving qualified support here and hesitant backing there. They are allies who cannot ultimately be trusted when the crunch comes. This was graphically demonstrated in the positions adopted by the Christian Democratic Party and the Roman Catholic hierarchy in Chile during the presidency of Salvador Allende. Political effectiveness demands loyalty, solidarity and resolute action, and these are qualities in which those who continually appeal to etherial values and transcendent criteria tend to be lacking. Nevertheless a critical commitment designed to secure the best in the circumstances is by no means excluded for those whose ultimate appeal is to a transcendent God.

It is important to distinguish between explicit use of the divine analogy and its unconscious influence. This corresponds to two quite different uses of the term 'ideology': first, the calculated use of a system of ideas to support or legitimate a political position; and, second, the widespread, implicit and generally unquestioned system of ideas and beliefs which a social group takes for granted. It is indeed likely that belief in, and worship of, an arbitrary, monolithic and absolute celestial being will dispose worshippers to a generally submissive attitude towards all officials, in church, state and family. Yet explicit arguments put forward to justify submission to such earthly powers, on the basis of the divine analogy, have sometimes rebounded on their authors. Occasionally the whole analogical mode will be questioned, as in the case of the Barthians of the twentieth century and many Puritan parliamentarians of the seventeenth century. At other times such arguments may even lead to a reassessment of the divine image. If monarchs are really as bad as this, is it proper to refer to God as 'king' at all?

Belief in a triune God, whose unity is a perfect harmony, might well incline people to think of earthly communities in terms of co-operation and community. Donne certainly thought it did. Yet at a recent Anglo-Catholic gathering in Loughborough one speaker attempted to show – with copious quotations from Charles Williams – that the structure of the Holy Trinity provides justification for a hierarchical ordering of social relations. Interestingly, however, he spoke of an 'inequality' of the divine persons, due to the dependence of the Son on the Father and of the Spirit on the Father (and the Son, in western theology).[12] The erroneous assumption that all forms of dependence imply inequality is one which I have considered in chapters 5 and 6.

Care must therefore be taken when assessing the relationship which obtains between divine and political images or concepts. It would, for instance, be wrong to suggest that Trinitarianism *logically* implies commitment to a communitarian political ideal or that such a conception of God inevitably leads to the acceptance of such an ideal. I have already rejected any idea that analogical argument can proceed in this 'coercive' manner. What we might properly say is that, if we are to have what Newman would have called a 'real' rather than a merely 'notional' idea of the triune God, we must have experienced co-operation and community here on earth, from which the divine analogy may come alive. Perhaps this is one good reason why those concerned with dogmatic orthodoxy should be interested in social and political structures. 'Human multiunity, or altogether-ness, actualized in reality', wrote Feodorov, 'is a necessary condition for the understanding of the Divine Triunity. As long as the

independence of individuals is expressed as enslavement, just so long
will altogetherness as a likeness of the Triunity be simply a thought,
an ideal.'[13]

Freedom, conflict and consent

Bakunin, Proudhon and Shelley believed in human freedom, and this
is indeed something that Christians too should hold in high regard. If
men and women are made in God's image and are responsible to him
and to one another, they should enjoy a maximum of effective
freedom. The current British government claims to believe in human
freedom. The 1987 Conservative Party manifesto stated that the
party is opposed to the 'all-powerful state' and wants people to have
'more freedom of choice'.[14] Some years ago Thatcher was rebuked
by a fellow Conservative for her libertarian rhetoric. Peregrine
Worsthorne maintained that 'social discipline' was a more fruitful
and rewarding theme for conservatism than individual freedom. 'The
truth at present', he asserted,

> is that all forms of discipline are breaking down. . . . The urgent
> need today is for the State to regain control over 'the people', to
> reassert its authority, and it is useless to imagine that this will be
> helped by some libertarian mish-mash drawn from the writings of
> Adam Smith, John Stuart Mill, and the warmed up milk of
> nineteenth century liberalism.[15]

Worsthorne was wrong. The libertarian rhetoric struck a chord with
an electorate which had become disillusioned with the bureaucratic
authoritarianism of the Callaghan–Heath consensus. The Labour party
had given little evidence of any solid commitment to human freedom.
Thatcher's rhetoric, however, proved to be empty. Power has
increasingly been centred in Westminster, Whitehall and the City of
London, with effective freedom being taken from local government,
trade unions, universities and other subsidiary bodies. Government
ministers have called on church leaders to legitimate this system by
reinforcing 'traditional moral values'.

Although much Christian iconography is indeed centred upon
political images of God which reflect domination and sovereignty,
there are also in Christian tradition and in Scripture ideas of God
which emphasise his participation in the world and co-operation with
human beings made in his likeness. Belief in the incarnation and in
the immanent presence of the Holy Spirit involves such ideas. Jesus

said that he did not call his disciples servants, for the servant simply obeys orders from his master without understanding; he called them friends (John 15: 15). Paul told his readers at Corinth that they were 'fellow workers with Christ' (2 Corinthians 6: 1). Prayer should be seen, as I have noted in my discussion of T.H. Green in chapter 3, not simply in terms of a child addressing a quite separate and distinct father or ruler, but as a sharing in the life of the Holy Trinity. All this suggests that the monarchical images of domination must be, if not replaced, supplemented by images which signify co-operation and participation.

Some popular theories of the atonement have in the past suggested almost a conflict of interest among the 'persons' of the Trinity. The Father, as strict and unbending judge, is placated by the loving, merciful and self-sacrificing Son. Most theologians, Catholic and Protestant alike, have scornfully rejected such theories. 'We cannot think or talk of the atonement', declared Hastings Rashdall, 'as involving any kind of transaction between the Father and the Son.'[16] Jürgen Moltmann praises certain Anglican writers of an earlier generation, including C.E. Rolt and Studdert Kennedy, for insisting that the suffering Christ is a revelation of the eternal nature of the Father.[17]

Although Moltmann rightly attacks a modalistic Christology, which portrays the incarnation in terms of the eternal God merely veiling his majesty in the manhood of Jesus, his own theology tends towards a kind of 'modalistic patrology', in which the suffering of Jesus is automatically ascribed to the Father.[18] His wish to assert a dynamic relationship between Father and Son in the Trinity is betrayed by his refusal to acknowledge the possibility of the Son having characteristics ascribed to him which are not ascribed to the Father. Although it is true that the Father 'sent' or 'gave' the Son, this does not imply that he necessarily shares in all the experiences of the Son. Indeed much traditional Christian language suggests otherwise. The Epistle to the Hebrews pictures Christ as interceding or pleading before the Father on behalf of his people (Hebrews 7: 25). While it would undoubtedly derogate from divine perfection to assert that there are within the godhead what Marxists would call 'antagonistic contradictions', an undialectical consensus or unison might be just as bad. Talk of 'the suffering of the Father' is based upon just that kind of uniformity in the godhead which Moltmann wishes to deny. Thus, while I would not seek to replace a 'consensus' model of the triune God by a 'conflict' model, it may be well to acknowledge what bishops call a 'fruitful tension' in our inevitably crude attempts to portray relations between the persons of the divine Trinity.

Though I do not wish to follow Catholic theorists like Joseph de Maistre, Juan Donoso Cortés and Christopher Dawson by suggesting that political heresy is always founded upon theological deviance, it would not be entirely implausible to see a denial of God's transcendence on the one hand and of his immanence on the other as manifesting totalitarian and tyrannical tendencies respectively. The former tradition goes back from the Balliol idealists to Hegel, Herder and Spinoza; the latter from Barth through the eighteenth-century deists to Hobbes and Bodin. A God who is unambiguously immanent may too easily be used to sanctify a current political system, while a merely transcendent being, ruling over an alien world, readily provides a model, and thus a potential legitimation, for arbitrary political rule. As Feodorov observed, both pantheism and deism tend towards 'the acknowledgment, worship and service of blind force', which is the negation of true religion.[19] Immanence without transcendence suggests a harmony, coherence and integration which ought not to be expected in this order of things, for 'here we have no continuing city'. Transcendence without immanence suggests a notion of domination which excludes participation and co-operation.

A God who is immanent through the incarnation of the divine Son and the indwelling of the Holy Spirit, yet who cannot be contained within this universe, and whose transcendence is symbolised by the ascended Christ and the eternal Father, might be said to provide the most satisfactory model from the standpoint of its political consequences. When we think of the 'internal' life of the Trinity, the Spirit is generally seen as constituting the bond which links Father and Son; when thinking of the 'economic' Trinity, however, it is the incarnate but risen Son who mediates between the transcendent Father and the immanent Holy Spirit. As the adequacy of moral principles may be assessed by the status of the consequences they entail, so Christian doctrines may be judged in the light of their outcome: 'By their fruits you shall know them' (Matthew 7: 16).

Contemporary images and the Christian community

Is there not a danger, though, in judging the validity of our images of God according to this kind of pragmatism, which looks at political or social consequences for a criterion?[20] Was it not precisely this feature of Gordon Kaufman's theological system which I found unsatisfactory in chapter 5's discussion? Kaufman's assumption that his own twentieth-century 'bourgeois' western beliefs about personality and humanity in some way transcend the social context within which he writes is rather remarkable. It is unlikely that these beliefs are shared by Hindu pundits, by the followers of Ayatollah Khomeini, or even by fellows of All Souls' College, Oxford.[21] While in theology, as in ethics, it may indeed be the case that the kind of reasoning which is appropriate, in defending one's judgments, should appeal downward to consequences – or perhaps sideways to analogous cases – rather than upwards to general principles, this does assume some *particular community* within which there is likely to be agreement about the status of these consequences and cases. It is for this reason that writers like W.G. Ward, in the last century, and Stanley Hauerwas in our own day, lay such emphasis upon a 'community of character'. Ward saw the church's encouragement of and respect for saintliness as forming the basis of its authority, both moral and doctrinal.[22]

The attempt to find fixed criteria by which to assess the validity of the images used of God results in a wild-goose chase. It is rather a question of adjusting and balancing a number of these images in such a way that they reflect the judgment and conscience of Christians. Many of these images are derived from Scripture; others have become current at some stage in the history of the church and have been generally received by the faithful as authentically representing their beliefs. Others again are perhaps in the process of emerging in the life of the contemporary church. There are no wholly 'objective' criteria to which we can appeal that are free from the taint of cultural context. Therefore the dialogue between different world religions must proceed otherwise than by attempts to find some universal standards by which each may be assessed. David Tracy has important things to say on this question in his book *The Analogical Imagination.*[23] Appeals 'downwards' from images and concepts of God to the kind of moral consequences – individual and social – which they entail is no solution. Different religious traditions assess these consequences differently and they cannot therefore constitute an agreed criterion to which appeal may be made. Within a particular tradition, however, where general agreement does exist, such appeals may be of considerable value in determining the appropriateness of competing images.

It is principally in the devotional and spiritual life of the church that images of God emerge and come to life. While it is important that Christians are open to new representations of the divine, they should also remember that, in the words of a gloomy dean, he who marries the spirit of the age will soon find himself a widower. In the church's scramble to be 'relevant' there is the danger that Christians will merely reflect current prejudices and enthusiasms and fail to stand as a challenge to the world. Ancient images of kingship, judgment and even military leadership may still represent something which the church must proclaim and the world needs to hear. Even the God of Daniel, who so impressed King Darius, may have something to teach this generation:

> For he is the living God,
> enduring for ever;
> his kingdom shall never be destroyed,
> and his dominion shall be to the end.
> He delivers and rescues
> he works signs and wonders
> in heaven and on earth. (Daniel 6: 26–7)

It is recorded of the black entertainer Sammy Davis Junior that, when he announced his conversion to Judaism, he declared that Christians are always talking about a God of love, but what the oppressed of this world need is justice.[24] Modern western Christians have indeed invented a God without enemies, a God who does not take sides, but spends his time conciliating and manipulating, like a celestial personnel manager. He is the God of the comfortable and contented. An English priest recalls meeting a Salvadorean woman who had just received news of her son's death:

An eyewitness, herself wounded, related how soldiers had cut off his hands and feet, slashed his face and partially skinned him before he died. The mother, quiet and dignified in her grief, didn't even know which of her two sons was involved: a 12-year-old or his 14-year-old brother.[25]

Such experiences lead to demands for a God who is concerned to vindicate the oppressed and to punish the wicked.

> Behold the storm of the Lord!
> Wrath has gone forth,
> a whirling tempest;
> it will burst upon the head of the wicked.
> The anger of the Lord will not turn back
> until he has executed and accomplished
> the intents of his mind. (Jeremiah 23: 19–20)

The modern emphasis on welfare images of God must be judged as unbalanced – uncritically reflecting, as they do, the ideology of a welfare state. In fact, as we have noted, the state has become a gigantic engine for preserving the privileges of the better-off and for transferring wealth from the poor to the rich. It makes increasing demands upon the loyalty and submission of its citizens and by the myths of 'consent' and 'representation' and by the claim to embody their 'real will' and 'true interests' has acquired, in the eyes of many, a sacred status. 'The secularization of social life', observed Harold Laski in 1943, 'has meant the increasing assumption by the state of the character of a church.'[26]

The dominance of the welfare images of God may already be in decline. The God of the new radical right is the decisionist God once more, the God who issues arbitrary commands. Any resemblance this God bears to Yahweh of the Old Testament is purely superficial, for instead of supporting the poor and the outcast he is a God who reinforces the structures of domination, legitimating the wealth of the successful and encouraging the rest to use 'their fleeting lives in this world to prepare themselves for the next', in the words of Margaret Thatcher.[27]

What kind of new pictures of God are required today to balance the dominant images of power and benevolence? Sallie McFague in a recent book on *Models of God*, makes a number of suggestions. She develops the images of God as mother, lover and friend in an imaginative and constructive way. None of these is, of course, new and all of them have a tendency to strengthen the dominant 'welfare' conception of God discussed in earlier chapters. Brian Wren also employs the concept of lover in one of his hymns:

> Self-giving lover, since you dare
>   to join us in our history,
>   embracing all our destiny,
> we'll come and go with praise and care.

Wren also employs feminine images:

> Midwife of Changes,
>   skilfully guiding,
> drawing us out through the shock of the new,
> Woman of Wisdom,
>   deeply perceiving,
>   never deceiving,
> freeing and leading in all that we do.[28]

In order to bring out that aspect of God's co-operation with humankind in transforming this order of things, so that 'the kingdoms of the world become the kingdoms of our God and his Christ', the notion of God as friend can be valuable. When purged of some of its sentimental connotations it stands for participation in a common endeavour. We may also look to such images as the conductor of an orchestra, who can be said in certain ways to relate to the musicians as God relates to us. A conductor solicits from each what he or she can contribute and, without coercion, weaves the whole into a dynamic harmony. The manager or captain of a football team might also be an appropriate and more popular image (if only their tenure of office were less transient!). They use the skill and ability of each team member to develop a coherent pattern of play, which may be discernible only in part to the individual player.

The notion of the universe as God's work of art, which Schleiermacher proposed, has recently been revived by the Doctrine Commission of the Church of England.[29] The German theologian liked the idea of the universe as God's *Kunstwerk* (work of art) because it excludes notions of reciprocity and accords with the feeling of absolute dependence which is the essence of religion. The Commission is evidently uneasy with these connotations and points out that the woodcarver, for example, respects and responds to the nature of the material and modifies the carving according to the grain of the wood as it becomes manifest. Nevertheless the wood itself is entirely passive.

Another image that may be used of God's relationship to the universe is that of the skilled author of a play to the characters within it. Although the characters of the play are indeed ultimately the creation of the playwright, even so they each develop a personality of their own as the play proceeds; they acquire a relative autonomy, prescribing in some respects the limits within which the author may proceed. There is a kind of dialogue between the author and the characters, so that the author may even be affected by the way things develop. It is of course necessary to say 'skilled author', for a bad one will impose upon the characters actions and responses which are quite 'out of character'. Incarnationalists will go on to speak of the author actually becoming a character in the play, in dialogue with the other characters. However, all attempts to speak of God, conceptually or metaphorically, are defective in some way and these images are intended not to replace but to supplement more traditional language.

In the opening chapter I drew attention to the ceiling of the Sheldonian Theatre, where Theology, among the other disciplines, is pictured as imploring the assistance of Truth. I observed how the idea of truth has in the modern world increasingly been called into question. In determining which images of God and the state are true or appropriate, it will be evident that there is no such thing as a clear, objective and unambiguous criterion. The images are not, however, arbitrarily applied but emerge in the context of a tradition and a community of discourse. Those wishing to introduce new images or revive old ones must appeal to the conscience and experience of this community.

Christians believe that the normative images are given in divine revelation and that the church is guided by the Holy Spirit in interpreting this revelation and in developing new images for new situations.[30] Although all these images are influenced by the cultural context in which they emerge, they point to the existence of a transcendent being who is the author of truth, whose nature we can only dimly conceive and imperfectly imagine. Discussing the confused ideas proposed some years ago by an Anglican bishop, Max Horkheimer observed, 'Truth – eternal truth outlasting human error – cannot as such be separated from theism. . . . The death of God is also the death of eternal truth.'[31] Today, when all disciplines – not least the natural sciences – are in danger of being swamped by an all-embracing relativism which threatens to undermine the idea of truth itself, theology by its very definition witnesses to a transcendent reality which alone is able to give substance to the concept of truth. Robert Streater's seventeenth-century painting in the Sheldonian Theatre has Theology imploring the assistance of Truth; perhaps a late-twentieth-century artist will be inspired to portray Truth imploring the assistance of Theology.

Notes

1 INTRODUCTION

1. See Mary B. Hesse, *The Structure of Scientific Inference* and *Models and Analogies in Science*; Thomas S. Kuhn, *The Structure of Scientific Revolutions*; Rom Harré, *The Principles of Scientific Thinking*; and Andrew Ortony, ed., *Metaphor and Thought*.
2. H. Richard Niebuhr, *The Responsible Self*, p. 14.
3. K. Marx, 'Contribution to the Critique of Hegel's Philosophy of Law', in K. Marx and F. Engels, *Collected Works*, III, pp. 174–5.
4. Friedrich Meinecke, *Historism*, p. 17.
5. A forthcoming series of books, 'Theology in Social Context' (to be published by Basil Blackwell), aims to help fill this gap.
6. Gregory Baum, 'Sociology and Theology', *Concilium*, 1: 10, January 1974, p. 23. I would quarrel with the word 'reflection', however, which suggests a somewhat undialectical relationship between religion and culture.
7. For example, F. Sontag, *Divine Perfection*; Keith Ward, *The Concept of God*; H.P. Owen, *Concepts of Deity*.
8. G.W.H. Lampe, in Church of England Doctrine Commission, *Christian Believing*, p. 103.
9. F. Engels, 'The Condition of England' (1843), in K. Marx and F. Engels, *Collected Works*, III, pp. 463–4.
10. G. Puente Ojea, *Ideología e historia: La formación del cristianismo como fenómeno ideológico*; Louis Boisset, *La Théologie en procès, face à la critique marxiste*; Georges Casalis, *Les Idées justes ne tombent pas du ciel*; José Vives, 'El dios trinitario y la comunión humana', *Estudios Eclesiásticos*, 52, 1977, pp. 129ff.; Alfredo Fierro, 'Histoire de Dieu', *Lumière et Vie*, 128, 1976; François Houtart, 'Sociologie de discours sur

Dieu', in M. Caudron, ed., *Foi et société*; Adolphe Gesché, 'Dieu et société', *Revue Théologique de Louvain*, 7, 1976, pp. 274ff.; Pierre Watté, 'Le Prince, le maître, et Dieu', *Revue Théologique de Louvain*, 9, 1978, pp. 436ff.; J. van Haeperen, 'Expériences politiques de la puissance et tout-puissance de Dieu', *Revue Théologique de Louvain*, 9, 1978, pp. 287ff. But see also, on the impact of Marxism on theology, Nicholas Lash, *A Matter of Hope*. On political aspects of Trinitarianism, see Conclusion, note 5.

11. M.F. Wiles, *The Making of Christian Doctrine*, p. 27.
12. G.W.F. Hegel, in H.S. Harris, *Hegel's Development: Towards the Sunlight, 1770–1801*, pp. 31–2. But compare the comment of an eminent 'Oxbridge' theologian on this subject, 'Perhaps it is easier to see the political setting in the seventeenth century than in our own, alas' (on a postcard to the author). On the theological vocabulary of modern politics see Carl Schmitt (note 41 below), echoed by Christopher Dawson, *Religion and the Modern State*, p. 44; Nathaniel Micklem, *The Theology of Politics*, pp. xv and 38; and Karl Löwith, *Meaning in History*. But see the critical study by Hans Blumenberg, *The Legitimacy of the Modern Age*.
13. Clifford Geertz, 'Centers, Kings and Charisma: Reflections on the Symbolics of Power', in *Local Knowledge*, pp. 121ff.
14. See Sallie McFague, *Metaphorical Theology: Models of God in Religious Language*, p. 167; Janet Soskice, *Metaphor and Religious Language*.
15. See David Burrell, 'Argument in Theology: Analogy and Narrative', in Carl A. Raschke, ed., *New Dimensions in Philosophical Theology*; Richard J. Bernstein, *Beyond Objectivism and Relativism*. For a discussion of a similar issue in politics see Ronald Beiner, *Political Judgment*.
16. Charles Darwin, *The Origin of Species*, p. 50.
17. Owing to restrictions of space I have to omit discussion of political images of God among the 'religions of the oppressed'. I hope to deal with this subject in a later work.
18. E.H. Kantorowicz, *Selected Studies*, p. 388.
19. E.H. Kantorowicz, *The King's Two Bodies*, p. 223.
20. D. Erasmus, *The Education of a Christian Prince*, pp. 170–1.
21. On Duvalier's use of supernatural imagery see David Nicholls, *From Dessalines to Duvalier*, p. 297.
22. For a discussion of these issues see Virginia Mollenkott, *The Divine Feminine: The Biblical Imagery of God as Female*; Rosemary R. Ruether, *Sexism and God-Talk: Toward a Feminist Theology*; Sallie McFague, *Metaphorical Theology* and *Models of God: Theology for an Ecological Nuclear Age*, especially chapters 3 and 4.
23. Sebastian Brock, *The Holy Spirit in the Syriac Baptismal Tradition*, pp. 3ff. Brock has elaborated on this matter in an unpublished paper

given to the Ecumenical Society of the Blessed Virgin Mary in Oxford; I am grateful for his advice on this question.

24. Christian Duquoc, 'Monotheism and Unitary Ideology', in Claude Geffré and Jean-Pierre Jossua, *Monotheism* (*Concilium*, 117, 1985), p. 66; see also J.B. Metz, ed., 'Perspectives of a Political Ecclesiology', *Concilium*, 66, 1971.

25. K. Barth, in E. Brunner and K. Barth, *Natural Theology*, p. 125.

26. Peter Brown, *The World of Late Antiquity*, p. 37; J.M. Sallmann, 'Image et fonction du saint dans la région de Naples à la fin du XVIIe siècle et au début du XVIIIe siècle', *Mélange de l'Ecole Français de Rome*, 91, 1979, p. 871.

27. J. Boissevain, *Friends of Friends*, p. 80.

28. Michael Kenny, 'Patterns of Patronage in Spain', *Anthropological Quarterly*, 33, 1960, pp. 14ff.; M. Bax, 'Patronage Irish Style: Irish Politicians as Brokers', *Sociologische Gids*, 17, 1970, pp. 179ff.

29. Shailer Mathews, *The Growth of the Idea of God*, p. 160.

30. J.-J. Rousseau, *Du contrat social*, 4: 8, in *The Political Writings*, II, p. 124. Feuerbach wrote, 'polytheism must exist so long as there are various nations', *The Essence of Christianity*, p. 175n. M. Bakunin, *God and the State*, p. 73.

31. Karl Kautsky, *Foundations of Christianity: A Study in Christian Origins*, pp. 180–1.

32. Max Weber, *The Sociology of Religion*, p. 23.

33. J.H. Breasted, *The Dawn of Conscience*, pp. 19 and 275; for a more sophisticated treatment see Henri Frankfort, *Kingship and the Gods: A Study of Ancient Near Eastern Religion as the Integration of Society and Nature*.

34. E. Peterson, *Theologische Traktate*, p. 91, quoted in J. Moltmann, *The Trinity and the Kingdom of God*, p. 248.

35. John S. Mbiti, *Concepts of God in Africa*, p. 71; see also C. Cagnolo, *The Akikuyu*, p. 26; and G.E. Swanson, *The Birth of the Gods*, p. 75.

36. B. Lang, 'No God but Yahweh! The Origin and Character of Biblical Monotheism', *Concilium*, 177, 1985, p. 48. See also B. Lang, ed., *Monotheism and the Prophetic Minority*. An earlier debate on the same theme is brought together in Robert J. Christen and H.E. Hazelton, eds, *Monotheism and Moses*.

37. G.E. Swanson, *The Birth*, p. 5.

38. G. Lenski, *Human Societies: A Macrolevel Introduction to Sociology*, p. 134; R. Underhill, 'Economic and Political Antecedents of Monotheism: a Cross-Cultural Study', *American Journal of Sociology*, 80, 1975, pp. 841ff.; D. Sheils, 'An Evolutionary Explanation of Supportive Monotheism', *International Journal of Comparative Sociology*, 15: 1–2, 1974, pp. 47ff.

39. F. Houtart, 'Sociologie du discours sur Dieu', in M. Caudron, ed., *Foi et*

société; A. Gesché, 'Dieu et société', *Lumière et Vie*, 128, 1976.

40. Raymond Williams, *Marxism and Literature*, pp. 121ff.
41. C. Schmitt, *Political Theology*, p. 36.
42. Perry Miller, *The New England Mind: The Seventeenth Century*, pp. 376–7.
43. E. Fromm, *The Dogma of Christ*, pp. 35 and 11.
44. F. Engels, 'Zur Geschichte des Urchristentums', *Die Neue Zeit*, 13: 1, September 1894, quoted in K. Kautsky, *Foundations*, p. 462. For recent work on the subject see R.M. Grant, *Early Christianity and Society*, pp. 11 and 79ff.; G. Theissen, *The First Followers of Jesus*, p. 46; Abraham J. Malherbe, *Social Aspects of Early Christianity*, chapters 1 and 2.
45. Nicholas Tyacke, 'Puritanism, Arminianism and Counter-Revolution', in Conrad Russell, ed., *The Origins of the English Civil War*, p. 128. The author goes on to speak of the historian's attempt to 'reconstruct the religious history' of a period. The idea that the historian's task is reconstruction, rather than construction, is perhaps the key to Tyacke's extraordinary remark on hindsight.
46. Jon Elster, *Leibniz et la formation de l'esprit capitaliste*.
47. David Nicholls, *Haiti in Caribbean Context: Ethnicity, Economy and Revolt*, pp. 220ff.
48. Max Weber, *The Protestant Ethic and the Spirit of Capitalism*, p. 103.
49. *Church Times*, 31 August 1984.
50. A.J. Balfour, *Essays and Addresses*, p. 273, and *Foundations of Belief*, pp. 216ff. I hope to examine this analogy of the sceptical basis for authoritarian images of God and the state in the writings of certain nineteenth-century writers on another occasion. But see David Nicholls, 'Few are Chosen: Reflections on the Politics of A.J. Balfour', *The Review of Politics*, 30: 1, 1968, pp. 33–42; and Nicholls, 'Conscience and Authority in the Thought of W.G. Ward', *Heythrop Journal*, 26: 4, 1985, pp. 416–29.
51. From 'Misa Campesina Nicaraguense', reprinted in *Cantos del pueblo para el pueblo*, p. 6.
52. Dionysius of Fourna, *The Painter's Manual*, pp. 88 and 41.
53. G. Winstanley, *The Law of Freedom and other Writings*, p. 93.
54. It is surprising how many authors make this mistake; see, for example, Carl J. Friedrich and Z.K. Brzezinski, *Totalitarian Dictatorship and Autocracy*, p. 205, and Judith N. Shklar, *Men and Citizens: A Study of Rousseau's Social Theory*, pp. 152–3.
55. William Shakespeare, *Richard II*; John Donne, *The Sermons of John Donne*, IV, p. 251.
56. J. Carswell, *From Revolution to Revolution: England 1688–1776*, p. 29; see also J. Plumb, *The Growth of Political Stability in England, 1675–1725*.

57. Peter Abelard, 'O quanta qualia', reprinted in *English Hymnal*, no. 465.
58. W.J.H. Campion, in Charles Gore, ed., *Lux Mundi: A Series of Studies in the Religion of the Incarnation*, p. 444.
59. Church of England General Synod, Board for Social Responsibility, *Changing Britain: Social Diversity and Moral Unity*. It is indeed curious to find the Archbishop of York and the Board for Social Responsibility falling into this discredited Parsonian functionalism. Sara Maitland, in a brief 'Note of Reservation', made this point; see her longer statement in *Jubilee News*, Michaelmas 1987.
60. Campion, in Gore, ed., *Lux Mundi*, p. 444.
61. Gore, 'Preface', *Lux Mundi*, p. ix. See also David Nicholls and Rowan Williams, *Politics and Theological Identity*, pp. 31–2; Nicholls, 'The Totalitarianism of Thomas Arnold', *The Review of Politics*, 29: 1, 1967, pp. 518f.; and Nicholls, *The Pluralist State*.
62. Campion, in Gore, ed., *Lux Mundi*, p. 445.
63. Campion, in ibid., p. 450.
64. James Barr, 'The Bible as a Political Document', *Bulletin of the John Rylands University Library of Manchester*, 62: 2, 1980, p. 273.
65. For a discussion of the extensive literature see Clinton D. Morrison, *The Powers That Be: Earthly Rulers and Demonic Powers in Romans 13: 1–7*, and Oscar Cullmann, *The State in the New Testament*, pp. 95–114.
66. Ernst Käsemann, *Commentary on Romans*, p. 354. See also his classic discussion of the question in 'Römer 13, 1–7 in unserer Generation', *Zeitschrift für Theologie und Kirche*, 56, 1959, pp. 316ff.
67. See the excellent work of Carole Pateman, *The Problem of Political Obligation: A Critique of Liberal Theory*; also David Nicholls, 'A Comment on "Consent"', *Political Studies*, 27: 1, 1979, pp. 120ff.
68. J.-J. Rousseau, *Du contrat social*, 3: 15, in *The Political Writings of Jean-Jacques Rousseau*, I, pp. 95ff.
69. Hanna Pitkin, *The Concept of Representation*, p. 232.
70. In February 1976 the Synod passed a resolution that 'urges all political parties to adopt a preferential system of proportional representation as a policy commitment for future elections', Church of England, *Proceedings of the General Synod*, 7: 2 (1976), p. 335.
71. For a consideration of early Christian attitudes to property see Martin Hengel, *Property and Riches in the Early Church*, and Luke T. Johnson, *Sharing Possessions: Mandate and Symbol of Faith*.
72. Church of England, *Faith in the City: A Call for Action by Church and Nation*, pp. 63 and 48. Duncan Forrester also refers more than once to the social 'implications' of the gospel, in *Christianity and the Future of Welfare*, pp. 33, 39 and elsewhere. This work contains some acute observations and criticisms.
73. W.G. Ward, *Essays on the Philosophy of Theism*, II, p. 90. See Nicholls, 'Conscience and Authority in the Thought of W.G. Ward', pp. 420ff.

74. P.-J. Proudhon, *Idée générale de la révolution*, in *Œuvres complètes de P.-J. Proudhon*, IV, p. 208.
75. Frankfort, *Kingship and the Gods*.

2 WELFARE GOD AND PATERNAL STATE I

1. Joseph Butler, *The Analogy of Religion, Natural and Revealed, to the Constitution and Course of Nature*, 1: 1: 3.
2. D. Fraser, *The Evolution of the British Welfare State*, pp. 108–9; see also M. Bruce, *The Coming of the Welfare State*, pp. 13ff.
3. David Roberts, *Victorian Origins of the British Welfare State*, p. 99.
4. J.B. Brebner, 'Laissez-faire and state intervention in nineteenth century Britain', *Journal of Economic History*, supp. VIII, 1948, pp. 59ff. On the relationship between individualism and collectivism see David Nicholls, *The Pluralist State*, pp. 31ff. and 57.
5. J.S. Mill, *Principles of Political Economy*, 5: 11: 2, p. 569.
6. J.S. Mill, *Essay on Liberty*, chapter 4, p. 137.
7. R. Currie, *Industrial Politics*, p. vii.
8. Matthew Arnold, *Culture and Anarchy*, p. 159; see also p. 36, and *Mixed Essays*, pp. 42ff.
9. Beatrice Webb, *My Apprenticeship*, p. 123, quoted in K. Woodroffe, *From Charity to Social Work in England and the United States*, p. 21.
10. *Angels in Marble* is the title of a book, by R.T. Mackenzie and A. Silver, on working-class conservatives.
11. Peter Taylor-Gooby, 'Disquiet and State Welfare: Clinging to Nanny' (an unpublished paper, presented at the 6th Urban Change and Conflict Conference, University of Kent, September 1987), p. 10. I am grateful to him for letting me have a copy of this paper.
12. On the working of the NEB see the excellent report of four trades councils, *State Intervention in Industry: A Workers' Enquiry*.
13. David Edwards, *The State of the Nation*, p. 24.
14. R. Bacon and W.A. Eltis, *Britain's Economic Problems*, pp. 13ff.
15. M. Beloff and G. Peele, *The Government of the United Kingdom*, p. 310.
16. Lord Redcliffe-Maud and B. Wood, *English Local Government Reformed*, p. 95.
17. K. Newton, *Second-City Politics*, p. 87; G.W. Jones, *Borough Politics*, p. 87.
18. See J.A.G. Griffith, *The Politics of the Judiciary*.
19. S. Peak, *Troops in Strikes*.
20. 'The Parole System: Executive "Justice" ', in Colin Brewer et al., *Criminal Welfare on Trial*, pp. 25ff.
21. George Jackson, *Soledad Brother: Prison Letters*.

22. See the excellent critique of the welfare state in Ian Gough, *The Political Economy of the Welfare State*.

23. Quoted by A.H. Halsey, in *The Welfare State in Crisis*, p. 15.

24. R.M. Titmuss, in J.L. and J.K. Roach, eds, *Poverty*, p. 321.

25. Quoted in Raymond Carr, *Puerto Rico: A Colonial Experiment*, p. 219.

26. T.H. Marshall, *Social Policy in the Twentieth Century*, p. 83; U.K. Hicks, *British Public Finances, their Structure and Development, 1880–1952*, chapter 1; A.T. Peacock and J. Wiseman, *The Growth of Public Expenditure in the United Kingdom*, chapter 2.

27. *Social Insurance and Allied Services*, para. 8.

28. G. Therborn, 'The Prospects of Labour and the Transformation of Advanced Capitalism', *New Left Review*, 145, May/June 1984, pp. 27ff.

29. See the OECD report of 1976, *Public Expenditure on Incomes Maintenance Programmes*.

30. Steps have, however, lately been taken to remove the earnings-related element in state pension schemes.

31. B. Abel-Smith, 'Whose Welfare State?', in N. Mackenzie, ed., *Conviction*, p. 56. See also B. Abel-Smith and P. Townsend, *The Poor and the Poorest*; Priscilla Polanyi, 'An End to Poverty', in R. Boyson, ed., *Down with the Poor*, pp. 111ff.

32. Figures taken from the Treasury's document, *The Government's Expenditure Plans, 1987/90*, II, p. 8, and quoted in Taylor-Gooby, 'Disquiet', table 2.

33. John Atherton, *The Scandal of Poverty*, p. 38; N. Bosanquet and P. Townsend, *Labour and Equality*; Frank Field, *Inequality in Britain: Freedom, Welfare and the State*; David G. Green, *The Welfare State: For Rich or for Poor?*; Julien Le Grand, *The Strategy of Equality*.

34. Frank Field, *Inequality*, chapter 6.

35. Church of England, Board for Social Responsibility, *Not Just for the Poor: Christian Perspectives on the Welfare State*, chapter 6.

36. See R.M. Titmuss, *The Gift Relationship*; Richard Flathman, *The Practice of Rights*.

37. T.H. Marshall, *Social Policy in the Twentieth Century*, p. 83.

38. Ibid., p. 14.

39. I am indebted to the Rev. J.H. Sadler for drawing my attention to the wedding.

40. P. Gregg, *The Welfare State*, pp. 3–4, cites Temple's use of the term in *Citizen and Churchman*; Temple had, however, used the term earlier, see note 69 below. Curiously Alan Suggate in his recent book, *William Temple and Christian Social Ethics Today*, says almost nothing about his ideas on the welfare role of the state.

41. J.D. Carmichael and H.S. Goodwin, *William Temple's Political Legacy*. This hostile and not particularly sophisticated volume makes no

attempt to relate Temple's theology to his social and political teaching.

42. F.A. Iremonger, *William Temple, Archbishop of Canterbury: His Life and Letters.*

43. William Temple, *Nature, Man and God*, p. 220; Temple, in B.H. Streeter et al., *Foundations*, p. 245. The term 'world process' appeared, however, in his tract *The Education of Citizens* of 1905; I am grateful to Stephen Spencer for referring me to this tract.

44. William Temple, *Mens Creatrix*, p. 3; *Nature*, p. 398. On his appreciation of Thomism, see his lecture, *Thomism and Modern Needs*, printed in Temple, *Religious Experience and Other Essays and Addresses*. Some critics deny he was a genuine realist; see R.C. Miller, 'Is Temple a Realist?', *Journal of Religion*, 19: 1, 1936, pp. 44ff.

45. Temple, *Nature*, p. 396.

46. William Temple, *Essays in Christian Politics*, p. 57; *Nature*, p. 189. Earlier, however, he had criticised the adequacy of this dictum; see *Mens Creatrix*, p. 206.

47. Quoted in Iremonger, *William Temple*, p. 322.

48. William Temple, *Christianity and Social Order*, pp. 21–3.

49. William Temple, in *Malvern, 1941: The Life of the Church and the Order of Society, being the Proceedings of the Archbishop of York's Conference*, p. 218; Temple, *Mens Creatrix*, p. 33.

50. I made this error myself in *Church and State in Britain since 1820*, pp. 17ff.

51. On the sanctity of personality see Temple, *Nature*, p. 191, and *Christianity and Social Order*, p. 64; on principles and axioms see *Malvern, 1941*, pp. vii and 218.

52. Temple, *Mens Creatrix*, p. 2.

53. Temple, *Nature*, p. 335; *Christus Veritas*, p. 284; *Christianity and the State*, pp. 32–3. See also *Essays*, pp. 67 and 208, where the notion of God's sovereignty is assumed.

54. William Temple, *Church and Nation*, p. 154. See also p. 155, where he writes of 'a joint sovereignty' without any indication of what this might involve.

55. Temple, *Nature*, p. 54; and Temple, *The Hope of a New World*, p. 57.

56. Rudolf Hermann Lotze, *Microcosmus*, 9: 4: 4.

57. See Temple's lectures on *The Nature of Personality*. Typical of this tendency were the contributions to Henry Sturt, ed., *Personal Idealism: Philosophical Essays by Eight Members of the University of Oxford.*

58. Temple, *Christian Faith and Life*, p. 49.

59. Temple, in Streeter et al., *Foundations*, p. 220; Temple, *Repton School Sermons*, p. 220. See also C.E. Rolt, *The World's Redemption*, and B.H. Streeter, 'The Suffering of God', *Hibbert Journal*, April 1914, pp. 603ff.

60. Temple, *The Education of Citizens*, p. 5.

61. Temple, *Nature*, pp. 267–8; Temple, *Repton*, p. 74. On the theme of

'service' see Temple, *Repton*, pp. 13, 51, 225, and Temple, *Christus Veritas*, p. 207.

62. Temple, *Christianity and Social Order*, p. 19; Temple, *Mens Creatrix*, p. 204.

63. Temple, *Repton*, pp. 161–3. Elsewhere he wrote of 'the interest of the whole community' and 'the welfare of the whole community', Temple, *Essays*, pp. 46 and 53. More recent writings on this subject include C.J. Friedrich, ed., *The Public Interest*; Brian Barry, *Political Argument*, chapters 11–13; and R.E. Flathman, *The Public Interest*.

64. Temple, *Essays*, pp. 54 and 67. See also Temple, *Christianity and the State*, p. 158.

65. Temple, *Christianity and Social Order*, p. 23.

66. Temple, *Hope*, p. 66.

67. Temple, *Education*, p. 5 (my italics).

68. Temple, *Nature*, pp. 192 and 194; Temple, *Essays*, p. 67.

69. Temple, *Christianity and the State*, pp. 169–70. See also Temple, *Citizen and Churchman*, pp. 26 and 35.

70. Temple, *Christianity and Social Order*, pp. 73–4.

71. Jose Harris, *William Beveridge: A Biography*, p. 42.

72. Ibid., pp. 3–4.

73. Ibid., p. 55.

74. Ibid., p. 102. For his attitude to friendly societies see William H. Beveridge, *Voluntary Action, passim*.

75. William H. Beveridge, *Full Employment in a Free Society*, pp. 36–7.

76. William H. Beveridge, *The Pillars of Security*, p. 42.

77. Ibid., p. 40.

78. R. Miliband, *Capitalist Democracy in Britain*.

79. Streeter et al., *Foundations*, p. 7.

80. F.W. Bussell, *Christian Theology and Social Progress*, preface and p. 331.

81. B.F. Westcott, 'The Educational Value of Co-operation', *The Economic Review*, 1: 1, 1891, p. 7. On 'incarnationalism' see David Nicholls, 'Two Tendencies in Anglo-Catholic Political Theology', in David Nicholls and Rowan Williams, *Politics and Theological Identity: Two Anglican Essays*, pp. 27ff. On Maurice's theology see A.R. Vidler, *The Theology of F.D. Maurice*, and A.M. Ramsey, *F.D. Maurice and the Conflicts of Modern Theology*; for a more recent discussion see E.R. Norman, *The Victorian Christian Socialists*.

82. See Stephen Paget, *Henry Scott Holland*, p. 170; also, on the CSU, G.L. Prestige, *The Life of Charles Gore: A Great Englishman*, pp. 91ff., and M.B. Reckitt, *Maurice to Temple: A Century of the Social Movement in the Church of England*, pp. 136f.

83. 'Editorial – a Programme', *The Economic Review*, 1: 1, 1891, p. 1.

84. Reckitt, *Maurice to Temple*, p. 138.

85. Hastings Rashdall, *Doctrine and Development*, p. 278.
86. F.H. Bradley, *Appearance and Reality*, pp. 396–7.
87. Rashdall, *Doctrine*, pp. 277–8 and 80.
88. Hastings Rashdall, *God and Man*, p. 55.
89. Hastings Rashdall, *Philosophy and Religion*, p. 55, and 'Personality, Human and Divine', in Sturt, ed., *Personal Idealism*, pp. 372 and 375. For Rashdall's racialism see *Christus in Ecclesia*, p. 282; *Ideas and Ideals*, pp. 30 and 65; *God and Man*, pp. 163, 165 and 176; *The Theory of Good and Evil*, I, p. 290.
90. Hastings Rashdall, *Conscience and Christ*, p. ix.
91. Rashdall, *God and Man*, p. 163.
92. 'To feed upon Christ's body and Christ's blood means to absorb His teaching into the soul', Rashdall, *Christus in Ecclesia*, p. 34.
93. Hastings Rashdall, *The Idea of Atonement in Christian Theology*, p. 457.
94. Rashdall, *The Theory*, I, p. 304; see also 'Punishment and Forgiveness', in *Principles and Precepts*, pp. 73ff.
95. Rashdall, *Principles*, p. 74.
96. Rashdall, *Ideas and Ideals*, p. 37.
97. Rashdall, *God and Man*, p. 186; *The Theory*, I, p. 269. For a recent discussion of these issues see David Miller, *Social Justice*.
98. See E. Lyttelton, *The Mind and Character of Henry Scott Holland*, p. 11. Holland would not have made a good dentist!
99. J.H. Heidt, *The Social Theology of Henry Scott Holland*, p. 9.
100. H.S. Holland, *The Real Problem of Eschatology*, p. 30.
101. H.S. Holland, *God's City and the Coming of the Kingdom*, pp. 39 and 7.
102. On the religious aspects of English idealism see J.S. Boys Smith 'The Interpretation of Christianity in Idealistic Philosophy in Great Britain in the Nineteenth Century', *The Modern Churchman*, 31: 5, 6 and 7, 1941, pp. 251ff. The author concentrates particularly on the tension between idealist metaphysics and the historical elements in Christianity. See also a 'somewhat sprawling essay' (the author's own words) by D.M. Mackinnon, 'Some Aspects of the Treatment of Christianity by the British Idealists', *Religious Studies*, 20: 1, 1983, pp. 133ff.
103. Opening words of Henry Scott Holland's well-known hymn (*English Hymnal*, no. 423).
104. R.C. Moberly, *Atonement and Personality*, p. 66.
105. W.H. Moberly, in Streeter et al., *Foundations*, p. 291.
106. Ibid., p. 293.
107. W.H. Moberly, 'Some Ambiguities in the Retributive Theory of Punishment', in *Proceedings of the Aristotelian Society*, NS, 25, 1925, pp. 289ff., and *The Ethics of Punishment*. There is a discussion of his ideas in E.R. Moberly, *Suffering, Innocent and Guilty*, chapter 5. J.M.E.

McTaggart put forward a similar idea of punishment in *Studies in Hegelian Cosmology*, chapter 5.

108. J.R. Illingworth, *Personality Human and Divine*, p. 121.
109. H.S. Holland, in C. Gore, ed., *Lux Mundi*, pp. 41–2; Prestige, *The Life of Charles Gore*, p. 18.
110. Gordon D. Kaufman, *God the Problem*, p. 107. On Kaufman, see pp. 154ff.
111. Illingworth, *Personality Human and Divine*, pp. 192 and 75; *The Doctrine of the Trinity*, p. 143. See also W. Richmond, 'God is a fellowship, a communion of persons', *An Essay on Personality*, II, p. 18.
112. H.S. Holland, 'Property and Personality', in Charles Gore et al., *Property: Its Duties and Rights*, p. 192.
113. Charles Gore, in S. Paget, *Henry Scott Holland*, p. 246. On Donne see David Nicholls, 'The Political Theology of John Donne', *Theological Studies*, 49: 1, 1988.
114. H.S. Holland, in J.E. Hand, ed., *Good Citizenship*, p. 278; Holland, *Facts of the Faith*, p. 20; and Gore, in Paget, *Henry Scott Holland*, p. 248.
115. Gore et al., *Property*, pp. xi–xii and 187–8.
116. 'Every Man his own Grandmother', reprinted in J. Adderley, ed., *Scott Holland's Goodwill*, p. 55.
117. Holland, in Hand, ed., *Good Citizenship*, p. 298.
118. J.S. Mill, *Essay on Liberty*, chapter 1.
119. H.S. Holland, *Logic and Life*, p. 248.
120. H.S. Holland, 'The State', in B.F. Westcott et al., *The Church and New Century Problems*, pp. 45 and 51.
121. Ibid., p. 52.
122. Holland, in Hand, ed., *Good Citizenship*, pp. 300 and 302.

3 WELFARE GOD AND PATERNAL STATE II

1. Wallas and Hobhouse were both in fact sons of evangelical Anglican clergymen. See Peter Clarke, *Liberals and Social Democrats*, pp. 9–10 and 46; also Martin J. Wiener, *Between Two Worlds: The Political Thought of Graham Wallas*.
2. R.S. Churchill, *Young Statesman, 1901–14, Winston S. Churchill*, II, pp. 30ff.; B.S. Rowntree, *Poverty: A Study of Town Life*; Charles Booth, *Life and Labour of the People of London*.
3. T. Jones, *Lloyd George*, p. 41; quoted in Andrew Vincent and Raymond Plant, *Philosophy, Politics and Citizenship*, p. 51; and W.S. Churchill, *Liberalism and the Social Problem*, p. xxii.
4. José Harris, *Unemployment and Politics: A Study in English Social*

Policy, 1886–1914, pp. 285ff., and *William Beveridge: A Biography*, pp. 146ff.

5. Quoted by E.P. Hennock, in W.J. Mommsen, ed., *The Emergence of the Welfare State in Britain and Germany*, p. 89. See also Hennock, *British Social Reform and German Precedents*.

6. C.G. Hanson, 'Welfare before the Welfare State', in R.M. Hartwell et al., *The Long Debate on Poverty*, pp. 118ff. A more conservative estimate of 4¼ to 4½ million is given by B.B. Gilbert, *The Evolution of National Insurance in Great Britain: The Origins of the Welfare State*, pp. 165ff. See also P.H.J.H. Gosden, *The Friendly Societies in England, 1815–1875* and *Self-Help*; also William Beveridge, *Voluntary Action*, E.W. Brabrook, *Provident Societies and Industrial Welfare*, and J.F. Wilkinson, *The Friendly Society Movement*.

7. Henry Bunbury, ed., *Lloyd George's Ambulance Wagon*, pp. 71ff. and 212.

8. Hennock, in Mommsen, ed., *The Emergence*, p. 102.

9. David G. Green, *The Welfare State: For Rich or for Poor?*, p. 29.

10. David Nicholls, 'Positive Liberty: 1880–1914', *American Political Science Review*, 56: 1, 1962, pp. 114ff. A good deal of the argument of this section is based on the article.

11. This point is, of course, strongly made by Isaiah Berlin in his celebrated essay 'Two Concepts of Liberty', reprinted in Berlin, *Four Essays on Liberty*. Unfortunately, however, he fails to make the distinction between those, on the one hand, with a basically empirical conception of liberty (like Hobson and Hobhouse) who recognise that people can be said to be free to do something only if they have the power and the means, and those on the other who speak of liberty as the power to do what is right or reasonable or in line with their true nature. This distinction is also ignored by Vincent and Plant, *Philosophy*, chapter 5. The two positions, however, are based on quite distinct philosophical assumptions and have significantly different practical consequences.

12. Henry Jones, *The Working Faith of the Social Reformer*, pp. 143–4.

13. 'An individual right ... cannot conflict with the common good, nor could any right exist apart from the common good', wrote L.T. Hobhouse (*Liberalism*, p. 127). On property see Hobhouse's essay in Charles Gore et al., *Property: Its Duties and Rights*, pp. 1–31. On rights see William Wallace, 'Natural Rights', in Wallace, *Lectures and Essays on Natural Theology and Ethics*, pp. 213ff., and D.G. Ritchie, *Natural Rights*.

14. Stefan Collini, *Liberalism and Sociology*, p. 47. Cliffe Leslie as quoted in Nicholls, 'Positive Liberty', pp. 116 and 122; I also cited Lord Acton in this context.

15. Collini, *Liberalism and Sociology*, pp. 46–7; Nicholls, 'Positive Liberty', p. 128.

16. H.H. Asquith, *Memories and Reflections of the Earl of Oxford and Asquith*, I, p. 19. See also J.A. Spender and H. Asquith, *The Life of Herbert Henry Asquith, Lord Oxford and Asquith*, I, p. 36; and Asquith, Introduction to H. Samuel, *Liberalism*, pp. ix–x.
17. Asquith, *Memories and Reflections*, I, p. 113.
18. H.J.W. Hetherington, *Life and Letters of Sir Henry Jones*, p. 20n.; Henry Jones, *The Working Faith*, pp. 262ff.
19. Vincent and Plant, *Philosophy*, p. 81; H. Jones, *The Principles of Citizenship*.
20. Jones, 'The Idealism of Jesus', in G. Tyrrell et al., *Jesus or Christ?* (*The Hibbert Journal*, Supplement for 1909), p. 92; H. Jones, *Social Powers*, p. 98.
21. Collini, *Liberalism and Sociology*, p. 144.
22. L.T. Hobhouse, *Social Evolution and Political Theory*, p. 202; cf. also J.A. Hobson, *The Crisis of Liberalism*, pp. 92–3.
23. Hobhouse, *Liberalism*, p. 123; *Democracy and Reaction*, p. 47.
24. Hobhouse, *Liberalism*, p. 23.
25. L.T. Hobhouse, *The Metaphysical Theory of the State*, p. 36.
26. Ibid., p. 29.
27. Hobhouse, *Liberalism*, pp. 24 and 29; Hobhouse, *Democracy and Reaction*, pp. 37–8.
28. Hobhouse, *Liberalism*, p. 91.
29. J.A. Hobson, *The Crisis of Liberalism*, p. 94, and Hobson, *The Social Problem*, pp. 10 and 96.
30. Herbert Spencer, *The Man Versus the State*, p. 80.
31. Herbert Spencer, *Principles of Sociology*, II, pp. 240ff.
32. T.H. Huxley, 'Evolution and Ethics', in Huxley, *Collected Essays*, p. 81.
33. D.G. Ritchie, *Principles of State Interference*, p. 50; Ritchie, *Darwinism and Politics*, p. 82.
34. Hobson, 'The Ethics of Industrialism', in Stanton Coit, ed., *Ethical Democracy: Essays in Social Dynamics*, p. 107.
35 'The Difficulties of Individualism', printed in Sidney Webb, *Socialism and Individualism*, p. 22.
36. Webb, *Socialism in England*, p. 13.
37. See Trevelyan's preface to H. Langshaw, *Socialism and the Historic Function of Liberalism*.
38. J.A. Hobson and M. Ginsberg, *L.T. Hobhouse: His Life and Work*, pp. 63 and 66.
39. Hobson, *The Crisis of Liberalism*, p. 93.
40. Vincent and Plant, *Philosophy*, p. 47.
41. Henry Pelling, 'The Working Class and the Origins of the Welfare State', in *Popular Politics and Society in Late Victorian Britain*, pp. 1ff.; H.C.G. Matthew et al., 'The Franchise Factor in the Rise of the Labour Party', *English Historical Review*, 91, 1976, pp. 723ff.

42. José Harris, 'The Transition to High Politics, 1880–1914', in M. Bentley and J. Stevenson, eds, *High and Low Politics in Modern Britain*, pp. 66–7. G.L. Bernstein, *Liberalism and Liberal Politics in Edwardian England*, points to the tensions which existed among the Liberals over these issues. While many party leaders saw a need to court the working-class vote, the rank and file were generally unprepared to modify traditional policies to this end.

43. Harris opposes sectional interests (trade unions, friendly societies, doctors and businessmen) to class interests, as though classes could be considered apart from the 'sections' which compose them. The working class, unless it is to be a total abstraction, must be seen as composed of such groups as trade unions and friendly societies.

44. Michael Freeden, *The New Liberalism*, p. 21.

45. Ibid., p. 55.

46. Ibid., p. 23.

47. Ibid., p. 47. In the real world principles do not move by their own logic into vacuums. 'The general process of investing traditional liberal concepts with new meaning' (ibid., p. 44), to which he refers, does not operate by some kind of mystical necessity, but by the actions of individuals and groups. Freeden is unclear in what he says about the relationship between liberalism and *laissez-faire*. Discussing Hobhouse's position he writes, 'If indeed there had been an association between liberalism and *laissez-faire* at any time, it had had regrettable consequences for liberalism' (ibid., p. 35). Surely he is not questioning whether there had been such an association. Again he speaks of 'a denial that *laissez-faire* was *ever* part of the liberal ideology *at the time*' (ibid., p. 33n.). What is the relationship between the 'ever' and 'at the time'?

48. Matthew, *The Liberal Imperialists*, p. vii.

49. Spencer, *The Man Versus the State*, chapter 1.

50. S.A. and H.O. Barnett, *Towards Social Reform*, p. 240.

51. Ibid., p. 255.

52. Ibid., p. 260.

53. S.A. Barnett, *The Service of God*, p. 337.

54. W. Picht, *Toynbee Hall and the English Settlement Movement*.

55. Gilbert, *The Evolution of National Insurance in Great Britain*, p. 44; Vincent and Plant, *Philosophy*, p. 147. See C.R. Attlee, *The Social Worker*.

56. S.A. Barnett, *Religion and Politics*, p. 4.

57. S.A. and H.O. Barnett, *Practicable Socialism*, p. 144, and Barnett, *The Service of God*, pp. 26 and 34.

58. Barnett, *Religion and Politics*, pp. 31–2.

59. Barnett, *The Service of God*, p. 99.

60. Barnett and Barnett, *Towards Social Reform*, p. 32. See S.T. Coleridge, *Lay Sermons*.

61. Barnett and Barnett, *Towards Social Reform*, p. 22.
62. Barnett, *The Service of God*, p. 253.
63. Barnett and Barnett, *Towards Social Reform*, p. 32.
64. J. Scott Lidgett, *The Fatherhood of God*, p. 1.
65. Ibid., p. 143.
66. Ibid., p. 206.
67. Ibid., p. 244.
68. For Moberly see above, p. 58; Lidgett rejected the image of a 'smiling and indulgent' father, claiming that the concept of fatherhood incorporates ideas of judicial righteousness and kingly rule, in J.S. Lidgett, *The Spiritual Principle of the Atonement*, p. 230.
69. Lidgett, *Fatherhood*, pp. 303 and vii.
70. Ibid., p. 343.
71. J.S. Lidgett, *The Idea of God and Social Ideals*, p. 101.
72. See Peter Hinchliff, *Benjamin Jowett and the Christian Religion*.
73. 'Reminiscence', in Arnold Toynbee, *Lectures on the Industrial Revolution of the Eighteenth Century in England*, p. xx.
74. Edward Caird, *Essays on Literature and Philosophy*, I, pp. 224-5; see also Caird, *The Evolution of Religion*, I, pp. 64ff.
75. T.H. Green, *Prolegomena to Ethics*, p. 220.
76. Quoted by R.L. Nettleship, 'Memoir', in *The Works of Thomas Hill Green*, III, p. cviii; Edward Caird, *Lay Sermons and Addresses*, p. 192.
77. 'I reckon religion and morality properly identical', Green to Henry Scott Holland, 6 October 1872, in S. Paget, *Henry Scott Holland*, p. 66.
78. T.H. Green, 'Lecture on Liberal Legislation and Freedom of Contract', in *Works*, III, p. 367.
79. Caird, *Evolution*, II, p. 320.
80. Caird, *Lay Sermons*, p. 111.
81. In Toynbee, *Industrial Revolution*, p. xx.
82. Green, 'Essay on Christian Dogma', in *Works*, III, pp. 170ff.; ibid., p. 182. 'One need not be an orthodox trinitarian to see that, if arianism had had its way, the theology of christianity would have become of a kind in which no philosopher who had outgrown the daemonism of ancient systems could for a moment acquiesce' (ibid., p. 172). See A. Harnack, *What is Christianity?*, p. 304. Despite this theoretical disagreement, the religion of Green and Harnack seems very similar.
83. See David Nicholls, 'The Totalitarianism of Thomas Arnold', *Review of Politics*, 29: 4, 1967, pp. 518ff.
84. Caird, *Lay Sermons*, pp. 111 and 218; Green, in Paget, *Henry Scott Holland*, p. 31, and in 'Four Lectures on the English Revolution', in Green, *Works*, III, p. 282. For J.N. Figgis see 'On Some Political Theories of the Early Jesuits', *Transactions of the Royal Historical Society*, NS, IX, 1897, pp. 89ff., and *Studies of Political Thought from Gerson to Grotius, 1414-1625*, pp. 146ff.

85. Nettleship, in Green, *Works*, III, p. cxxii; Toynbee, *Industrial Revolution*, p. 256.
86. Green, 'Fragment of an Address on the Text "the Word is nigh thee"', *Works*, III, p. 221; 'The Witness of God', *Works*, III, p. 244.
87. Green, 'Fragment', *Works*, III, p. 221.
88. Caird, *Essays*, I, p.141.
89. Caird, *Lay Sermons*, p. 80.
90. Green, *Prolegomena to Ethics*, pp. 218ff., and Green to Holland, 29 December 1868, in Paget, *Henry Scott Holland*, p. 29.
91. Toynbee, *Industrial Revolution*, p. 250.
92. Green, 'Principles of Political Obligation', in *Works*, II, p. 344.
93. Ibid., II, pp. 344ff.
94. Green, 'Liberal Legislation', in *Works*, III, p. 375.
95. Green, 'Principles', in *Works*, II, p. 515.
96. Green, 'Liberal Legislation', in *Works*, III, pp. 370–2. I have discussed some of these issues in 'Positive Liberty', pp. 114ff.
97. Toynbee, *Industrial Revolution*, p. 250.
98. Ibid., pp. 249 and 237.
99. Green, 'Liberal Legislation', in *Works*, III, p. 374.
100. M. Richter, *The Politics of Conscience*, p. 342.
101. Milner, in Toynbee, *Industrial Revolution*, p. xxvii.
102. Milner, in ibid., p. xxv.
103. J. Reulecke, in Mommsen, ed., *The Emergence*, pp. 32ff.
104. J. Tampke, in ibid., p. 73.
105. W.H. Dawson, *Social Insurance in Germany, 1883–1911*, p. 3.
106. See David Nicholls, 'Modifications and Movements', *Journal of Theological Studies*, NS, 25: 2, 1974, pp. 393ff.
107. Bismarck, quoted in H. Rothfels, 'Bismarck's Social Policy and the Problem of State Socialism in Germany', *Sociological Review*, 30: 1, 1938, p. 92.
108. Bismarck, quoted in Dawson, *Social Insurance*, pp. 1–2.
109. Dawson, *Social Insurance*, p. 11.
110. G.V. Rimlinger, *Welfare Policy and Industrialization in Europe, America and Russia*, p. 112.
111. Ibid., p. 118.
112. Bismarck, *Gesammelte Werke*, 13, p. 403, quoted in Rimlinger, *Welfare Policy*, p. 121.
113. See Rimlinger, *Welfare Policy*, p. 113.
114. Quoted in Dawson, *Social Insurance*, p. 13.
115. See Otto Ritschl, *Albrecht Ritschl's Leben*.
116. Ibid., II, p. 181.
117. James Richmond appears to believe that such a label does Ritschl some grave injustice: *Ritschl: A Reappraisal*, pp. 20ff.
118. It should perhaps be noted that Ritschl himself rejected the term

'liberal' for his theology, which had too close associations with neo-Hegelian rationalism, preferring the term 'modern' for the conservative reconstruction of theology which he was proposing.

119. A. Ritschl, 'Instruction in the Christian Religion', printed as an appendix to A.T. Swing, *The Theology of Albrecht Ritschl*, pp. 233, 263 and 240.

120. A. Ritschl, *A Critical History of the Christian Doctrine of Justification and Reconciliation*, pp. 209 and 14. This is an English translation of the first volume of *Die christliche Lehre von der Rechtfertigung und Versöhnung*.

121. A. Ritschl, *The Christian Doctrine of Justification and Reconciliation*, p. 239. This is volume III of *Die christliche Lehre*.

122. 'Instruction in the Christian Religion', printed as an appendix to Swing, *The Theology of Albrecht Ritschl*, p. 190.

123. Ritschl, *The Christian Doctrine*, p. 319.

124. Paul Tillich, *Perspectives on Nineteenth and Twentieth Century Protestant Theology*, p. 218.

125. W. Herrmann, Preface to A. Harnack and W. Herrmann, *Essays on the Social Gospel*, p. vii.

126. *The Communion of the Christian with God* is the title of a book by Wilhelm Herrmann.

127. Adolf Harnack, *What is Christianity?*, p. 57.

128. See Max Weber, *Jugendbriefe*, pp. 298ff. See also J.P. Mayer, *Max Weber and German Politics*.

129. Weber and Meinecke believed that they were 'pulling on the same rope' (F. Meinecke, *Machiavellism: The Doctrine of Raison d'Etat and its Place in Modern History*, p. xxxix). Meinecke later renounced this doctrine of *raison d'état*, but adopted an equally unsatisfactory belief in an individualistic liberalism which he saw as the political expression of the Christian religion (*The German Catastrophe*, p. 6).

130. H. von Treitschke, *Bundesstaat und Einheitsstaat*, Aufsatz 2, p. 152; quoted in Meinecke, *Machiavellism*, p. 399.

131. Max Weber, 'Politics as a Vocation', in H. Gerth and C.Wright Mills, eds, *From Max Weber*, p. 78.

132. Gerth and Mills, eds, *From Max Weber*, p. 82.

133. Max Weber, *The Sociology of Religion*, p. 103.

134. Ibid., p. 26.

135. Max Weber, 'Parlament und Regierung im neugeordneten Deutschland', in *Gesammelte Politische Schriften*, p. 138.

136. Ibid., pp. 139ff.

137. Gerth and Mills, eds, *From Max Weber*, p. 42.

138. Mayer, *Max Weber and German Politics*, pp. 30ff.

139. Weber, *The Sociology of Religion*, p. 143.

140. Max Weber, *The Protestant Ethic and the Spirit of Capitalism*, p. 103.
141. H. Richard Niebuhr, *The Kingdom of God in America*, p. 193.

4 NO KING BUT CAESAR

1. For a brief discussion of the concept of social henotheism, see H.R. Niebuhr, *Radical Monotheism and Western Culture*, pp. 27ff.
2. Nicolas Berdyaev, *The Divine and the Human*, p. 45.
3. V.I. Lenin, 'Certain Features of the Historical Development of Marxism' (*Zvezda*, 2, 23 December 1923) and 'Our Revolution' (*Pravda*, 117, 30 May 1923), both reprinted in V.I. Lenin, *Against Revisionism*, pp. 134ff. and 576.
4. Quoted by Karl Löwith, *Meaning in History*, p. 24.
5. Reprinted in Michael Oakeshott, *The Social and Political Doctrines of Contemporary Europe*, p. 166.
6. Carl J. Friedrich and Zbigniew K. Brzezinski, *Totalitarian Dictatorship and Autocracy*, p. 5.
7. See David Nicholls, *The Pluralist State*.
8. Hannah Arendt, *The Origins of Totalitarianism*, p. 348n.
9. See Alex Inkeles, 'The Totalitarian Mystique', in C.J. Friedrich, ed., *Totalitarianism*, pp. 87ff.; and L.B. Schapiro, *Totalitarianism*, pp. 123ff.
10. J.L. Talmon, *The Origins of Totalitarian Democracy*. See also Carl Schmitt's discussion of Rousseau and the Jacobins, *Political Romanticism* (1919), p. 59: 'Politics becomes a religious matter. The political organ becomes a priest of the republic.' Berdyaev also referred to Jacobinism as 'totalitarian in character' (*The Divine*, p. 117).
11. See Robert A. Dahl, *A Preface to Democratic Theory* and *Polyarchy, Participation and Opposition*; Edward Shils, *The Torment of Secrecy*. Some of these are discussed in David Nicholls, *Three Varieties of Pluralism*, chapter 3; and in William Connolly, ed., *The Bias of Pluralism*.
12. See, for example, the writings of Wyndham Lewis; also the trenchant criticisms made by the Portuguese dictator Salazar, from an authoritarian, though not totalitarian, standpoint.
13. Herbert Marcuse, *One Dimensional Man*, p. 20. See also Robert Paul Wolff et al., *The Limits of Pure Tolerance*, and Wolff, *The Poverty of Liberalism*.
14. J. Moltmann, *The Crucified God*, p. 328; on Davidson see below pp. 153–4.
15. Robert A. Pois, *National Socialism and the Religion of Nature*, p. 67; Alfred Rosenberg, 'Totaler Staat?', *Völkischer Beobachter*, 9 January 1934, reprinted in Robert A. Pois, ed., *Alfred Rosenberg: Selected Writings*, p. 192.

16. Adolf Hitler, quoted in *Zeitschrift der Akademie für deutsches Recht*, 4: 4, 1937, p. 97, see J.W. Bendersky, *Carl Schmitt: Theorist for the Reich*, pp. 221–2; see also A. Hitler, *Mein Kampf*, 2: 2, pp. 386ff.

17. Hermann Rauschning, *Hitler Speaks*, p. 232.

18. Ian Kershaw, *The 'Hitler Myth'*, p. 20; see also W. Struve, *Elites against Democracy: Leadership Ideals in Bourgeois Political Thought in Germany, 1890–1933*.

19. Oakeshott, *Social and Political Doctrines*, p. 193.

20. Alfred Rosenberg, *Der Mythus des 20. Jahrhunderts*, pp. 78–9; quoted by Oakeshott, *Social and Political Doctrines*, p. 193n.

21. *Christliche Welt*, 1930, p. 1162; quoted in E. Bethge, *Dietrich Bonhoeffer: Man of Vision, Man of Courage*, p. 157.

22. J.S. Conway, *The Nazi Persecution of the Church, 1933–45*, p. 45; on the theological ideas of the 'Deutsche Christen', see Kurt Meier, *Die Deutschen Christen: Das Bild einer Bewegung im Kirchenkampf des Dritten Reiches*, and Hans-Joachim Sonne, *Die politische Theologie der Deutschen Christen*.

23. Conway, *The Nazi Persecution*, p. 47.

24. Ibid., p. 11; G. Van Norden, *Kirche in der Krise*, p. 94.

25. E. Bethge, in F.H. Littell and H.G. Locke, eds, *The German Church Struggle and the Holocaust*, p. 178. For the role of Protestant churches in the Weimar period see Kurt Nowak, *Evangelische Kirche und Weimarer Republik*, and Jonathan Wright, *'Above Parties': The Political Attitudes of the German Protestant Church Leadership, 1918–1933*.

26. J. Beckmann, *Artgemässes Christentum oder schriftgemäss* (1933), quoted in Conway, *The Nazi Persecution*, p. 46.

27. Rosenberg, *Der Mythus*, in Pois, ed., *Alfred Rosenberg*, pp. 114–15.

28. Bormann (1942), quoted in George L. Mosse, *Nazi Culture: Intellectual, Cultural and Social Life in the Third Reich*, p. 245.

29. Hesse and Goebbels, in Conway, *The Nazi Persecution*, pp. 50 and 115.

30. Cajus Fabricius, *Positive Christianity in the Third Reich*, p. 33.

31. Dr Reinhold Krause, quoted in Conway, *The Nazi Persecution*, p. 52.

32. F.O. Bonkovsky, 'The German State and Protestant Elites', in Littell and Locke, eds, *The German Church Struggle*, p. 137.

33. Heinrich Forck, quoted by Bethge in Littell and Locke, eds, *The German Church Struggle*, p. 180.

34. Dietrich Bonhoeffer, *No Rusty Swords*, p. 218.

35. G. Zahn, *German Catholics and Hitler's Wars*, p. 73; see also Guenter Lewy, *The Catholic Church and Nazi Germany*.

36. Jean-Loup Seban, 'The Theology of Nationalism of Emanuel Hirsch', *Princeton Seminary Bulletin*, NS, 7: 2, 1986, p. 161. See also John Stroup, 'Political Theology and Secularization Theory in Germany, 1918–1939: Emanuel Hirsch as a Phenomenon of his Time', *Harvard Theological Review*, 80: 3, 1987, pp. 321ff.

37. E. Hirsch, *Das kirchliche Wollen der Deutschen Christen*, quoted in R.P. Ericksen, *Theologians under Hitler*, p. 146; on Hirsch see also Sonne, *Die politische Theologie*, pp. 119ff.
38. Paul Tillich, quoted in Ericksen, *Theologians*, p. 180. Tillich's open letter to Hirsch, of 1934, is to be found in *Theologische Blätter* (ed. K.L. Schmidt), 13, 1934.
39. Paul Althaus, *Politisches Christentum*, pp. 19 and 9, quoted in Ericksen, *Theologians*, pp. 92–3; and Althaus, *Theologie der Ordnungen*. See also Sonne, *Die politische Theologie*, pp. 106–7.
40. Paul Althaus, *Kirche und Staat nach lutherischer Lehre*, pp. 9–10, quoted in Ericksen, *Theologians*, p. 106.
41. Paul Althaus, in E. Gerstenmeier, ed., *Kirche, Volk und Staat*, p. 30; quoted in Ericksen, *Theologians*, p. 94.
42. Paul Althaus, *Obrigkeit und Führertum*, pp. 47ff.
43. For details of Schmitt's life see J.W. Bendersky, *Carl Schmitt*.
44. Carl Schmitt, *Political Theology: Four Chapters on the Concept of Sovereignty*, p. 58; Schmitt, quoted in Bendersky, *Carl Schmitt*, p. 87.
45. Schmitt, *Political Theology*, p. 7.
46. Schmitt, *Political Theology*, p. 5; *The Crisis of Parliamentary Democracy*, p. 43; for his views on dictatorship see *Die Diktatur*.
47. Schmitt, *Political Theology*, p. 15.
48. Antonio de Oliveira Salazar, *Doctrine and Action*, p. 269.
49. Carl Schmitt, *The Concept of the Political*, p. 71.
50. Schmitt, *The Crisis*, p. 35.
51. Schmitt, *The Concept*, p. 75.
52. Ibid., p. 77.
53. Ibid., p. 74.
54. Schmitt, *The Crisis*, p. 6.
55. Ibid., pp. 16 and 7.
56. Ibid., p. xix.
57. See the critical comments by Richard Thoma, 'On the Ideology of Parliamentarism', reprinted in Schmitt, *The Crisis*, pp. 79–80.
58. Thoma, 'On the Ideology of Parliamentarism', p. 80.
59. See, for example, the literature discussed in Peter Bachrach and Morton S. Baratz, *The Theory of Democratic Elitism*. The continental theorists include Mosca, Pareto, Weber and Schumpeter.
60. Schmitt, *The Crisis*, p. 4.
61. Ibid., p. 1; and Thoma, 'On the Ideology of Parliamentarism', p. 82.
62. Carl Schmitt, *The Necessity of Politics*, p. 56.
63. George Schwab, *The Challenge of the Exception*, p. 19.
64. Schmitt, 'Wesen und Werden des faschistischen Staates' (1929), in *Positionen und Begriffe im Kampf mit Weimar–Genf–Versailles*, p. 110 (quoted in G. Lukács, *The Destruction of Reason*, p. 659).
65. Schmitt, *The Necessity of Politics*, p. 56.

66. See George Schwab, in Schmitt, *Political Theology*, p. xiii.

67. Schmitt, *Political Theology*, pp. 18ff. On Schmitt's relationship to Hobbes, see Carl Schmitt, *Der Leviathan in der Staatslehre des Thomas Hobbes*, and Helmut Rumpf, *Carl Schmitt und Thomas Hobbes*.

68. Quoted in J. Noakes and G. Pridham, eds, *Documents on Nazism*, p. 254.

69. Schmitt, 'Das Zeitalter der Neutralisierungen und Entpolitisierungen' (1929), in *Positionen und Begriffe*, pp. 120ff.

70. Schmitt, *Political Theology*, p. 65; on the Frankfurt School see Martin Jay, *The Dialectical Imagination*, and J. Habermas, *Toward a Rational Society*.

71. Schmitt, *The Concept*, p. 49, and 'Staatsethik und pluralistischer Staat' (1930), in *Positionen und Begriffe*, pp. 133ff. Figgis was, however, prepared to recognise that the state is an association of a peculiar kind, charged with the duty of reconciling conflicts and maintaining order. See David Nicholls, *The Pluralist State*, pp. 79ff.

72. In Schmitt, *The Concept*, p. 39n.

73. Ibid., pp. 38–9.

74. Schmitt, *Uber die drei Arten*, quoted in Schwab, *The Challenge*, p. 122.

75. Schmitt, 'Weiterentwicklung des totalen Staates in Deutschland' (1933), in *Positionen und Begriffe*, p. 187.

76. Schmitt, *Staat, Bewegung, Volk: Die Dreigliederung der politischen Einheit*, pp. 42–3 (reprinted in G.L. Mosse, *Nazi Culture*, p. 326).

77. Schmitt, *Political Theology*, p. 36. On Bacon, see David Nicholls, 'Deity and Domination II', *New Blackfriars*, 776, February 1985, p. 47.

78. Schmitt, *Political Theology*, pp. 36–7.

79. Ibid., pp. 44–5.

80. Ibid., p. 46.

81. Schmitt, *Political Romanticism*, pp. 58–9.

82. Schmitt, *Politische Theologie II: Die Legende von der Erledigung jeder politischen Theologie*, p. 101n.

83. Hans Blumenberg, *The Legitimacy of the Modern Age*, p. 94.

84. Karl Barth, *Church Dogmatics*, 1: 1, p. x.

85. In K. Barth and E. Thurneysen, *Revolutionary Theology in the Making*, p. 14.

86. F.-W. Marquardt, *Theologie und Sozialismus: das Beispiel Karl Barths*; Eberhard Jüngel, *Karl Barth: A Theological Legacy*, p. 104.

87. The reception of Barth's theology in Britain makes an interesting contrast. In Scotland his admirers tended to be rather conservative Presbyterians. In England some of his disciples were Anglican liberal Catholics in search of an ideology, like Sir Edwyn Hoskyns and the circle around him at Corpus Christi College, Cambridge, who were socially conservative and politically authoritarian, with a certain sympathy for Nazism and Fascism.

88. On Barth's political ideas see Marquardt, *Theologie und Sozialismus*; G. Hunsinger, ed., *Karl Barth and Radical Politics*; also R.E. Hood, *Contemporary Political Orders and Christ*. There is a perceptive discussion of Barth's political theology in chapter VI:B of R.E. Willis, *The Ethics of Karl Barth*.

89. Barth, *The Epistle to the Romans (Römerbrief)*, 1st edn, p. 380.

90. Barth, *The Epistle to the Romans*, pp. 483 and 460.

91. Barth 'The Christian Community in the Midst of Political Change' (1948), in Barth, *Against the Stream*, pp. 80 and 94.

92. Jüngel, *Karl Barth*, pp. 39–40.

93. Barth, 'Basic Problems of Christian Social Ethics: A Discussion with Paul Althaus', in James M. Robinson, ed., *The Beginnings of Dialectic Theology*, p. 48. See Paul Althaus, *Grundriss der Ethik*.

94. Barth, 'The Christian Community and the Civil Community' (1946), in Barth, *Against the Stream*, pp. 21f. (my italics) and 40.

95. Barth, *Church Dogmatics*, 3: 4, pp. 19ff.; and Barth, *Against the Stream*, pp. 28–9 and 31.

96. Barth, *Against the Stream*, pp. 49 and 40.

97. Barth, *Against the Stream*, pp. 17 and 24.

98. See T.A. Gill, in Littell and Locke, eds, *The German Church Struggle*, p. 287.

99. Karl Barth, *The Church and the Political Problem of our Day*, p. 33.

100. Barth, *The Church*, p. 32.

101. Barth, *Church Dogmatics*, 2: 1, p. 174.

102. T.H. Gill, in Littell and Locke, eds, *The German Church Struggle*, p. 286.

103. Barth to H. von Soden, 5 December 1934, in *Karl Barth–Rudolf Bultmann Letters, 1922–1966*, p. 137; and Barth, *The Church*, pp. 43, 38 and 22. See also *How I Changed my Mind* (originally published as an article in 1938).

104. See Wright, 'Above Parties', p. 168.

105. Barth, *Church Dogmatics*, 1: 1, p. 178.

106. Schmitt, *Political Theology*, p. 36.

107. Karl Barth, *The Humanity of God*, pp. 33 and 41.

108. Barth, *Church Dogmatics*, 2: 1, pp. 23, 325 and 31.

109. Karl Barth, *God Here and Now*, p. 17; Barth, *How I Changed my Mind*, p. 48. See also Barth, *The Word of God and the Word of Man*, p. 248.

110. Barth, *God Here and Now*, p. 29.

111. K. Barth and J. Hamel, *How to Serve God in a Marxist Land*, p. 58.

112. Emil Brunner, 'An Open Letter to Karl Barth', in Barth, *Against the Stream*, pp. 106ff., and Reinhold Niebuhr, 'Why is Barth Silent about Hungary?', *The Christian Century*, 74: 19, 23 January 1957, pp. 108ff.

113. Barth, *Church Dogmatics*, 2: 2, p. 520.

114. Ibid., 2: 2, p. 522.

115. Ibid., 2: 2, p. 665 (German edition, *Kirchliche Dogmatik*, 2: 2, p. 741).
116. Barth, *Church Dogmatics*, 2: 2, pp. 631ff., and 1: 2 (revised edn), p. 364 (quoted in Jüngel, *Karl Barth*, p. 121).
117. Barth, *Church Dogmatics*, 2: 2, p. 651.
118. Ibid., 2: 2, p. 660.
119. Barth, *The Epistle to the Romans*, p. 490.
120. Barth, *Church Dogmatics*, 4: 1, p. 451.
121. Ibid., 2: 2, pp. 683ff.
122. Ibid., 3: 4, p. 449.
123. Ibid., 2: 2, pp. 676–7.
124. Ibid., 2: 1, pp. 541–2.
125. Ibid., 2: 2, p. 677–8.
126. Ibid., 2: 1, p. 379.
127. Ibid., 2: 1, p. 538.
128. Ibid., 4: 1, pp. 181ff.
129. Karl Barth, *Dogmatics in Outline*, p. 48; Barth, *The Humanity*, pp. 67–8.
130. Barth, *Church Dogmatics*, 3: 2, p. 148.
131. Karl Barth, *Evangelical Theology: An Introduction*, p. 10.
132. Barth, *God Here and Now*, p. 17; Barth, *The Humanity*, pp. 42ff. and 73.
133. On Barth's Trinitarianism see Eberhard Jüngel, *The Doctrine of the Trinity*, and Rowan Williams, 'Barth on the Triune God', in Stephen Sykes, ed., *Karl Barth: Studies of his Theological Method*, pp. 147ff.
134. Barth, *Church Dogmatics*, 1: 1, p. 454, and 4: 1, p. 202.
135. Christopher Read, *Religion, Revolution and the Russian Intelligentsia, 1900–1912*.
136. See Berdyaev's autobiography, *Dream and Reality*.
137. Berdyaev, *Dream and Reality*, p. 50.
138. James Pain and Nicolas Zernov, eds, *A Bulgakov Anthology*.
139. See S.L. Frank, ed., *A Solovyov Anthology*; and N.F. Feodorov, in Alexander Schmemann, ed., *Ultimate Questions: An Anthology of Modern Russian Religious Thought*, pp. 175ff.; also Stephen Lukashevich, *N.F. Fedorov (1828–1903): A Study in Russian Eupsychian and Utopian Thought*.
140. N.A. Berdyaev, *The Meaning of History*, p. 89.
141. Ibid., p. 131; and N.A. Berdyaev, *Freedom and the Spirit*, pp. 303ff.
142. In more recent years C.F. von Weizsäcker has maintained that 'The modern world can largely be understood as the result of a secularization of Christianity' (*The Relevance of Science*, p. 162) and Karl Löwith has also restated the thesis (*Meaning in History*). Hans Blumenberg has mobilised some excessively heavy artillery in the attempt to demolish what is, after all, a rather modest construction

(*The Legitimacy of the Modern Age*). See also Judith N. Shklar, *After Utopia*, chapter 5.

143. N.A. Berdyaev, *The Realm of Spirit and the Realm of Caesar*, p. 53.
144. Ibid., p. 177.
145. Berdyaev, *Dream and Reality*, p. 98.
146. Ibid., p. 46.
147. Ibid., p. 56.
148. Berdyaev, *The Meaning of History*, p. 52; see also *Dream and Reality*, p. 181.
149. N.A. Berdyaev, *Solitude and Society*, p. 97; *The Realm of Spirit*, p. 39; and *Slavery and Freedom*, p. 83.
150. Berdyaev, *Freedom and the Spirit*, pp. 70ff.
151. Ibid., p. 83; see Paul Tillich, *Dynamics of Faith*, especially chapter 3.
152. Berdyaev, *The Realm of Spirit*, p. 38.
153. Berdyaev, *The Meaning of History*, p. 48.
154. Berdyaev, *The Divine and the Human*, p. 22.
155. Ibid., p. 6.
156. Berdyaev, *Dream and Reality*, pp. 57–8; *Slavery and Freedom*, pp. 83ff.
157. Berdyaev, *Freedom and the Spirit*, p. 147. Paul Tillich later developed this conception of theonomy in his *Systematic Theology*, III, pp. 264ff. See also Auguste Sabatier, *La Religion et la culture moderne*.
158. Berdyaev, *Freedom and the Spirit*, p. 149, and *Dream and Reality*, p. 180.
159. Berdyaev, *Slavery and Freedom*, p. 82.
160. Berdyaev, *Spirit and Reality*, p. 185, and *Freedom and the Spirit*, p. 140. There is also a somewhat confusing discussion of power in *The Divine and the Human*, pp. 105ff.
161. Berdyaev, *Slavery and Freedom*, p. 39.
162. Berdyaev, *The Divine and the Human*, p. 110; *Freedom and the Spirit*, pp. 189 and 214ff.; see also *Dream and Reality*, p. 180.
163. Berdyaev, *Slavery and Freedom*, p. 70.
164. Berdyaev, *Slavery and Freedom*, p. 89, and *Spirit and Reality*, p. 147.
165. Berdyaev, *Slavery and Freedom*, pp. 90ff.
166. Berdyaev, *The Divine and the Human*, p. 13.
167. Berdyaev, *Dream and Reality*, p. 112.
168. Berdyaev, *The Meaning of History*, pp. 171–2.
169. Berdyaev, *Slavery and Freedom*, p. 146. I have discussed the question of sovereignty in Nicholls, *The Pluralist State*, chapter 3.
170. Berdyaev, *Spirit and Reality*, p. 190.
171. Berdyaev, *The Realm of Spirit*, p. 70.
172. Ibid., p. 72.
173. Berdyaev, *Slavery and Freedom*, pp. 149–50, and *Solitude and Society*, p. 185.

174. Berdyaev, *Slavery and Freedom*, pp. 147–8.
175. Berdyaev, *Dream and Reality*, pp. 110 and 222.
176. Berdyaev, *Dream and Reality*, p. 48; see also *The Realm of Spirit*, pp. 109–10.
177. Berdyaev, *The Realm of Spirit*, pp. 109–10.
178. Berdyaev, *Solitude and Society*, p. 189. For Schmitt see above pp. 99ff.
179. Berdyaev, quoted in E. Lampert, *Berdyaev and the New Middle Ages*, p. 87.
180. Berdyaev, 'K psikhologii revolyutsii', *Russkaya mysl'*, 7, 1908, p. 133; and Berdyaev, 'Revolyutsiya i kul'tura', *Polyarnaya zvezda*, 2, 1905, p. 148, both quoted in C. Read, *Religion*, p. 74.
181. Berdyaev, *Slavery and Freedom*, p. 84.
182. Berdyaev, *Dream and Reality*, p. 72.
183. Berdyaev, *Freedom and the Spirit*, pp. 144ff. On *sobornost* in Orthodox thinking about the church, see Pain and Zernov, *A Bulgakov Anthology*, pp. 126ff. It was central to the theology of A.S. Khomiakoff, see especially *L'Eglise latine et le protestantisme au point de vue de l'église d'orient*.
184. Berdyaev, *Slavery and Freedom*, p. 140, and *The Meaning of History*, pp. 160–1 and 170ff. Earlier writers to state this thesis include de Tocqueville, Ketteler, Acton, Maitland and Figgis (see Nicholls, *The Pluralist State*, chapter 2). It has been restated in more recent times by William Kornhauser in his *The Politics of Mass Society*.
185. Lampert, *Berdyaev*, pp. 63ff.
186. Berdyaev, *Slavery and Freedom*, p. 114.
187. M.G. Smith, in L. Kuper and M.G. Smith, eds, *Pluralism in Africa*, p. 29.
188. Ralf Dahrendorf, *Essays in the Theory of Society*, p. 44.
189. Dahrendorf, *Essays*, pp. 52ff. and 64.
190. David Frisby and Derek Sayer, *Society*, p. 122.
191. E. Durkheim, *The Elementary Forms of the Religious Life*, p. 258, and *Sociologie et philosophie*, p. 75.
192. Durkheim, *Sociologie et philosophie*, p. 70, quoted in Gillian Rose, *Hegel contra Sociology*, p. 15.
193. Rose, *Hegel*, p. 16.
194. For a brief discussion of this issue, see David Nicholls, *Haiti in Caribbean Context*, pp. 160ff., and *Three Varieties of Pluralism*, pp. 44ff.
195. See Nicholls, *The Pluralist State*, chapter 4.
196. F.A. von Hayek, *The Counter-Revolution of Science* (reprinting articles originally appearing in 1941), pp. 53ff.
197. F.A. von Hayek, *Individualism: True and False*, p. 7 (my italics).
198. Ibid., pp. 22 and 14.
199. F.A. von Hayek, *The Constitution of Liberty*, pp. 90 and 3.

200. Kurt H. Wolff, ed., *The Sociology of Georg Simmel*, p. 10.
201. Ibid., p. 258.

5 FEDERAL POLITICS AND FINITE GOD

1. A.N. Whitehead, *Religion in the Making*, p. 44.
2. Gordon D. Kaufman, *Theology for a Nuclear Age*, p. 39.
3. A. de Tocqueville, *Democracy in America*, p. 129 (chapter 11).
4. Henry B. Parkes, *The American Experience*, p. 64.
5. Robert Bellah, *Beyond Belief*; Clifford Geertz, *Local Knowledge*, chapter 6; Richard Neuhaus, *The Naked Public Square: Religion and Democracy in America*.
6. Peter Smith, 'Anglo-American Religion and Hegemonic Change in the World System, c.1870–1980', *British Journal of Sociology*, 37: 1, 1986. The argument is not very well pursued and most of the statistical evidence on religious practice which the author parades is irrelevant to the thesis, which purports to be about 'establishment religion'.
7. In the course of the present study this issue will arise from time to time and I hope to deal with it in a more systematic way elsewhere.
8. John Dewey, *Problems of Man*, p. 17; Dewey, *Reconstruction in Philosophy*, pp. 61 and 64ff. It is curious that a recent author, in a book which begins and ends with a discussion of Dewey, can make the following remark, without reference to his contribution in this field: 'until recently philosophers have paid little or no attention to the social context in which science takes place and the social consequences of science, but this is becoming an issue of much greater concern' (Richard J. Bernstein, *Philosophical Profiles*, p. 152).
9. Dewey, 'The Obligation to Knowledge of God', in John Dewey, *The Early Works, 1882–1898*, I, p. 61.
10. William James, *The Varieties of Religious Experience*, pp. 515ff.; see also James, *Pragmatism*, p. 97.
11. William James, *The Writings of William James*, pp. 807ff., 527 and 492.
12. William James, *The Will to Believe*, pp. 122 and 134; and *The Writings*, pp. 492, 527ff. and 803ff.
13. John Dewey, 'Christianity and Democracy' (1893), in *The Early Works*, IV, p. 7.
14. John Dewey, *Reconstruction in Philosophy*, pp. 203ff.; but see *The Public and its Problems*, pp. 73ff., where he envisages a more constructive role for the state.
15. Dewey, *Reconstruction*, p. 162; James, *The Writings*, p. 809; also James, *Pragmatism*, p. 257.
16. H.R. Niebuhr, *The Kingdom of God in America*, p. 183.
17. A.F. Bentley, *The Process of Government*. See also Paul F. Kress, *Social*

Science and the Idea of Process: The Ambiguous Legacy of Arthur F. Bentley; and Myron Q. Hale, 'The Cosmology of Arthur F. Bentley', in William E. Connolly, ed., *The Bias of Pluralism*, pp. 35–50.

18. A.J. Balfour, *Essays and Addresses*, pp. 238 and 267; also British Museum Add. MSS 49962:40. See David Nicholls, 'Few are Chosen: Some Reflections on the Politics of A.J. Balfour', *The Review of Politics*, 30: 1, 1968, pp. 33ff.

19. Morton White, *Social Thought in America: The Revolt against Formalism*, p. 13.

20. Mary Parker Follett, especially *The New State*, and 'Community is a Process', *Philosophical Review*, 28: 6, 1919, pp. 580ff.

21. W. Lippmann, *A Preface to Morals*, pp. 268ff.

22. Grant McConnell, *Private Power and American Democracy*; Arthur S. Miller, *The Modern Corporate State: Private Government and the American Constitution*.

23. C. Wright Mills, *The Power Elite*; Henry Kariel, *The Decline of American Pluralism*; Robert P. Wolff, *The Poverty of Liberalism*; Herbert Marcuse, *One Dimensional Man*; P. Bachrach and M.S. Baratz, *Power and Poverty*. There is an extensive literature on this subject, some of which is discussed in David Nicholls, *Three Varieties of Pluralism*.

24. A.N. Whitehead, *Process and Reality*, p. 345.

25. Ibid., pp. 349ff.

26. Ibid., p. 346.

27. Ibid., p. 342; see also A.N. Whitehead, *Adventures of Ideas*, p. 37.

28. Whitehead, *Religion in the Making*, pp. 44ff. and 139, and *Process*, p. 351.

29. Whitehead, *Adventures*, pp. 196ff.; and *Science and the Modern World*, p. 276.

30. D.D. Williams, *Essays in Process Theology*, p. 191, and Williams, 'Deity, Monarchy and Metaphysics: Whitehead's Critique of the Theological Tradition', in Ivor Leclerc, ed., *The Relevance of Whitehead*, p. 56.

31. E.H. Madden and P.H. Hare, *Evil and the Concept of God*, pp. 121ff., and L.S. Ford, 'Divine Persuasion and the Triumph of the Good', in Delwin Brown et al., eds, *Process Philosophy and Christian Thought*, pp. 283ff. See also Illtyd Trethowan, *Process Theology and the Christian Tradition*.

32. A.N. Whitehead, *The Aims of Education*.

33. Whitehead, *Science*, chapter 13.

34. Whitehead, *Adventures*, pp. 72–3.

35. A.H. Johnson, 'The Social Philosophy of Alfred North Whitehead', *The Journal of Philosophy*, 40: 10, 1943, pp. 261ff.; see also Johnson, 'A Philosophical Foundation for Democracy', *Ethics*, 68: 4, 1958, pp. 281ff.

36. Whitehead, *Process*, p. 343, and Williams, 'Deity, Monarchy and Metaphysics', p. 58.

37. For a recent attack on the whole enterprise of founding Christian faith on any metaphysic of being, see Joseph O'Leary, *Questioning Back: The Overcoming of Metaphysics in Christian Tradition*. For an earlier example see H.L. Mansel, *The Limits of Religious Thought*.

38. Charles Hartshorne, *The Divine Relativity*, p. 18.

39. See Richard E. Creel, *Divine Impassibility: An Essay in Philosophical Theology*, and the earlier works, Bertrand D. Brasnett, *The Suffering of the Impassible God*, and H. Wheeler Robinson, *Suffering, Human and Divine*.

40. John Macquarrie, *In Search of Deity*.

41. Charles Hartshorne, *Man's Vision of God*, p. xiv.

42. G.A. Studdert Kennedy, *The Unutterable Beauty*; see also Kennedy, *The Hardest Part*; William Temple, in B.H. Streeter et al., *Foundations: A Statement of Christian Belief in Terms of Modern Thought*, p. 220; B.H. Streeter, 'The Suffering of God', *The Hibbert Journal*, 47, 1914; C.E. Rolt, *The World's Redemption*; K. Kitamori, *Theology of the Pain of God*; J. Moltmann, *The Crucified God* and *The Trinity and the Kingdom of God*, chapter 2.

43. See a forthcoming book on 'Salvation', to be published by Blackwell in the series 'Theology in Social Context'.

44. Hartshorne, *Man's Vision*, p. 142.

45. Ibid., p. 51. 'Existence is essentially social, plural, free, and exposed to risk', Charles Hartshorne, *The Logic of Perfection*, p. 202; see also Hartshorne, *The Divine Relativity*, pp. 148ff., and Hartshorne, *Man's Vision*, p. xv.

46. P. Bachrach and M.S. Baratz, *Power and Poverty*, p. 43; A. Gramsci, *Selections from the Prison Notebooks*.

47. Charles Hartshorne, 'Politics and the Metaphysics of Freedom', in Fédération Internationale des Sociétés de Philosophie, *Enquête sur la liberté*; also Hartshorne, 'Individual Differences and the Ideal of Equality', *New South*, 18: 2, 1963.

48. Hartshorne, *Man's Vision*, p. 173.

49. Ibid., pp. 173 and xvi.

50. Eric Mascall, *The Openness of Being*, p. 162; see also Colin E. Gunton, *Becoming and Being*.

51. David Burrell, *Aquinas: God and Action*, chapters 2 and 6.

52. Wieman, in H.N. Wieman and W.M. Horton, *The Growth of Religion*, pp. 348 and 350.

53. H.N. Wieman, *The Wrestle of Religion with Truth*, p. 2,

54. H.N. Wieman , 'Some Blind Spots Removed', in *The Christian Century*, 56, 27 January 1939; and Wieman, in H.N. Wieman, with D.C. Macintosh and M.C. Otto, *Is There a God: A Conversation*, p. 15.

55. Wieman and Horton, *The Growth*, pp. 326ff.
56. H.N. Wieman, *Religious Experience and Scientific Method*, pp. 267–8.
57. Wieman and Horton, *The Growth*, p. 348; Wieman, in Wieman, with Macintosh and Otto, *Is There a God?*, p. 18.
58. H.N. Wieman, *Man's Ultimate Commitment*, pp. 226 and 228.
59. Wieman, *The Wrestle of Religion*, p. 3.
60. Shailer Mathews, *New Faith for Old*, p. 72. On the Chicago school see William J. Hynes, *Shirley Jackson Case and the Chicago School: The Socio-Historical Method*, and C.H. Arnold, *Near the Edge of Battle*.
61. S.J. Case, *The Evolution of Early Christianity*, p. 45.
62. Gerald Birney Smith, *Current Christian Thinking*, p. 165.
63. Shailer Mathews, 'Doctrines as Social Patterns', *The Journal of Religion*, 10: 1, 1930, p. 2.
64. Shailer Mathews, 'Social Patterns and the Idea of God', *The Journal of Religion*, 11: 2, 1931, p. 162.
65. Edward S. Ames, in Miles H. Krumbine, ed., *The Process of Religion: Essays in Honor of Dean Shailer Mathews*, pp. 68ff.
66. Shailer Mathews, *The Atonement and the Social Process*, p. 37; and 'Social Patterns and the Idea of God', pp. 170ff. This functionalist orientation in Mathews's thought is stressed by Edwin Aubrey, 'Theology and the Social Process', in Krumbine, ed., *The Process*, p. 47.
67. Shailer Mathews, *The Growth of the Idea of God*, p. 214.
68. Mathews, 'Social Patterns and the Idea of God', p. 174; Mathews, *Outline of Christianity*, III, p. 501; and Mathews, 'Theology and the Social Mind', *Biblical World*, 46, 1915, pp. 201ff.
69. Mathews, *The Growth*, p. 25; *The Atonement*, p. 11; see also *Patriotism and Religion*, pp. 17ff.; Mathews, 'Theology from the Point of View of Social Psychology', *The Journal of Religion*, 3, 1923, p. 343; Mathews, *Outline*, III, p. 83.
70. E.S. Ames, *The Psychology of Religious Experience*, p. 404. This aspect of Ames's thought is discussed by his colleague Gerald Birney Smith in *Current Christian Thinking*, pp. 161–2.
71. Ames, *The Psychology*, p. 397; and Ames, *Religion*, p. 133.
72. John Macquarrie, *Twentieth Century Religious Thought*, pp. 49ff.; John Passmore, *A Hundred Years of Philosophy*, pp. 73ff.
73. G.H. Howison, *The Limits of Evolution, and Other Essays*, p. 76; and Josiah Royce et al., *The Conception of God*, pp. 94ff.
74. Howison, *The Limits*, pp. 248ff. For a discussion of the ideas of Howison see J.W. Buckham and G.M. Stratton, *George Holmes Howison*.
75. H.A. Overstreet, 'The Democratic Conception of God', *Hibbert Journal*, 11: 2, 1913, pp. 400 and 410.
76. H.A. Overstreet, *The Enduring Quest*, p. 260.
77. Ibid., p. 265.

78. H.A. Overstreet, *The Great Enterprise*, p. 106.
79. Dores R. Sharpe, *Walter Rauschenbusch*.
80. Walter Rauschenbusch, *Christianity and the Social Crisis*, p. xxii.
81. Walter Rauschenbusch, *Christianizing the Social Order*, p. 61.
82. Walter Rauschenbusch, *A Theology for the Social Gospel*, pp. 174–6.
83. Ibid., pp. 173ff.
84. Ibid., p. 179.
85. Walter Rauschenbusch, *Prayers of the Social Awakening*, pp. 57 and 59.
86. Rauschenbusch, *A Theology*, p. 217.
87. Ibid., pp. 224ff.
88. Rauschenbusch, *Christianizing*, pp. 110, 274 and 368ff.
89. Washington Gladden, *The Church and the Kingdom*, p. 8. See also Josiah Strong, *The New Era or the Coming Kingdom*.
90. Robert A. Woods, 'Democracy: A New Unfolding of Human Power', in James H. Tufts et al., *Studies in Philosophy and Psychology by Former Students of Charles Edward Garman*, p. 91; on Woods, see Eleanor A. Woods, *Robert A. Woods: Champion of Democracy*.
91. Woods, 'Democracy', p. 98.
92. Thomas Davidson, 'American Democracy as a Religion', *International Journal of Ethics*, 10: 1, 1899, p. 26.
93. Ibid., p. 37.
94. Ibid., pp. 38–9.
95. Gordon Kaufman, *Theology for a Nuclear Age*, p. 33.
96. Gordon Kaufman, *God the Problem*, especially chapter 3.
97. Gordon Kaufman, *The Theological Imagination*, p. 198.
98. Ibid., p. 76.
99. Kaufman, *Theology for a Nuclear Age*, p. 42; *The Theological Imagination*, p. 47.
100. Kaufman, *Theology for a Nuclear Age*, p. 39.
101. Smith, *Current Christian Thinking*, pp. 169–70. See also E.S. Ames, who stated that the word 'God' should not be taken to refer to a particular person but to 'the order of nature including man and all the processes of an aspiring social life', *Religion*, p. 177.
102. Rauschenbusch, *Prayers*, pp. 49–50.
103. In the light of this sophisticated discussion of the natural world, it is amusing to read an earlier reference of his to canine existence, which is in the fullest sense of the word dogmatic! – 'man is a reflective being. (Dogs also die, but this does not lead them to despair over canine life, because they, presumably, are unable to anticipate their own death imaginatively and reflect on its meaning)' (Kaufman, *God the Problem*, p. 53).
104. R. Bellah, *The Broken Covenant*, p. 142.
105. Bellah, in R. Bellah and P.E. Hammond, *Varieties of Civil Religion*, p. 12.

106. Neuhaus, *The Naked Public Square: Religion and Democracy in America.*

6 IMPASSIBLE GOD AND AUTARKIC STATE

1. H. Heine, *Religion and Philosophy in Germany*, p. 79.
2. Ibid., pp. 102–3.
3. Alfred Cobban, *The Nation State and National Self-Determination*, p. 118.
4. For Fichte see below, pp. 162ff.; for Schiller see R.D. Miller, *Schiller and the Ideal of Freedom.*
5. For Kant's criticism of Herder see Immanuel Kant, *Werke*, V, pp. 180ff.; for Herder on language see his 'Essay on the Origin of Language', in F.M. Barnard, ed., *J.G. Herder on Social and Political Culture*, pp. 117ff.
6. Cited in Max Rouche, *La Philosophie de l'histoire de Herder*, p. 297n. On Herder see also A. Gillies, *Herder*; Robert Ergang, *Herder and the Foundations of German Nationalism*; and F.M. Barnard, *Herder's Social and Political Thought.*
7. J.G. Herder, *God, Some Conversations*, pp. 96–7.
8. K.S. Pinson, *Pietism as a Factor in the Rise of German Nationalism*; but for a warning that pietism was by no means a single coherent movement see H. Lehmann, 'Pietism and Nationalism: The Relationship between Protestant Revivalism and National Renewal in Nineteenth-Century Germany', *Church History*, 51: 1, 1982, pp. 39ff.
9. G.A. Kelly, *Idealism, Politics and History: Sources of Hegelian Thought*, p. 82.
10. F. Schiller, *Sämmtliche Werke*, 13, p. 278, quoted in Kelly, *Idealism*, p. 82.
11. For a brief discussion of Novalis see H.S. Reiss's Introduction to his *The Political Thought of the German Romantics*, pp. 24ff.
12. Adam Müller, *Vom Geist der Gemeinschaft*, cited in Eric Roll, *History of Economic Thought*, p. 226.
13. See G.A. Briefs, 'The Economic Philosophy of Romanticism', *Journal of the History of Ideas*, 2: 3, 1941, pp. 279ff.
14. R.A. Pois, *Friedrich Meinecke and German Politics in the Twentieth Century*, p. 15.
15. Ranke, 'Politisches Gespräch', translated in T.H. von Laue, *Leopold Ranke: The Formative Years*, p. 166.
16. Schleiermacher to F. Schlegel, 22 March 1813, in F.D.E. Schleiermacher, *Aus Schleiermachers Leben in Briefen*, III, pp. 428–9; cited in Pinson, *Pietism as a Factor in the Rise of German Nationalism*, p. 205.
17. J.G. Fichte, *Attempt at a Critique of all Revelation*, p. 63.
18. Ibid., p. 74.

19. J.G. Fichte, *Grundzüge des gegenwärtigen Zeitalters* (1804), *Sämmtliche Werke*, VII, pp. 3–256; Fichte, *Staatslehre: oder über das Verhältniss des Urstaates zum Vernüftreiche* (1813), *Sämmtliche Werke*, IV, pp. 369–600.

20. Fichte, *Sämmtliche Werke*, V, pp. 185–6; English trans. in P.L. Gardiner, ed., *Nineteenth Century Philosophy*, p. 25.

21. J.G. Fichte, *Der geschlossene Handelsstaat, Sämmtliche Werke*, III, p. 389; English trans. in H.S. Reiss, ed., *The Political Thought of the German Romantics*, p. 94.

22. Fichte, 'Addresses to the German Nation', Reiss, ed., *Political Thought*, p. 103.

23. Fichte, *Grundzüge des gegenwärtigen Zeitalters, Sämmtliche Werke*, VII, pp. 204ff.

24. J.G. Fichte, *Der Patriotismus und sein Gegenteil. Patriotische Dialoge*, in *Nachgelassene Werke*, III, pp. 228ff.; quoted in H.C. Engelbrecht, *Johann Gottlieb Fichte: A Study of his Political Writings with Special Reference to his Nationalism*, p. 97.

25. Fichte, *Addresses, Sämmtliche Werke*, VII, p. 466; English trans. in Reiss, ed., *Political Thought*, p. 107; and *Addresses*, 5: 64–5, *Sämmtliche Werke*, VII, p. 336f.

26. Fichte, *Addresses*, 8: 119 and 1: 7, *Sämmtliche Werke*, pp. 387 and 274.

27. Pinson, *Pietism*, p. 48.

28. See, for example, references to 'the new Caribbean man', in the writings of William Demas (*Change and Renewal in the Caribbean*, pp. 1ff.). This idea is also found in the works of Che Guevara.

29. Fichte, *Addresses*, 9: 168, p. 193.

30. Fichte, *Addresses*, 9: 160, p. 184.

31. J.G. Fichte, 'The Characteristics of the Present Age', *The Popular Works of Johann Gottlieb Fichte*, II, pp. 169 and 161.

32. John Burrow, Editor's Introduction to Wilhelm von Humboldt, *The Limits of State Action*, p. xiv.

33. See Otto von Gierke, *Natural Law and the Theory of Society, 1500–1800*, pp. 131ff.

34. J.G. Fichte, *Die Darstellung der Wissenschaftslehre, Sämmtliche Werke*, II, pp. 16–18, quoted in R.W. Stine, *The Doctrine of God in the Philosophy of Fichte*, p. 37.

35. Fichte, *Attempt*, p. 142.

36. J.G. Fichte, 'Aphorismen über Religion und Deismus' (1790), *Sämmtliche Werke*, V, p. 108; quoted in Stine, *The Doctrine of God*, p. 3.

37. J.G. Fichte, 'From a Private Paper' (1800), *Sämmtliche Werke*, III, p. 39; quoted in F.C. Copleston, *History of Philosophy*, VII, p. 82.

38. J.G. Fichte, 'The Nature of the Scholar', in *Popular Works*, I, p. 223, and Fichte, 'The Way Towards the Blessed Life' (1806), in *Popular Works*, II, p. 339.

39. Ibid., pp. 385, 423 and 315–16.
40. Fichte, 'Aphorismen', quoted in Stine, *The Doctrine of God*, p. 3, and *Attempt*, pp. 62–3.
41. X. Léon, *Fichte et son temps*, I, p. 526.
42. Fichte, 'Aphorismen', quoted in Stine, *The Doctrine of God*, pp. 3–4.
43. J.G. Fichte, *The Science of Rights*, p. 39.
44. J.G. Fichte, *The Vocation of Man*, in *Popular Works*, I, p. 406.
45. Ibid., pp. 411–12.
46. J.G. Fichte, *The Science of Knowledge*, p. 16.
47. Fichte, *Vocation*, *Popular Works*, I, pp. 419–21.
48. Fichte, *The Science of Rights*, p. 13.
49. Fichte, 'The Nature', *Popular Works*, I, p. 285.
50. See *Popular Works*, I, p. 140. The quotation comes from II, p. 443.
51. For the life of Schleiermacher, see the classic work of Wilhelm Dilthey, *Leben Schleiermachers*; for a bibliography see Terrence N. Tice, *Schleiermacher Bibliography*.
52. Quoted by R.M. Bigler, *The Politics of German Protestantism*, p. 169.
53. F.D.E. Schleiermacher, 'On the Concepts of Different Forms of the State', in Reiss, ed., *Political Thought*, p. 199.
54. F.D.E. Schleiermacher, *Soliloquies*, p. 17.
55. Ibid., pp. 58–9.
56. F.D.E. Schleiermacher, *The Christian Faith*, p. 76.
57. F.D.E. Schleiermacher, *On Religion: Speeches to its Cultured Despisers*, p. 212.
58. Schleiermacher, 'On the Concepts', p. 199.
59. Ibid., pp. 194ff.
60. Schleiermacher, *The Christian Faith*, pp. 468ff.
61. Schleiermacher, 'On the Concepts', p. 198. Stephen Sykes for some reason writes of Schleiermacher as 'at heart a republican', *The Identity of Christianity*, p. 120.
62. Schleiermacher, 'On the Concepts', p. 198.
63. Reiss, 'Introduction' to *The Political Thought*, p. 36.
64. F.D.E Schleiermacher to K. von Ranmer, quoted in *The Life of Schleiermacher as Unfolded in his Autobiography and Letters*, II, p. 202, and *Selected Sermons of Schleiermacher*, p. 80. See also J.F. Dawson, *Friedrich Schleiermacher: The Evolution of a Nationalist*.
65. Schleiermacher, *Selected Sermons*, p. 73.
66. F.D.E. Schleiermacher to Charlotte von Kathen, 20 June 1806, in *The Life of Schleiermacher*, II, p. 58.
67. Schleiermacher, *Speeches*, p. 50.
68. Schleiermacher, *Speeches*, p. 101.
69. Schleiermacher, *Speeches*, p. 31. It should, however, be emphasised that Schleiermacher did not intend to suggest that there is no relationship between religion and knowledge or action; it was reductionism to

which he objected. See Claude Welch, *Protestant Thought in the Nineteenth Century*, I, p. 66.

70. J. Calvin, *The Institutes of the Christian Religion*, 1: 14: 4, English trans., I, p. 144. Elie Kedourie (*Nationalism*, p. 26) mistakenly calls Schleiermacher a Lutheran. He was in fact a minister in the Reformed Church and described himself as 'a theologian who belongs decidedly to the reformed tradition': H. Mulert, ed., *Schleiermachers Sendschreiben über seine Glaubenslehre an Lücke*, p. 30. Kedourie also misdates the *Reden* by ten years.

71. Schleiermacher, *The Christian Faith*, p. 196.

72. Ibid., p. 748.

73. Ibid., pp. 200ff.

74. Ibid., p. 206; see also p. 750.

75. Ibid., p. 179.

76. Ibid., p. 219; for the earthly monarch see above, p. 174.

77. Schleiermacher, *The Christian Faith*, p. 214.

78. Ibid., pp. 743ff.

79. Schleiermacher, *The Life of Jesus*, p. 388; see also p. 395.

80. Schleiermacher, *The Christian Faith*, p. 673.

81. Schleiermacher, *Selected Sermons*, pp. 44 and 48–9.

82. Schleiermacher, Sermon on Trinity VI 1831, *Predigten, Werke* (Berlin, 1834–), III, p. 22.

83. K. Barth, *The Theology of Schleiermacher*, pp. 3ff.

84. Schleiermacher to Brinckmann, August 1833, *Aus Schleiermachers Leben in Briefen*, IV, p. 408 (my italics).

85. Robert R. Williams, *Schleiermacher the Theologian: The Construction of the Doctrine of God*, p. 184.

86. Ibid., p. 186.

87. Schleiermacher noted that a God who seeks a society to reflect his love loses his independence and as lover is affected by the beloved. R. Odebrecht, ed., *Friedrich Schleiermachers Dialektik*, pp. 255ff. For a discussion of this see R.R. Niebuhr, 'Schleiermacher and the Names of God', in R.W. Funk, ed., 'Schleiermacher as Contemporary', *Journal for Theology and the Church*, 7, 1970, pp. 190ff.

88. In Funk, ed., 'Schleiermacher', p. 29.

89. See Richard R. Niebuhr, *Schleiermacher on Christ and Religion*, pp. 248ff.

90. Schleiermacher, *The Life of Jesus*, p. 425.

91. G.W.F. Hegel, *Lectures on the Philosophy of Religion*, I, p. 247.

92. For the early life of Hegel see H.S. Harris, *Hegel's Development: Towards the Sunlight, 1770–1801*.

93. G.W.F. Hegel, *Hegels theologische Jugendschriften*; for an English translation of this material see *On Christianity: Early Theological Writings by Friedrich Hegel*.

94. G.W.F. Hegel, *Philosophy of Right*, sec. 349, pp. 218–19.

95. Ibid., para. 394, p. 46; and para. 549, p. 279.

96. Ibid., sec. 274, pp. 178–9.

97. For example, E. Kedourie writes, 'Hegel is not a nationalist ... his political thought is concerned with the state, not the nation', *Nationalism*, p. 36n. See also Shlomo Avineri, 'Hegel and Nationalism', in W. Kaufmann, ed., *Hegel's Political Philosophy*, pp. 109–36.

98. This aspect of Hegel's thought is brought out clearly by Ivan Soll, *An Introduction to Hegel's Metaphysics*, chapter 1.

99. Hegel quoted Aristotle to this effect in his *Natural Law*, p. 113.

100. Hegel, *Philosophy of Right*, p. 213.

101. K.R. Popper, *The Open Society and its Enemies*, II, pp. 1ff. Many criticisms have been made, but mostly in recent years. See Walter Kaufmann, 'The Hegel Myth and its Method', reprinted in Alasdair MacIntyre, ed., *Hegel: A Collection of Critical Essays*, pp. 21ff.

102. Hegel, *Philosophy of Right*, addition to para. 272, p. 285. The term he used was 'Irdisch-Göttliches' (literally: earthly divine).

103. Thomas Hobbes, *Leviathan*, chapter 17, p. 112.

104. Hegel uses the term in *Philosophy of Right*, para. 308, p. 200. See G. Heiman, in Z.A. Pelczynski, ed., *Hegel's Political Philosophy*, p. 135.

105. G.W.F. Hegel, 'The German Constitution', in *Hegel's Political Writings*, pp. 160ff.

106. Hegel, *Philosophy of Right*, para. 288, p. 189; and 'The German Constitution', p. 160. I noted the limits of Hegel's quasi-pluralism in *Authority in Church and State*, pp. 262ff., and in *The Pluralist State*, pp. 77ff. and 121.

107. Hegel, *Philosophy of Right*, para. 288, p. 189.

108. Ibid., addition to para. 274, pp. 286ff.

109. Ibid., para. 280, pp. 184–5.

110. Ibid., paras 275ff., pp. 179ff., and additions to paras 279ff., pp. 288ff.

111. Ibid., para. 331, p. 212.

112. See Quentin Lauer, *Hegel's Concept of God*, p. 48.

113. Hegel, *Lectures on the Philosophy of Religion*, II, p. 327.

114. Romans 8: 26 and 1 Corinthians 2: 11.

115. G.W.F. Hegel, *Lectures on the Philosophy of World History*, pp. 58–9; quoted by Lauer, *Hegel's Concept of God*, p. 307; see also Hegel, *Philosophy of Mind*, para. 567, p. 299.

116. Hegel, *Philosophy of Religion*, I, p. 198.

117. Hegel, *Philosophy of Religion*, I, p. 37.

118. Karl Barth, *From Rousseau to Ritschl*, p. 293.

119. *Hegel's Political Writings*, p. 145; see also Hegel's celebrated Preface to the *Philosophy of Right*, especially pp. 10–13.

120. Hegel appears to have welcomed the change in Württemberg from 'Calm satisfaction with the present, hopelessness, patient acquiescence

in a fate that is all too great and powerful' to 'hope, expectation, and a resolution for something different' ('On the Recent Domestic Affairs of Württemberg', in *Hegel's Political Writings*, p. 243).

121. For Italy see G. de Michelis, 'L'autarchia economica', *Nuovo Anthologia*, 375, 1934, pp. 95ff.; A. Garino Canina, 'L'autarchia economica e impero', *Nuovo Anthologia*, 391, 1937. For Germany see Ferdinand Fried, *Autarkie*, H. von Beckerath and F. Kern, *Autarkie oder internationale Zusammenarbeit*; F. Neumann discusses the issue in *Behemoth*, pp. 329ff. For Japan see K. Kobori, *The Idea of a Closed State*. More generally see J. Mattern, *Geopolitik: Doctrine of Self-Sufficiency and Empire*, and Jerzy Nowak, *L'Idée de l'autarchie économique*.

122. P.V. de Vastey, *Political Remarks on Some French Works and Newspapers concerning Hayti*.

123. See David Nicholls, 'Economic Dependence and Political Autonomy, 1804–1915', in *Haiti in Caribbean Context*, pp. 83ff.

124. L.J. Janvier, *Haïti aux Haïtiens*, pp. 10ff.

125. See E. Boorstein, *The Economic Transformation of Cuba*, pp. 191ff.; 'Notas sobre la estrategia cubana de desarrollo', in *Economía y Desarrollo*, October–December 1970, pp. 76ff.; Ernesto 'Che' Guevara, 'Against Bureaucratism', in John Gerassi, ed., *Venceremos*, p. 192.

126. Naomi Garrett, *The Renaissance of Haitian Poetry*; J. Michael Dash, *Literature and Ideology in Haiti, 1915–1961*; David Nicholls, *From Dessalines to Duvalier*.

127. *The Republic of Plato*, chapter 9; see also *Philebus*, 60c, quoted in Arthur O. Lovejoy, *The Great Chain of Being*, p. 42.

128. Aristotle, *On the Parts of Animals*, 2: 1; *Rhetoric*, 1: 6 and 1: 7; *Nicomachean Ethics*, 1: 7. Eric Voegelin is one of the few authors to notice the analogy in Aristotle between divine and political autarky, *Order and History: 3, Plato and Aristotle*, p. 313.

129. Aristotle, *Eudemian Ethics*, 7: 1244b.

130. Victor Ehrenberg, *The Greek State*, pp. 95–6.

131. Aristotle, *Politics*, 1: 2: 8.

132. Aristotle, *Politics*, 2: 2: 7.

133. Ecphantus, *Stobaeus*, 4: 7: 65; quoted in Ernest Barker, *From Alexander to Constantine*, pp. 370–1.

134. Barker, *From Alexander*, p. 373.

135. Irenaeus, *Contra baer*, 3: 8: 3; cf. Augustine, *De civitate dei*, 14: 8: 4; see G.L. Prestige, *God in Patristic Thought*, p. 4.

136. Origen, *In Num. Hom.*, 23: 2.

137. W.K.C. Guthrie, *A History of Greek Philosophy*, III, pp. 230–1.

138. Some of these issues are discussed by Illtyd Trethowan, in *Process Theology and the Christian Tradition*; see also Richard E. Creel, *Divine Impassibility: An Essay in Philosophical Theology*, and earlier by

Bertrand D. Brasnett, *The Suffering of the Impassible God*.

139. J.K. Mozley, *The Impassibility of God*, *passim*.
140. D.E. Jenkins, *Living with Questions*, pp. 56–7.

7 ATHEISTS AND ANARCHISTS

1. Eusebius, *Tricennial Oration*, 3: 4–5, quoted in Ernest Barker, *From Alexander to Constantine*, p. 478.
2. James I, *Defence of the Right of Kings*, in C.H. McIlwain, ed., *The Political Works of James I*, p. 333.
3. Lord King, *The Life and Letters of John Locke*, p. 90.
4. H. Heine, *Religion and Philosophy in Germany*, p. 102.
5. 'Gaudium et Spes', in W.M. Abbott, ed., *The Documents of Vatican II*, p. 217; Vincent Cosmao, *Changer le monde*, p. 148. See also Cornelio Fabro, *God in Exile*, p. 4.
6. Paul Tillich, *The Protestant Era*, p. xxix; see also J. Lagneau, *Célèbres, leçons et fragments*, p. 229.
7. Paul Tillich, *The Construction of the History of Religion in Schelling's Positive Philosophy*, p. 123. The reference is to F.W.J. von Schelling, *Sämtliche Werke*, VII, p. 149.
8. J.M.E. McTaggart, *Studies in Hegelian Cosmology*, p. 56.
9. J.S. Mill, *An Examination of Sir William Hamilton's Philosophy*, p. 129.
10. M. Bakunin, *God and the State*, p. 24. He was, of course, deliberately parodying Voltaire, who had written, 'If God did not exist it would be necessary to invent him.'
11. For a good recent discussion of the varieties of anarchism see David Miller, *Anarchism*, also James Joll, *The Anarchists*, and George Woodcock, *Anarchism*.
12. Quoted in Joll, *The Anarchists*, p. 142.
13. Ernst Bloch, *The Principle of Hope*, II, p. 573.
14. See Carl Schmitt, *Political Theology*, p. 65.
15. Joseph Butler, *The Analogy of Religion, Natural and Revealed, to the Constitution and Course of Nature*, p. 87.
16. Emma Goldman, *Anarchism and Other Essays*; Maxine Molyneux, 'No God, No Boss, No Husband: Anarchist Feminism in Nineteenth Century Argentina', *Latin American Perspectives*, 13: 1, 1986, pp. 119ff. On the relation of anarchism and feminism see also Miller, *Anarchism*, p. 149. See also Andres Ortiz-Osés, 'El dios patriarcal contra la materia', in Ortiz-Osés, *Comunicación y experiencia interhumana*.
17. M. Bakunin, 'La Religion', *Œuvres* (Paris, 1908), p. 295.
18. M. Bakunin, 'Federalism, Socialism and Anti-Theologism', in G.P. Maximoff, ed., *The Political Philosophy of Bakunin: Scientific Anarchism*, pp. 143–4.

19. Bakunin, *God and the State*, p. 10.
20. M. Bakunin, 'The Knouto-Germanic Empire and the Social Revolution', in *Œuvres*, III, p. 149n.
21. M. Bakunin, *Beichte aus der Peter-Paul-Festung an Zar Niklaus I*, p. 25; quoted in Eric Voegelin, *From Enlightenment to Revolution*, p. 207.
22. E.H. Carr, *Michael Bakunin*, p. 242.
23. Carr, *Michael Bakunin*; Woodcock, *Anarchism*, chapter 6; E. Lampert, *Studies in Rebellion*.
24. M. Bakunin, 'The Paris Commune and the State', in Maximoff, ed., *Political Philosophy*, p. 270.
25. M. Bakunin, 'Federalism', in Maximoff, ed., *Political Philosophy*, p. 269.
26. Bakunin, 'The Knouto-Germanic Empire', in Maximoff, ed., *Political Philosophy*, pp. 268–9.
27. M. Bakunin, 'The Bear of Berne and the Bear of St Petersburg' and 'Protestation of the Alliance', both in Maximoff, ed., *Political Philosophy*, p. 212.
28. Bakunin, 'The Knouto-Germanic Empire', in Maximoff, ed., *Political Philosophy*, p. 217.
29. Bakunin, 'The Paris Commune', in Maximoff, ed., *Political Philosophy*, p. 207.
30. Quoted in Joll, *The Anarchists*, p. 102.
31. Ibid., pp. 107–8.
32. Bakunin, *Œuvres*, V, p. 252, quoted in Joll, *The Anarchists*, p. 93.
33. Quoted in Carr, *Bakunin*, p. 380.
34. M. Bakunin, *Statism and Anarchy*, in Maximoff, ed., *Political Philosophy*, p. 211.
35. Ibid., p. 211.
36. Ibid., p. 210; and Bakunin, 'Federalism', in Maximoff, ed., *Political Philosophy*, p. 276.
37. M. Bakunin, 'Proposition motivée au comité central de la Ligue de la Paix et de la Liberté', in *Œuvres*, I, p. 13.
38. Bakunin, 'Federalism', in Maximoff, ed., *Political Philosophy*, p. 109.
39. Bakunin, 'The Knouto-Germanic Empire', in Maximoff, ed., *Political Philosophy*, p. 130.
40. Bakunin, *God and the State*, p. 73.
41. Ibid., p. 74.
42. Ibid., p. 28.
43. Ibid., p. 84.
44. Ibid., p. 24. 'God appears, man is reduced to nothing; and the greater Divinity becomes, the more miserable becomes humanity'; ibid., p. 53.
45. Ibid., p. 64.
46. Ibid., p. 85.
47. Bakunin, 'Federalism', in Maximoff, ed., *Political Philosophy*, p. 116.

48. Bakunin, 'The Knouto-Germanic Empire', in Maximoff, ed., *Political Philosophy*, p. 130.
49. M. Bakunin, 'A Circular Letter to my Friends in Italy', in Maximoff, ed., *Political Philosophy*, p. 120.
50. Bakunin, 'The Paris Commune', in Maximoff, ed., *Political Philosophy*, p. 56.
51. M. Bakunin, 'Integral Education', in Maximoff, ed., *Political Philosophy*, p. 102.
52. Bakunin, 'Federalism', in Maximoff, ed., *Political Philosophy*, p. 148.
53. M. Bakunin, 'A Member of the International Answers Mazzini', in Maximoff, ed., *Political Philosophy*, p. 65.
54. P.-J. Proudhon, *De la capacité politique des classes ouvrières*, in *Œuvres complètes de P.-J. Proudhon*, I, p. 89.
55. P.-J. Proudhon, *Système des contradictions économiques ou la misère de la philosophie*, in *Œuvres*, II, p. 412.
56. P.-J. Proudhon, *Idée générale de la révolution*, in *Œuvres*, IV, p. 304; English trans., Proudhon, *General Idea of the Revolution in the Nineteenth Century*, p. 248.
57. P.-J. Proudhon, *De la création de l'ordre*, note to second edition, in *Œuvres*, VI, p. 388n., and Proudhon, 'Résistance à la révolution', *La Voix du Peuple*, 64, 3 December 1849, in *Œuvres*, IV, p. 365. See also K.S. Vincent, *Pierre-Joseph Proudhon and the Rise of French Republican Socialism*, p. 178.
58. Proudhon, *Idée générale*, *Œuvres*, IV, p. 344; *General Idea*, p. 294.
59. Quoted in George Woodcock, *Pierre-Joseph Proudhon*, p. 7. 'Je pense à Dieu depuis que j'existe, et ne reconnais à personne plus qu'à moi le droit d'en parler': P.-J. Proudhon, *De la justice dans la révolution et dans l'église*, in *Œuvres*, IX, p. 283.
60. P.-J. Proudhon, *Qu'est-ce que la propriété?*, in *Œuvres*, V, p. 245, and Proudhon, *Du principe fédératif et de la nécessité de reconstituer le parti de la révolution*, English trans., *The Principle of Federation*, p. 58.
61. Proudhon, *Idée générale*, *Œuvres*, IV, p. 307; *General Idea*, pp. 251–2. See also Vincent, *Proudhon*, pp. 106–7.
62. Proudhon, *Système*, *Œuvres*, I, p. 377.
63. Ibid., pp. 396 and 385. On an earlier page he wrote of God: 'c'est sottise et lâcheté; Dieu, c'est hypocrisie et mensonge; Dieu, c'est tyrannie et misère; Dieu, c'est le mal', ibid., p. 384.
64. Proudhon, *De la justice*, *Œuvres*, IX, p. 366, and XI, p. 299.
65. Proudhon, *De la justice*, *Œuvres*, IX, p. 476.
66. Proudhon, *De la justice*, *Œuvres*, IX, p. 422; see also H. de Lubac, *The Unmarxian Socialist*, p. 181.
67. Pierre Haubtmann, *Pierre-Joseph Proudhon: genèse d'un antithéiste*, pp. 123ff.
68. Proudhon, *De la justice*, *Œuvres*, XII, p. 365.

69. P.-J. Proudhon, *De la célébration du dimanche*, in *Œuvres*, V, p. 38.

70. Proudhon, *De la justice*, *Œuvres*, IX, p. 225.

71. Ibid., p. 215.

72. Proudhon, *De la création de l'ordre*, *Œuvres*, VI, p. 63; *De la justice*, *Œuvres*, XI, p. 299.

73. P.-J. Proudhon, *Jésus et les origines du christianisme*, *Œuvres*, XIX, p. 528.

74. Proudhon, *Système*, quoted de Lubac, *The Unmarxian Socialist*, p. 178. Of man, he wrote: 'Ni il n'est Dieu, ni il ne saurait vivant, devenir Dieu', *Système*, *Œuvres*, I, p. 375.

75. Quoted in Pierre Haubtmann, *Pierre-Joseph Proudhon: sa vie et sa pensée*, p. 531.

76. Proudhon, *Idée générale*, *Œuvres*, IV, p. 308; *General Idea*, pp. 251–2.

77. Proudhon, *Idée générale*, *Œuvres*, IV, pp. 341–2; *General Idea*, pp. 290–1.

78. Proudhon, *Idée générale*, *Œuvres*, IV, pp. 200 and 297; *General Idea*, pp. 127 and 240; Proudhon, *De la justice*, *Œuvres*, XI, p. 71.

79. Proudhon, 'Notes et pensées', *Œuvres*, XV, p. 427.

80. Proudhon, *Idée générale*, *Œuvres*, IV, p. 208; *General Idea*, p. 137.

81. Proudhon, *Dimanche*, *Œuvres*, V, p. 55.

82. Proudhon, *Idée générale*, *Œuvres*, IV, p. 313; *General Idea*, p. 259. For a present-day example of the invalid use of such a concept see Albert Weale, 'Consent', *Political Studies*, 26: 1, 1978, pp. 65ff.; and David Nicholls, 'A Comment on "Consent"', *Political Studies*, 27: 1, 1979, pp. 120ff. See also the excellent book by Carole Pateman, *The Problem of Political Obligation: A Critique of Liberal Theory*. I plan to take up this issue in the sequel.

83. Proudhon, *Idée générale*, *Œuvres*, IV, pp. 191–2; *General Idea*, pp. 117–18.

84. Proudhon, *Idée générale*, *Œuvres*, IV, p. 156; *General Idea*, p. 76.

85. P. Nourrisson, *Histoire de la liberté d'association en France depuis 1789*, I, pp. 119–20; see also Vincent, *Proudhon*, p. 129.

86. Proudhon, *Propriété*, *Œuvres*, V, p. 327; see also de Lubac, *The Unmarxian Socialist*, pp. 211ff.

87. Proudhon, *De la capacité*, *Œuvres*, I, pp. 80ff.

88. Proudhon, *Propriété*, *Œuvres*, V, p. 148.

89. Proudhon, *Dimanche*, *Œuvres*, V, p. 94.

90. Proudhon to Gautier, quoted in Woodcock, *Proudhon*, p. 59.

91. Proudhon, *The Principle of Federation*, p. 28. See also *Idée générale*, *Œuvres*, IV, p. 156; *General Idea*, pp. 76–7. On Balfour see David Nicholls, 'Few are Chosen: Some Reflections on the Politics of A.J. Balfour', *Review of Politics*, 30: 1, 1968, pp. 33ff.

92. P.-J. Proudhon to Beslay, 25 October 1861, *Correspondance de P.-J. Proudhon*, XI, p. 247.

93. Proudhon, *Idée générale*, *Œuvres*, IV, p. 94; *General Idea*, p. 60.
94. Proudhon, *Idée générale*, *Œuvres*, IV, p. 298; *General Idea*, p. 241.
95. Proudhon, *The Principle of Federation*, p. 60.
96. Proudhon, *Idée générale*, *Œuvres*, IV, p. 344; *General Idea*, p. 293.
97. Proudhon, *Idée générale*, *Œuvres*, IV, p. 318; *General Idea*, p. 265.
98. Proudhon, *Propriété*, *Œuvres*, V, pp. 335 and 339.
99. Proudhon, 'Résistance à la révolution', *Œuvres*, IV, p. 365. Maine, however, constructed an authoritarian, but limited, state to enforce contracts and to maintain order.
100. Proudhon, *The Principle of Federation*, p. 46.
101. Ibid., p. 61.
102. Ibid., pp. 62 and 72.
103. Quoted in Woodcock, *Proudhon*, p. 249.
104. P.-J. Proudhon, 'A Pierre Leroux', *La Voix du Peuple*, 68, 7 December 1849, in *Œuvres*, IV, p. 391; see also de Lubac, *The Unmarxian Socialist*, p. 265.
105. Proudhon, *De la justice*, *Œuvres*, XII, p. 436; Proudhon to Micaud, 22 December 1844, *Correspondance*, IV, p. 348.
106. Printed in Haubtmann, *Proudhon: genèse d'un antithéiste*, p. 237.
107. Proudhon à Penet, 31 December 1863, *Correspondance*, XIII, pp. 217–18; quoted in Woodcock, *Proudhon*, p. 256.
108. Proudhon, *Dimanche*, *Œuvres*, V, p. 90.
109. Proudhon, *De la justice*, *Œuvres*, IX, p. 233.
110. Proudhon, *Idée générale*, *Œuvres*, IV, p. 308; *General Idea*, p. 252.
111. Proudhon à l'abbé X, 22 January 1849, quoted in *Œuvres*, I, p. 375n.
112. Shelley to Hunt, 22 June 1821, in P.B. Shelley, *The Letters of Percy Bysshe Shelley*, ed. F.L. Jones, no. 636, II, p. 304.
113. It should, however, be noted that when Shelley or Godwin used the term 'anarchy' they meant disorder and chaos, rather than the absence of coercive authority, and therefore attacked it. Godwin went so far as to assert that 'anarchy is perhaps a condition more deplorable than despotism': William Godwin, *An Enquiry Concerning Political Justice*, 7: 5, p. 664.
114. The best biographical study of Shelley is by Richard Holmes, *Shelley: The Pursuit*, and the best discussions of the political and religious aspects of his writings are to be found in Timothy Webb, *Shelley: A Voice not Understood*, and in the two books of K.N. Cameron, *The Young Shelley: Genesis of a Radical* and *Shelley: The Golden Years*.
115. J.E.E.D. Acton, *The History of Freedom*, p. xii. See also F.O. Darvall, *Popular Disturbances and Public Order in Regency England*, F.W. Chandler, *Political Spies and Provocative Agents*, and A.F. Freemantle, 'The Truth about Oliver the Spy', *English Historical Review*, 47: 4, 1932, pp. 601ff.
116. P.B. Shelley, Preface to *Hellas*, in Shelley, *The Poetical Works*, p. 448.

117. P.B. Shelley, *The Complete Works of Percy Bysshe Shelley*, VI, p. 82.
118. P.B. Shelley, 'A Philosophical View of Reform' (1820), *Complete Works*, VII, pp. 14–15; *Prometheus Unbound, Poetical Works*, p. 222; and 'Address to the Irish People' (1812), *Complete Works*, V, pp. 225–6.
119. *The Revolt of Islam, Poetical Works*, p. 338.
120. P.M.S. Dawson, *The Unacknowledged Legislator: Shelley and Politics*, pp. 68ff. Dawson's book contains an excellent discussion of Shelley's politics. Shelley attributed the failure of the revolution to its being the product of individual genius 'and out of general knowledge'. Dawson's interpretation of the last phrase is unconvincing. He claims that the poet 'expresses himself carelessly' and really means 'without' or 'not of' general knowledge. It is likely that Shelley means precisely what he says, contrasting general knowledge with a particular knowledge of a situation which is essential for a successful revolutionary. In his preface to *The Revolt of Islam* he wrote: 'The French Revolution may be considered as one of those manifestations of a general state of feeling among civilised mankind produced by a defect of correspondence between the knowledge existing in society and the improvement or gradual abolition of political institutions': Shelley, *Poetical Works*, p. 33.
121. Shelley to T.J. Hogg, 8 May 1811, *The Letters*, ed. Jones, no. 67, I, p. 80.
122. William Godwin, *Enquiry*, 2: 2, p. 176; 6: 1, p. 558; 5: 1, p. 408, and 3: 7, p. 253. On Godwin see J.P. Clark, *The Philosophical Anarchism of William Godwin*; also H.N. Brailsford, *Shelley, Godwin and their Circle*.
123. Godwin, *Enquiry*, 3: 6, pp. 239ff.; 5: 6, p. 440; 1: 5, p. 140; 1: 6, p. 148, and 5: 21, p. 538.
124. Shelley, *Complete Works*, V, p. 256; for Shelley's differences with Godwin see Holmes, *Shelley*, pp. 129ff.
125. C. Kegan Paul, *William Godwin: His Friends and Contemporaries*, I, p. 26.
126. W. Godwin, *Thoughts Occasioned by the Perusal of Dr Parr's Spital Sermon*, p. 8.
127. Godwin, *Sketches of History in Six Sermons*, p. 20.
128. Godwin, *Enquiry*, p. 350.
129. Godwin, *Thoughts*, pp. 72 and 91.
130. Ibid., pp. 69–70.
131. P.B. Shelley, 'Speculations on Morals', *Complete Works*, VII, p. 80; Shelley, 'On Christianity', *Complete Works*, VI, p. 249. 'Government is an evil; it is only the thoughtlessness and vices of men that make it a necessary evil': Shelley, 'Address to the Irish People', in *Complete Works*, V, p. 232. See also Shelley, *Declaration of Rights*, *Complete Works*, V, p. 275.

132. Shelley to anon., 12 August 1812. This letter is of dubious authenticity and is not included in *The Letters*, ed. Jones, but is printed in *The Letters of Percy Bysshe Shelley*, ed. R. Ingpen, p. 355.
133. Shelley, *Declaration, Complete Works*, V, p. 273.
134. Shelley to Lord Ellenborough, June 1812, in *The Letters of Percy Bysshe Shelley*, ed. R. Ingpen, I, p. 329; this was later published as a pamphlet.
135. Shelley, *Poetical Works*, pp. 205 and 211.
136. Ibid., p. 812.
137. Ibid., p. 822.
138. Shelley to Peacock, 7 November 1818, *The Letters*, ed. Jones, no. 485, II, p. 47.
139. P.B. Shelley, 'Fragment: Pater Omnipotens', *Poetical Works*, p. 634.
140. P.B. Shelley, 'Essay on the Devil and Devils', *Complete Works*, VII, p. 89.
141. P.B. Shelley, 'On the Devil', *Complete Works*, VII, p. 95.
142. Dawson, *Unacknowledged Legislator*, pp. 113ff. See Psalm 68: 18 and Ephesians 4: 8.
143. Bodleian Library, Oxford, Shelley MS, e 9, p. 211; quoted in Webb, *Shelley*, p. 158. Isaiah 14: 5.
144. Shelley, *Poetical Works*, pp. 338–9 and 344. R.J. White condemned Shelley's *Mask* as 'ignorant injustice' (*From Waterloo to Peterloo*, p. 70). Whether Sidmouth had intended a confrontation at St Peter's Fields is debatable. It is likely that he knew of and approved the Manchester magistrates' plan to arrest Hunt. The government certainly gave strong support to them after the event. D. Read maintains that the Liverpool government did not plan the massacre as a repressive gesture (*Peterloo*, p. 207) but see comments of E.P. Thompson (*The Making of the English Working Class*, p. 750).
145. Shelley, 'Philosophical View', *Complete Works*, VII, pp. 48–9; and Shelley, 'The Death of the Princess Charlotte' (1817), *Complete Works*, VI, p. 77.
146. Shelley, 'Address to the Irish People', *Complete Works*, V, p. 229.
147. Shelley, *Declaration, Complete Works*, V, p. 272.
148. Shelley to Byron, 20 November 1816, in *The Letters*, ed. Jones, no. 370, I, p. 513.
149. Shelley to Peacock, August 1819, in *The Letters*, ed. Jones, no. 511, II, p. 115.
150. It is this 'Marcusian' belief which sheds doubt upon the notion that Demogorgon, in *Prometheus*, is a symbol of the masses – 'people-monster' – as has been suggested. If this interpretation were correct Shelley would not have portrayed Demogorgon as playing a leading part in the liberation of Prometheus, who is generally held to represent the intellectual or the poet, for in his prose works he saw precisely the reverse happening. See Holmes, *Shelley*, p. 505, and G.M. Matthews,

'A Volcano's Voice in Shelley', in R.B. Woodings, *Shelley: Modern Judgements*, pp. 162ff. E.P. Thompson suggests that the name 'Demogorgon' may be derived from the radical journal *Gorgon*, published at the time. Paul Foot has also interpreted *Prometheus* in this way, in *Red Shelley*.

151. Shelley to Hitchener, 7 January 1812, *The Letters*, ed. Jones, no. 158, I, p. 223; and Shelley to Hitchener, 27 February 1812, *The Letters*, ed. Jones, no. 172, I, p. 263.

152. Shelley, *Poetical Works*, p. 214.

153. Shelley, *Philosophical View*, *Complete Works*, VII, p. 46.

154. Shelley to Hunt, November 1819, *The Letters*, ed. Jones, no. 530, II, p. 153.

155. See Rosa Luxemburg, *Social Reform or Revolution* (1900).

156. Shelley, *Poetical Works*, pp. 572–3 and 574.

157. Shelley, *Complete Works*, VII, p. 57; 'Nothing is more idle than to reject a limited benefit because we cannot without great sacrifices obtain an unlimited one', ibid., VII, p. 46.

158. Shelley, *Philosophical View*, *Complete Works*, VII, p. 46.

159. Shelley to Thomas Hookham, ? 15 February 1813, *The Letters*, ed. Jones, no. 224, I, p. 353.

160. Shelley, *Poetical Works*, p. 342.

161. Shelley to Elizabeth Hitchener, 10 August 1811, *The Letters*, ed. Jones, no. 104, I, p. 133.

162. Shelley to Hitchener, ? 19 August 1811, *The Letters*, ed. Jones, no. 107, I, p. 136; and Shelley to Hitchener, 25 July 1811, *The Letters*, ed. Jones, no. 99, I, p. 125.

163. Shelley, *Philosophical View*, *Complete Works*, VII, p. 25; Shelley, 'Two Fragments on Reform', *Complete Works*, VI, p. 295.

164. Shelley, 'A Defence of Poetry', *Complete Works*, VII, p. 127; Shelley, *The Revolt of Islam*, *Poetical Works*, p. 63.

165. Shelley to Hitchener, 11 June 1811, *The Letters*, ed. Jones, no. 82, I, pp. 99–100.

166. Angela Leighton, *Shelley and the Sublime*, p. 28.

167. Shelley to T.J. Hogg, 3 January 1811, *The Letters*, ed. Jones, no. 35, I, p. 35.

168. Shelley, *Poetical Works*, p. 812; Shelley to Hitchener, 11 June 1811, *The Letters*, ed. Jones, no. 82, I, p. 101; Shelley, 'On Christianity', *Complete Works*, VI, p. 231; and Shelley to Hitchener, 2 January 1812, *The Letters*, ed. Jones, no. 156, I, p. 215.

169. Shelley to Hitchener, 11 June 1811, *The Letters*, ed. Jones, no. 82, I, p. 100.

170. Shelley, *The Necessity of Atheism*, *Complete Works*, V, p. 209.

171. Shelley to Godwin, 10 January 1812, *The Letters*, ed. Jones, no. 159, I, p. 228.

172. Shelley, 'Essay on Christianity', *Complete Works*, VI, p. 230.
173. Shelley, 'On the Punishment of Death', *Complete Works*, VI, p. 185; Shelley, 'Essay on Christianity', *Complete Works*, VI, p. 233.
174. Thomas Merton, *Contemplation in a World of Action*, p. 172.
175. Ann Oakley to D. Reisman, quoted in Reisman, *State and Welfare: Tawney, Galbraith and Adam Smith*, p. 83.
176. J.F. Stephen, *Liberty, Equality, Fraternity*, pp. 243–4.
177. Thomas Hobbes, *Leviathan*, 1: 10, p. 56.
178. F.D. Maurice, *The Kingdom of Christ*, III, p. 76; W.J.H. Campion, 'Christianity and Politics', in Charles Gore, ed., *Lux Mundi: A Series of Studies in the Religion of the Incarnation*, p. 444.
179. 2 Corinthians 3: 17. There is a perceptive discussion of the issues dealt with in this chapter in Aurelio Orensanz, *Anarquía y christianismo*.
180. David Nicholls, 'Stepping out of Babylon: Sin, Salvation and Social Transformation in Christian Tradition', in K. Leech and R. Williams, eds, *Essays Catholic and Radical*, pp. 38ff.

8 CONCLUSION

1. G.A. Studdert Kennedy, *The Hardest Part*, pp. 1ff. and 138ff.; Kazoh Kitamori, *Theology of the Pain of God*; see also J. Moltmann, *The Crucified God*.
2. David Nicholls, *From Dessalines to Duvalier*, p. 297.
3. Peter Brown, *The Cult of the Saints*, p. 63.
4. Karl Mannheim, *Ideology and Utopia*.
5. Conrad Noel, *Socialism and Church Tradition*, pp. 7–8; quoted in Rowan Williams, *Arius: Heresy and Tradition*, pp. 13–14; see also Kenneth Leech, *The Social God*; Jan M. Lochman, 'The Trinity and Human Life', *Theology*, 78, 1975, pp. 173–83; Thomas D. Parker, 'The Political Meaning of the Doctrine of the Trinity', *Journal of Religion*, 60: 2, 1980, pp. 165–85; Daniel L. Migliore, 'The Trinity and Human Liberty', *Theology Today* 36: 4, 1980, pp. 497ff.; Gerd Decke, 'Trinity, Church and Community', *Lutheran World*, 32: 1, 1976, pp. 41ff.
6. N.F. Feodorov, 'The Restoration of Kinship Among Mankind', in Alexander Schmemann, ed., *Ultimate Questions*, pp. 175–223. On Donne see David Nicholls, 'Divine Analogy: The Theological Politics of John Donne', *Political Studies*, 32: 4, 1984, pp. 570ff., and David Nicholls, 'The Political Theology of John Donne', *Theological Studies*, 49: 1, 1988.
7. J. Moltmann, *The Trinity and the Kingdom of God*, pp. 129ff. and 192. A Trinitarianism which is 'economic' denies any real distinction between the persons of the Godhead, and insists that it is legitimate to speak of the three persons only in the context of the divine economy – that is, with respect to God's relations with the universe.

8. Robert Caspar, 'The Permanent Significance of Islam's Monotheism', *Concilium*, 177, 1985, p. 73.

9. Franz Rosenzweig, *Der Stern der Erloung*, pp. 192ff., and A. Heschel, *The Prophets*, pp. 252ff. Quoted by J. Moltmann, 'The Inviting Unity of the Triune God', *Concilium*, 177, 1985, pp. 54–5. For Donne see *The Sermons of John Donne*, ed. G.R. Potter and E.M. Simpson, 3, p. 264.

10. J. Moltmann, 'The Inviting Unity', p. 50, and *The Trinity*, pp. 191–2.

11. I plan to deal with some seventeenth-century facets of this theme in volume 2. See also David Nicholls, 'Deity and Domination I', *New Blackfriars*, 775, January 1985, pp. 21–31.

12. I refer to a paper by Brian Horne. Compare the *Quicunque vult* (Athanasian Creed), which states, 'In this Trinity none is afore, or after other: none is greater, or less than another; but the whole three Persons are co-eternal together: and co-equal' (reprinted in the *Book of Common Prayer*).

13. Feodorov, 'The Restoration', p. 191. See also my 1978 'civic sermon' in the Borough of Milton Keynes, *Principalities and Powers*.

14. Conservative Party, *The Next Move Forward*, p. 27.

15. P. Worsthorne, 'Too Much Freedom', in Maurice Cowling, ed., *Conservative Essays*, pp. 148–9.

16. Hastings Rashdall, *The Idea of the Atonement in Christian Theology*, p. 445.

17. Moltmann, *The Trinity*, pp. 25 and 31ff.

18. Moltmann, *The Crucified God*, p. 265.

19. Feodorov, 'The Restoration', pp. 177–8.

20. See the remarks of Judith Shklar, *After Utopia: The Decline of Political Faith*, pp. 172ff.

21. I am thinking, of course, of Derek Parfit's book, *Reasons and Persons*. Parfit appears, like Kaufman, to assume that his own peculiar beliefs are universally shared. He continually appeals to what 'we' think or feel, in order to reject alternative conclusions from the ones he wishes the reader to adopt. 'Most of us believe that . . . . It is very hard to believe . . .' (pp. 232–3); 'we are inclined to believe . . .' (p. 239); 'Most of us are strongly inclined to reject this view . . . it is hard to believe that . . .' (p. 278). After appealing throughout to such criteria it is curious to find the author finally asserting a position which almost nobody is inclined to believe! See also Michael B. Foster, ' "We" in Modern Philosophy', in Basil Mitchell, ed., *Faith and Logic*, pp. 194–220.

22. David Nicholls, 'Conscience and Authority in the Thought of W.G. Ward', *Heythrop Journal*, 26: 4, 1985, pp. 416–29. See Stanley Hauerwas, *A Community of Character, The Peaceable Kingdom*, etc.

23. David Tracy, *The Analogical Imagination: Christian Theology and the Culture of Pluralism*, especially chapter 11. (But see my review of this book in *Theology*, March 1983.)

24. Quoted in William Barclay, *Ethics in a Permissive Society*, p. 74.
25. From a private letter to the author.
26. Harold J. Laski, *Reflections on the Revolution of our Time*, p. 180; see also Edward R. Norman, who comments on those who complain that the church is 'becoming involved in politics', that it is 'the State that is becoming involved in the traditional concerns of religion', 'Christianity and Politics', in Cowling, ed., *Conservative Essays*, p. 71.
27. Margaret Thatcher (1978), quoted by A.M.C. Waterman, in W. Block and I. Hexham, eds, *Religion, Economics and Social Thought*, p. 99.
28. I am grateful to Brian Wren for sending me copies of some of his recent work.
29. Church of England, Doctrine Commission, *We Believe in God*, pp. 151ff.
30. For a consideration of the relation between revelation and divine images see Austin Farrer's brilliant Bampton Lectures, *The Glass of Vision*.
31. Max Horkheimer, *Critique of Instrumental Reason*, pp. 47–8.

Bibliography

Abbott, Walter M., *The Documents of Vatican II*, New York, 1966

Abel-Smith, B. and Townsend, P., *The Poor and the Poorest*, London, 1965

Acton, John E.E.D., *The History of Freedom and Other Essays*, London, 1907

Adderley, J., ed., *Scott Holland's Goodwill*, London, n.d.

Adorno Theodor W., et al., *The Positivist Dispute in German Sociology*, London, 1976

Althaus, Paul, *Grundriss der Ethik,* Gütersloh, 1953
  Kirche und Staat nach Lutherischer Lehre, Leipzig, 1935
  Obrigkeit und Führertum, Gütersloh, 1936
  Politisches Christentum, Leipzig, 1935
  Theologie der Ordnungen, Gütersloh, 1935

Ames, Edward S., *The Psychology of Religious Experience*, Boston, 1910
  Religion, New York, 1919

Arendt, Hannah, *The Origins of Totalitarianism*, Cleveland, 1958

Arnold, C.H., *Near the Edge of Battle*, Chicago, 1966

Arnold, Matthew, *Culture and Anarchy*, London, 1901
  Mixed Essays, London, 1880

Asquith, Herbert H., *Memories and Reflections of the Earl of Oxford and Asquith*, London, 1919

Atherton, John, *The Scandal of Poverty*, Oxford, 1983

Attlee, Clement R., *The Social Worker*, London, 1920

Bachrach, Peter, *The Theory of Democratic Elitism*, Boston and Toronto, 1967

Bachrach, Peter and Baratz, M.S., *Power and Poverty*, New York, 1970

Bacon, R. and Eltis, W.A., *Britain's Economic Problems*, London, 1976

Bakunin, Mikhail, *Beichte aus der Peter-Paul-Festung an Zar Niklaus I*, ed. K. Kersten, Berlin, 1926
　God and the State, New York, 1970
　Œuvres, Paris, 1895–1913
Balfour, Arthur J., *Essays and Addresses*, London, 1893
　Foundations of Belief, London, 1895
Barclay, William, *Ethics in a Permissive Society*, London, 1971
Barker, Ernest, *From Alexander to Constantine*, Oxford, 1956
Barnard, F.M., *Herder's Social and Political Thought*, Oxford, 1965
　ed., J.G. *Herder on Social and Political Culture*, Cambridge, 1969
Barnett, Samuel A., *Religion and Politics*, London, 1911
　The Service of God, London, 1897
Barnett, S.A. and H.O., *Practicable Socialism*, London, 1888
　Towards Social Reform, London, 1909
Barry, Brian, *Political Argument*, London, 1965
Barth, Karl, *Against the Stream*, London, 1954
　The Church and the Political Problem of our Day, London, 1939
　Church Dogmatics, Edinburgh, 1932
　Dogmatics in Outline, London, 1949
　The Epistle to the Romans (1919 and 1921), London, 1933
　Evangelical Theology: an Introduction, New York, 1963
　From Rousseau to Ritschl, London, 1959
　God Here and Now, New York, 1964
　The Hope of a New World, London, 1940
　How I Changed my Mind, Richmond, Va., 1966
　The Humanity of God, London, 1967
　The Theology of Schleiermacher, Edinburgh, 1982
　The Word of God and the Word of Man, London, 1928
Barth, K. and Hamel, J., *How to Serve God in a Marxist Land*, New York, 1959
Barth, K. and Thurneysen, E., *Revolutionary Theology in the Making*, London, 1964
Beckerath, H. von and Kern, F., *Autarkie oder internationale Zusammenarbeit*, Berlin, 1932
Beiner, Ronald, *Political Judgment*, London, 1983
Bellah, Robert, *Beyond Belief*, New York, 1970
　The Broken Covenant, New York, 1975
Bellah, Robert and Hammond, P.E., *Varieties of Civil Religion*, San Francisco, 1980
Beloff, M. and Peele, G., *The Government of the United Kingdom: Political Authority in a Changing Society*, London, 1980
Bendersky, J.W., *Carl Schmitt: Theorist for the Reich*, Princeton, 1983
Bentley, Arthur F., *The Process of Government*, Cambridge, Mass., 1967

Bentley, M. and Stevenson J., eds, *High and Low Politics in Modern Britain*, Oxford, 1983

Berdyaev, Nicolas A., *The Divine and the Human*, London, 1949
Dream and Reality, London, 1950
Freedom and the Spirit, London, 1935
The Meaning of History, London, 1936
The Realm of Spirit and the Realm of Caesar, London, 1952
Slavery and Freedom, London, 1943
Solitude and Society, London, 1938
Spirit and Reality, London, 1939

Berlin, Isaiah, *Four Essays on Liberty*, Oxford, 1969

Bernstein, G.L., *Liberalism and Liberal Politics in Edwardian England*, London, 1986

Bernstein, Richard J., *Beyond Objectivism and Relativism*, Oxford, 1983
Philosophical Profiles, Cambridge, 1986

Bethge, Eberhard, *Dietrich Bonhoeffer: Man of Vision, Man of Courage*, New York and Evanston, 1970

Beveridge, William H., *Full Employment in a Free Society*, London, 1944
The Pillars of Security, London, 1943
Voluntary Action, London, 1948

Bigler, R.M., *The Politics of German Protestantism*, Berkeley and Los Angeles, 1972

Bloch, Ernst, *The Principle of Hope*, Oxford, 1986

Block, Walter and Hexham, I. eds, *Religion, Economics and Social Thought*, Vancouver, 1986

Blumenberg, Hans, *The Legitimacy of the Modern Age*, Cambridge, Mass., 1983 (reprint of 2nd rev. edn of 1976)

Boisset, Louis, *La Théologie en procès, face à la critique marxiste*, Paris, 1974

Boissevain, Jeremy, *Friends of Friends*, Oxford, 1974
Saints and Fireworks, London, 1965

Bonhoeffer, Dietrich, *No Rusty Swords*, London, 1970

Boorstein, E., *The Economic Transformation of Cuba*, New York, 1968

Booth, Charles, *Life and Labour of the People of London*, London, 1889–

Bosanquet, N. and Townsend, P., *Labour and Equality*, London, 1980

Boyson, Rhodes, ed., *Down with the Poor*, London, 1971

Brabrook, E.W., *Provident Societies and Industrial Welfare*, London, 1898

Bradley, F.H., *Appearance and Reality*, Oxford, 1930 (1st edn 1893)

Brailsford, H.N., *Shelley, Godwin and their Circle*, London, 1913

Brasnett, Bertrand D. *The Suffering of the Impassible God*, London, 1928

Breasted, J.H., *The Dawn of Conscience*, New York, 1933

Brewer, Colin, et al., *Criminal Welfare on Trial*, London, 1981

Brock, Sebastian, *The Holy Spirit in the Syriac Baptismal Tradition*, Poona, 1979

Brown, Delwin, et al., eds, *Process Philosophy and Christian Thought*, Indianapolis, 1971

Brown, Peter, *The Cult of the Saints*, London, 1981
  The World of Late Antiquity, London, 1971

Bruce, Maurice, *The Coming of the Welfare State*, London, 1972

Brunner, Emil and Barth, Karl, *Natural Theology*, London, 1946

Buckham, J.W. and Stratton, G.M., *George Holmes Howison*, Berkeley, 1934

Bunbury, Henry, ed., *Lloyd George's Ambulance Wagon*, London, 1957

Burrell, David B., *Aquinas: God and Action*, London and Henley, 1979

Bussell, F.W., *Christian Theology and Social Progress*, London, 1907

Butler, Joseph, *The Analogy of Religion, Natural and Revealed, to the Constitution and Course of Nature*, Dublin, 1736

Cagnolo, C., *The Akikuyu*, Nyeri, 1933

Caird, Edward, *Essays on Literature and Philosophy*, Glasgow, 1892
  The Evolution of Religion, Glasgow, 1899
  Lay Sermons and Addresses, Glasgow, 1907

Calvin, John, *The Institutes of the Christian Religion*, London, 1957

Cameron, K.N., *The Young Shelley: Genesis of a Radical*, New York, 1951
  Shelley: The Golden Years, Cambridge, Mass., 1974

Cantos del pueblo para el pueblo, Santo Domingo, DR, n.d.

Carmichael, J.D. and Goodwin, H.S., *William Temple's Political Legacy*, London, 1963

Carr, E.H., *Michael Bakunin*, London, 1937

Carr, Raymond, *Puerto Rico: A Colonial Experiment*, New York and London, 1984

Carswell, J., *From Revolution to Revolution: England 1688–1776*, London, 1973

Casalis, Georges, *Les Idées justes ne tombent pas du ciel*, Paris, 1977

Case, Shirley Jackson, *The Evolution of Early Christianity*, Chicago, 1914

Caudron, Marc, ed., *Foi et société*, Gembloux, Belgium, 1978

Chandler, F.W., *Political Spies and Provocative Agents*, Sheffield, 1933

Christen, Robert J. and Hazelton, H.E., eds, *Monotheism and Moses*, Lexington, Mass., 1969

Church of England, Archbishops' Commission on Urban Priority Areas, *Faith in the City: A Call for Action by Church and Nation*, London, 1985

Church of England, Board for Social Responsibility, *Not Just for the Poor: Christian Perspectives on the Welfare State*, London, 1986

Church of England, Board for Social Responsibility, *Changing Britain*, London, 1987

Church of England, Doctrine Commission, *Christian Believing*, London, 1976

Church of England, Doctrine Commission, *We Believe in God*, London, 1987

Churchill, Randolph S., *Young Statesman, 1901–14, Winston S. Churchill*, London, 1967

Churchill, Winston S., *Liberalism and the Social Problem*, London, 1909

Clark, J.P., *The Philosophical Anarchism of William Godwin*, Princeton, 1977

Clarke, Peter, *Liberals and Social Democrats*, Cambridge, 1978

Cobban, Alfred, *The Nation State and National Self-Determination*, London, 1969

Coit, Stanton, ed., *Ethical Democracy: Essays in Social Dynamics*, London, 1900

Coleridge, Samuel T., *Lay Sermons*, London, 1852

Collini, S., *Liberalism and Sociology: L.T. Hobhouse and Political Argument in England, 1880–1915*, Cambridge, 1979

Connolly, William E., ed., *The Bias of Pluralism*, New York, 1969

Conservative Party, *The Next Move Forward*, London, 1987

Conway, J.S., *The Nazi Persecution of the Church, 1933–45*, New York, 1968

Copleston, Frederick C., *History of Philosophy*, London, 1946

Cosmao, Vincent, *Changer le monde*, Paris, 1979

Cowling, Maurice, ed., *Conservative Essays*, London, 1978

Creel, Richard E., *Divine Impassibility: An Essay in Philosophical Theology*, Cambridge, 1986

Cullman, Oscar, *The State in the New Testament*, London, 1957

Currie, R., *Industrial Politics*, Oxford, 1979

Dahl, Robert A., *Polyarchy, Participation and Opposition*, New Haven, Conn., 1971

A Preface to Democratic Theory, Chicago, 1956

Dahrendorf, Ralf, *Essays in the Theory of Society*, Stanford, 1968

Darvall, F.O., *Popular Disturbances and Public Order in Regency England*, Oxford, 1934

Darwin, Charles, *The Origin of Species*, London, 1900

Dash, J.M., *Literature and Ideology in Haiti, 1915–1961*, London, 1981

Dawson, Christopher, *Religion and the Modern State*, London, 1935

Dawson, J.F., *Friedrich Schleiermacher: The Evolution of a Nationalist*, Austin, Tex., 1966

Dawson, P.M.S., *The Unacknowledged Legislator: Shelley and Politics*, Oxford, 1980

Dawson, W.H., *Social Insurance in Germany, 1883–1911*, London, 1912

Demas, William G., *Change and Renewal in the Caribbean*, Bridgetown, Barbados, 1975

Dewey, John, *The Early Works, 1882–1898*, Carbondale and Edwardsville, Ill., 1969–

Problems of Man, New York, 1946

The Public and its Problems, London, n.d.

Reconstruction in Philosophy, 1966 (1st edn 1920)

Reconstruction in Philosophy, 1966 (1st edn 1920)

Dilthey, Wilhelm, *Leben Schleiermachers*, Berlin, 1870

Dionysius of Fourna, *The Painter's Manual*, London, 1981

Donne, John, *The Sermons of John Donne*, ed. G.R. Potter and E.M. Simpson, Berkeley, 1953–62

Durkheim, Emile, *The Elementary Forms of the Religious Life*, London, 1915
Sociologie et philosophie, Paris, 1979

Edwards, David, *The State of the Nation*, London, 1976

Ehrenberg, Victor, *The Greek State*, London, 1969

Elster, Jon, *Leibniz et la formation de l'esprit capitaliste*, Paris, 1975

Engelbrecht, H.C., *Johann Gottlieb Fichte: A Study of his Political Writings with Special Reference to his Nationalism*, PhD thesis, Columbia University, New York, 1933

Erasmus, D., *The Education of a Christian Prince* (1516), ed. L.K. Brown, New York, 1936

Ergang, Robert R., *Herder and the Foundations of German Nationalism*, New York, 1931

Ericksen, R.P., *Theologians under Hitler*, New Haven and London, 1985

Fabricius, Cajus, *Positive Christianity in the Third Reich*, Dresden, 1937

Fabro, Cornelio, *God in Exile*, Westminster, Md., 1968

Farrer, Austin, *The Glass of Vision*, London, 1948

Fédération Internationale des Sociétés de Philosophie, *Enquête sur la liberté*, Paris, 1953

Feuerbach, Ludwig, *The Essence of Christianity*, New York, 1957

Fichte, Johann Gottlieb, *An Attempt at a Critique of all Revelation*, Cambridge, 1978
Nachgelassene Werke, Bonn, 1834
The Popular Works of Johann Gottlieb Fichte, London, 1889
Sämmtliche Werke, ed. I.H. Fichte, Berlin, 1845–6
The Science of Knowledge, New York, 1970
The Science of Rights, London, 1889

Field, Frank, *Inequality in Britain: Freedom, Welfare and the State*, London, 1981

Figgis, John Neville, *Studies of Political Thought from Gerson to Grotius, 1414–1625*, Cambridge, 1923

Flathman, Richard, *The Practice of Rights*, Cambridge, 1976
The Public Interest, New York, 1966

Follett, Mary P., *The New State*, New York, 1918

Foot, Paul, *Red Shelley*, London, 1980

Forrester, Duncan B., *Christianity and the Future of Welfare*, London, 1985

Frank, S.L., ed., *A Solovyov Anthology*, London, 1950

Frankfort, Henri, *Kingship and the Gods*, Chicago, 1948

Fraser, D., *The Evolution of the British Welfare State*, London, 1973

Freeden, Michael, *The New Liberalism: an Ideology of Social Reform*, Oxford, 1978

Fried, Ferdinand, *Autarkie*, Jena, 1932

Friedrich, Carl J., ed., *The Public Interest, Nomos* V, New York, 1962
  ed., *Totalitarianism*, New York, 1964

Friedrich, Carl J. and Brzezinski, Z.K., *Totalitarian Dictatorship and Autocracy*, New York, 1961

Frisby, David and Sayer, Derek, *Society*, Chichester and London, 1986

Fromm, E., *The Dogma of Christ*, London, 1963

Funk, Robert, *Schleiermacher as Contemporary* (vol. 7 of *Journal for Theology and the Church*), New York, 1970

Gardiner, Patrick, ed., *Nineteenth Century Philosophy*, New York, 1969

Garrett, Naomi, *The Renaissance of Haitian Poetry*, Paris, 1963

Geertz, Clifford, *Local Knowledge: Further Essays in Interpretive Anthropology*, New York, 1983

Gerassi, John, ed., *Venceremos: The Speeches and Writings of Ernesto Che Guevara*, London, 1968

Gerstenmeier, E., ed., *Kirche, Volk und Staat*, Berlin, 1937

Gerth, H.H. and Mills, C. Wright, eds, *From Max Weber*, London, 1948

Gierke, Otto von, *Das deutsche Genossenschaftsrecht*, Berlin, 1868–1913
  The Development of Political Theory, London, 1939
  Natural Law and the Theory of Society, Cambridge, 1950

Gilbert, B.B., *The Evolution of National Insurance in Great Britain: The Origins of the Welfare State*, London, 1966

Gill, Robin, *The Social Context of Theology*, Oxford, 1975
  Theology and Social Structure, Oxford, 1977

Gillies, A., *Herder*, Oxford, 1945

Gladden, Washington, *The Church and the Kingdom*, London, 1894

Godwin, William, *An Enquiry Concerning Political Justice*, Harmondsworth, 1976 (reprint of 3rd edition of 1798)
  Sketches of History in Six Sermons, London, 1784
  Thoughts Occasioned by the Perusal of Dr Parr's Spital Sermon, London, 1801

Goldman, Emma, *Anarchism and Other Essays*, New York, 1969

Gore, Charles, ed., *Lux Mundi: A Series of Studies in the Religion of the Incarnation*, London, 1890

Gore, Charles, et al., *Property: Its Duties and Rights*, London, 1913

Gosden, P.H.J.H., *The Friendly Societies in England, 1815–1875*, Manchester, 1961
  Self-Help, London, 1973

Gough, Ian, *The Political Economy of the Welfare State*, London, 1979

Gough, J.W., *Social Contract*, Oxford, 1957

Gramsci, Antonio, *Selections from the Prison Notebooks*, London, 1971

Grant, Robert M., *Early Christianity and Society*, London, 1978

Green, David G., *The Welfare State: For Rich or for Poor?*, London, 1982

Green, Thomas Hill, *Prolegomena to Ethics*, Oxford, 1899
  The Works of Thomas Hill Green, ed. R.L. Nettleship, London, 1885

Gregg, P. *The Welfare State*, London, 1967

Griffith, J.A.G., *The Politics of the Judiciary*, London, 1977

Gunton, Colin E., *Becoming and Being: The Doctrine of God in Charles Hartshorne and Karl Barth*, Oxford, 1978

Guthrie, W.K.C., *A History of Greek Philosophy*, Cambridge, 1962

Habermas, Jürgen, *Toward a Rational Society*, London, 1973

Hand, J.E., ed., *Good Citizenship*, London, 1899

Harnack, Adolf, *What is Christianity?*, London, 1904

Harnack, Adolf and Herrmann, W., *Essays on the Social Gospel*, London, 1907

Harré, Rom, *The Principles of Scientific Thinking*, London, 1970

Harris, H.S., *Hegel's Development: Towards the Sunlight, 1770–1801*, Oxford, 1972

Harris, José, *Unemployment and Politics: A Study in English Social Policy, 1886–1914*, Oxford, 1972

William Beveridge: A Biography, Oxford, 1977

Hartshorne, Charles, *The Divine Relativity*, New Haven, Conn., 1948

The Logic of Perfection, Lasalle, Ill., 1962

Man's Vision of God, Chicago and New York, 1941

Hartwell, R.M., et al., *The Long Debate on Poverty*, London, 1974

Haubtmann, Pierre, *Pierre-Joseph Proudhon: genèse d'un antithéiste*, Paris, 1969

Pierre-Joseph Proudhon: sa vie et sa pensée, Paris, 1982

Hauerwas, Stanley, *Character and the Christian Life: A Study in Theological Ethics*, San Antonio, Tex., 1985

A Community of Character: Toward a Constructive Christian Social Ethic, Notre Dame, Ind., 1981

The Peaceable Kingdom: A Primer in Christian Ethics, Notre Dame, Ind., 1985

Hayek, F.A. von, *The Constitution of Liberty*, London, 1960

The Counter-Revolution of Science, New York, 1955

Individualism: True and False, Dublin, 1946

Hegel, G.W.F., *Hegel's Political Writings*, Oxford, 1964

Hegels theologisches Jugendschriften, ed. Herman Nohl, Tübingen, 1907

Lectures on the Philosophy of Religion, Together with a Work on the Proofs for the Existence of God (1832), London, 1895

Lectures on the Philosophy of World History, Cambridge, 1975

Natural Law, Philadelphia, 1975

On Christianity: Early Theological Writings by Friedrich Hegel, New York, 1961

Philosophy of Right, Oxford, 1953

Heidt, J.H. *The Social Theology of Henry Scott Holland*, D. Phil. thesis, Oxford, 1975

Heimert, Alan, *Religion and the American Mind*, Cambridge, Mass., 1966

Heine, H., *Religion and Philosophy in Germany*, Boston, 1959

Hengel, Martin, *Property and Riches in the Early Church*, London, 1974

Hennock, E.P., *British Social Reform and German Precedents: the Case of Social Insurance, 1880–1914*, Oxford, 1987

Herder, J.G., *God, Some Conversations*, Indianapolis, 1940

Herrmann, Wilhelm, *The Communion of the Christian with God*, London, 1906

Heschel, Abraham, *The Prophets*, New York, 1962

Hesse, Mary B., *Models and Analogies in Science*, Notre Dame, Ind., 1966
The Structure of Scientific Inference, London, 1974

Hetherington, H.J.W., *Life and Letters of Sir Henry Jones*, London, 1924

Hicks, U.K., *British Public Finances, their Structure and Development, 1880–1952*, London, 1954

Hinchliffe, Peter, *Benjamin Jowett and the Christian Religion*, Oxford, 1988

Hirsch, Emanuel, *Das kirchliche Wollen der Deutsche Christen*, Berlin, 1933

Hitler, Adolf, *Mein Kampf*, Boston, 1943

Hobbes, Thomas, *Leviathan: or the Matter, Forme and Power of a Commonwealth, Ecclesiastical and Civil* (1651), Oxford, 1946

Hobhouse, L.T., *Democracy and Reaction*, London, 1904
Liberalism, London, n.d.
The Metaphysical Theory of the State, London, 1918
Social Evolution and Political Theory, London, 1911

Hobson, J.A., *The Crisis of Liberalism: New Issues of Democracy*, London, 1909
The Social Problem, London, 1901

Hobson, J.A. and Ginsberg, M., *L.T. Hobhouse: His Life and Work*, London, 1931

Holland, Henry Scott, *Facts of the Faith*, London, 1919
God's City and the Coming of the Kingdom, London, 1897
Logic and Life, London, 1885
The Real Problem of Eschatology, London, 1916

Holmes, Richard, *Shelley: The Pursuit*, London, 1976

Hood, Robert E., *Contemporary Political Orders and Christ*, Allison Park, Pa., 1985

Horkheimer, Max, *Critical Theory, Selected Essays*, New York, 1972
Critique of Instrumental Reason, New York, 1974

Howison, George H., *The Limits of Evolution, and Other Essays*, New York, 1901

Humboldt, Wilhelm von, *The Limits of State Action*, Cambridge, 1969

Hunsinger, G., ed., *Karl Barth and Radical Politics*, Philadelphia, 1976

Huxley, T.H., *Collected Essays*, London, 1895

Hynes, William J., *Shirley Jackson Case and the Chicago School: The Socio-Historical Method*, Chico, Calif., 1981

Illingworth, J.R., *The Doctrine of the Trinity*, London, 1907

Personality Human and Divine, London, 1894

Institute of Economic Affairs, *The Long Debate on Poverty*, London, 1972

Iremonger, F.A., *William Temple, Archbishop of Canterbury: His Life and Letters*, London, 1948

Jackson, George, *Soledad Brother: Prison Letters*, Harmondsworth, 1971

James, William, *Pragmatism*, London, 1907

    The Varieties of Religious Experience, London, 1904

    The Will to Believe, London, 1897

    The Writings of William James, New York, 1967

Janvier, Louis J., *Haiti aux haitiens*, Paris, 1884

Jay, Martin, *The Dialectical Imagination: A History of the Frankfurt School and the Institute of Social Research, 1923–50*, London, 1973

Jenkins, David E., *Living with Questions*, London, 1967

Johnson, Luke T., *Sharing Possessions: Mandate and Symbol of Faith*, Philadelphia, 1981

Joll, James, *The Anarchists*, New York, 1964

Jones, G.W., *Borough Politics: A Study of the Wolverhampton Town Council, 1888–1964*, London, 1969

Jones, Henry, *The Principles of Citizenship*, London, 1919

    Social Powers, Glasgow, 1913

    The Working Faith of the Social Reformer, London, 1910

Jones, Thomas, *Lloyd George*, Oxford, 1951

Jüngel, Eberhard, *The Doctrine of the Trinity: God's Being is in Becoming*, Edinburgh, 1976

    Karl Barth: A Theological Legacy, Philadelphia, 1986

Kant, Immanuel, *Werke*, Berlin, 1912–22

Kantorowicz, Ernst H., *The King's Two Bodies: A Study in Medieval Political Theology*, Princeton, 1957

    Selected Studies, Locust Valley, NY, 1965

Kariel, Henry, *The Decline of American Pluralism*, Stanford, 1961

Karl Barth–Rudolf Bultmann Letters, 1922–1966, Grand Rapids, Mich., 1981

Käsemann, Ernst, *Commentary on Romans*, London, 1980

Kaufman, Gordon D., *God the Problem*, Cambridge, Mass., 1972

    The Theological Imagination, Philadelphia, 1981

    Theology for a Nuclear Age, Manchester, 1985

Kaufmann, Walter, ed., *Hegel's Political Philosophy*, New York, 1970

Kautsky, Karl, *Foundations of Christianity: A Study in Christian Origins*, New York, 1925

Kedourie, E., *Nationalism*, London, 1966

Kegan Paul, C., *William Godwin: His Friends and Contemporaries*, London, 1976

Kelly, George A., *Idealism, Politics and History: Sources of Hegelian Thought*, Cambridge, 1969

Kennedy, G. Studdert, *The Hardest Part*, London, 1919
  The Unutterable Beauty, London, 1927
Kershaw, Ian, *The Hitler Myth*, Oxford, 1987
Khomiakoff, A.S., *L'Eglise latine et le protestantisme au point de vue de l'église d'orient*, Lausanne and Vevey, 1872
King, Lord, *The Life and Letters of John Locke*, London, 1864
Kitamori, Kazoh, *Theology of the Pain of God*, London, 1968
Kobori, K., *The Idea of a Closed State*, Tokyo, 1951
Kornhauser, William, *The Politics of Mass Society*, New York, 1959
Kress, Paul F., *Social Science and the Idea of Process: The Ambiguous Legacy of Arthur F. Bentley*, Urbana, Chicago and London, 1970
Kropotkin, Peter, *Mutual Aid*, New York and London, 1907
Krumbine, Miles H., ed., *The Process of Religion: Essays in Honor of Dean Shailer Mathews*, New York, 1933
Kuhn, Thomas S., *The Structure of Scientific Revolutions*, Chicago, 1962
Kuper, Leo and Smith, M.G., eds, *Pluralism in Africa*, Berkeley and Los Angeles, 1969
Lagneau, J., *Célèbres, leçons et fragments*, Paris, 1950
Lampert, E., *Berdyaev and the New Middle Ages*, London, n.d.
  Studies in Rebellion, London, 1957
Lang, Bernhard, ed., *Monotheism and the Prophetic Minority: An Essay in Biblical History and Sociology*, Sheffield, 1983
Langshaw, H., *Socialism and the Historic Function of Liberalism*, London, 1925
Lash, Nicholas, *A Matter of Hope*, London, 1981
Laski, Harold J., *Reflections on the Revolution of our Time*, London, 1943
Laue, Theodore H. von, *Leopold Ranke: The Formative Years*, Princeton, 1950
Lauer, Quentin, *Hegel's Concept of God*, Albany, NY, 1982
Leclerc, Ivor, ed., *The Relevance of Whitehead*, London, 1961
Leech, Kenneth, *The Social God*, London, 1981
Leech, Kenneth and Williams, Rowan, *Essays Catholic and Radical*, London, 1983
Le Grand, Julian, *The Strategy of Equality: Redistribution and the Welfare Services*, London, 1982
Leighton, Angela, *Shelley and the Sublime*, Cambridge, 1984
Lenin, V.I., *Against Revisionism*, Moscow, 1959
Lenski, G., *Human Societies: A Macrolevel Introduction to Sociology*, New York, 1970
Léon, Xavier, *Fichte et son temps*, Paris, 1924
Lessnoff, Michael, *Social Contract*, London, 1986
Lewy, G., *The Catholic Church and Nazi Germany*, New York, 1964
Lidgett, J. Scott, *The Fatherhood of God*, Edinburgh, 1902
  The Idea of God and Social Ideals, London, 1938

The Spiritual Principle of the Atonement, London, 1898

Lippmann, Walter, *A Preface to Morals*, London, 1929

Littell, Franklin H. and Locke, H.G., eds, *The German Church Struggle and the Holocaust*, Detroit, 1974

Lotze, Rudolf Hermann, *Microcosmus*, Edinburgh, 1885

Lovejoy, Arthur O., *The Great Chain of Being*, New York, 1960

Löwith, Karl, *Meaning in History*, Chicago and London, 1949

Lubac, Henri de, *The Unmarxian Socialist: A Study of Proudhon*, London, 1948

Lukács, Georg, *The Destruction of Reason*, London, 1980

Lukashevich, Stephen, *N.F. Fedorov (1828–1903): A Study in Russian Eupsychian and Utopian Thought*, Cranbury, NJ, 1977

Luxemburg, Rosa, *Social Reform or Revolution*, New York, 1973

Lyttelton, Edward, *The Mind and Character of Henry Scott Holland*, London, 1926

McConnell, Grant, *Private Power and American Democracy*, New York, 1966

McFague, Sallie, *Metaphorical Theology: Models of God in Religious Language*, Philadelphia, 1982

Models of God: Theology for an Ecological Nuclear Age, Philadelphia, 1987

McIlwain, C.H., ed., *The Political Works of James I*, Cambridge, Mass., 1918

MacIntyre, Alasdair, ed., *Hegel*, New York, 1972

McKenzie, Norman, ed., *Conviction*, London, 1958

Mackenzie, R.T. and Silver, A., *Angels in Marble: Working Class Conservatives in Urban England*, London, 1964

Macquarrie, John, *In Search of Deity*, London, 1984

Twentieth Century Religious Thought, New York and Evanston, 1963

McTaggart, John M.E., *Studies in Hegelian Cosmology*, Cambridge, 1901

Madden, E.H. and Hare, P.H., *Evil and the Concept of God*, Springfield, Ill., 1968

Malherbe, Abraham J., *Social Aspects of Early Christianity*, Philadelphia, 1983

Malvern, 1941: The Life of the Church and the Order of Society, being the Proceedings of the Archbishop of York's Conference, London, 1941

Mannheim, Karl, *Ideology and Utopia*, New York, 1954

Mansel, Henry L., *The Limits of Religious Thought*, London, 1858

Marcuse, Herbert, *One Dimensional Man*, London, 1968

Marquardt, F.-W., *Theologie und Sozialismus: das Beispiel Karl Barths*, Munich, 1972

Marshall, T.H., *Social Policy in the Twentieth Century*, London, 1975

Marx, Karl and Engels, F., *Collected Works*, London, 1975–

Mascall, Eric, *The Openness of Being*, London, 1971

Mathews, Shailer, *The Atonement and the Social Process*, New York, 1930

The Faith of Modernism, New York, 1924

The Growth of the Idea of God, New York, 1931

New Faith for Old, New York, 1936

Patriotism and Religion, New York, 1918

The Spiritual Interpretation of History, Cambridge, Mass., 1916

ed., *Outline of Christianity*, volume 3, Toronto and New York, 1926

Mattern, J., *Geopolitik: Doctrine of Self-Sufficiency and Empire*, Baltimore, 1942

Matthew, H.C.G., *The Liberal Imperialists*, Oxford, 1973

Maurice, Frederick D., *The Kingdom of Christ*, London, 1838

Maximoff, G.P., ed., *The Political Philosophy of Bakunin: Scientific Anarchism*, New York, 1964

Mayer, J.P., *Max Weber and German Politics*, London, 1944

Mbiti, John S., *Concepts of God in Africa*, London, 1975

Meier, Kurt, *Die Deutschen Christen: Das Bild einer Bewegung im Kirchenkampf des Drittes Reiches*, Göttingen, 1964

Meinecke, Friedrich, *The German Catastrophe*, Boston, 1963

Historism: The Rise of a New Historical Outlook, London, 1972

Machiavellism: the Doctrine of Raison d'Etat and its Place in Modern History, New York, 1965

Merton, Thomas, *Contemplation in a World of Action*, London, 1980

Micklem, Nathaniel, *The Theology of Politics*, London, 1941

Miliband, R., *Capitalist Democracy in Britain*, Oxford, 1982

Mill, John Stuart, *Essay on Liberty*, London, 1910 (1st edn 1859)

An Examination of Sir William Hamilton's Philosophy, London, 1889

Principles of Political Economy, London, 1883 (1st edn 1848)

Utilitarianism, Liberty and Representative Government, London, 1910

Miller, Arthur S., *The Modern Corporate State: Private Government and the American Constitution*, Westport, Conn., 1976

Miller, David, *Anarchism*, London, 1984

Social Justice, Oxford, 1976

Miller, Perry, *Errand into the Wilderness*, Boston, 1956

The New England Mind: The Seventeenth Century, Boston, 1939

Miller, R.D., *Schiller and the Ideal of Freedom*, Oxford, 1970

Mills, C. Wright, *The Power Elite*, New York, 1959

Mitchell, Basil, ed., *Faith and Logic*, London, 1957

Moberly, E.R., *Suffering, Innocent and Guilty*, London, 1978

Moberly, R.C., *Atonement and Personality*, London, 1901

Moberly, W.H., *The Ethics of Punishment*, London, 1968

Mollenkott, Virginia, *The Divine Feminine: The Biblical Imagery of God as Female*, New York, 1983

Moltmann, Jürgen, *The Crucified God*, London, 1974

The Trinity and the Kingdom of God, London, 1981

Mommsen, W.J., ed., *The Emergence of the Welfare State in Britain and Germany*, London, 1981

Morrison, Clinton D., *The Powers That Be: Earthly Rulers and Demonic*

Powers in Romans 13: 1–7, London, 1960

Mosse, George L., *Nazi Culture: Intellectual, Cultural and Social Life in the Third Reich*, New York, 1968

Mozley, J.K., *The Impassibility of God*, Cambridge, 1926

Mulert, H., ed., *Schleiermachers Sendschreiben über seine Glaubenslehre an Lücke*, Giessen, 1908

Nettleship, R.L., ed., *The Works of Thomas Hill Green*, London, 1888

Neuhaus, Richard, *The Naked Public Square: Religion and Democracy in America*, Grand Rapids, Mich., 1984

Neumann, F., *Behemoth: The Structure and Practice of National Socialism, 1933–1945*, 1966

Newton, Kenneth, *Second-City Politics: Democratic Process and Decision Making in Birmingham*, Oxford, 1976

Nicholls, David, 'Authority in Church and State: Aspects of the Thought of J.N. Figgis and his Contemporaries', Cambridge PhD thesis, History Faculty, 1962

From Dessalines to Duvalier, Cambridge, 1979

Haiti in Caribbean Context, London, 1985

The Pluralist State, London, 1975

Principalities and Powers (Jubilee Group Pamphlet), London, 1978

Three Varieties of Pluralism, London, 1974

Nicholls, David, ed., *Church and State in Britain since 1820*, London, 1967

Nicholls, David and Williams, Rowan, *Politics and Theological Identity: Two Anglican Essays*, London, 1984

Niebuhr, H. Richard, *The Kingdom of God in America*, New York, 1959

Radical Monotheism and Western Culture, New York, 1960

The Responsible Self, New York, 1963

Niebuhr, Richard R., *Schleiermacher on Christ and Religion*, London, 1965

Noakes, Jeffrey and Pridham, G., eds, *Documents on Nazism*, London, 1974

Noel, Conrad, *Socialism and Church Tradition*, London, 1909

Norman, Edward R., *The Victorian Christian Socialists*, Cambridge, 1987

Nourrisson, P. *Histoire de la liberté d'association en France depuis 1789*, Paris, 1920

Nowak, Jerzy, *L'Idée de l'autarchie économique*, Paris, 1924

Nowak, Kurt, *Evangelische Kirche und Weimarer Republik*, Göttingen, 1985

Oakeshott, Michael, *The Social and Political Doctrines of Contemporary Europe*, London, 1940

Odebrecht, R., ed., *Friedrich Schleiermachers Dialektik*, Leipzig, 1942

O'Leary, Joseph, *Questioning Back: The Overcoming of Metaphysics in Christian Tradition*, Minneapolis, 1985

Orensanz, Aurelio L., *Anarquía y christianismo*, Madrid, 1978

Ortiz-Osés, Andrés, *Comunicación y experiencia interhumana*, Bilbao, 1977

Ortony, Andrew, ed., *Metaphor and Thought*, Cambridge, 1979

Overstreet, Harry A., *The Enduring Quest*, New York, 1931

The Great Enterprise, London, 1953

Owen, H.P., *Concepts of Deity*, London, 1971

Paget, S., *Henry Scott Holland*, London, 1921

Pain, James and Zernov, Nicolas, eds, *A Bulgakov Anthology*, London, 1976

Parfit, Derek, *Reasons and Persons*, Oxford, 1984

Parkes, Henry B., *The American Experience*, New York, 1959

Parsons, Talcott, *The Social System*, London, 1951

Passmore, John, *A Hundred Years of Philosophy*, London, 1957

Pateman, Carole, *The Problem of Political Obligation: A Critique of Liberal Theory*, London, 1979

Peacock, A.T. and Wiseman, J., *The Growth of Public Expenditure in the United Kingdom*, London, 1961

Peak, Steve, *Troops in Strikes: Military Intervention in Industrial Disputes*, London, 1984

Pelczynski, Z.A., ed., *Hegel's Political Philosophy: Problems and Perspectives*, Cambridge, 1971

Pelling, Henry, *Popular Politics and Society in Late Victorian Britain*, London, 1968

Peterson, E. *Theologische Traktate*, Munich, 1951

Picht, Werner, *Toynbee Hall and the English Settlement Movement*, London, 1914

Pinson, K.S., *Pietism as a Factor in the Rise of German Nationalism*, New York, 1934

Pitkin, Hanna, *The Concept of Representation*, Berkeley and Los Angeles, 1972

Plato, *The Republic*, New York, 1945

Plumb, J., *The Growth of Political Stability in England, 1675–1725*, London, 1967

Pois, Robert A., *Friedrich Meinecke and German Politics in the Twentieth Century*, Los Angeles, Berkeley and London, 1972
National Socialism and the Religion of Nature, New York, 1986

Pois, Robert A. ed., *Alfred Rosenberg: Selected Writings*, London, 1970

Popper, Karl R., *The Open Society and its Enemies*, London, 1957

Prestige, G.L., *God in Patristic Thought*, London, 1936
The Life of Charles Gore: A Great Englishman, London, 1935

Proudhon, Pierre-Joseph, *Correspondance de P.-J. Proudhon*, Paris, 1875
General Idea of the Revolution in the Nineteenth Century, London, 1923
Œuvres complètes de P.-J. Proudhon, Paris, 1923–
The Principle of Federation, translated and introduced by Richard Vernon, Toronto, 1979

Public Expenditure on Incomes Maintenance Programmes, OECD, Paris, 1976

Puente Ojea, G., *Ideología e historia: La formación del cristianismo como fenómeno ideológico*, Madrid, 1974

Ramsey, A.M., *F.D. Maurice and the Conflicts of Modern Theology*, Cambridge, 1951

Raschke, Carl A., ed., New Dimensions in Philosophical Theology, *Journal of* the American Academy of Religious Studies, 1982

Rashdall, Hastings, *Christus in Ecclesia*, Edinburgh, 1904

Conscience and Christ: Six Lectures on Christian Ethics, London, 1916

Doctrine and Development: University Sermons, London, 1898

God and Man, Oxford, 1930

The Idea of Atonement in Christian Theology, London, 1920

Ideas and Ideals, Oxford, 1928

Philosophy and Religion, London, 1909

Principles and Precepts, Oxford, 1927

The Theory of Good and Evil, Oxford, 1907

Rauschenbusch, Walter, *Christianity and the Social Crisis*, New York, 1964

Christianizing the Social Order, New York, 1912

Prayers of the Social Awakening, London, 1927

A Theology for the Social Gospel, New York, 1917

Rauschning, Hermann, *Hitler Speaks*, London, 1939

Read, Christopher, *Religion, Revolution and the Russian Intelligentsia, 1900–1912*, London, 1979

Read, D., *Peterloo*, Manchester, 1957

Reckitt, Maurice B., *Maurice to Temple: A Century of the Social Movement in the Church of England*, London, 1947

Redcliffe-Maud, Lord and Wood, B., *English Local Government Reformed*, London, 1974

Reisman, David, *State and Welfare: Tawney, Galbraith and Adam Smith*, London, 1982

Reiss, H.S., ed., *The Political Thought of the German Romantics*, Oxford, 1955

Richmond, James, *Ritschl: A Reappraisal*, London, 1978

Richmond, W., *An Essay on Personality*, London, 1900

Richter, M., *The Politics of Conscience: T.H. Green and his Age*, London, 1964

Rimlinger, Gaston V., *Welfare Policy and Industrialization in Europe, America and Russia*, New York, 1971

Ritchie, David G., *Darwinism and Politics*, London, 1889

Natural Rights, London, 1895

Principles of State Interference, London, 1902

Ritschl, Albrecht, *The Christian Doctrine of Justification and Reconciliation*, Edinburgh, 1900

A Critical History of the Christian Doctrine of Justification and Reconciliation, Edinburgh, 1872

Ritschl, Otto, *Albrecht Ritschls Leben*, Freiburg, 1892 and 1896

Roach, J.L. and J.K., eds, *Poverty*, London, 1972

Roberts, David, *Victorian Origins of the British Welfare State*, Hamden, Conn., 1969

Robinson, H. Wheeler, *Suffering, Human and Divine*, London, 1939

Robinson, James M., ed., *The Beginnings of Dialectic Theology*, Richmond, Va., 1968

Roll, Eric, *History of Economic Thought*, London, 1961

Rolt, C.E., *The World's Redemption*, London, 1913

Rose, Gillian, *Hegel contra Sociology*, London, 1981

Rosenberg, Alfred, *Der Mythus des 20. Jahrhunderts*, Munich, 1930

Rosenzweig, Franz, *Der Stern der Erloung*, Heidelberg, 1954

Rouche, Max, *La Philosophie de l'histoire de Herder*, Paris, 1940

Rousseau, Jean-Jacques, *The Political Writings of Jean-Jacques Rousseau*, ed. C.E. Vaughan, Oxford, 1962

Rowntree, B.S., *Poverty: A Study of Town Life*, London, 1901

Royce, Josiah, et al., *The Conception of God*, New York, 1898

Ruether, Rosemary R., *Sexism and God-Talk: Toward a Feminist Theology*, Boston, 1983

Rumpf, Helmut, *Carl Schmitt und Thomas Hobbes*, Berlin, 1982

Russell, Conrad, ed., *The Origins of the English Civil War*, London, 1973

Sabatier, Auguste, *La Religion et la culture moderne*, Paris, 1897

Salazar, Antonio de Oliveira, *Doctrine and Action*, London, 1939

Samuel, Herbert, *Liberalism: An Attempt to State the Principles of Contemporary Liberalism*, London, 1902

Schapiro, Leonard B., *Totalitarianism*, London, 1972

Schelling, F.W.J. von, *Sämtliche Werke*, Stuttgart, 1856–61

Schiller, F., *Sämtliche Werke*, Munich and Leipzig, n.d.

Schleiermacher, F.D.E., *Aus Schleiermachers Leben in Briefen*, ed. W. Dilthey, Berlin, 1858–63

The Christian Faith, Edinburgh, 1928

The Life of Jesus, Philadelphia, 1975

The Life of Schleiermacher as Unfolded in his Autobiography and Letters, London, 1860

On Religion: Speeches to its Cultured Despisers, New York, 1958

Sämtliche Werke, Berlin, 1834–64

Selected Sermons of Schleiermacher, London, 1890

Soliloquies, Chicago, 1957

Schmemann, Alexander, ed., *Ultimate Questions: An Anthology of Modern Russian Religious Thought*, London and Oxford, 1977

Schmitt, Carl, *The Concept of the Political* (1927 and 1932), New Brunswick, NJ, 1976

The Crisis of Parliamentary Democracy (1923 and 1926), Cambridge, Mass., 1985

Die Diktatur. Von den Anfangen des modernen Souveranitätsgedankens bis zum proletarischen Klassenkampf, Munich and Leipzig, 1921

Der Leviathan in der Staatslehre des Thomas Hobbes, Hamburg, 1938

The Necessity of Politics (1923), London, 1931

Political Romanticism (1919 and 1925), Cambridge, Mass., 1986

Political Theology (1922 and 1934), Cambridge, Mass., 1985

Politische Theologie, Munich, 1922

Politische Theologie II: Die Legende von der Erledigung jeder Politischen Theologie, Berlin, 1970

Positionen und Begriffe im Kampf mit Weimar–Genf–Versailles, Hamburg, 1940

Staat, Bewegung, Volk: Die Dreigliederung der politischen Einheit, Hamburg, 1933

Uber die drei Arten des rechtswissenschaftslichen Denken, Hamburg, 1934

Schwab, George, *The Challenge of the Exception*, Berlin, 1970

Sharpe, Dores R., *Walter Rauschenbusch*, New York, 1942

Shelley, Percy Bysshe, *The Complete Works of Percy Bysshe Shelley*, ed. R. Ingpen and W.E. Peck, London, 1924

The Letters of Percy Bysshe Shelley, ed. R. Ingpen, London, 1912

The Letters of Percy Bysshe Shelley, ed. F.L. Jones, Oxford, 1964

The Poetical Works, ed. T. Hutchinson, London, 1952

Shils, Edward, *The Torment of Secrecy*, Glencoe, 1956

Shklar, Judith N., *After Utopia: The Decline of Political Faith*, Princeton, 1969

Men and Citizens: A Study of Rousseau's Social Theory, Cambridge, 1969

Smith, Gerald Birney, *Current Christian Thinking*, Chicago, 1928

Social Insurance and Allied Services (Cmd 6404), London, 1942

Soll, Ivan, *An Introduction to Hegel's Metaphysics*, Chicago, 1969

Sonne, Hans-Joachim, *Die politische Theologie der Deutschen Christen*, Göttingen, 1982

Sontag, Frederick, *Divine Perfection*, London, 1962

Soskice, Janet M., *Metaphor and Religious Language*, Oxford, 1985

Spencer, Herbert, *The Man Versus the State* (1884), London, 1940

Principles of Sociology, London, 1877

Spender, J.A. and Asquith, H., *The Life of Herbert Henry Asquith, Lord Oxford and Asquith*, London, 1932

State Intervention in Industry: A Workers' Inquiry, Newcastle upon Tyne, 1980

Stephen, James F., *Liberty, Equality, Fraternity*, London, 1874

Stine, R.W., *The Doctrine of God in the Philosophy of Fichte*, University of Pennsylvania, PhD thesis, Philadelphia, 1945

Streeter, B.H., et al., *Foundations: A Statement of Christian Belief in Terms of Modern Thought*, London, 1912

Strong, Josiah, *The New Era or the Coming Kingdom*, New York, 1893

Struve, W., *Elites Against Democracy: Leadership Ideals in Bourgeois Political Thought in Germany, 1890–1933*, Princeton, 1973

Sturt, Henry, ed., *Personal Idealism: Philosophical Essays by Eight Members of the University of Oxford*, London, 1902

Suggate, Alan, *William Temple and Christian Social Ethics Today*, Edinburgh, 1987

Swanson, Guy E., *The Birth of the Gods*, Ann Arbor, 1960

Swing, A.T., *The Theology of Albrecht Ritschl*, New York, 1901

Sykes, Stephen, *The Identity of Christianity*, London, 1984
  ed., *Karl Barth: Studies of his Theological Method*, Oxford, 1979

Talmon, J.L., *The Origins of Totalitarian Democracy*, London, 1952

Temple, William, *Christian Faith and Life*, London, 1934
  Christianity and Social Order, Harmondsworth, 1942
  Christianity and the State, London, 1929
  Christus Veritas, London, 1924
  Church and Nation, London, 1916
  Citizen and Churchman, London, 1941
  The Education of Citizens, London, 1905
  Essays in Christian Politics, London, 1927
  The Hope of a New World, London, 1940
  Mens Creatrix, London, 1917
  Nature, Man and God, London, 1934
  The Nature of Personality, London, 1911
  Religious Experience and Other Essays and Addresses, London, 1958
  Repton School Sermons, London, 1913

Theissen, Gerd, *The First Followers of Jesus*, London, 1978
  Sociology of Early Palestinian Christianity, London, 1978

Thompson, E.P., *The Making of the English Working Class*, Harmondsworth, 1963

Tice, Terrence N., *Schleiermacher Bibliography*, Princeton, 1966

Tillich, Paul, *The Construction of the History of Religion in Schelling's Positive Philosophy*, Cranbury, NJ, 1974
  Dynamics of Faith, New York, 1957
  Perspectives on Nineteenth and Twentieth Century Protestant Theology, London, 1967
  The Protestant Era, London, 1951
  Systematic Theology, III, Chicago, 1963
  Twentieth Century Religious Thought, New York, 1963

Titmuss, Richard M., *The Gift Relationship*, London, 1970

Tocqueville, Alexis de, *Democracy in America*, London, 1946

Toynbee, Arnold, *Lectures on the Industrial Revolution of the Eighteenth Century in England*, London, 1908

Tracy, David, *The Analogical Imagination: Christian Theology and the Culture of Pluralism*, London, 1981

Treitschke, H. von, *Bundesstaat und Einheitsstaat*, Aufsatz 2

Trethowan, Illtyd, *Process Theology and the Christian Tradition*, Still River, Mass., 1985

Tufts, James H., et al., eds, *Studies in Philosophy and Psychology by Former Students of Charles Edward Garman*, Boston and New York, 1906

Tyrrell, George, et al., *Jesus or Christ?* (*The Hibbert Journal*, Supplement for 1909), London, 1909

Van Norden, G., *Kirche in der Krise*, Düsseldorf, 1963

Vastey, Baron P.V. de, *Political Remarks on Some French Works and Newspapers concerning Hayti*, London, 1818

Vidler, Alec R., *The Theology of F.D. Maurice*, London, 1948

Vincent, Andrew and Plant, Raymond, *Philosophy, Politics and Citizenship: The Life and Thought of the British Idealists*, Oxford, 1984

Vincent, K. Steven, *Pierre-Joseph Proudhon and the Rise of French Republican Socialism*, Oxford, 1984

Voegelin, Eric, *From Enlightenment to Revolution*, Durham, NC, 1975
Order and History, Baton Rouge, Louisiana, 1956

Wallace, William, *Lectures and Essays on Natural Theology and Ethics*, Oxford, 1898

Ward, Keith, *The Concept of God*, Oxford, 1974

Ward, Wilfrid, *William George Ward and the Catholic Revival*, London, 1893

Ward, William G., *Essays of the Philosophy of Theism*, London, 1884

Webb, Beatrice, *My Apprenticeship*, London, 1926

Webb, Sidney, *Socialism and Individualism*, London, 1908
Socialism in England, London, 1890

Webb, Timothy, *Shelley: A Voice not Understood*, Manchester, 1977

Weber, Max, *Gesammelte Politische Schriften*, Munich, 1921
Jugendbriefe, Tübingen, 1936
The Protestant Ethic and the Spirit of Capitalism, New York, 1958
The Sociology of Religion, Boston, 1963

Weizsäcker, C.F. von, *The Relevance of Science*, New York, 1965

Welch, Claude, *Protestant Thought in the Nineteenth Century*, New Haven, Conn., and London, 1972
The Welfare State in Crisis, OECD, Paris, 1981

Westcott, B.F., et al., *The Church and New Century Problems*, London, n.d. (*c.* 1901)

White, Morton, *Social Thought in America: The Revolt against Formalism*, Boston, 1957

White, R.J., *From Waterloo to Peterloo*, London, 1957

Whitehead, Alfred N., *Adventures of Ideas*, Harmondsworth, 1942
The Aims of Education, New York, 1929
Process and Reality, New York, 1978
Religion in the Making, Cambridge, 1930
Science and the Modern World, New York, 1931

Wieman, Henry N., *Man's Ultimate Commitment*, Carbondale, Ill., 1958
Religious Experience and Scientific Method, New York, 1926
The Wrestle of Religion with Truth, New York, 1927

Wieman, Henry N. and Horton, W.M., *The Growth of Religion*, Chicago and New York, 1938

Wieman, Henry N. with Macintosh, D.C. and Otto, M.C., *Is There a*

God? A Conversation, Chicago, 1932

Wiener, Martin J., *Between Two Worlds: the Political Thought of Graham Wallas*, Oxford, 1971

Wiles, M.F., *The Making of Christian Doctrine*, Cambridge, 1967

Wilkinson, J.F., *The Friendly Society Movement*, London, 1891

Williams, Daniel D., *Essays in Process Theology*, Chicago, 1985

Williams, Raymond, *Marxism and Literature*, Oxford, 1977

Williams, Robert R., *Schleiermacher the Theologian: The Construction of the Doctrine of God*, Philadelphia, 1978

Williams, Rowan, *Arius: Heresy and Tradition*, London, 1987

Willis, R.E., *The Ethics of Karl Barth*, Leiden, 1971

Winstanley, Gerrard, *The Law of Freedom and other Writings*, ed. C. Hill, Harmondsworth, 1973

Wolff, Kurt H., ed., *The Sociology of Georg Simmel*, New York, 1950

Wolff, Robert Paul, *The Poverty of Liberalism*, Boston, 1968

Wolff, Robert Paul, et al., *The Limits of Pure Tolerance*, Boston, 1969

Woodcock, George, *Anarchism*, Harmondsworth, 1963

Pierre-Joseph Proudhon, London, 1956

Woodings, R.B., *Shelley: Modern Judgements*, Nashville and London, 1970

Woodroofe, K., *From Charity to Social Work in England and the United States*, London, 1962

Woods, Eleanor A., *Robert A. Woods: Champion of Democracy*, Boston, 1929

Wright, Jonathan, *'Above Parties': The Political Attitudes of the German Protestant Church Leadership, 1918–1933*, Oxford, 1974

Yates, Frances, *Astrea: The Imperial Theme in the Sixteenth Century*, Harmondsworth, 1977

Zahn, G., *German Catholics and Hitler's Wars*, New York, 1962

Index

314